SIGNS OF LIFE

LOS ANGELES IS THE CITY OF NEON

Photographs from the Collection of the Los Angeles Public Library

Essay by J. Eric Lynxwiler

Edited by Christina Rice

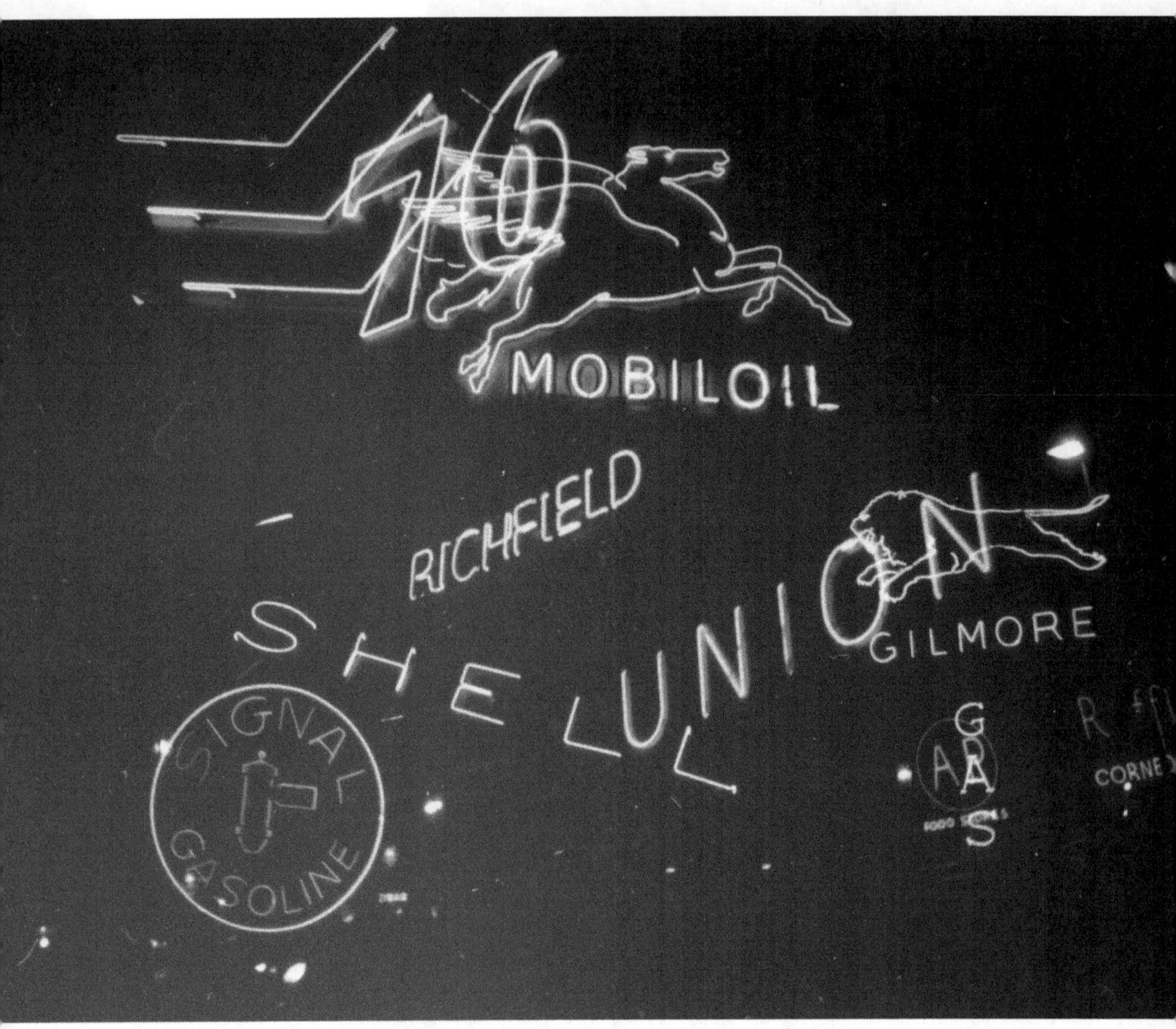

A flurry of neon advertises various petroleum companies.
(Circa 1937, Herman J. Schultheis Collection)

CONTENTS

Pages 4-5 and pages 7-11: Prior to the invention of neon, individual incandescent light bulbs were used to create illuminated signage as shown on these early Los Angeles buildings.

INTRODUCTION

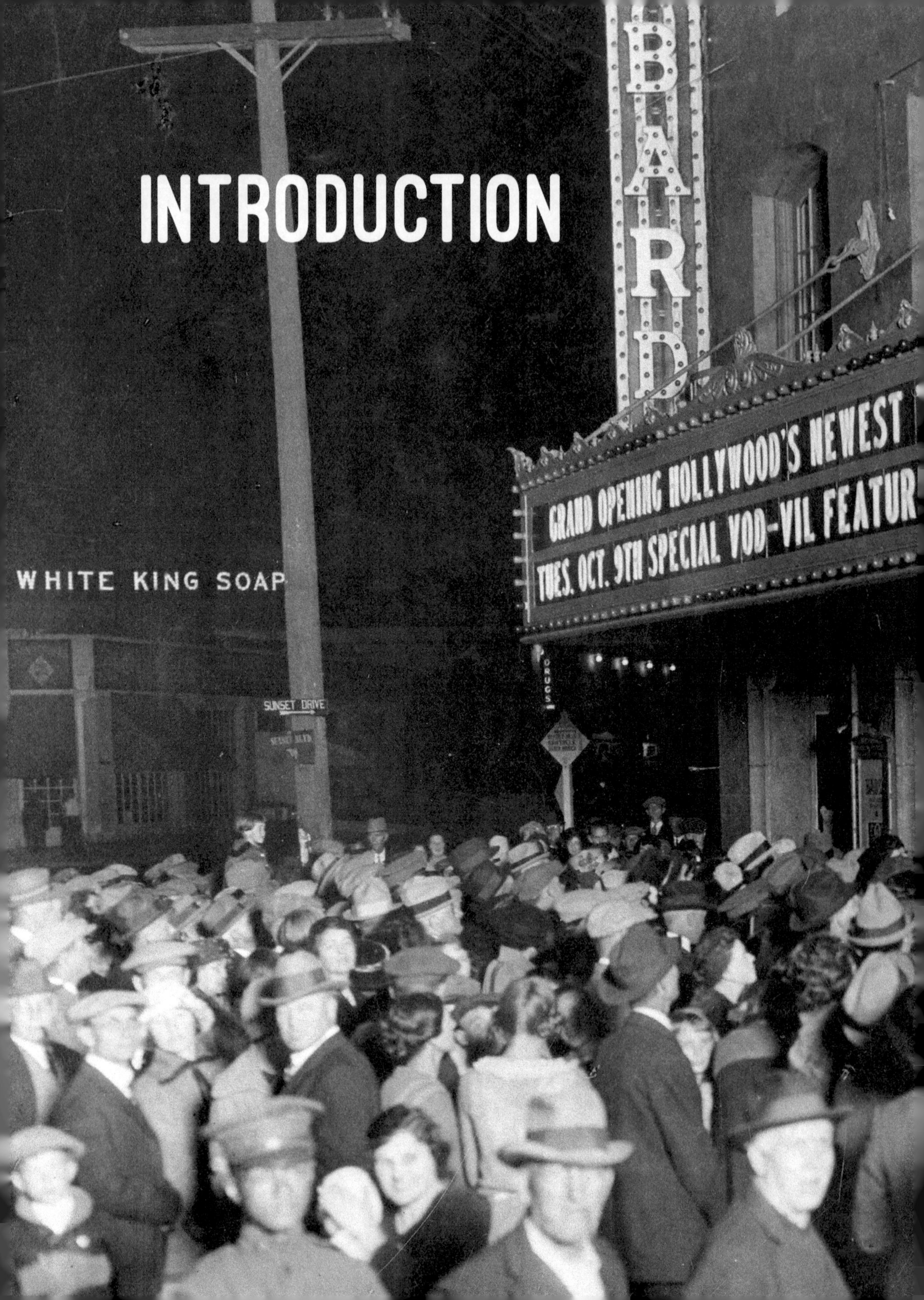

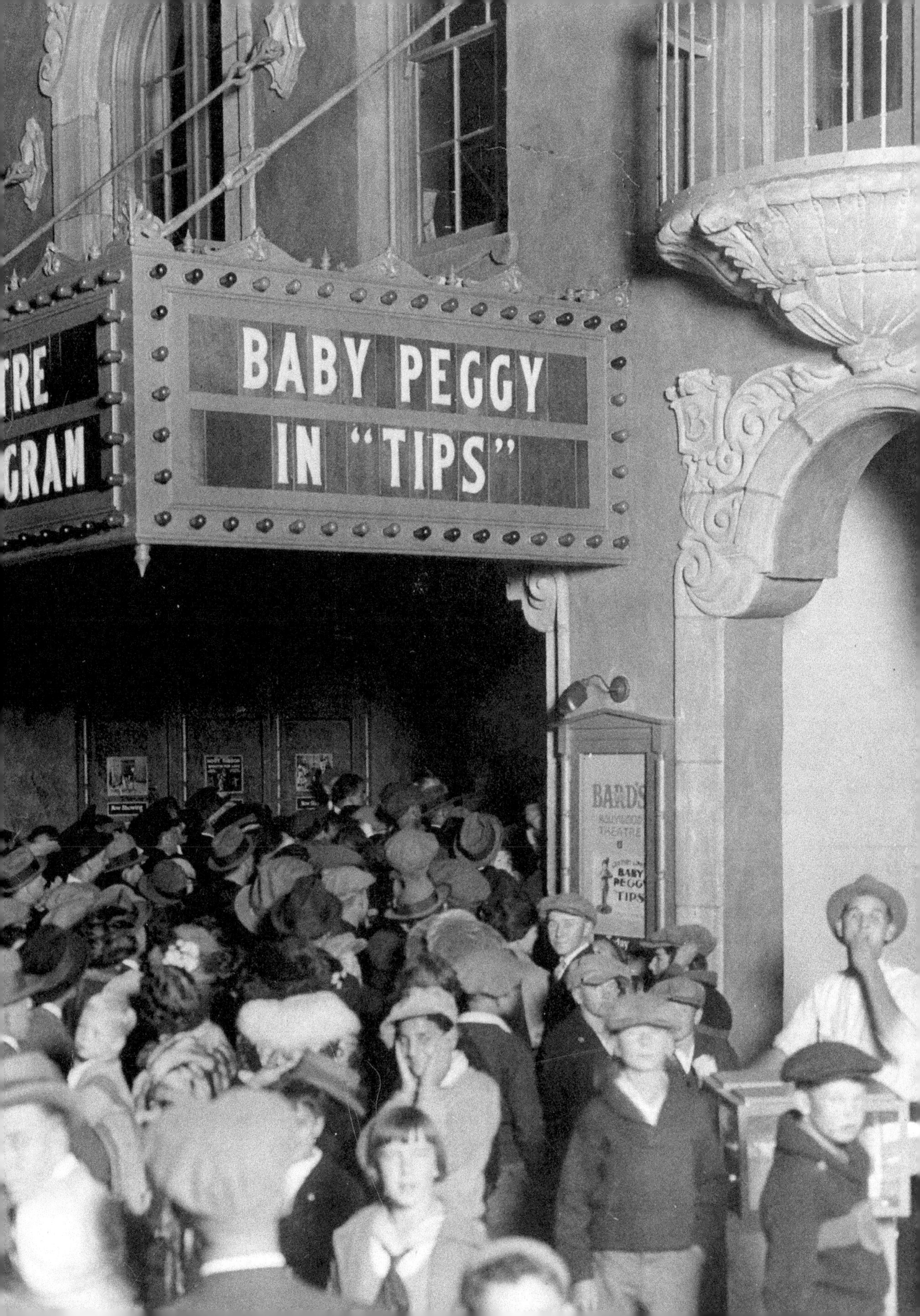
TRE
GRAM
BABY PEGGY
IN “TIPS”
BARD'S

Neon isn't native to Los Angeles, but it's difficult to picture the city without it. Every aspect of our lives has been spelled out in neon tubes across the United States, but Los Angeles is the king of that advertising glow. No other landscape could match its sheer quantity of signs in this city that grew up with the automobile. It was indeed a visual cacophony as the neon sign vied for the eye of the pedestrian and, primarily, motorists.

Mile after mile, the streets of Los Angeles stretched across valleys and into the hillsides and mountains carrying neon messages for drug stores, coffee shops, doctor's offices, car repair and juke joints into infinity. There was nothing neon couldn't announce in bright, eye-catching colors and Los Angeles businesses that wanted to be modern, and up to date, had one if not five neon signs promoting their wares.

The brightest points on the city's map were the Hollywood & Vine and Downtown Broadway shopping districts, with kudos going to Wilshire's Miracle Mile and Chinatown. In the neighborhood of Hollywood, Vine Street was the headquarters for nationwide radio broadcasts drawing celebrities and tourists alike for work and play in theaters, nightclubs, and restaurants such as the Brown Derby. Downtown's Broadway district drew thousands of shoppers to its numerous department stores with towering, vertical neon signs and movie palaces with glittering theater marquees.

The first neon tubes in the nation were imported from Paris, France, in the early 1920s and peaked early on. This heyday of jazzy neon followed the rise of the American automobile, but slowly waned in the 1960s as cheaper materials such as plastic signs replaced aging neon. More than anything else however, it was an active movement against roadside advertising that brought an end to its run. The quantity of neon signs clogging the streets of Los Angeles became an eyesore to some and "City Beautiful" campaigns began to eradicate and illegalize them.

Today, one may cruise Los Angeles and see numerous vestiges of its neon past, lit and unlit, here and there in older parts of town. Although tens of thousands of its neon signs are gone, when compared to the rest of the nation, Los Angeles still has more neon than any other city, Las Vegas included. And that is a fact that needs to be recognized and celebrated – **here is Los Angeles, City of Neon.**

—J. Eric Lynxwiler

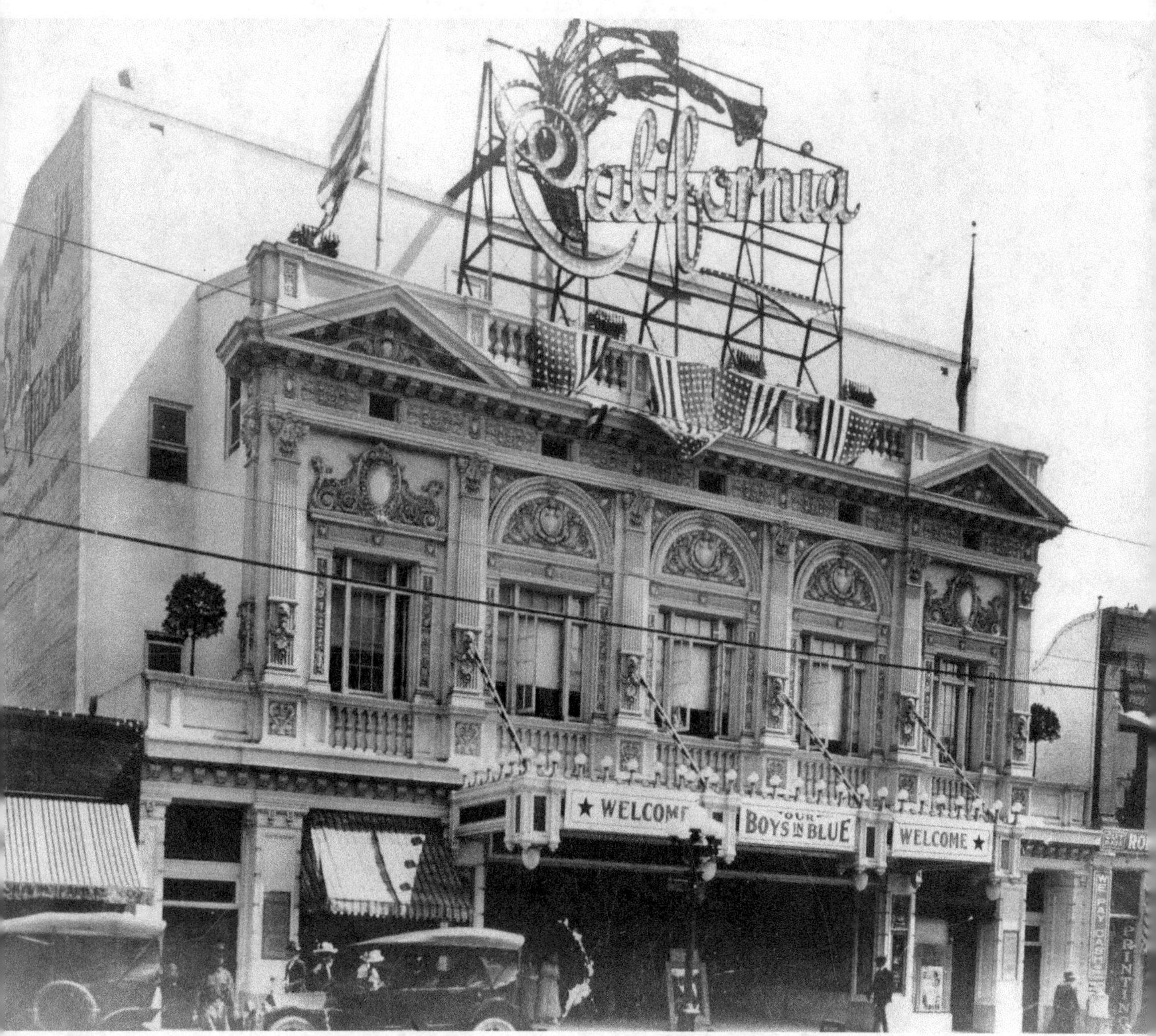

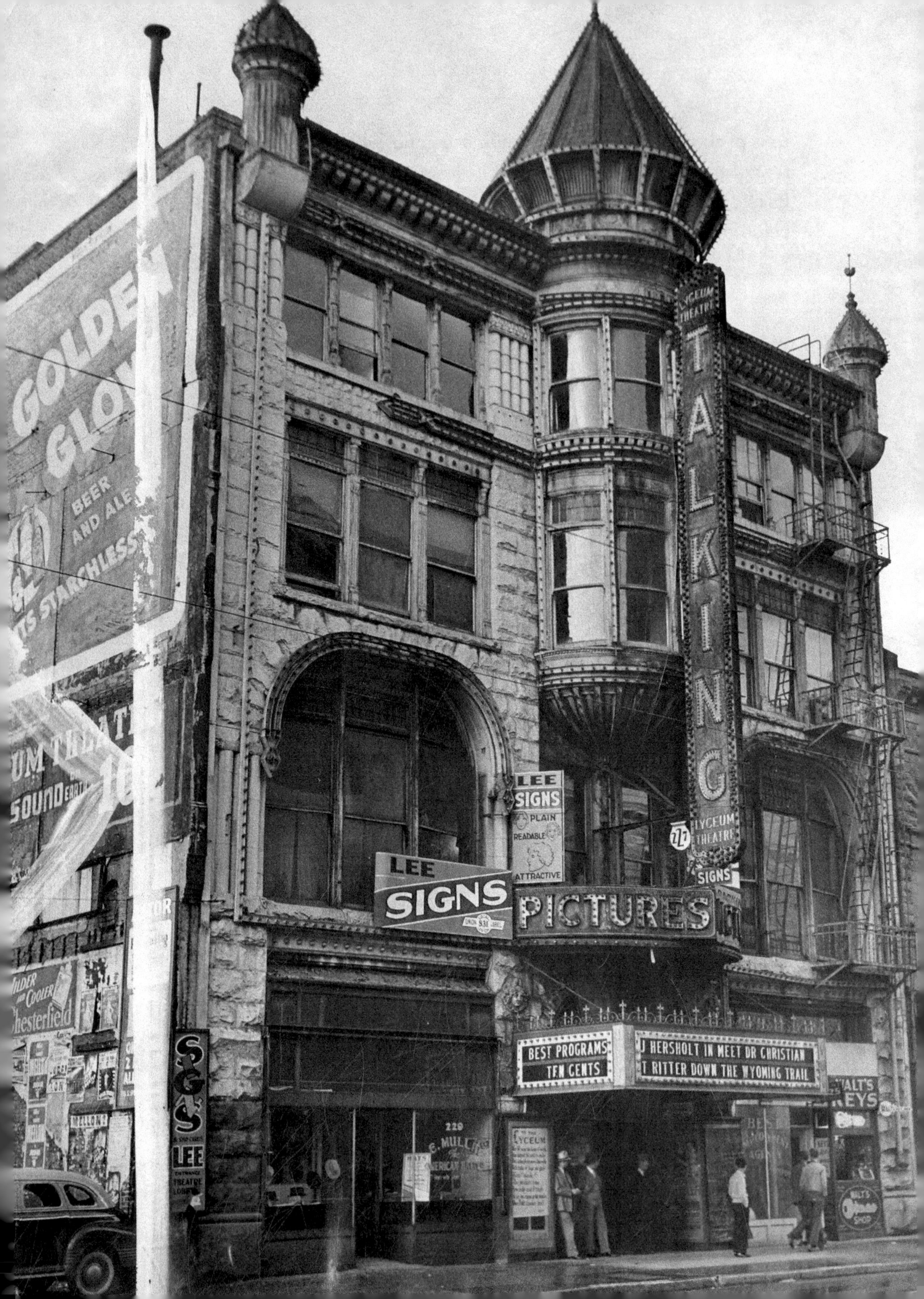
GOLDEN
BEER AND ALE
LYCEUM THEATRE
TALKING
LYCEUM THEATRE
LEE
SIGNS
PLAIN
READABLE
ATTRACTIVE
LEE
SIGNS
PICTURES
SIGNS
BEST PROGRAMS
TEN CENTS
J HERSHOLT IN MEET DR CHRISTIAN
T RITTER DOWN THE WYOMING TRAIL
Chesterfield
LEE
229
LYCEUM

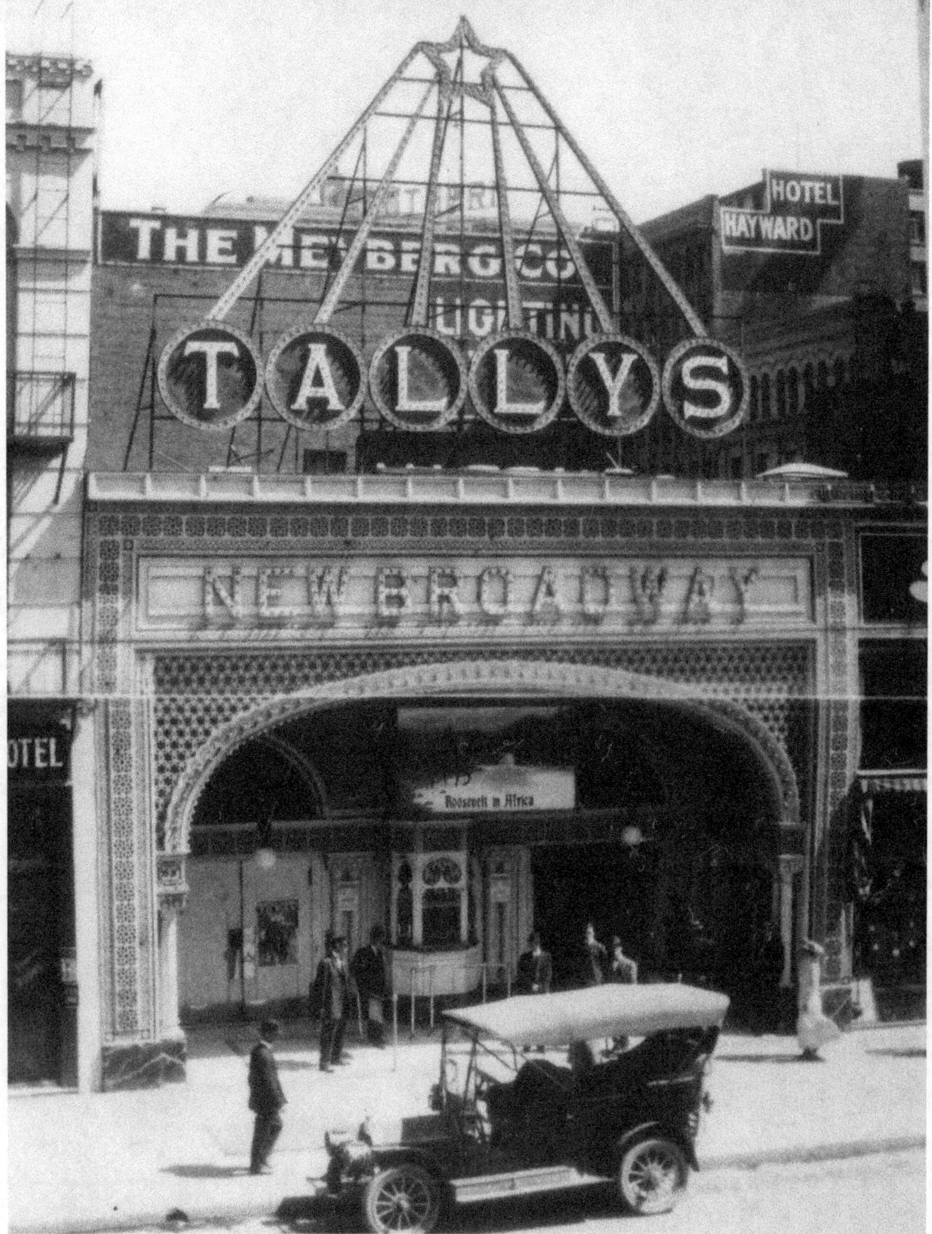

Before neon was introduced to Los Angeles, it was the traditional, incandescent bulb that illuminated the cityscape at night. Numerous businesses utilized the medium, but it was theaters that made fanciful use of the light bulb. Downtown's California, Lyceum, and Tally's Theatres glowed with bulb signs, even decorating the outlines of their facades with light. Hollywood's Warner Bros. Theatre utilized the light bulb with elegance on its marquee and backlit its slumped glass movie lettering with even more.

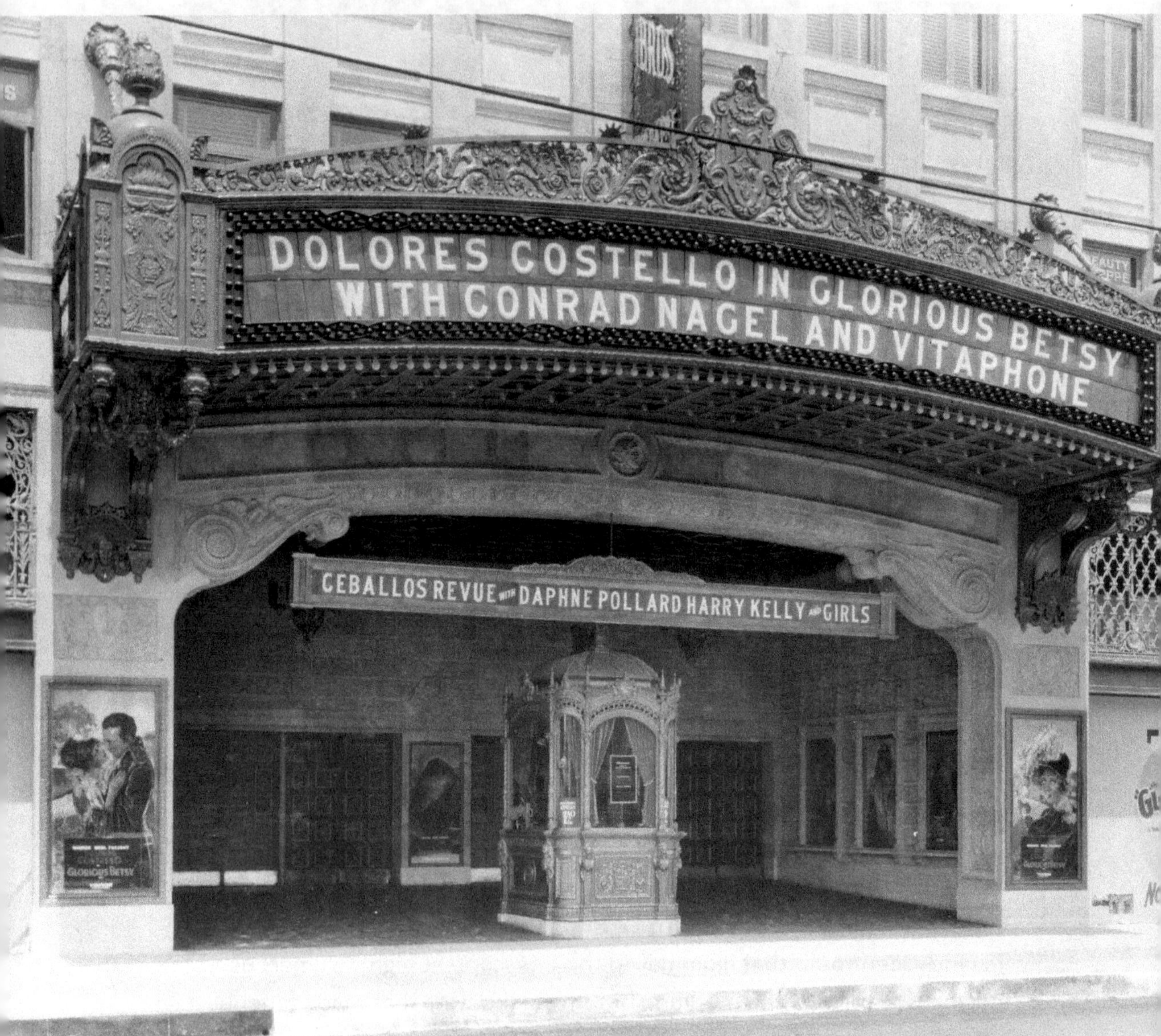
DOLORES COSTELLO IN GLORIOUS BETSY
WITH CONRAD NAGEL AND VITAPHONE
CEBALLOS REVUE WITH DAPHNE POLLARD HARRY KELLY AND GIRLS

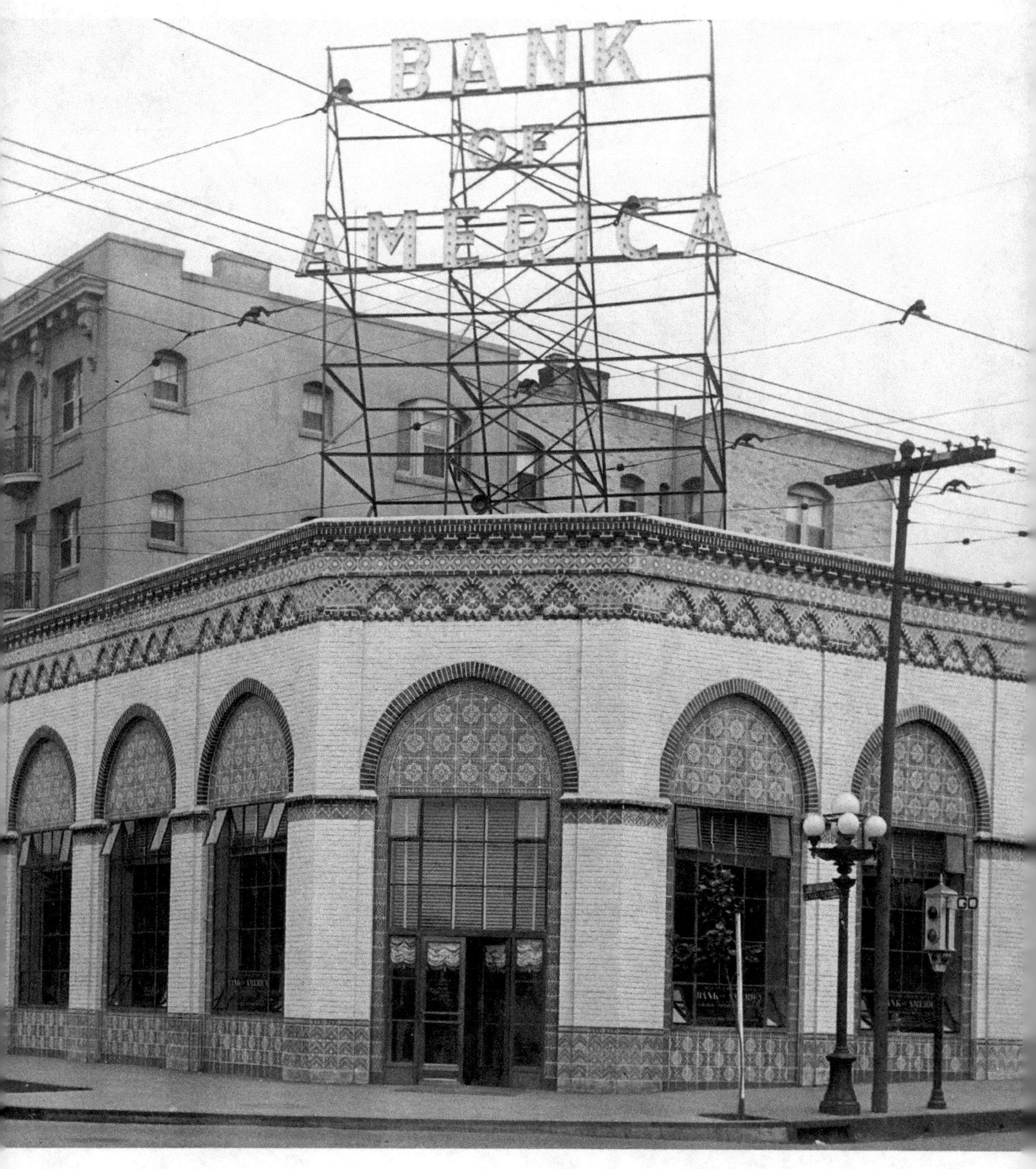
BANK
OF
AMERICA
GO

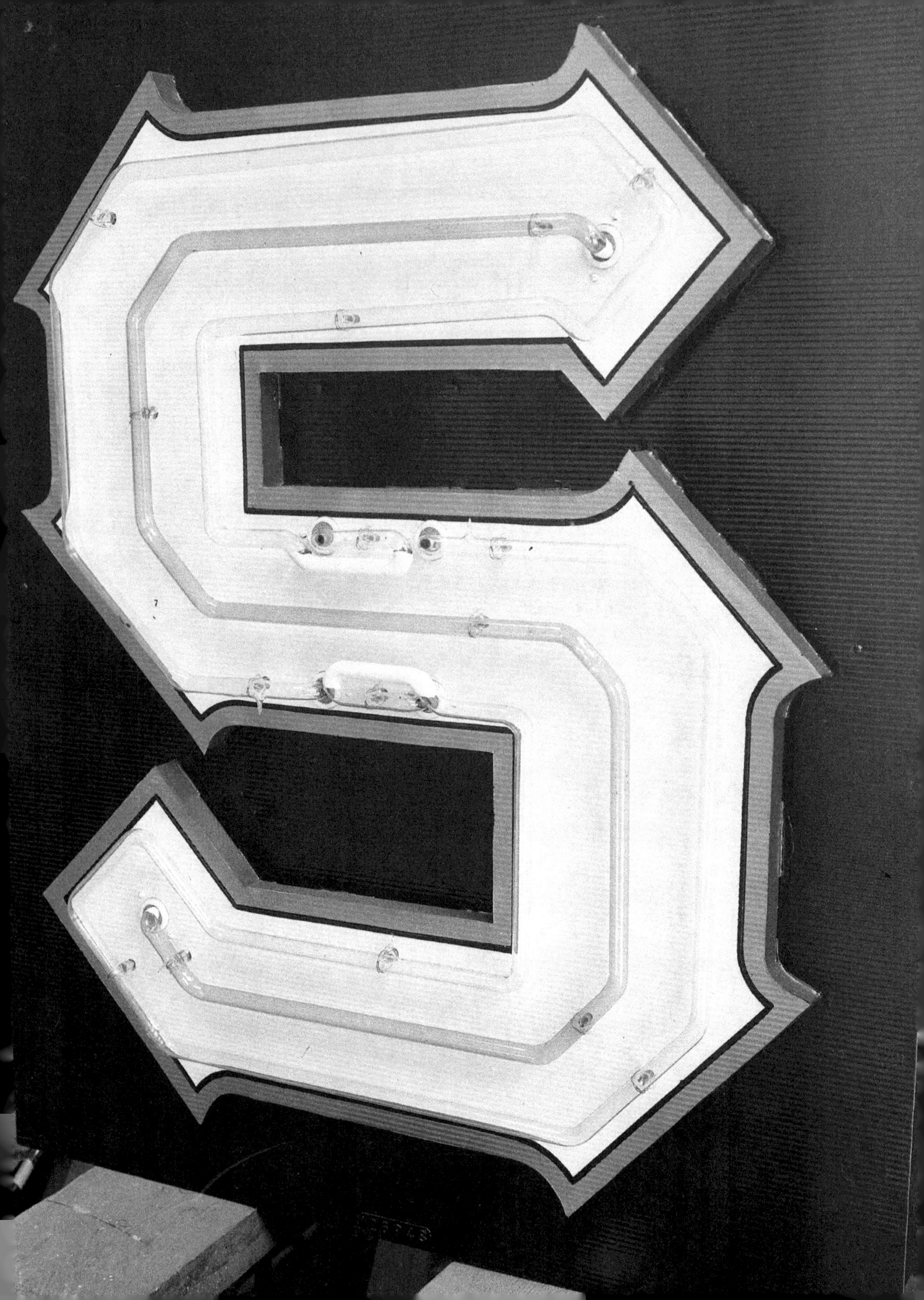

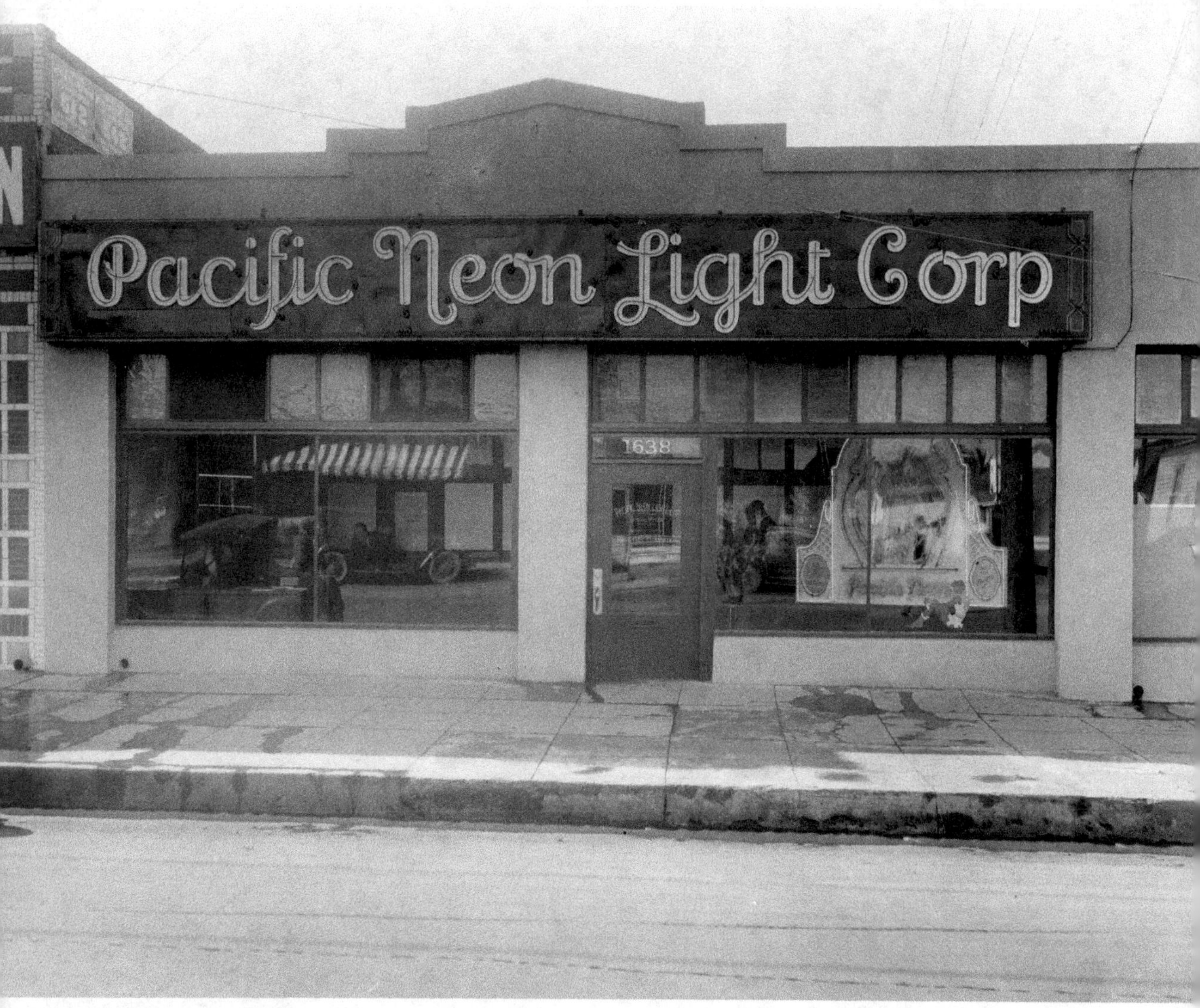

The Pacific Neon Light Corp. at 1638 W. Washington Boulevard uses appropriate signage to advertise its services. (1928, Los Angeles Herald Examiner Collection)

Opposite: Detailed view of neon-decorated letter. (Undated, Security Pacific National Bank Collection)

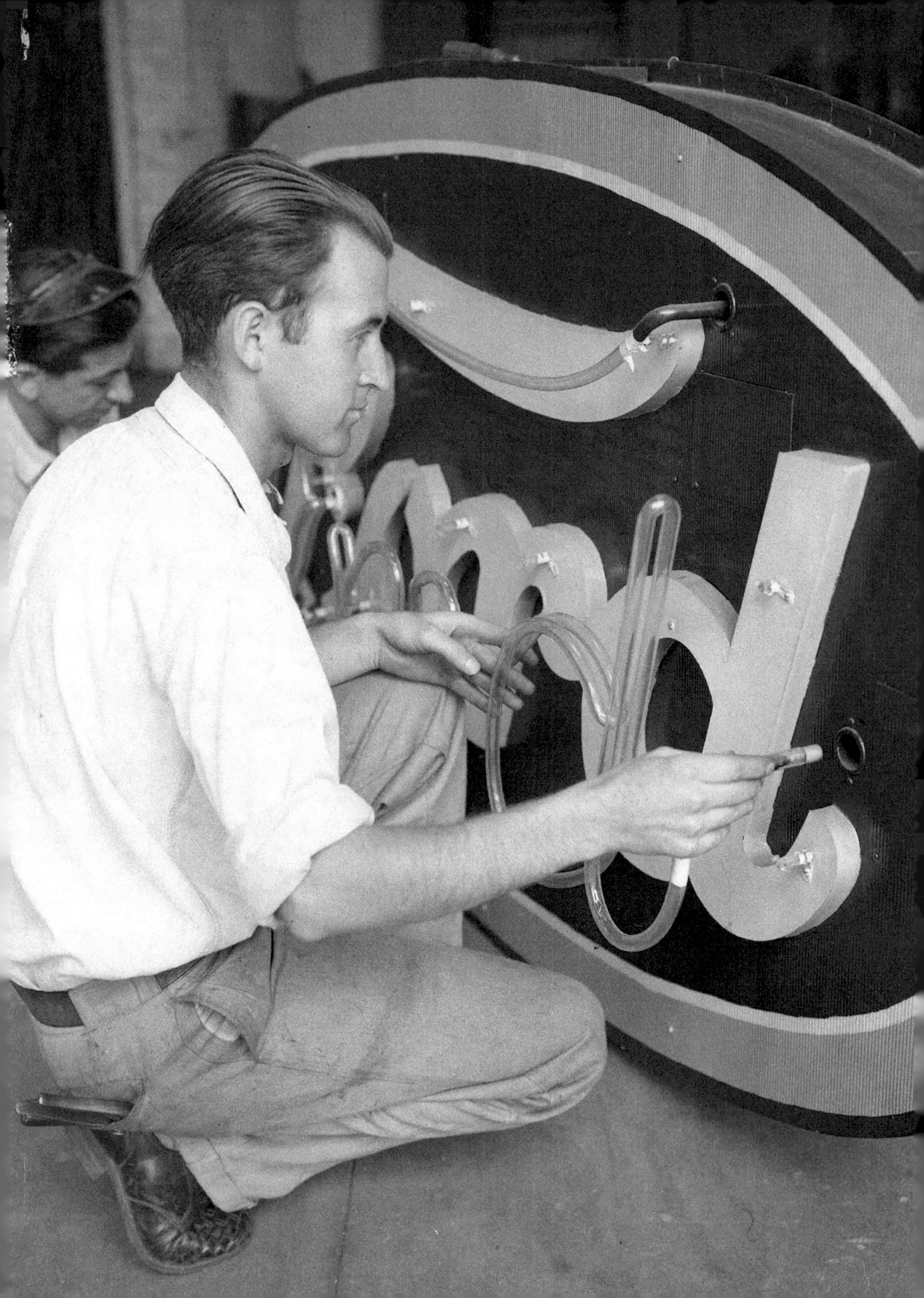

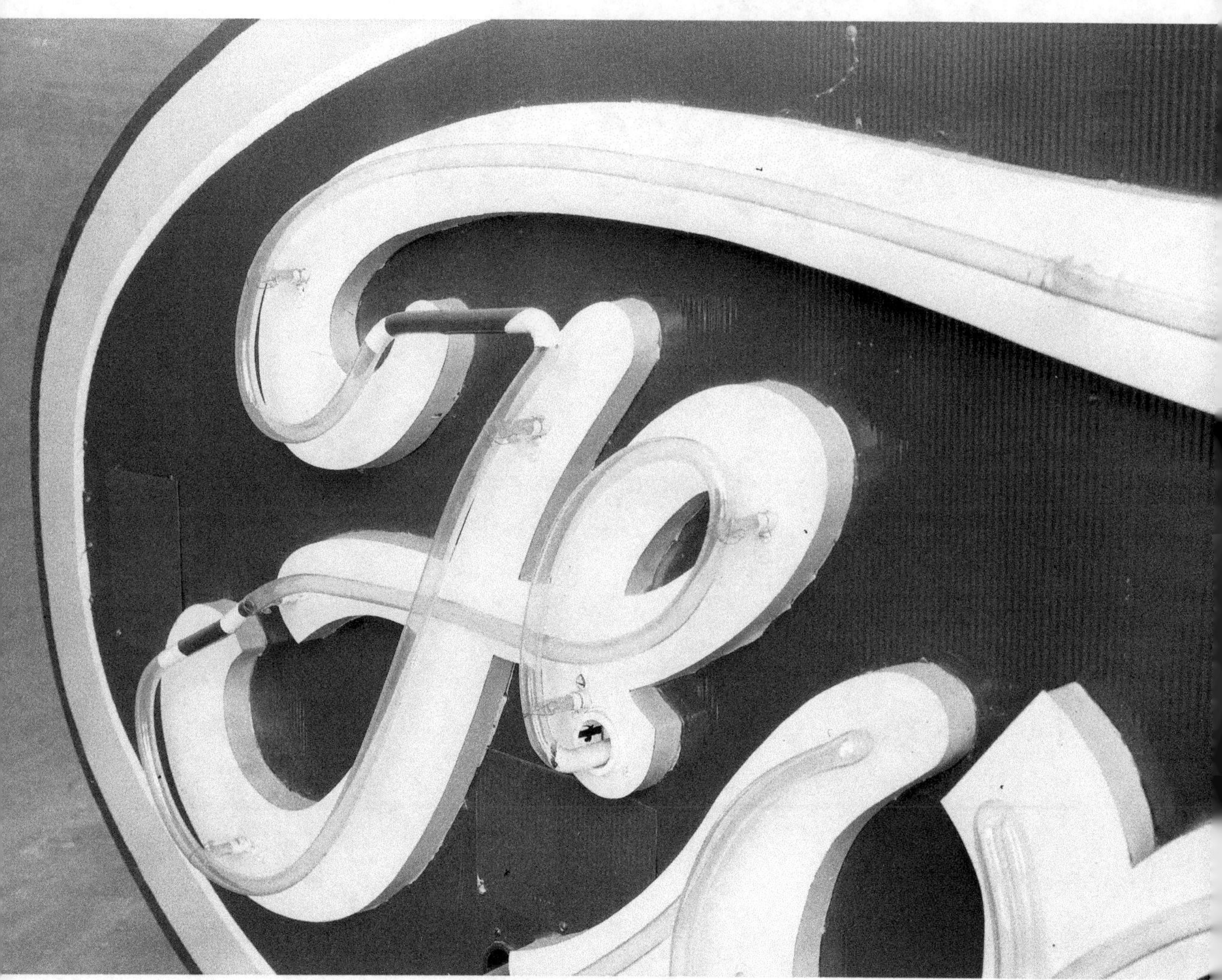

Opposite: Neon is installed onto a Ford sign. (Undated, Security Pacific National Bank Collection)

Above: Closer view of the Ford sign. (Undated, Security Pacific National Bank Collection)

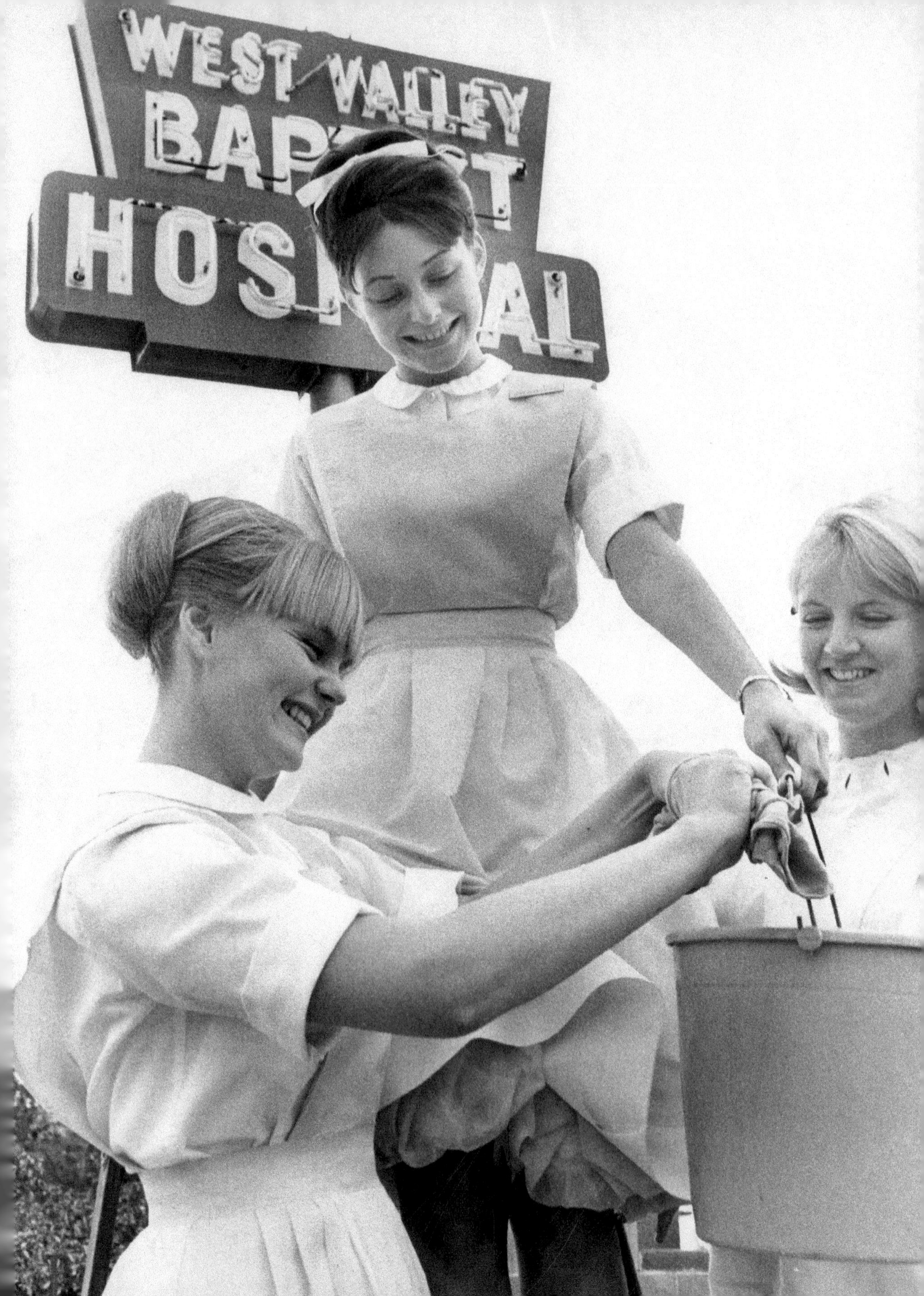
WEST VALLEY

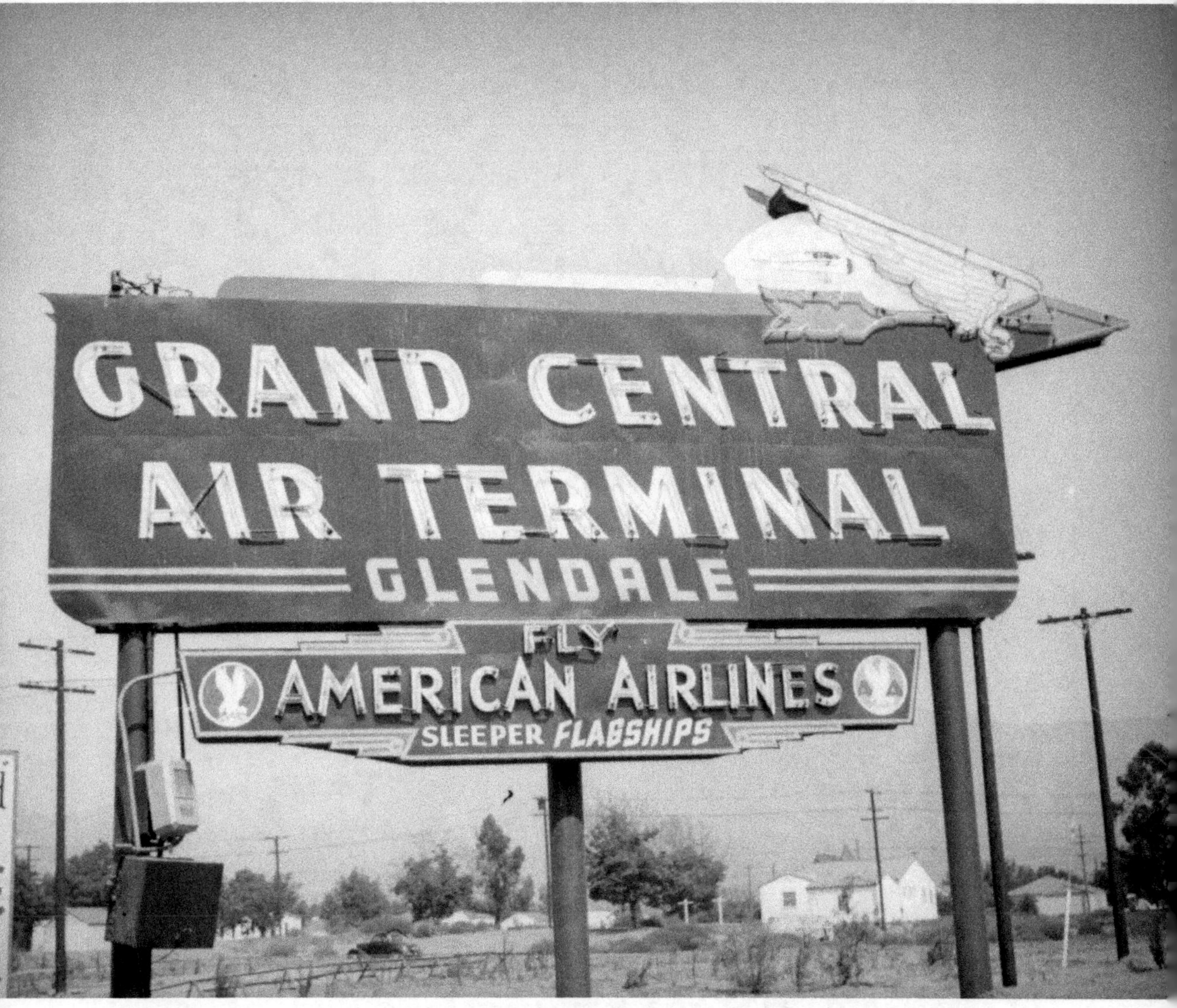

The Grand Central Air Terminal in Glendale takes full advantage of neon with this sign. (Circa 1937, Herman J. Schultheis Collection)

Opposite: Every business needed a neon sign, including Encino's West Valley Baptist hospital. Three volunteers wash the sign in preparation for National Hospital Week attesting to the value of advertising. (1964, George Brich/Valley Times Collection)

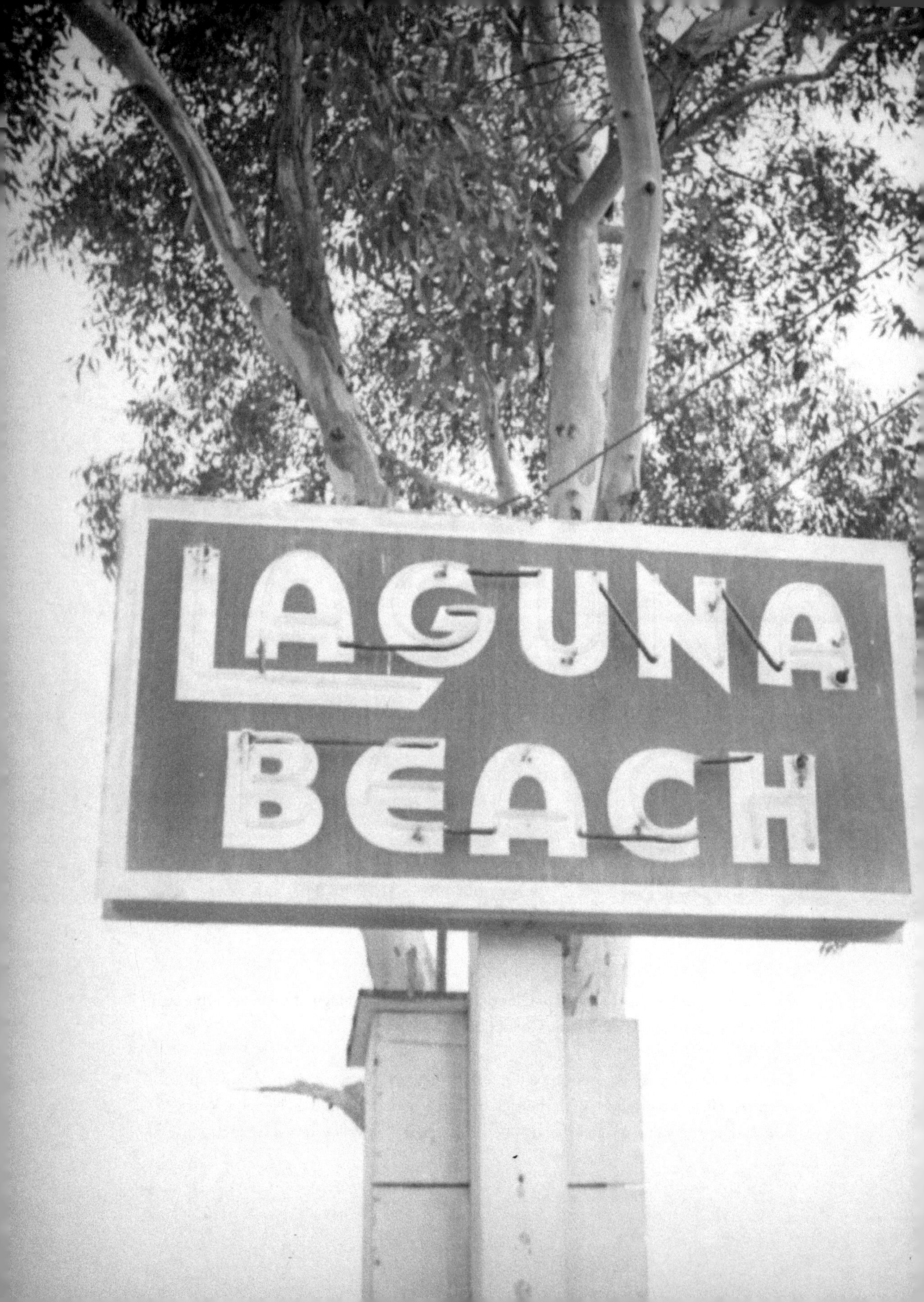

LAGUNA
BEACH

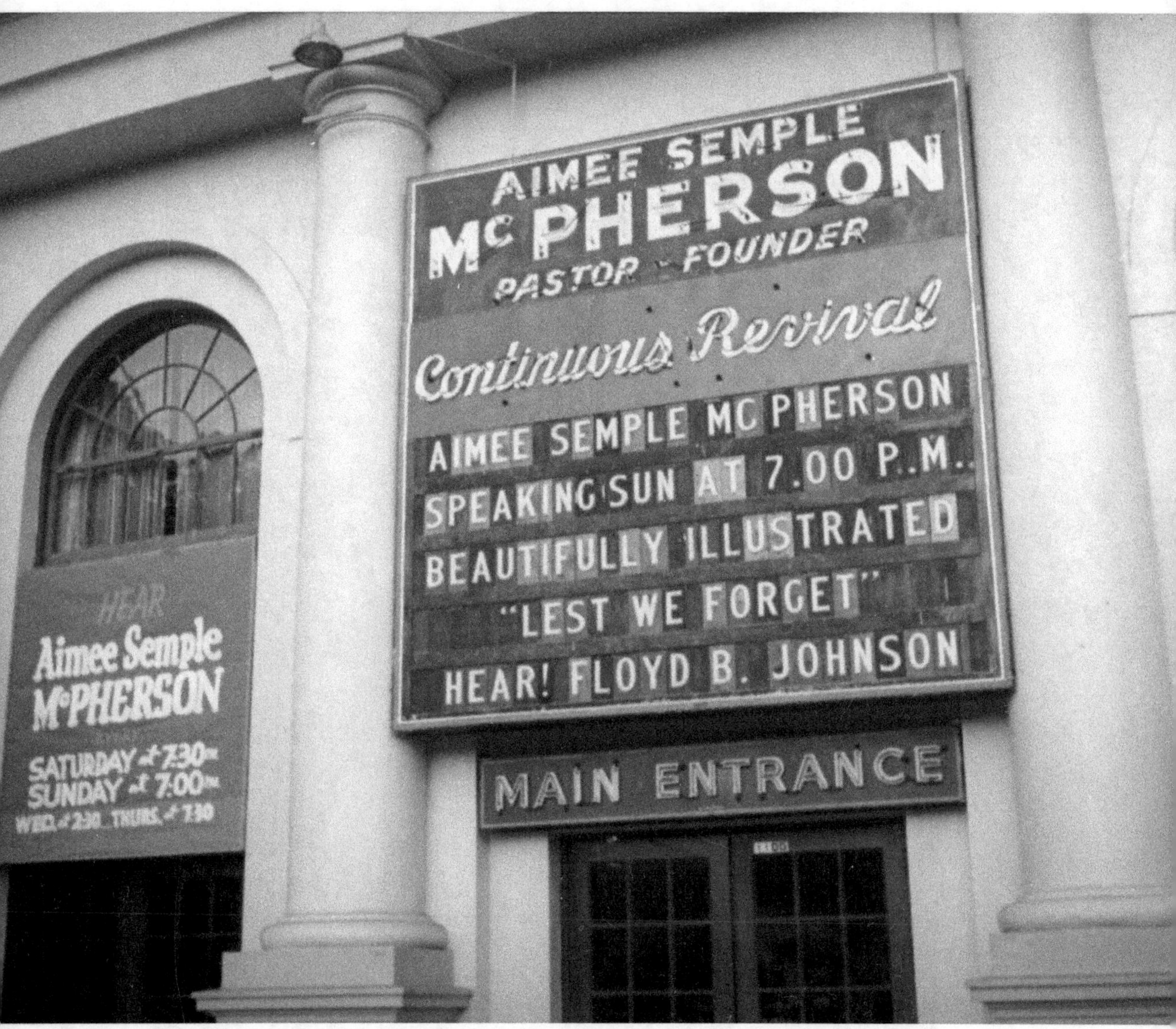

No establishment was above using neon to attract patrons, including Aimee Semple McPherson's Angelus Temple in Echo Park. (Circa 1937, Herman J. Schultheis Collection)

Opposite: Neon is used to indicate to passersby that they are in Laguna Beach. (Circa 1937. Herman J. Schultheis Collection)

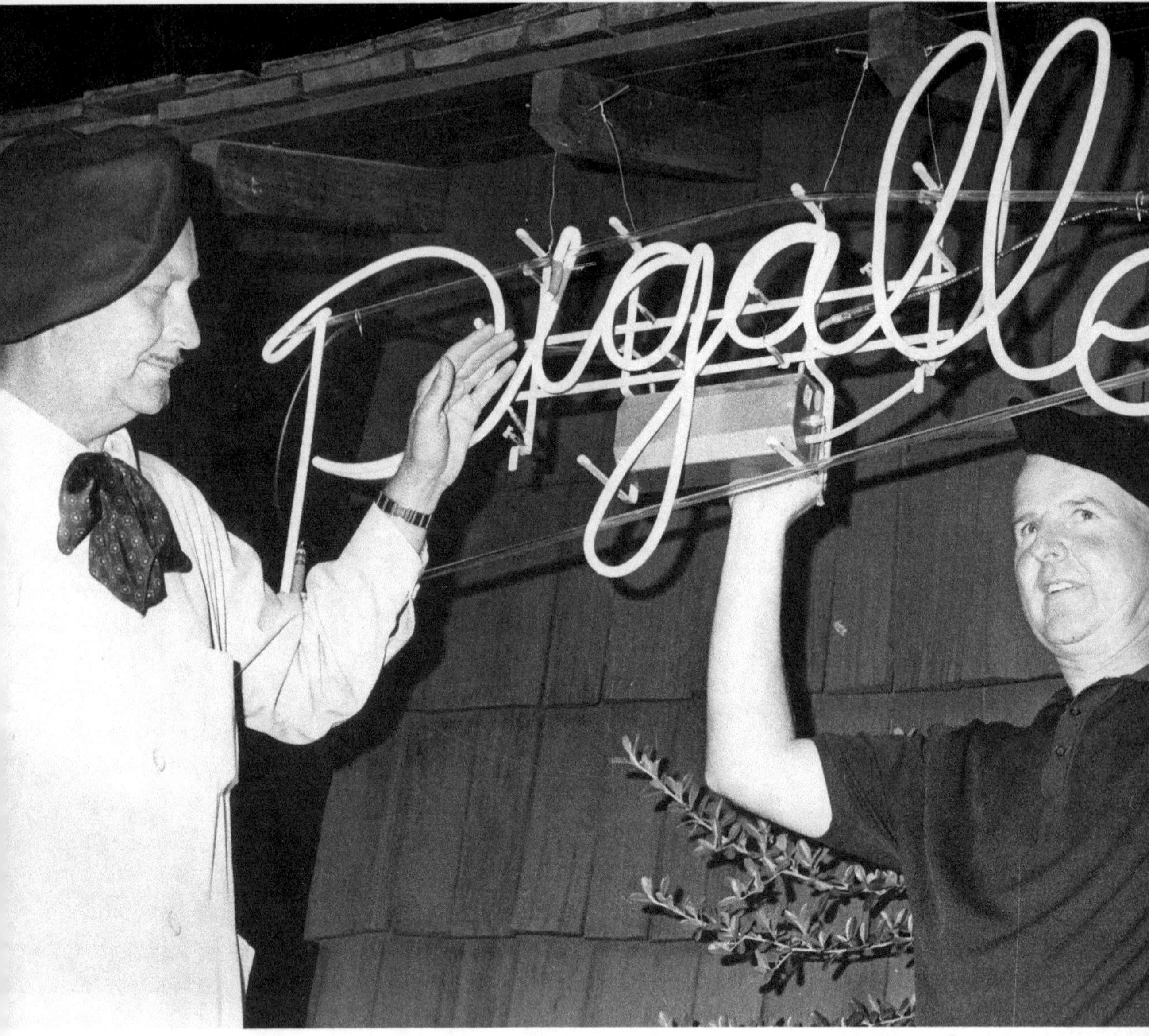

Two men attend to a neon side at a sidewalk café in the Valley. (1961, Valley Times Collection)

Opposite: With great aspirations, the then-rural community of Torrance proclaimed itself the "Industrial City" in welcoming neon signage. Besides the stray oil derricks, it's a dichotomy of hope and reality in one long-lost neon sign. (1937, Herman J. Schultheis Collection)

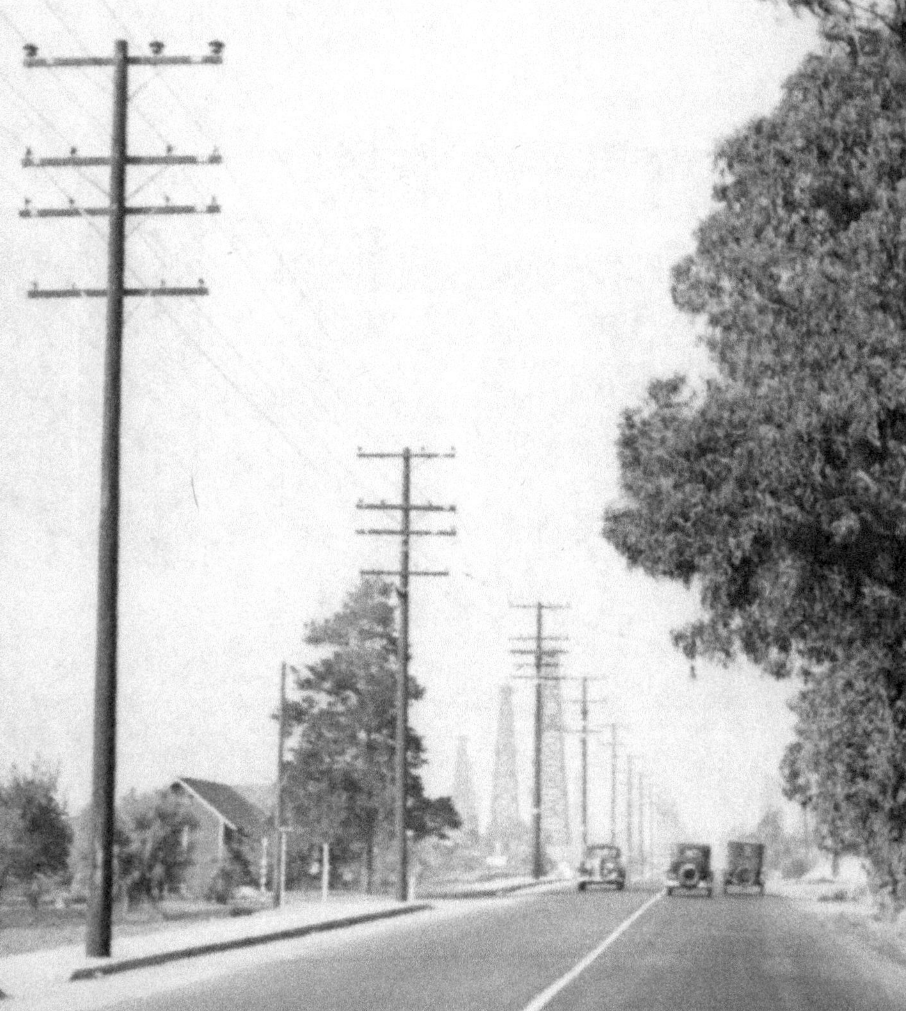
The Modern Industrial City
Torrance

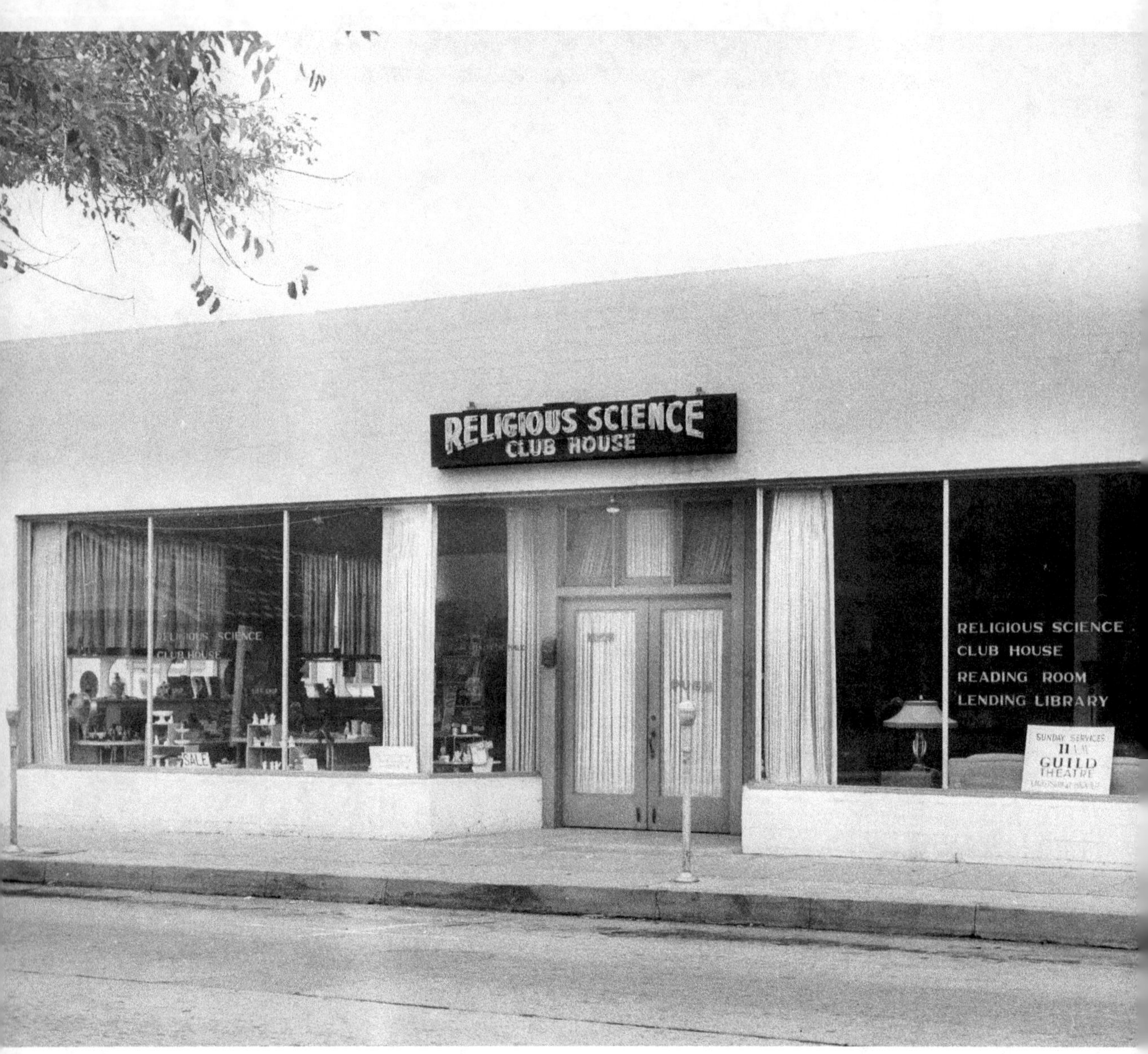

A simple neon sign advertises the Church of Religious Science in North Hollywood. (1963, Valley Times Collecton)

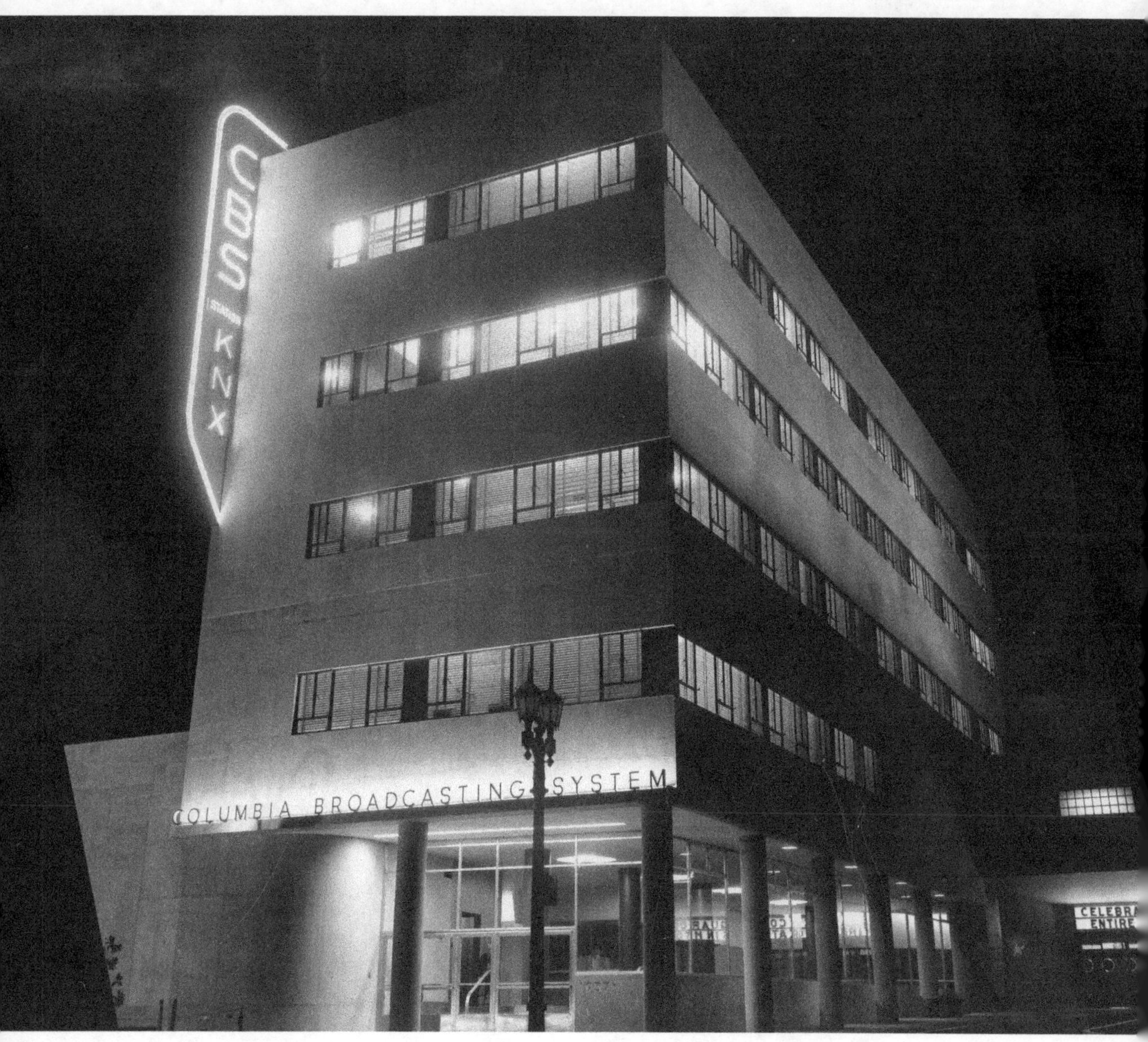

A neon blade sign brands one of the buildings at CBS Columbia Square in Hollywood. (1939, Works Progress Administration Collection)

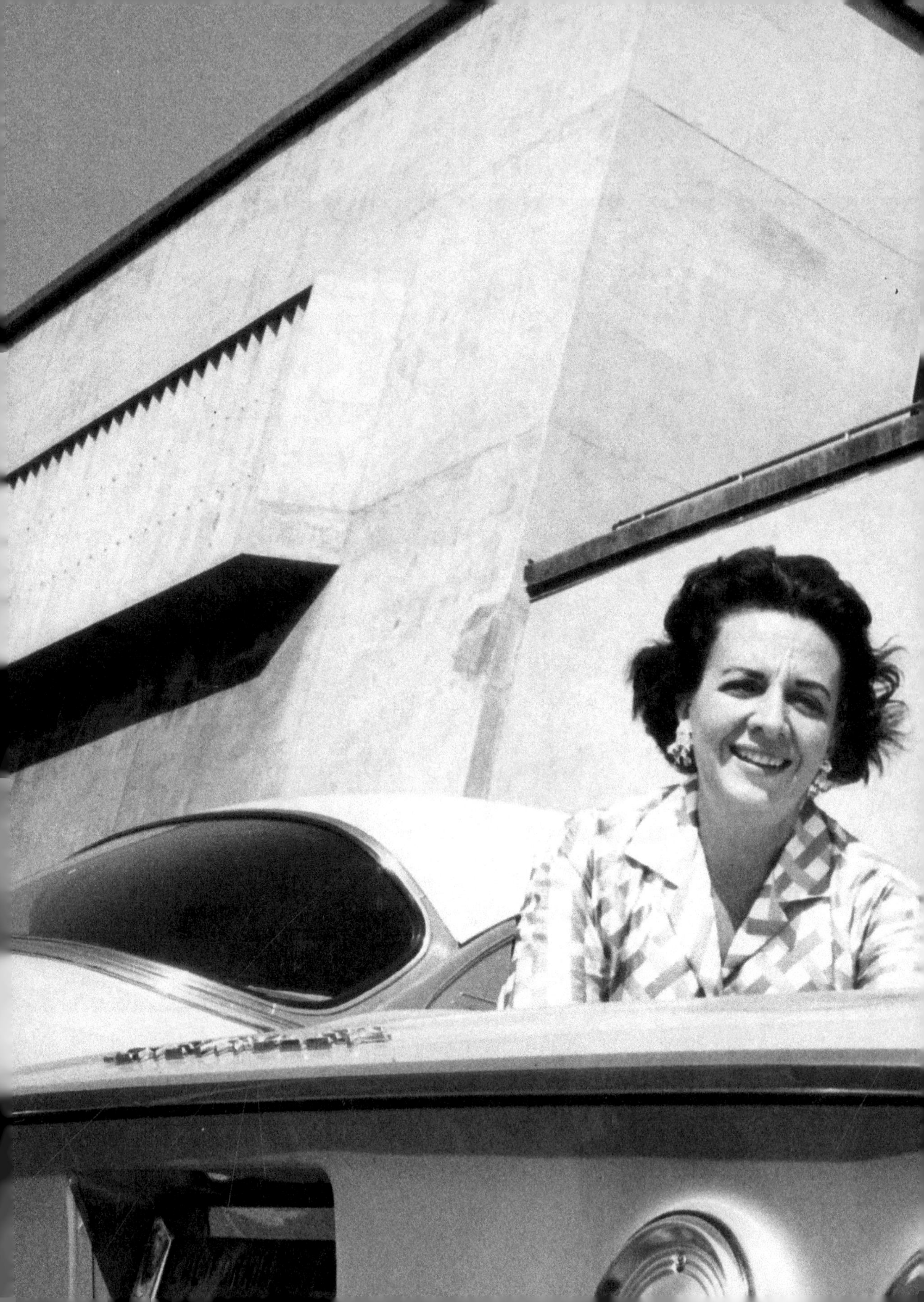

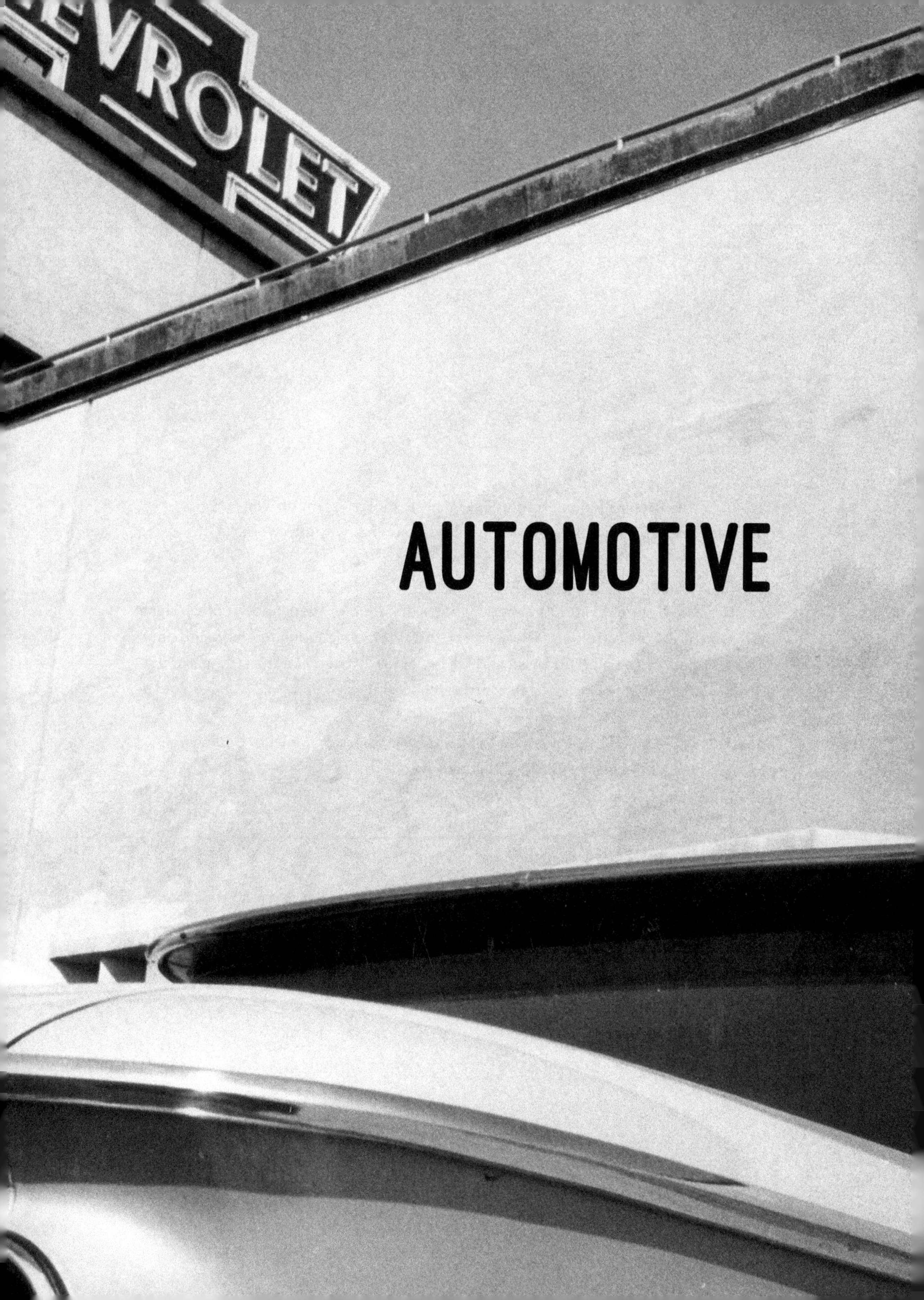

AUTOMOTIVE

Overleaf: Mrs. Thomas Rollo, secretary at General Motors plant on Van Nuys Boulevard, pauses beneath a neon Chevrolet sign on her way into work. (1960, George Brich/Valley Times Collection)

Opposite: Pep Boys auto supply aimed high with its double-sided, neon rooftop signs built upon scads of scaffolding. Every arm of the automobile industry embraced neon and, regardless of the medium's rise and fall in popularity, neon kept a strong bond with car culture. (Circa 1930s, Ralph Morris Collection)

Pages 28-29: A view of the iconic neon at Casa de Cadillac on Ventura Boulevard in Sherman Oaks. (1958, Valley Times Collection)

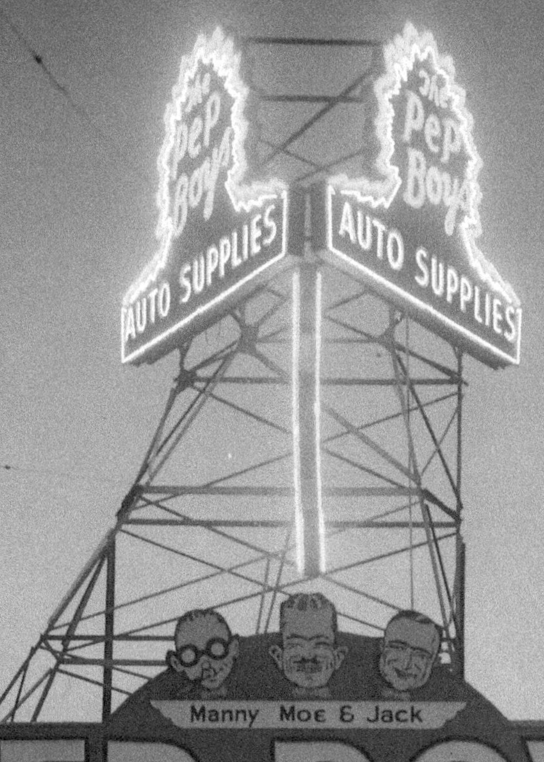
The Pep Boys
AUTO SUPPLIES
The Pep Boys
AUTO SUPPLIES

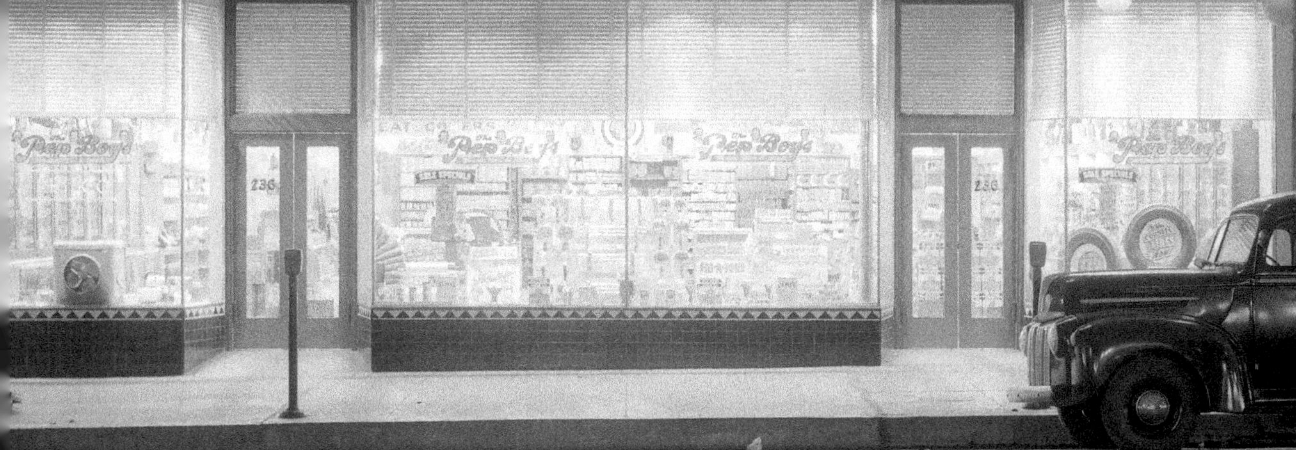
Manny Moe & Jack
The PEP BOYS
AUTO
PPLIES
CYCLES
TIRES
TUBES
AUTO SUPPLIES
The Pep Boys
The Pep Boys
The Pep Boys
The Pep Boys
236
236

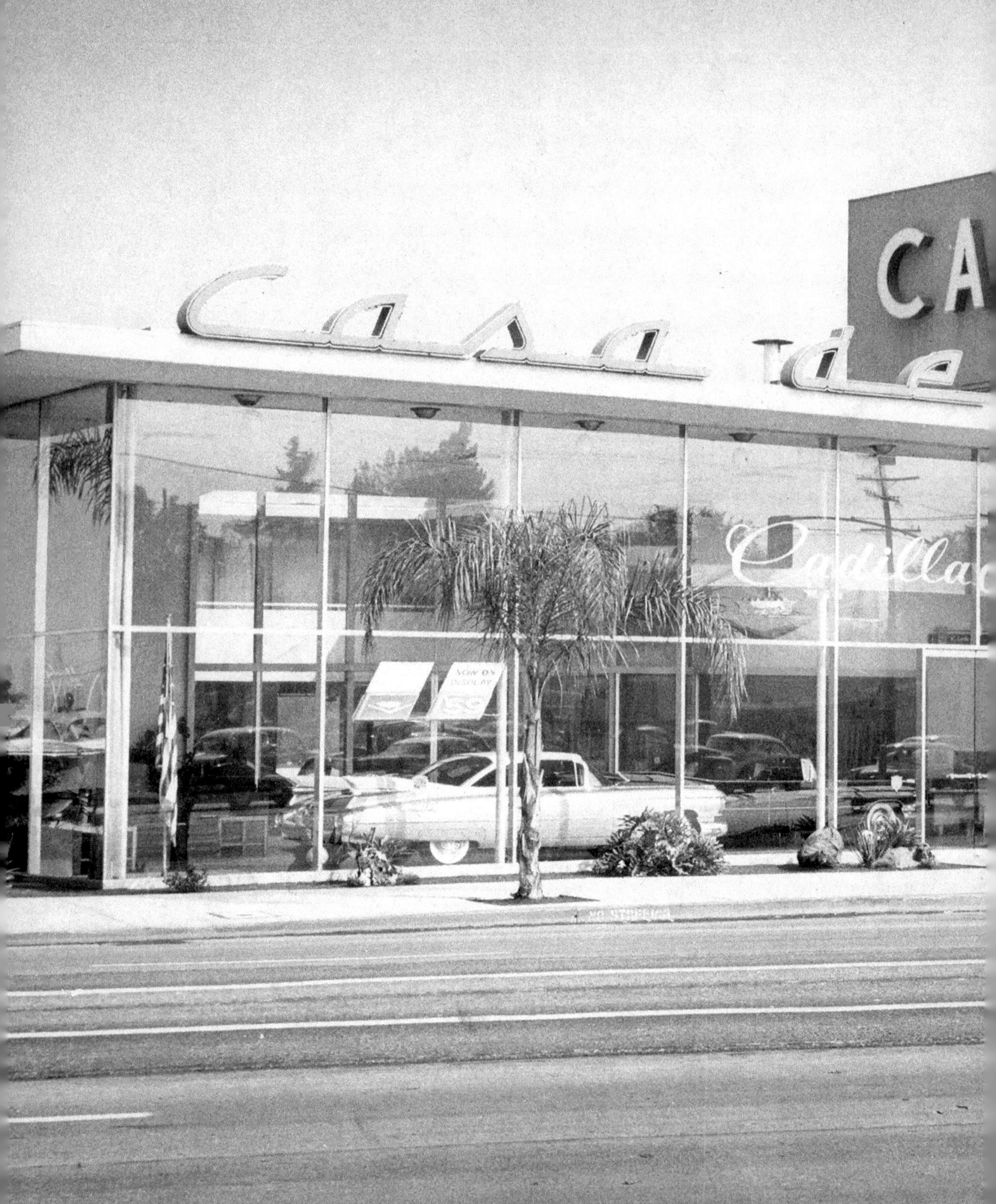
CA
Casa de
NOW ON
DISPLAY

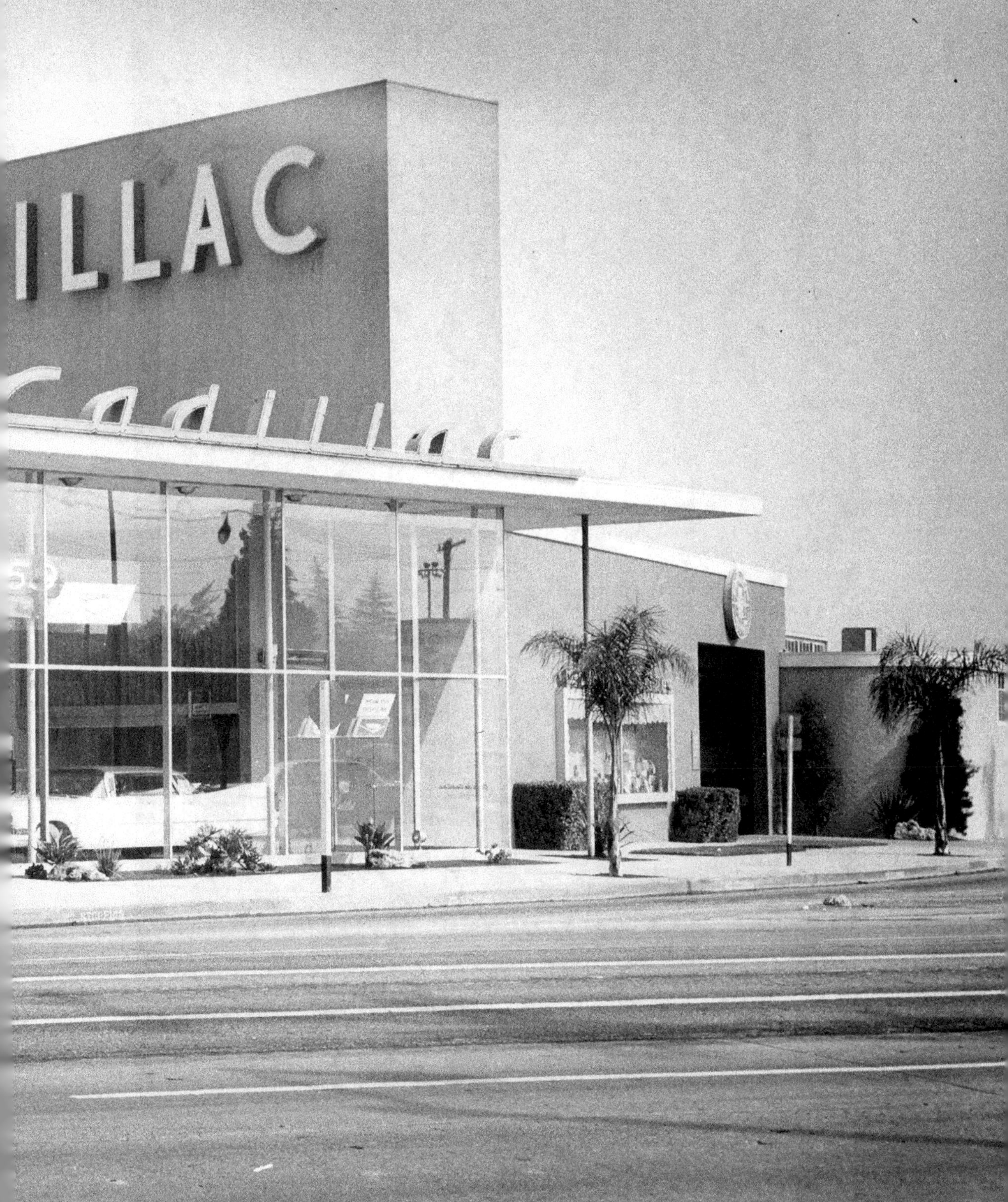
ILLAC

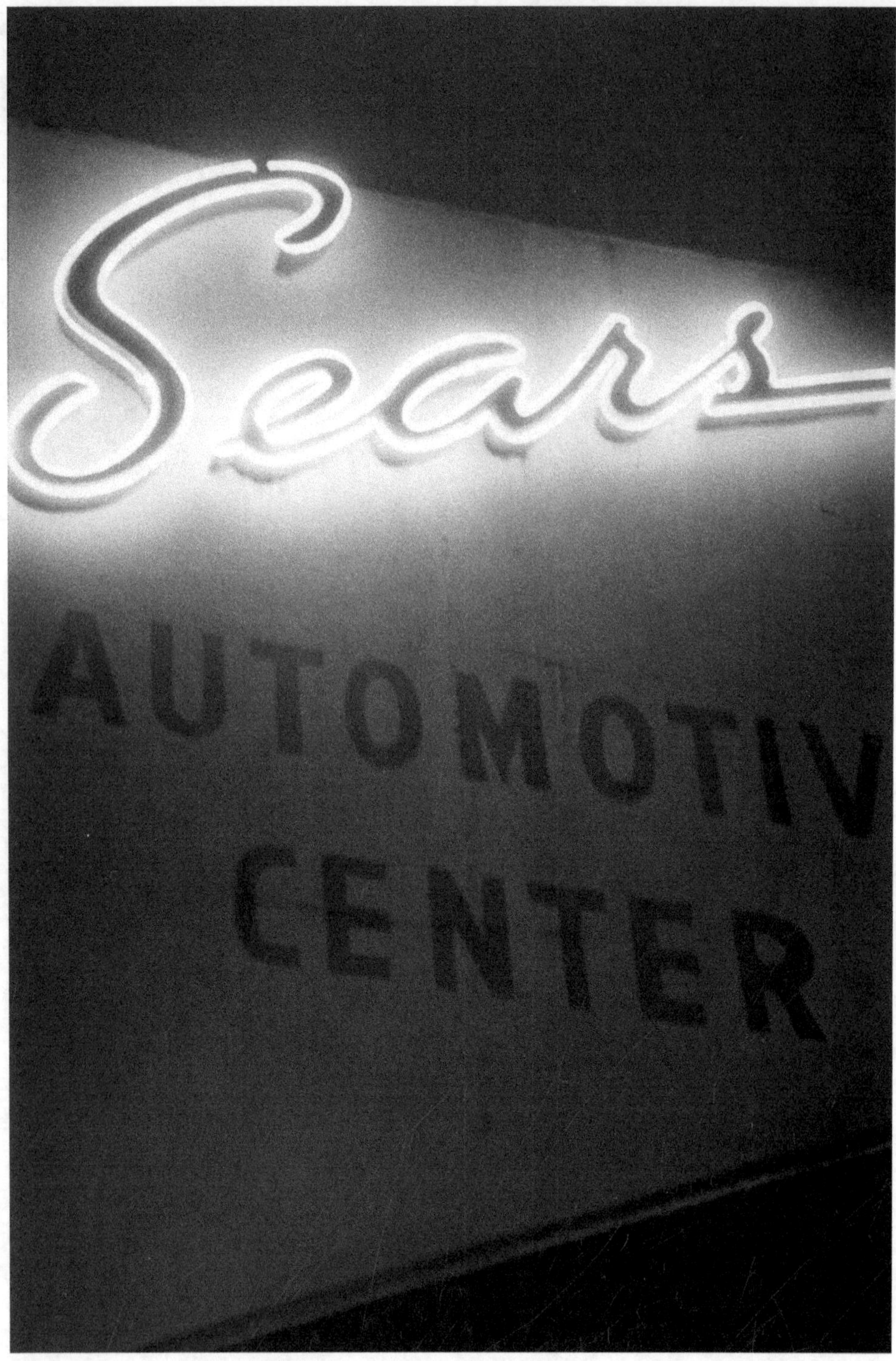
Sears
AUTOMOTIV
CENTER

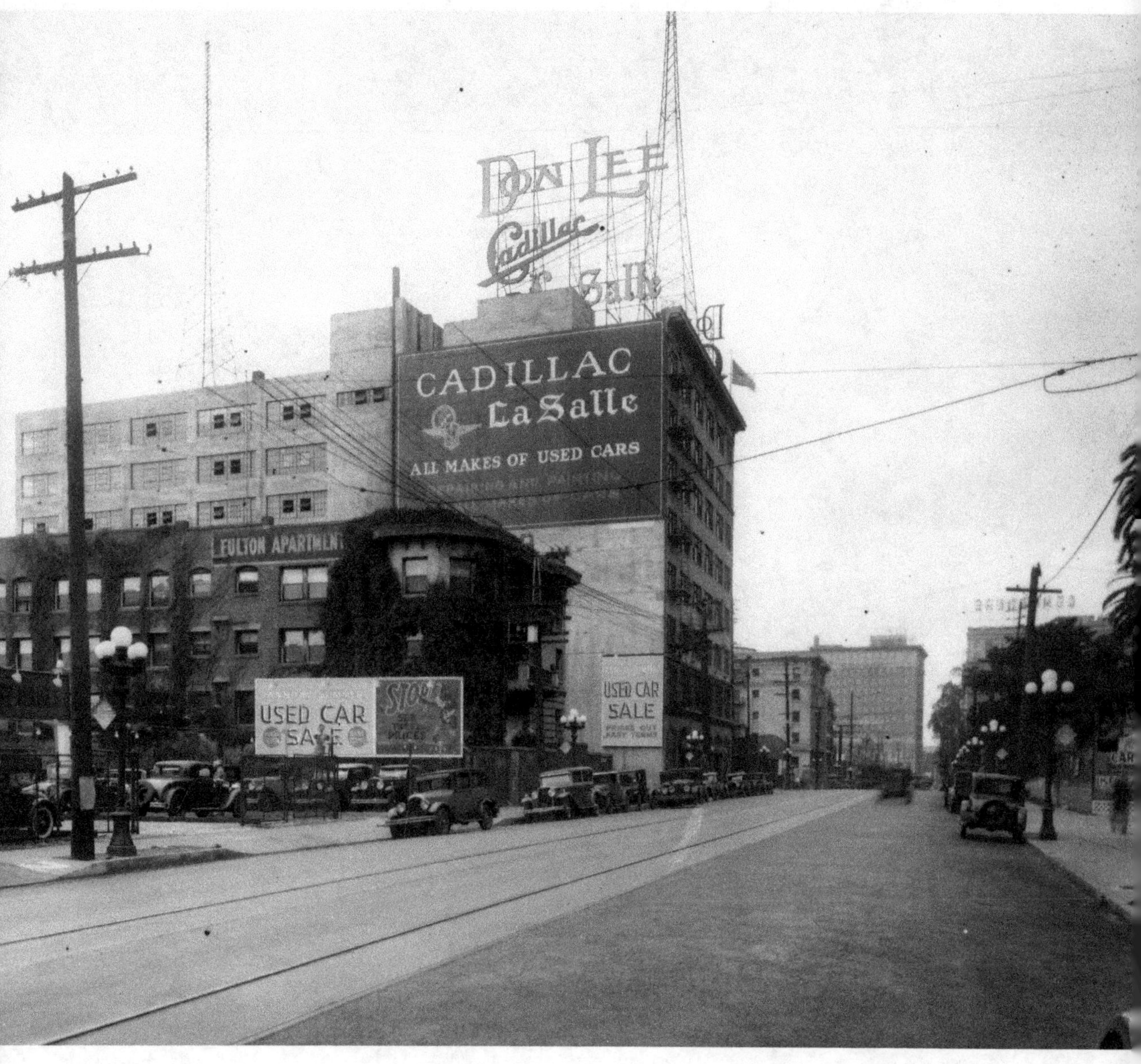

A large neon sigh sits atop the Don Lee Cadillac and LaSalle car dealership, located at 1076 West 7th Street and Bixel. (Circa 1920s, Security Pacific National Bank Collection)

Opposite: Night view of the neon sign for the Sears automotive department in Santa Monica (1988, Carol Westwood)

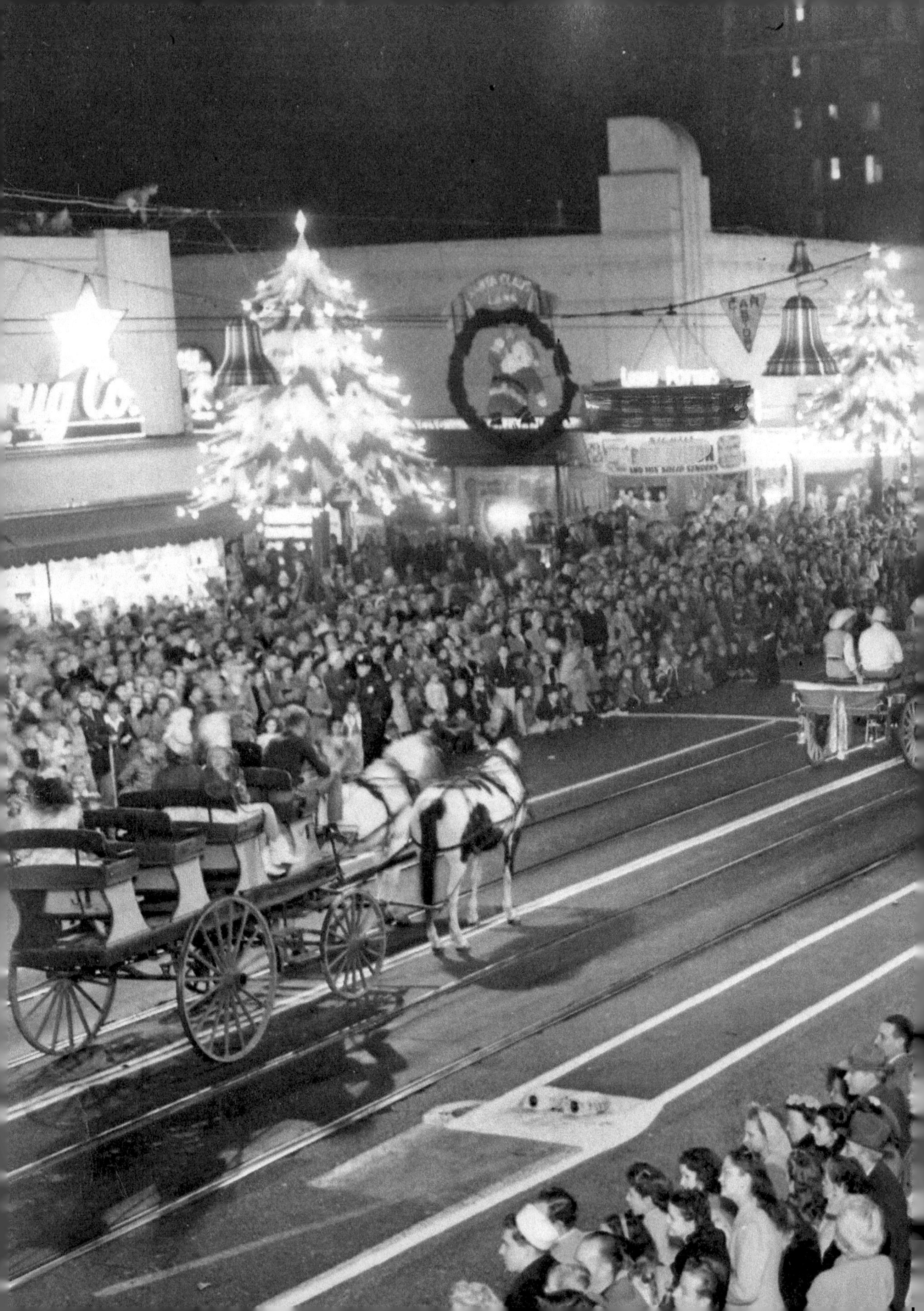
rug Co.

BOULEVARD / LANDSCAPES

Overleaf: Hollywood Boulevard's usual illumination gets a boost from holiday decorations during the annual Santa Claus Lane Parade. (1945, Howard Ballew/ Los Angeles Herald Examiner Collection)

Opposite: This view of Broadway from 10th Street (now Olympic) highlights why it became known as the "Great White Way of the West." (1931, Security Pacific National Bank Collection)

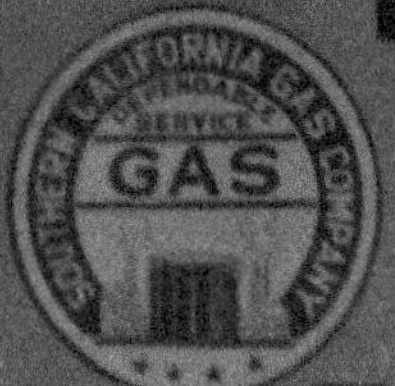
SOUTHERN CALIFORNIA GAS COMPANY
DEPENDABLE SERVICE
GAS

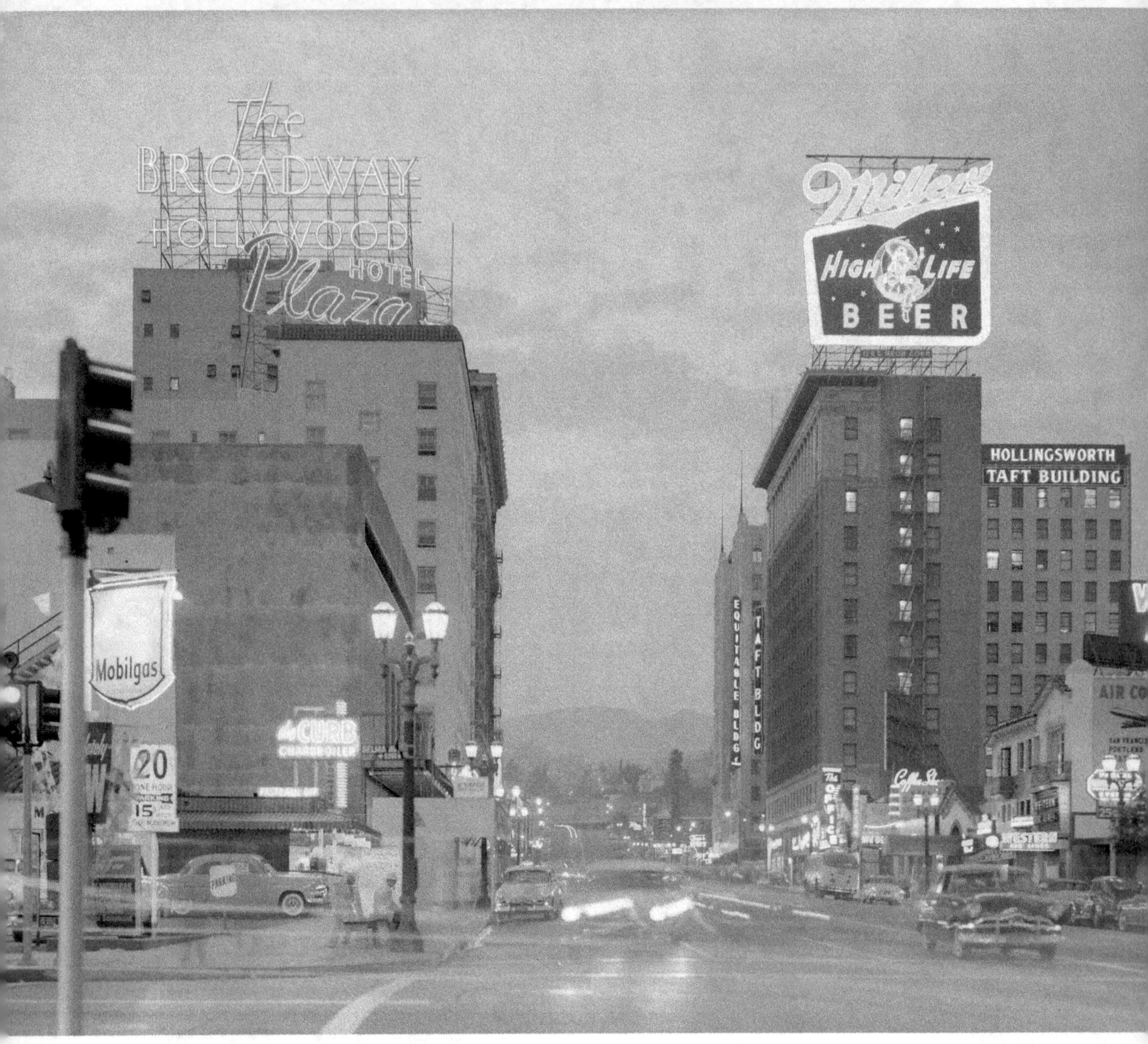

Hollywood is awash in neon in this view of Vine Street looking north from Selma Avenue. (Circa 1940/Ralph Morris Collection)

Opposite: The neon tower of the Richfield Building dominates Flower Street in this view from Wilshire Boulevard. (1966, Los Angeles Herald Examiner Collection)

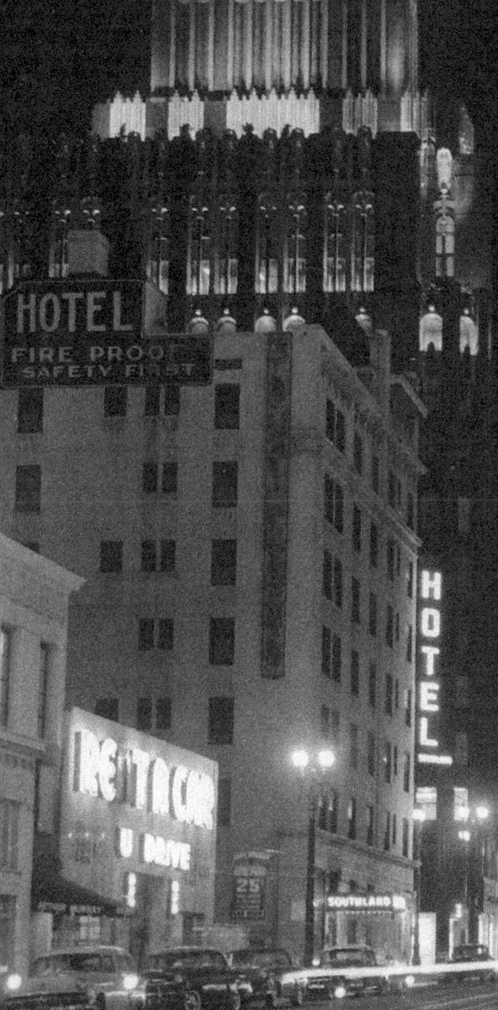
RICHFIELD
HOTEL
FIRE PROOF
SAFETY FIRST
HOTEL
U DRIVE
SOUTHLAND

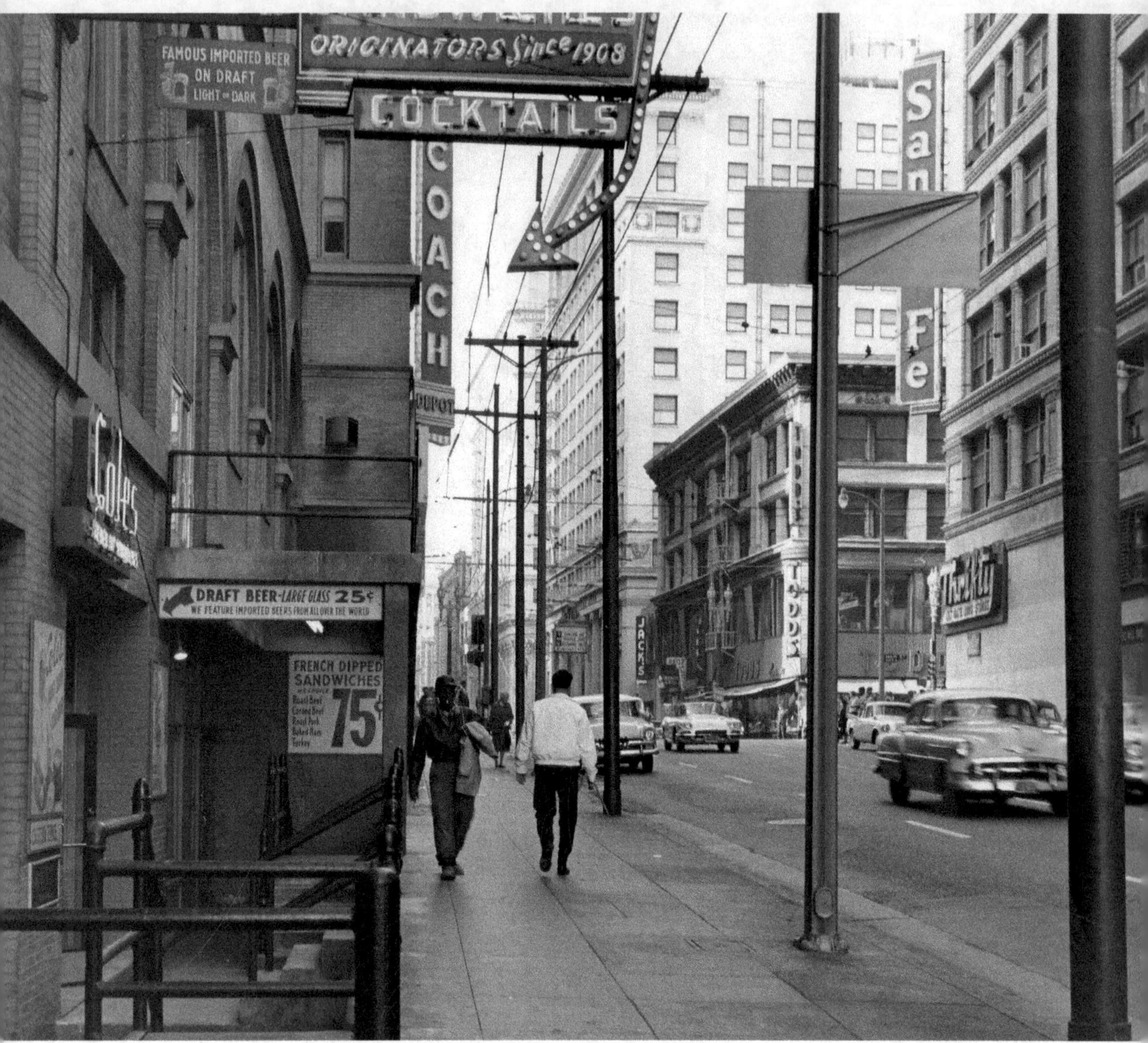

The commercial businesses visible in this image are long gone from the intersection of 6th and Main, but Cole's Pacific Electric Buffet lives on. Open in the same location since 1908, the landmark eatery is among the oldest in the city. It retains its 1940s neon signage which promotes its most famous sandwich, a Los Angeles original, the French Dip. (1962, William Reagh Collection)

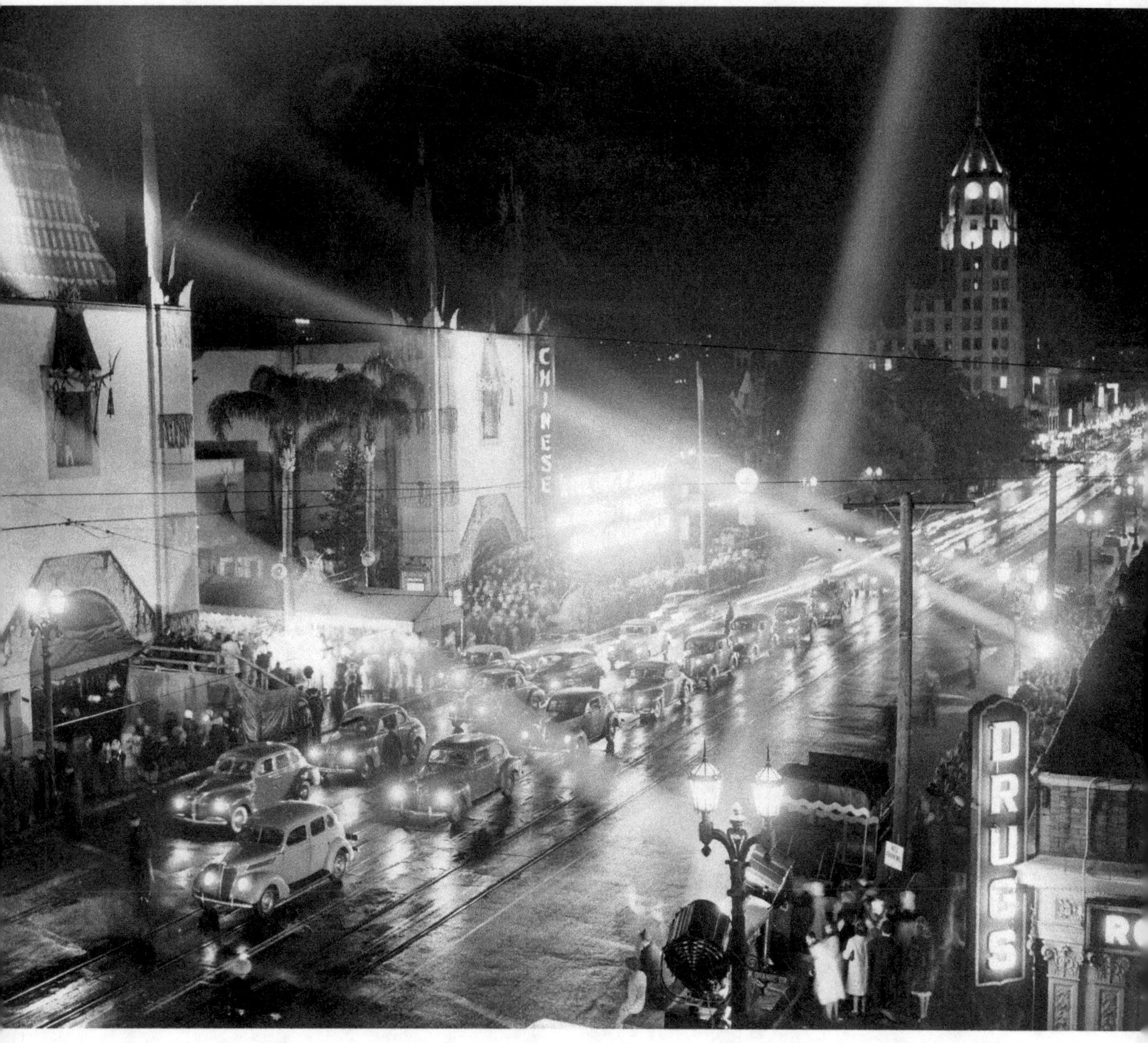

Klieg lights compliment the neon of Hollywood Boulevard during the premiere of *A Tree Grows in Brooklyn* at Grauman's Chinese Theatre. (1945, Security Pacific National Bank)

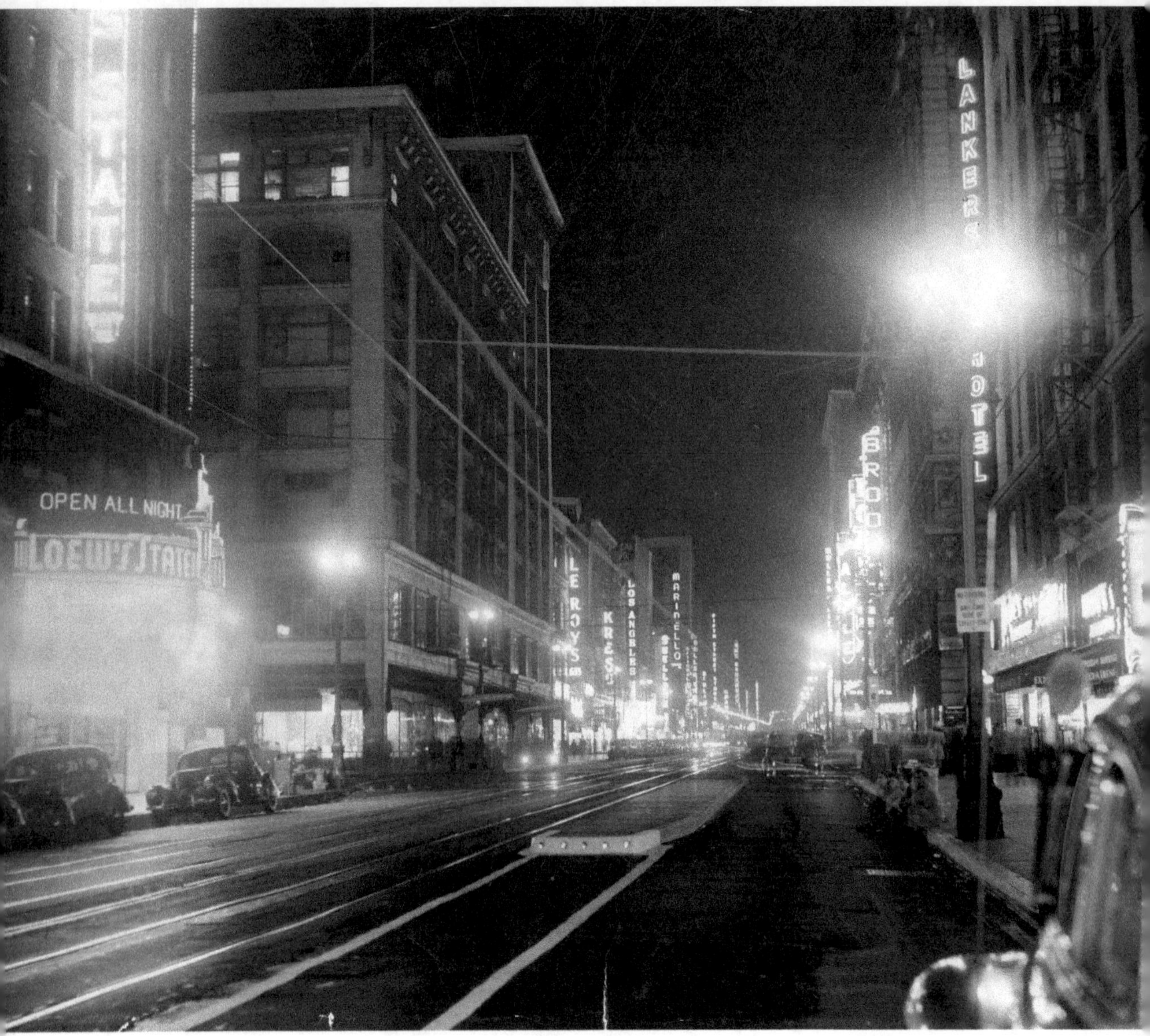

Los Angeles' office and commercial buildings stretch to infinity along Broadway, the city's premiere theater district in the early twentieth century. Loew's State Theatre dominates the corner at 7th Street with an eye-catching marquee as a plethora of vertical signs march onward. (1946. Los Angeles Herald Examiner Collection)

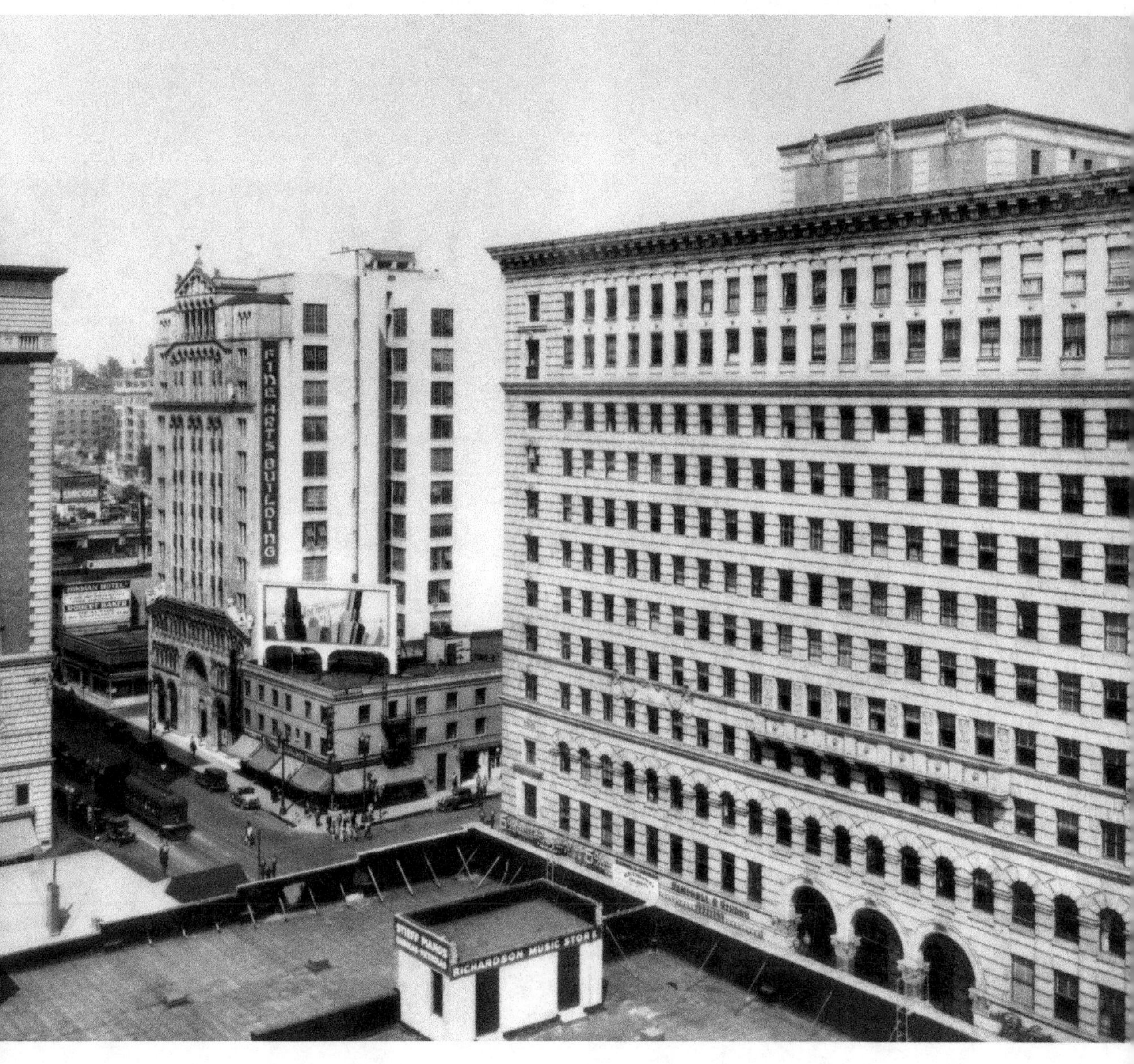

A daytime view shows neon dotting the buildings at 7th & Flower Streets.
(1930, Security Pacific National Bank)

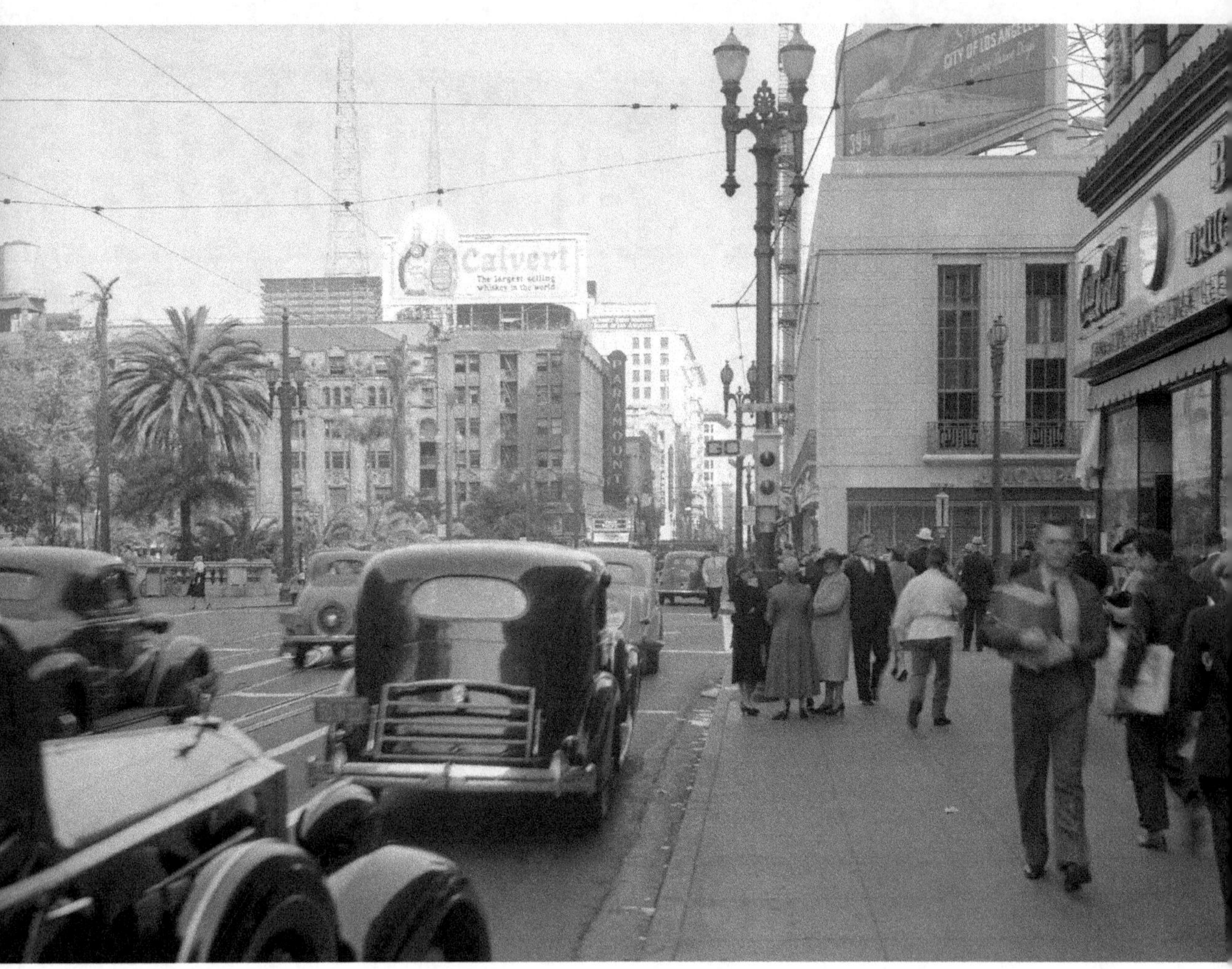

Plenty of neon is to be found in the daytime view of 6th Street, looking east at Olive Street. (Circa 1939, Blackstock Negative Collection)

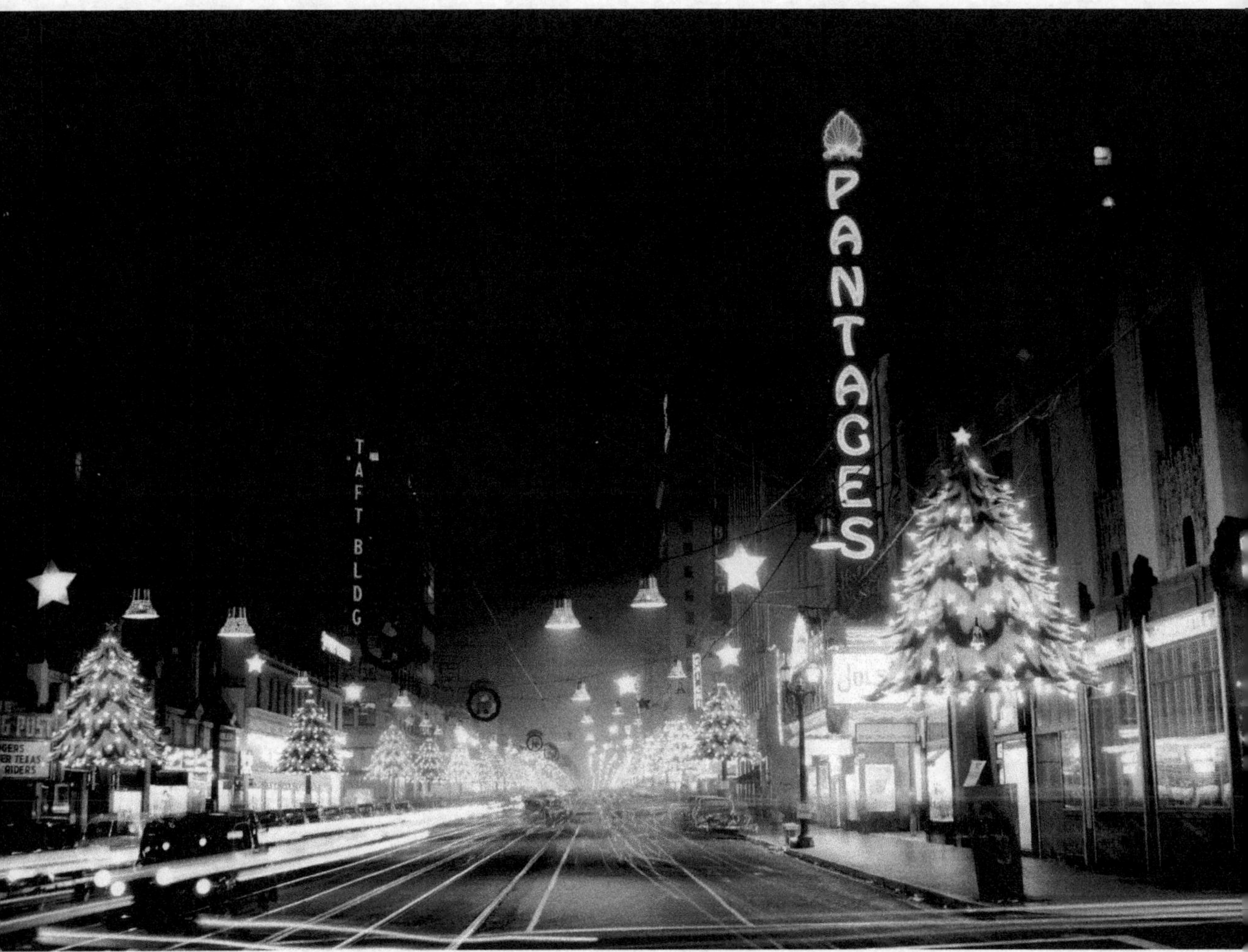

Hollywood Boulevard was even more aglow in the holiday season as stylized Christmas trees were alight with hundreds of colored, electric light bulbs. The neighborhood's Chamber of Commerce put on quite a show for its Hollywood Christmas Parade. At the Hitching Post Theatre, left, Roy Roger's *Rainbow over Texas* plays across the street from the Pantages Theatre's *Al Jolson Story*. (1946, Security Pacific National Bank Collection)

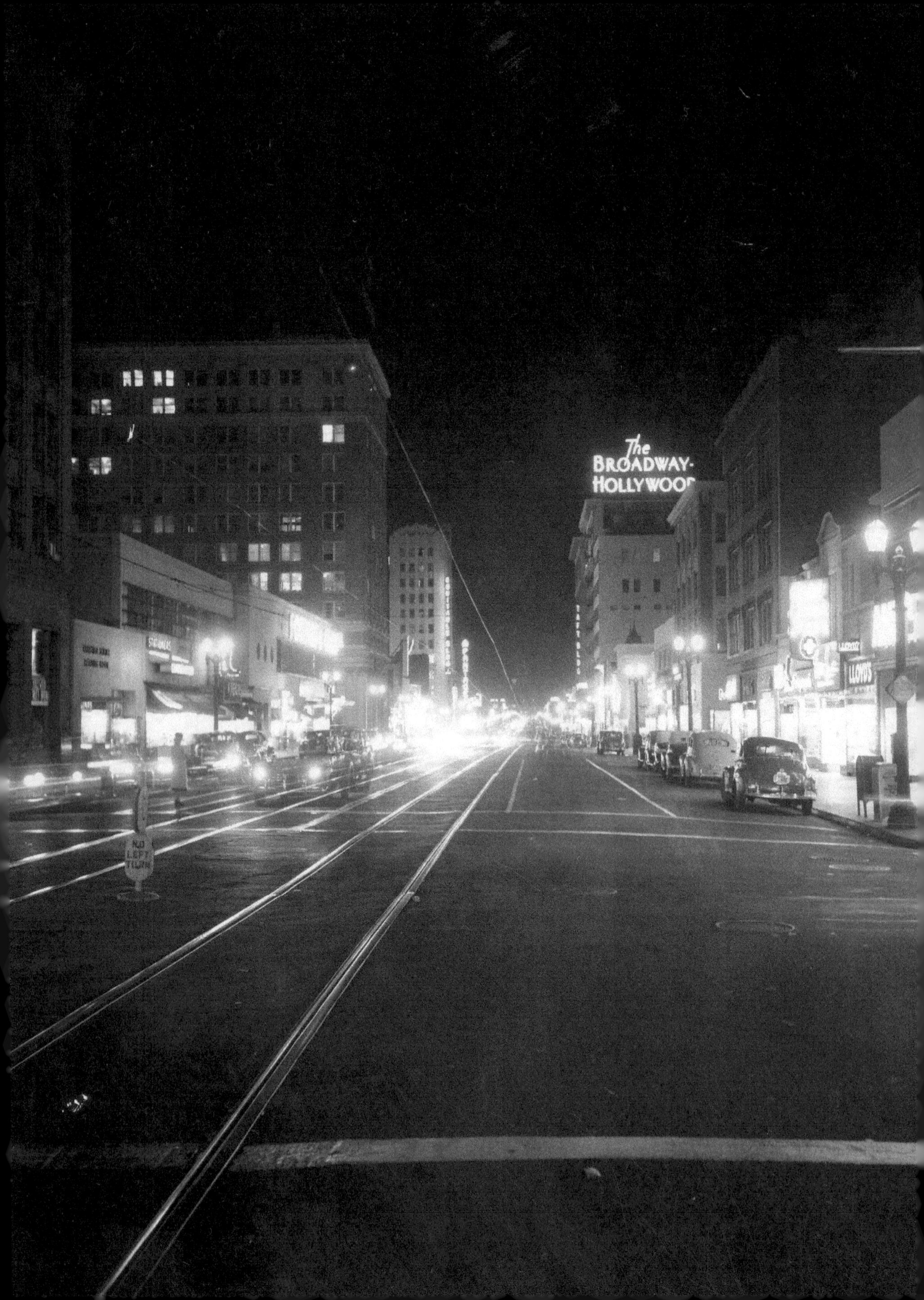

The
BROADWAY-
HOLLYWOOD
NO
LEFT
TURN
LLOYD'S

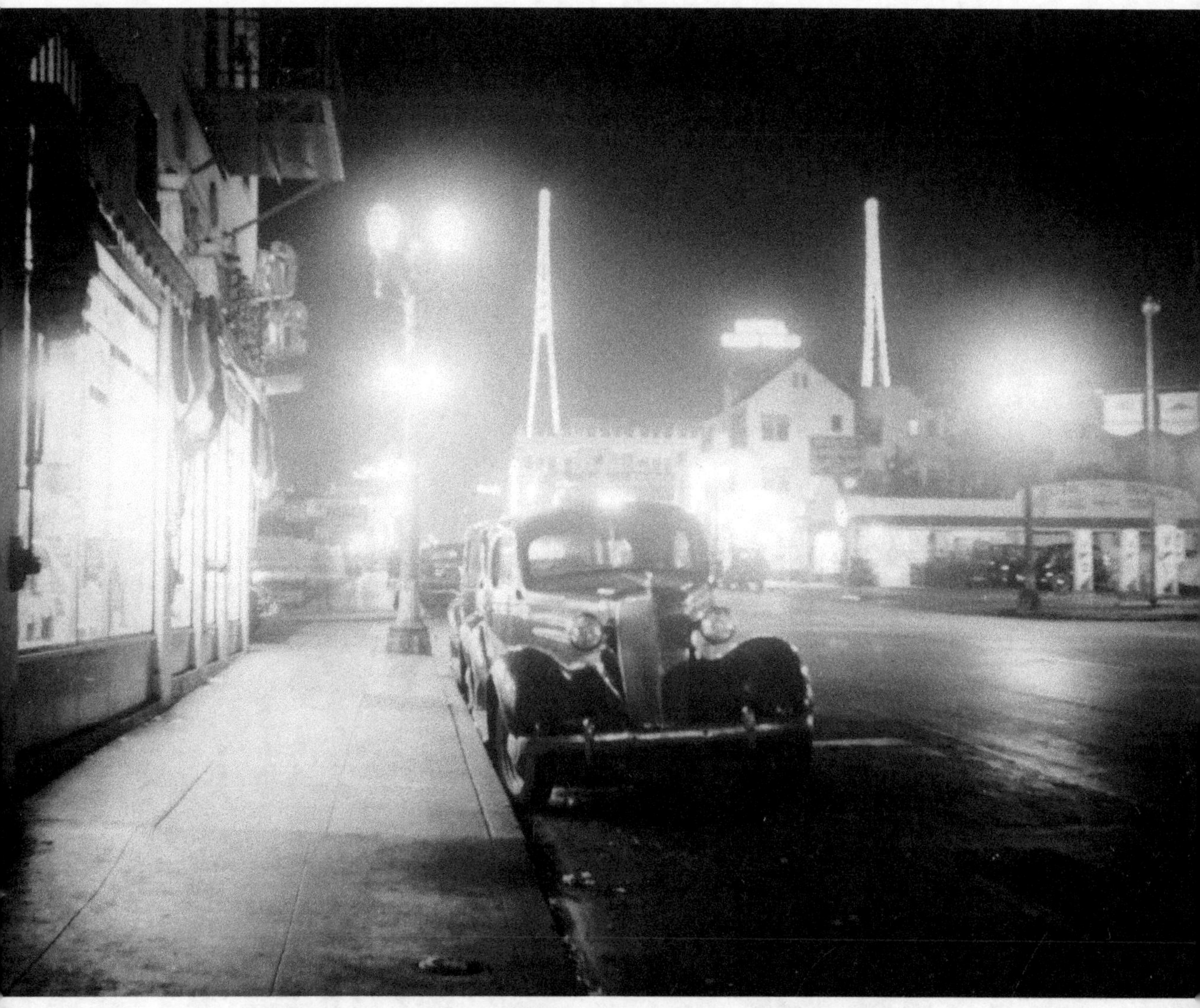

Photographer Herman Schultheis captured a moment of Hollywood noir as streetlights and neon signs blurred together in a moody, nighttime shot. The large, neon and light bulb encrusted radio towers of KFWB rise in the background atop the Warner Bros. Theatre. Residential rooftop crowns, the neon signs that sit atop apartment buildings, are also visible: the Hotel Mark Twain to the right, the Lido and Mayfair Apartments in the far distance. (1937, Herman J. Schultheis Collection)

Opposite: Looking east on Hollywood Boulevard, the Broadway Hollywood sign stands out against the night sky. (Circa 1940s, Ralph Morris Collection)

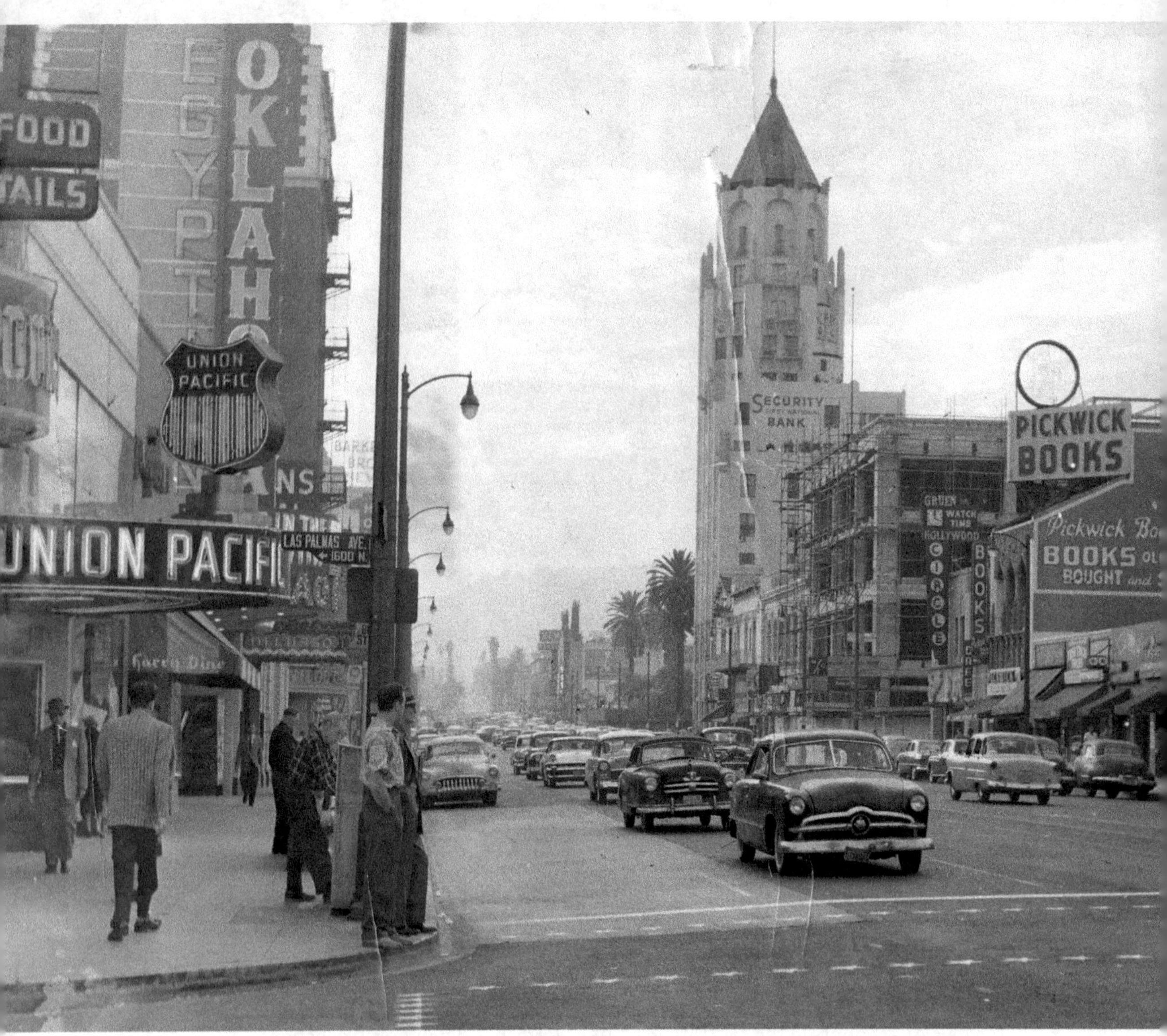

A Union Pacific neon sign provides some illumination in this dramatic shot of the intersection at Hollywood Boulevard and Las Palmas Ave. (Circa 1955, Security Pacific National Bank Collection)

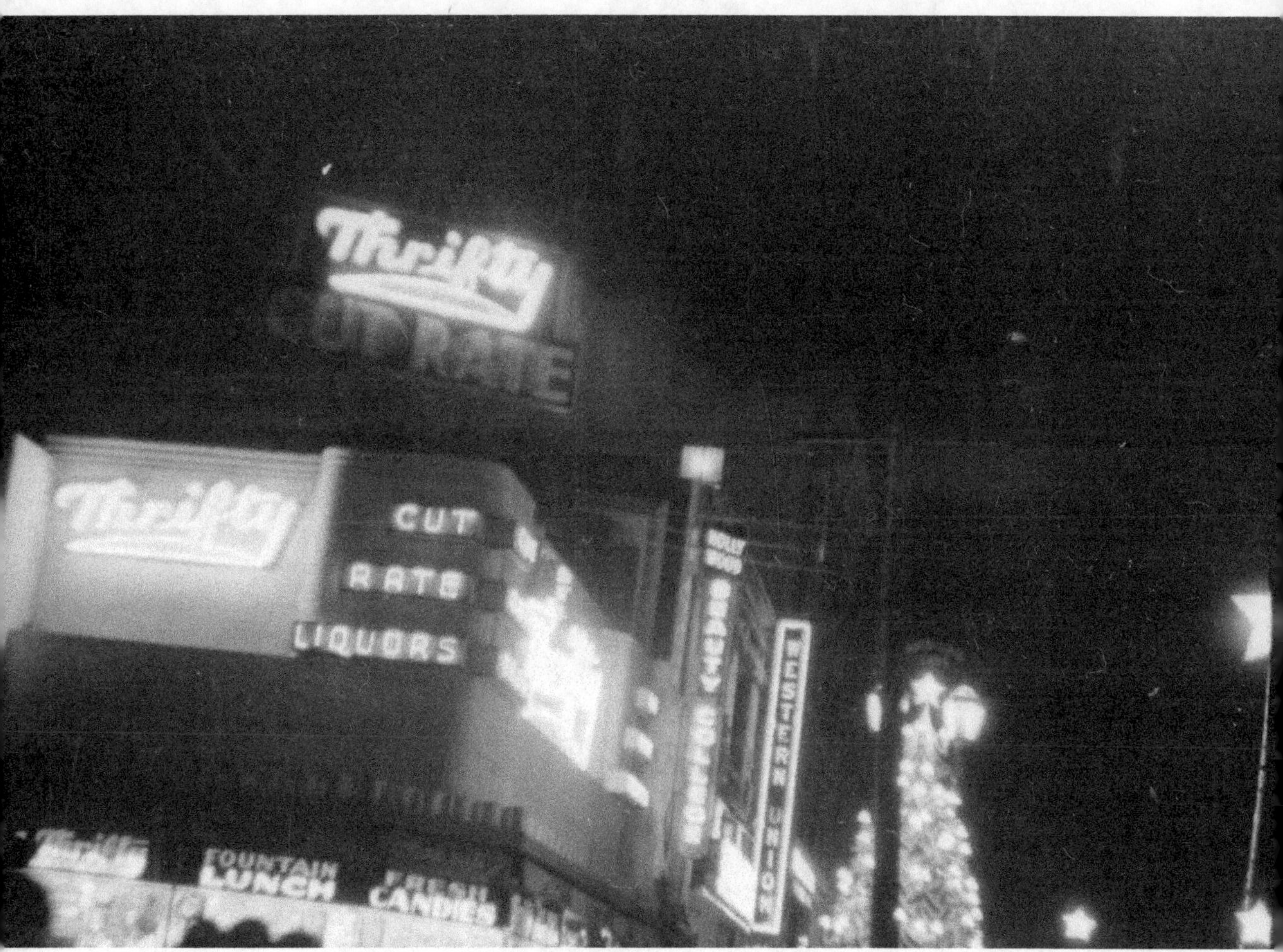

A view of Hollywood Boulevard and Ivar Avenue presents a wide variety of neon signage. (Circa 1930s, Herman J. Schultheis Collection)

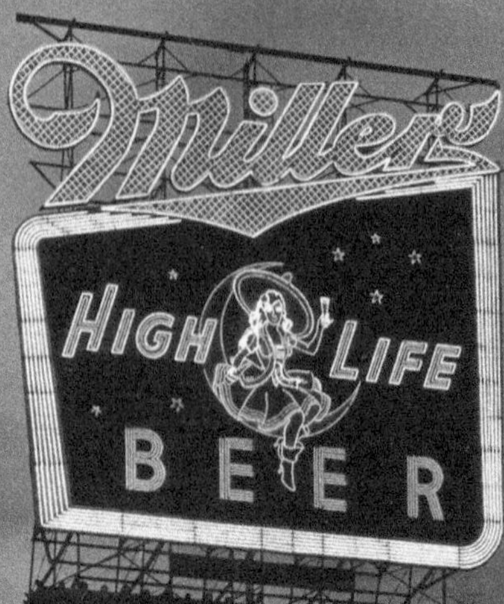
Miller
HIGH LIFE
BEER

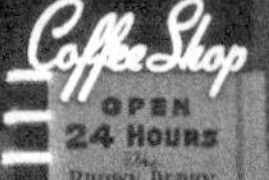
Coffee Shop
OPEN
24 HOURS
The
BROWN DERBY

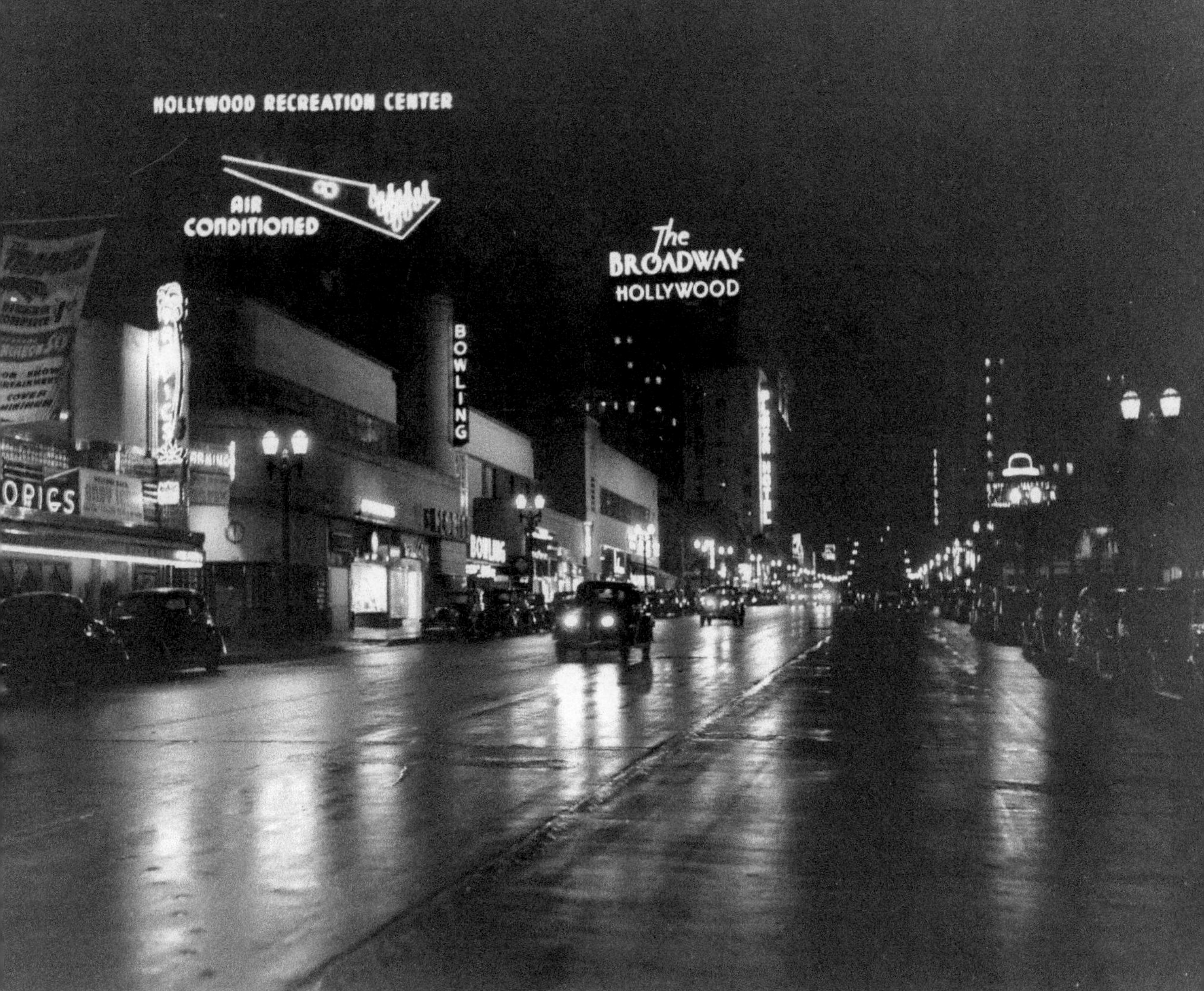

The neon of Vine Street is reflected on the pavement below. (Circa 1940s, Security Pacific National Bank Collection)

Opposite: Vine Street was the city's epicenter of national radio programing, the symbolic heart of Hollywood, and a major destination for fans of neon signage. Along with downtown's Broadway and the nearby Hollywood Boulevard, little compared to the bright lights of Vine which glittered like the many stars and celebrities at the ABC, NBC, and CBS radio stations. The animated Miller High Life Beer sign was among the best in the city and was visible for miles. It sat high above the Brown Derby restaurant and its quick-bite Coffee Shop, below. Although the famed Miller neon sign is long gone, the Brown Derby's rooftop sign and Coffee Shop lettering survives at the Museum of Neon Art (MONA, www.neonmona.org). (Circa 1950s, Security Pacific National Bank Collection)

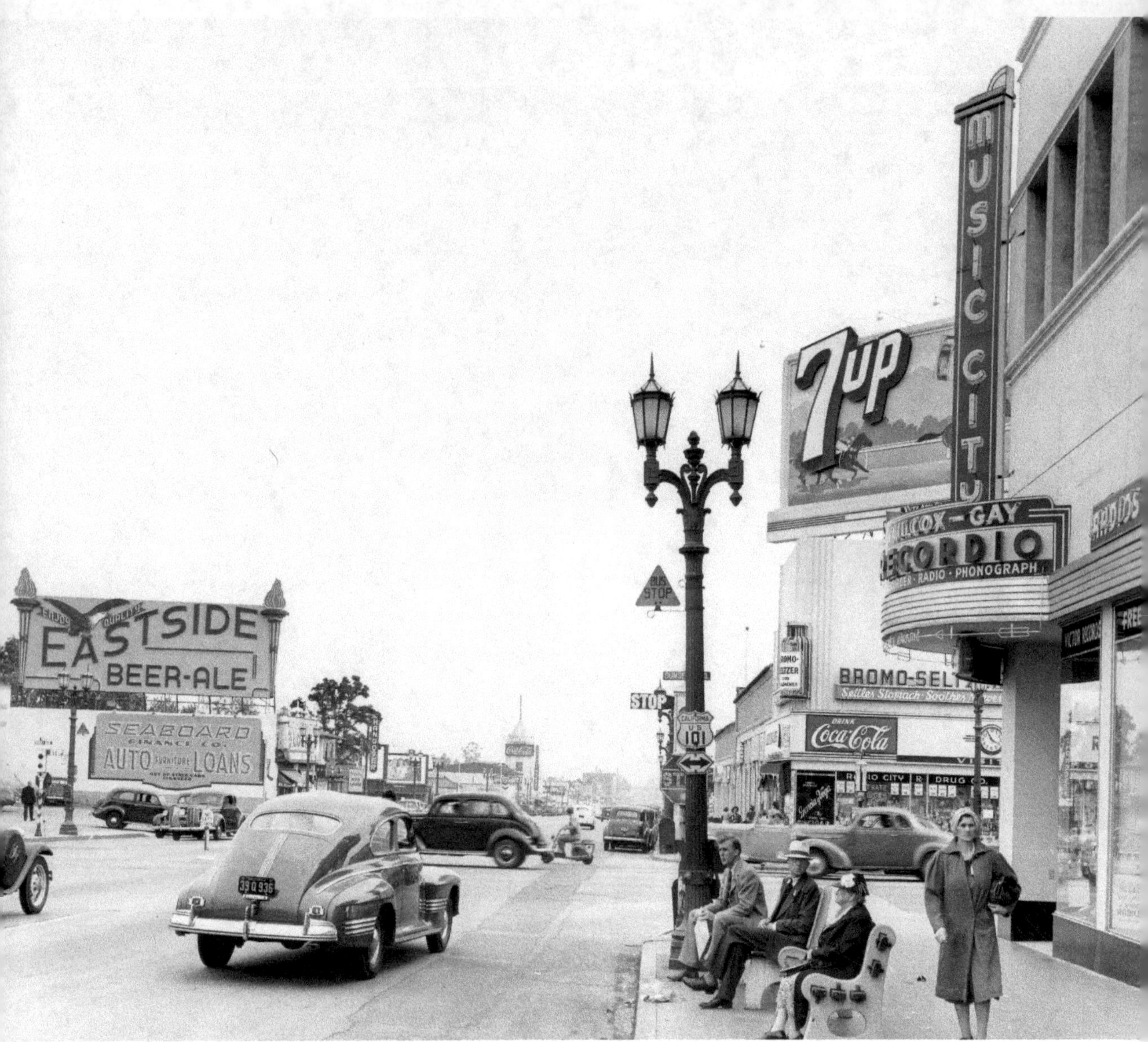

Pedestrians and commuters are surrounded by neon signage at the intersection of Sunset and Vine in Hollywood. (Circa 1940s. Security Pacific National Bank Collection)

Neon is present in almost every corner in this image of Hollywood. (Circa 1930s, Security Pacific National Bank Collection)

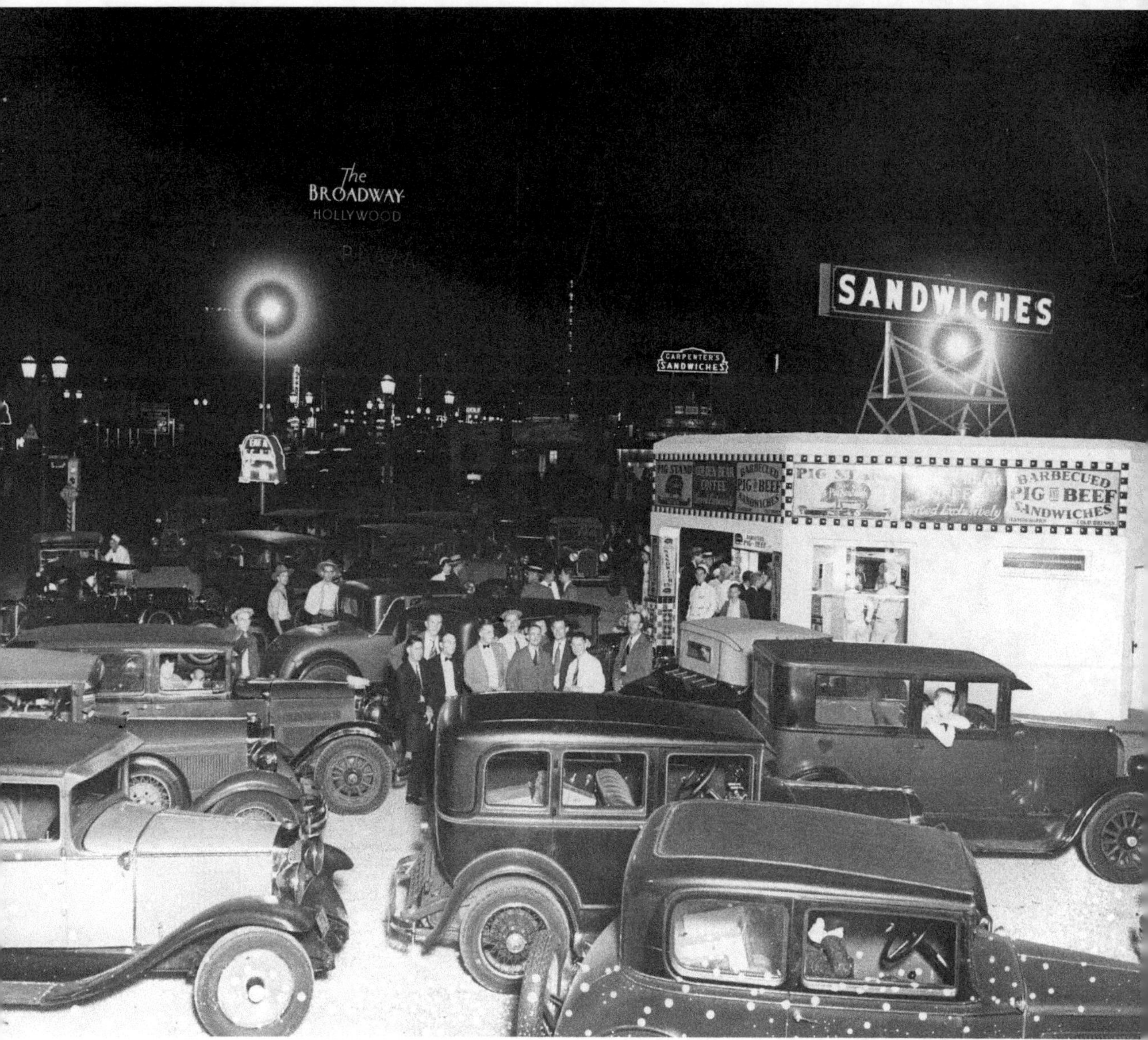

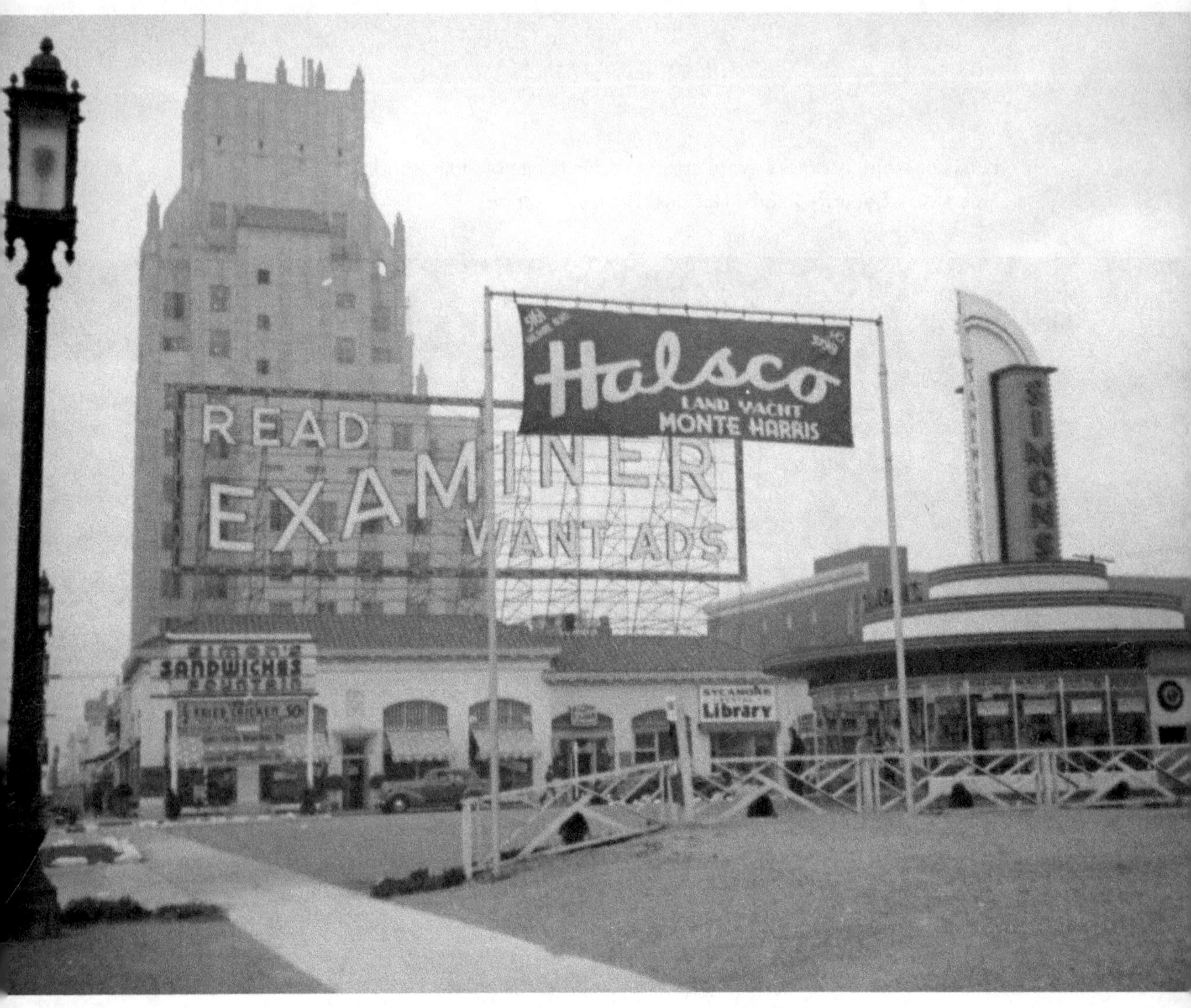

The Art Deco the E. Clem Wilson Building stands tall above signage for Simon's Drive-In and the Los Angeles Examiner Newspaper on Wilshire Boulevard. (Circa 1937, Herman J. Schultheis Collection)

Opposite: A Beverly Hills portion of Wilshire Boulevard shows off its neon in daylight. (Circa 1937, Security Pacific National Bank Collection)

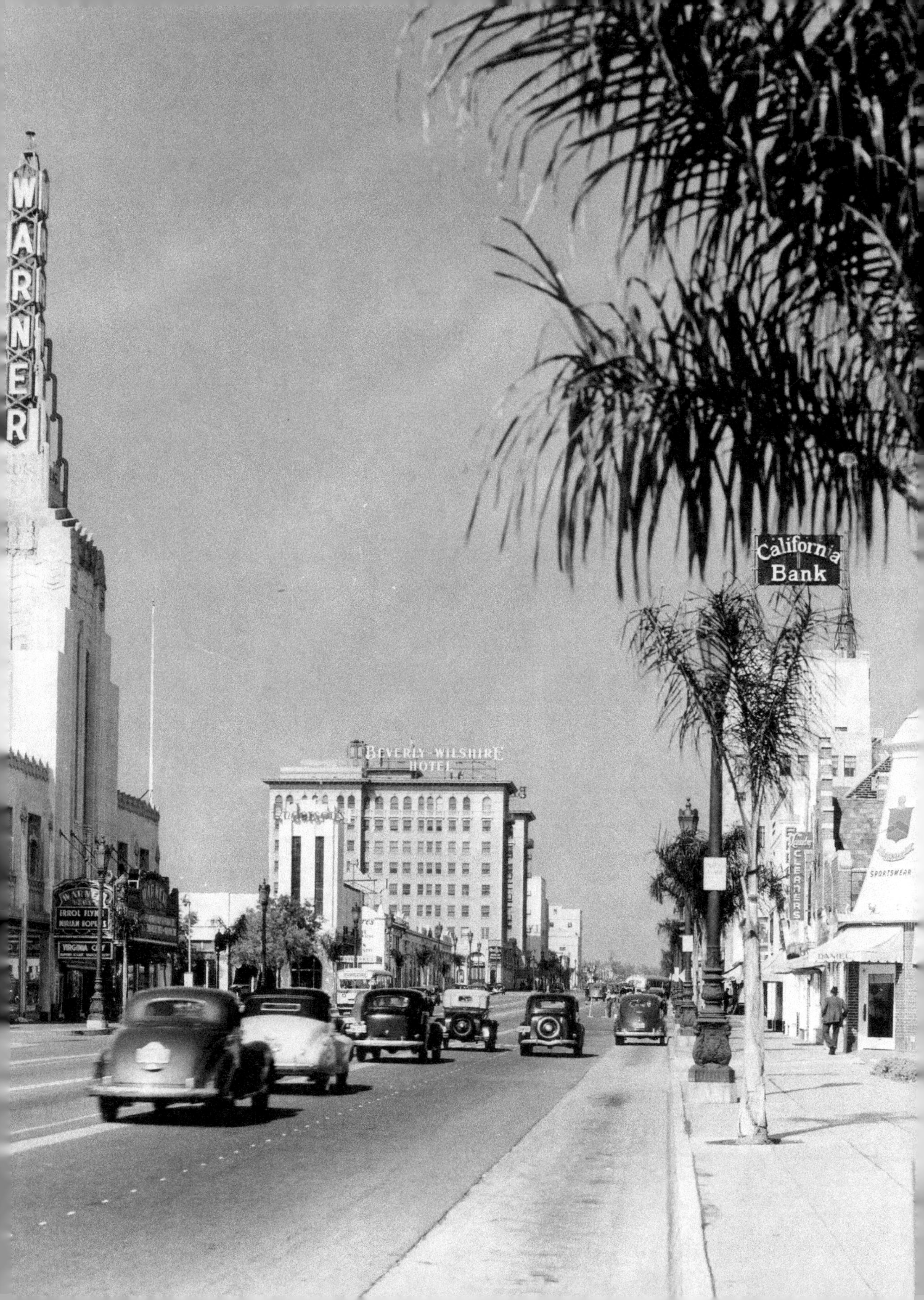
WARNER
BEVERLY WILSHIRE
HOTEL
California Bank
VIRGINIA CITY
CLEANERS
SPORTSWEAR

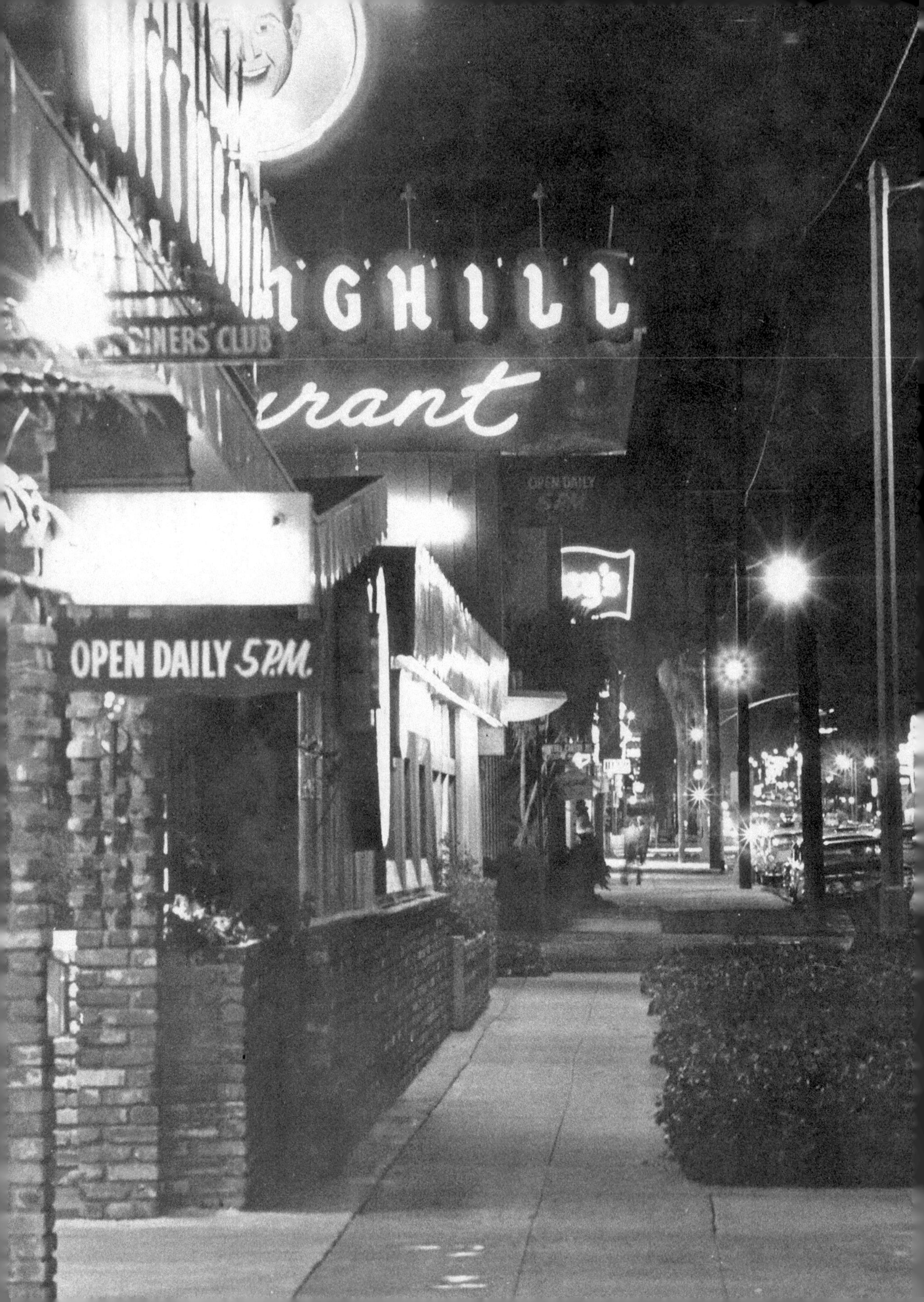

GHILL
INERS' CLUB
rant
OPEN DAILY 5 P.M.

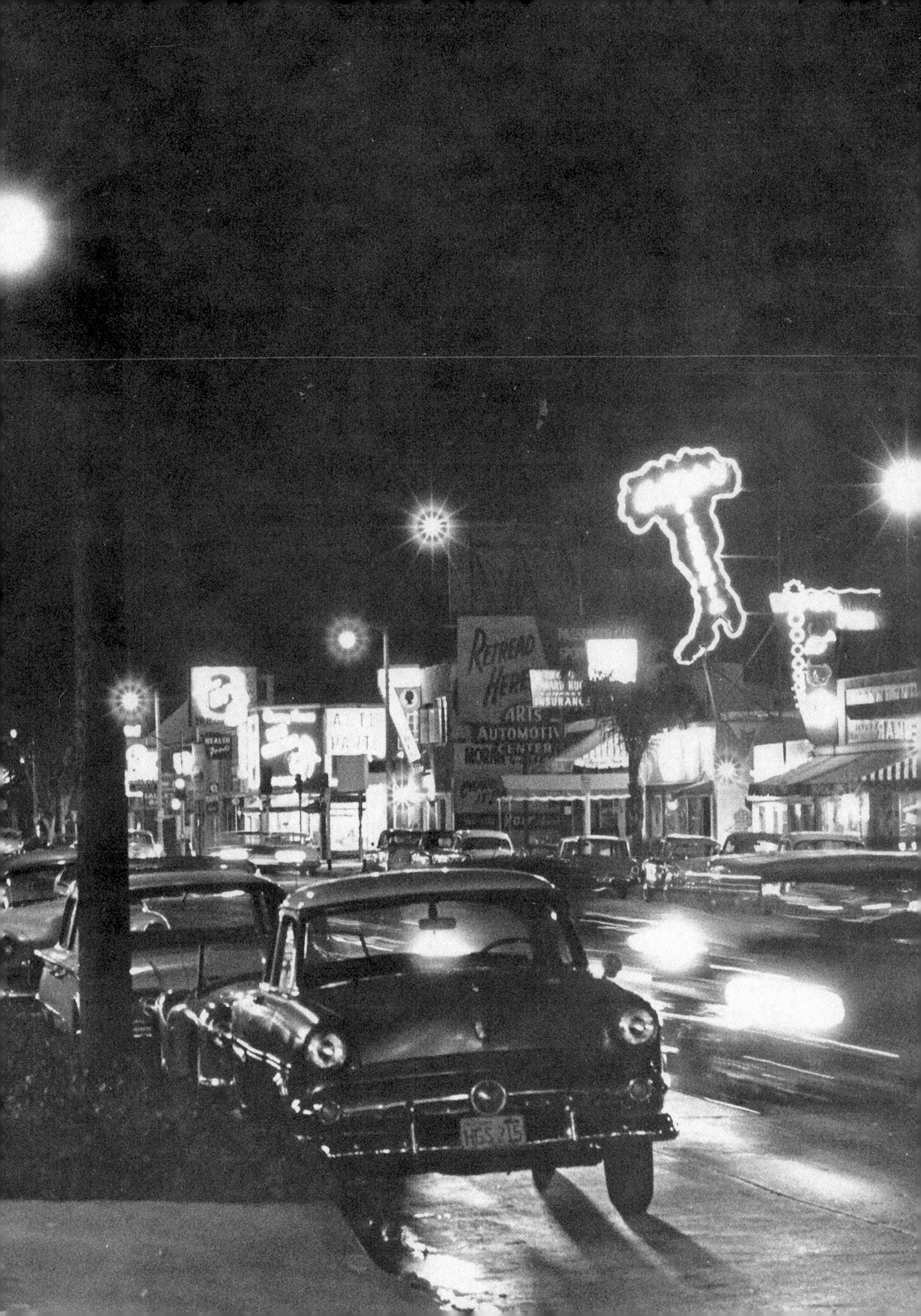
Retread
AUTOMOTIV
CENTER
INSURANCE

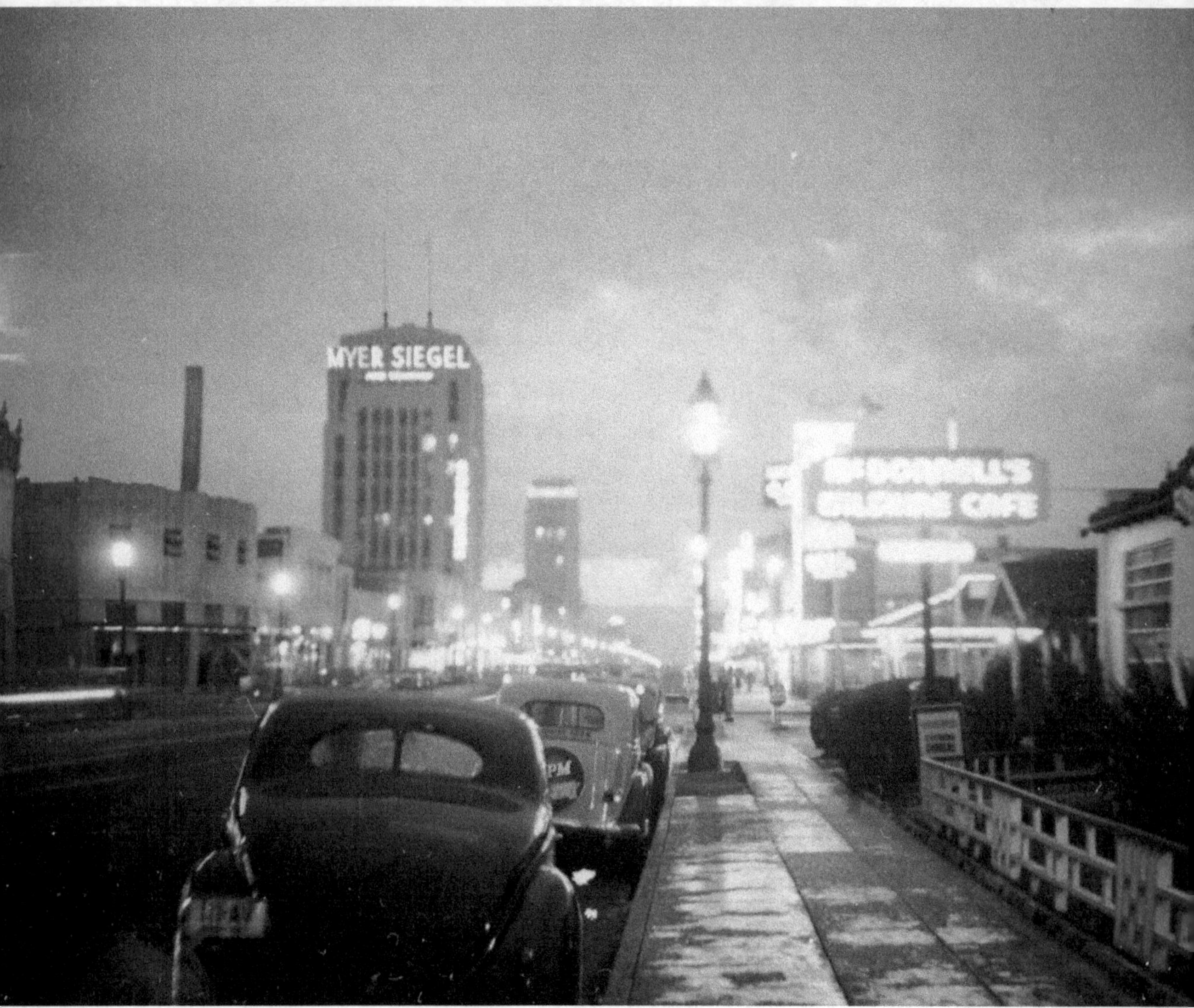

The seemingly infinite streets of Los Angeles were lit with countless neon signs. To appear modern, every business had to present itself with neon signage or detailing in at least one way, shape, or form. Myer Siegel clothiers and Desmond's haberdashery, beyond, are the tallest in this Miracle Mile street scene and were visible for miles. (1937, Herman J. Schultheis Collection)

Overleaf: Neon lights the way on a Sherman Oaks segment of Ventura Boulevard. (Circa 1960, George Brich/Valley Times Collection)

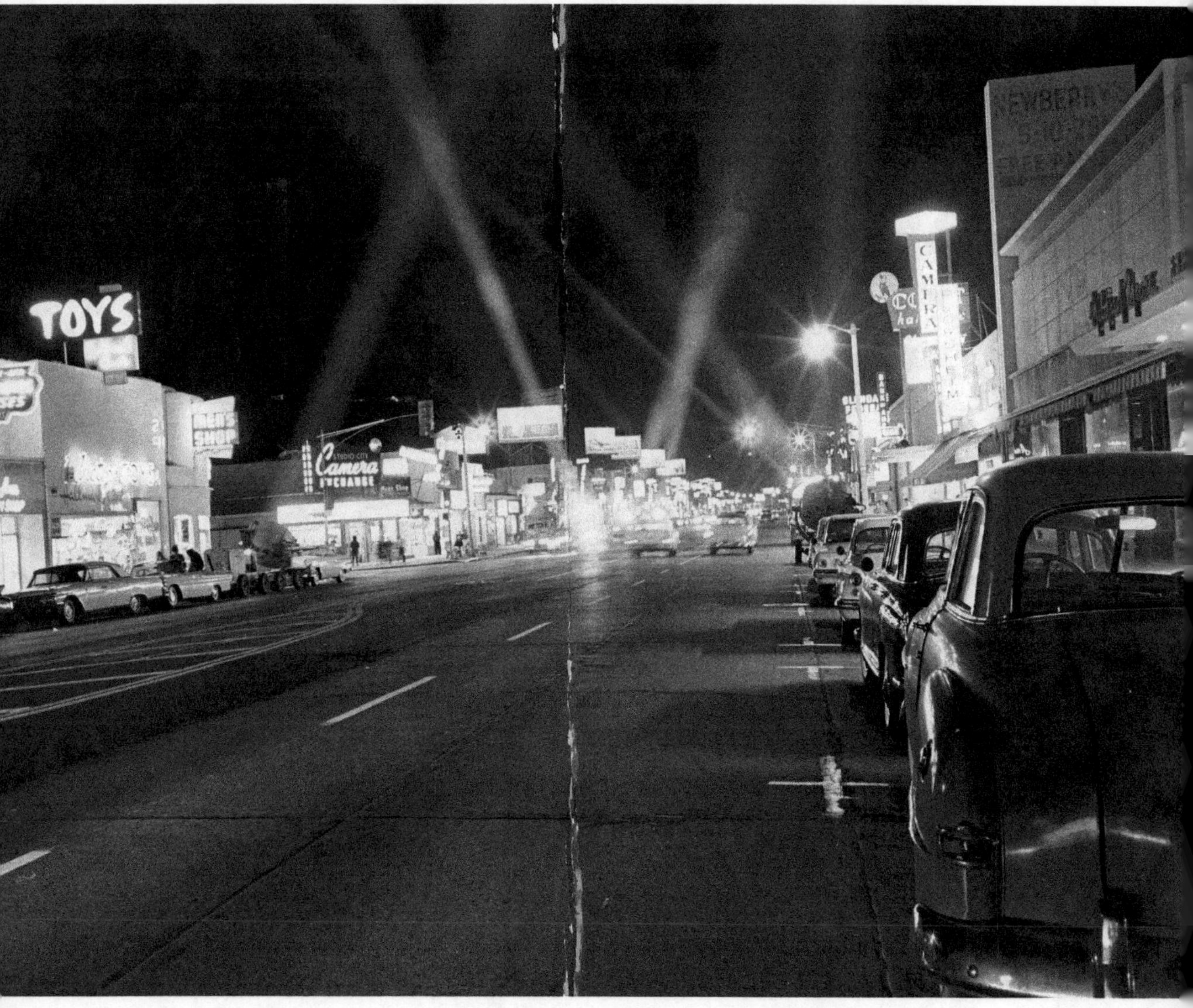

The streets of Los Angeles were unlike any other city; the quantity of neon and illuminated signs stretched as far as the road would travel. Every commercial corridor was bedazzled. Los Angeles businesses competed along the streetscape with window neon, fascia neon, over-sidewalk neon, and rooftop neon just name a few sign examples. The Studio City Camera Exchange neon sign, at left, has been donated to the Museum of Neon Art in Glendale, California (MONA, www.neonmona.org). (1962, Jeff Goldwater/Valley Times Collection)

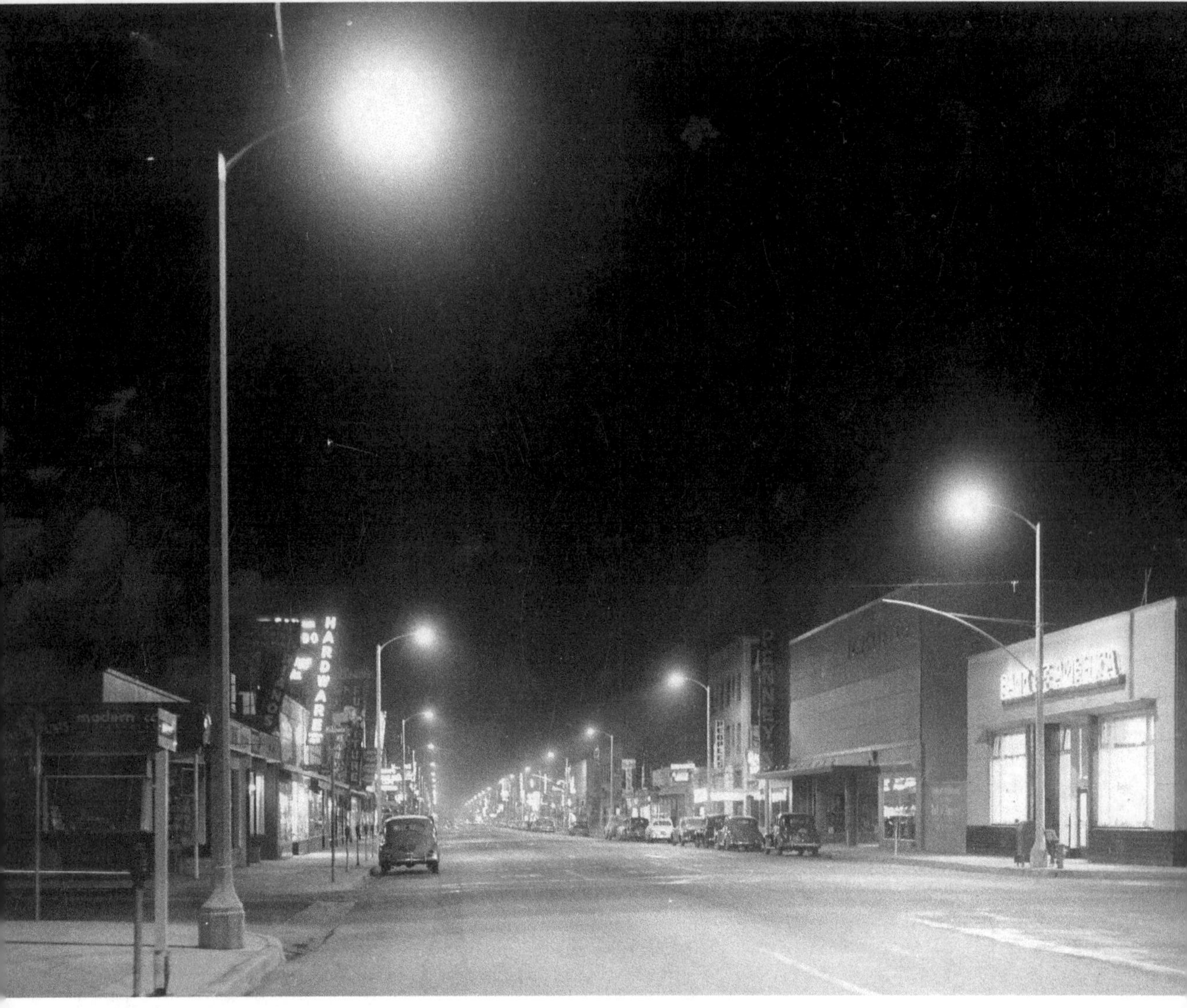

The neon of San Fernando Road in the city of San Fernando is joined by lumen street lamps which had recently been installed at the time this image was taken. (1954, Valley Times Collection)

Opposite: Neon signs are as ubiquitous to the Los Angeles skyline as its palm trees, as demonstrated in this view of Van Nuys Boulevard in the San Fernando Valley. In fact, it's difficult to imagine Los Angeles without such icons although neither are native to the region. (1960, George Brich/Valley Times Collection)

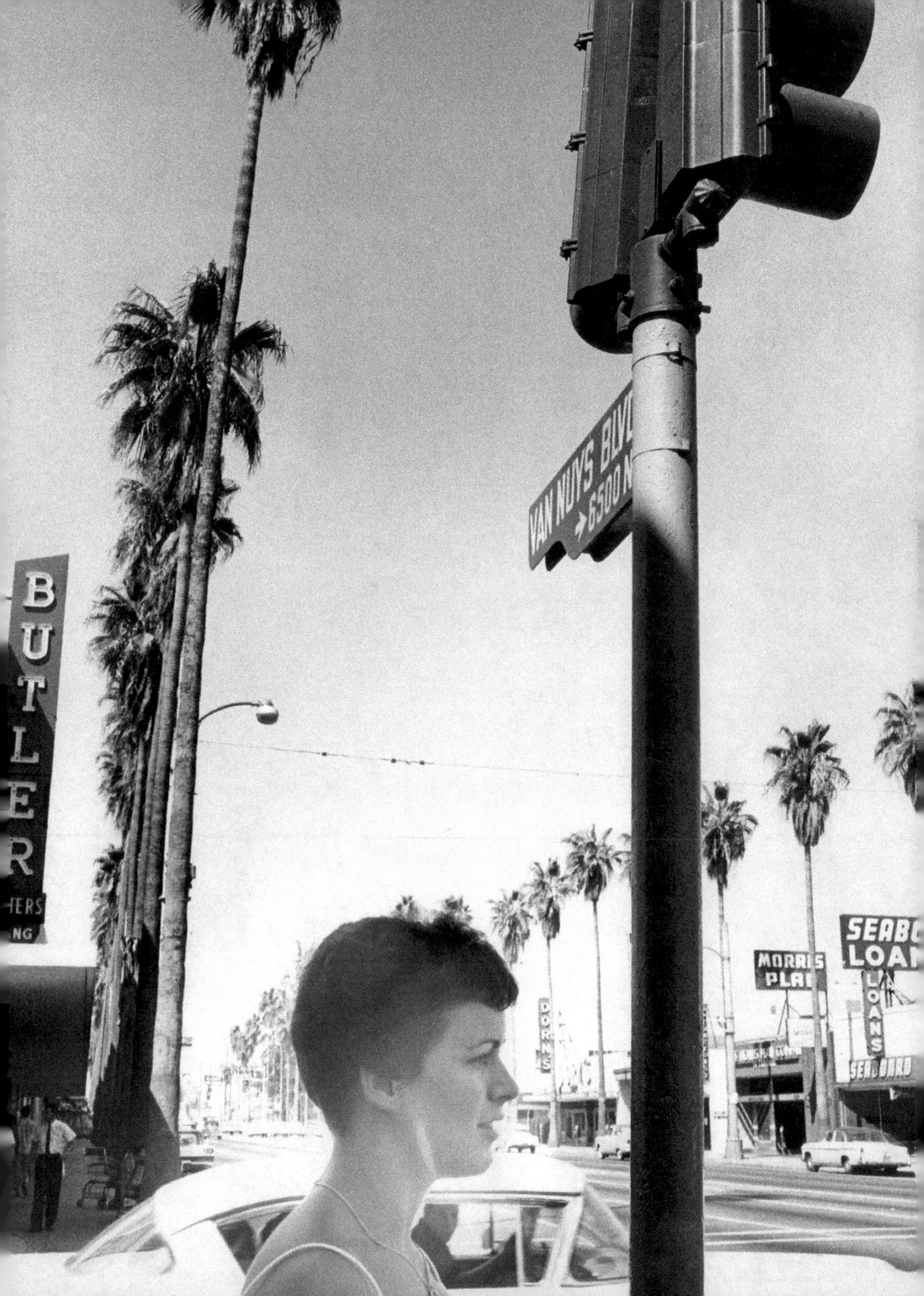
BUTLER
VAN NUYS BLV
6500 N
DORNS
LOANS
SEABOARD

CHINATOWN

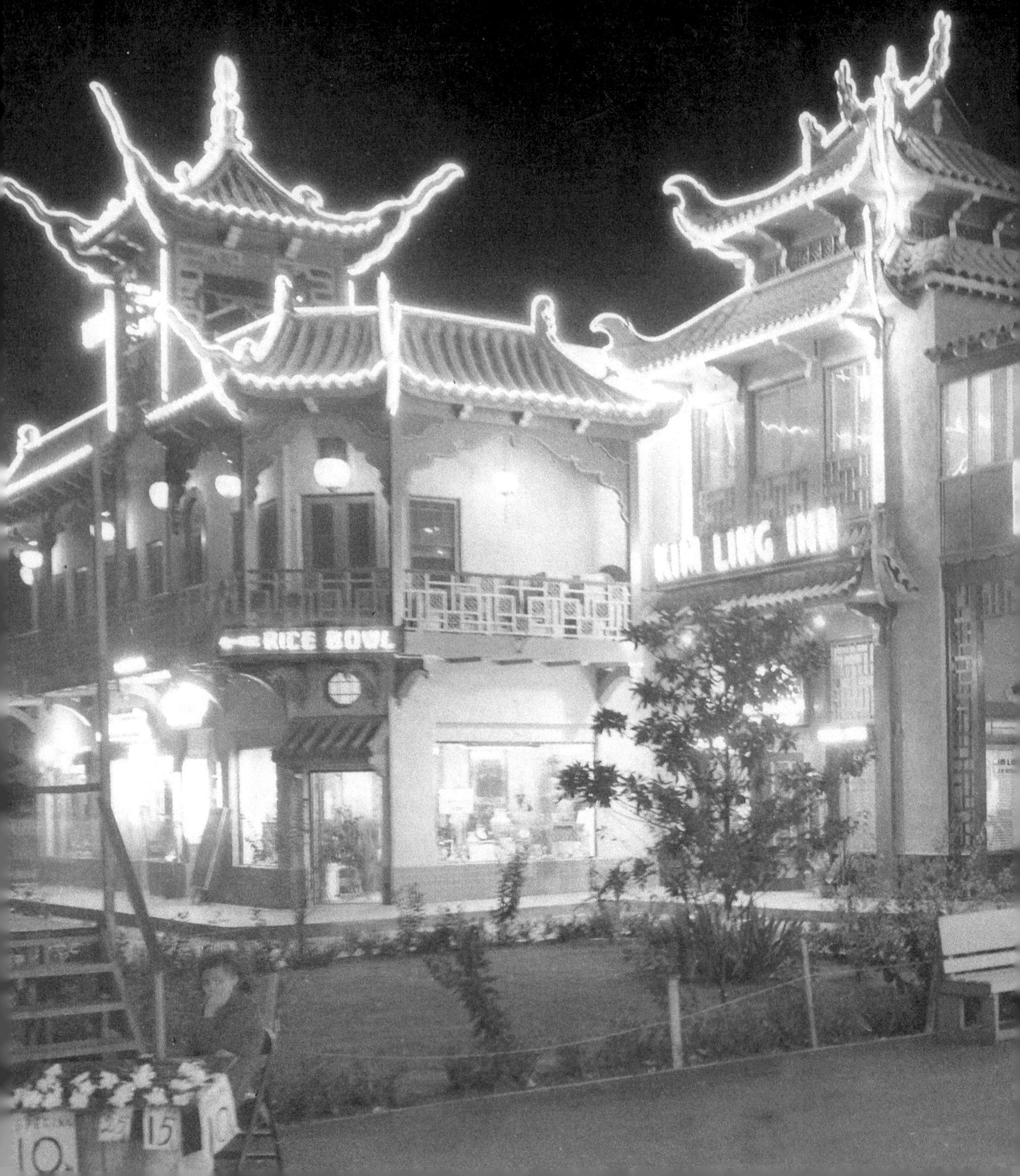

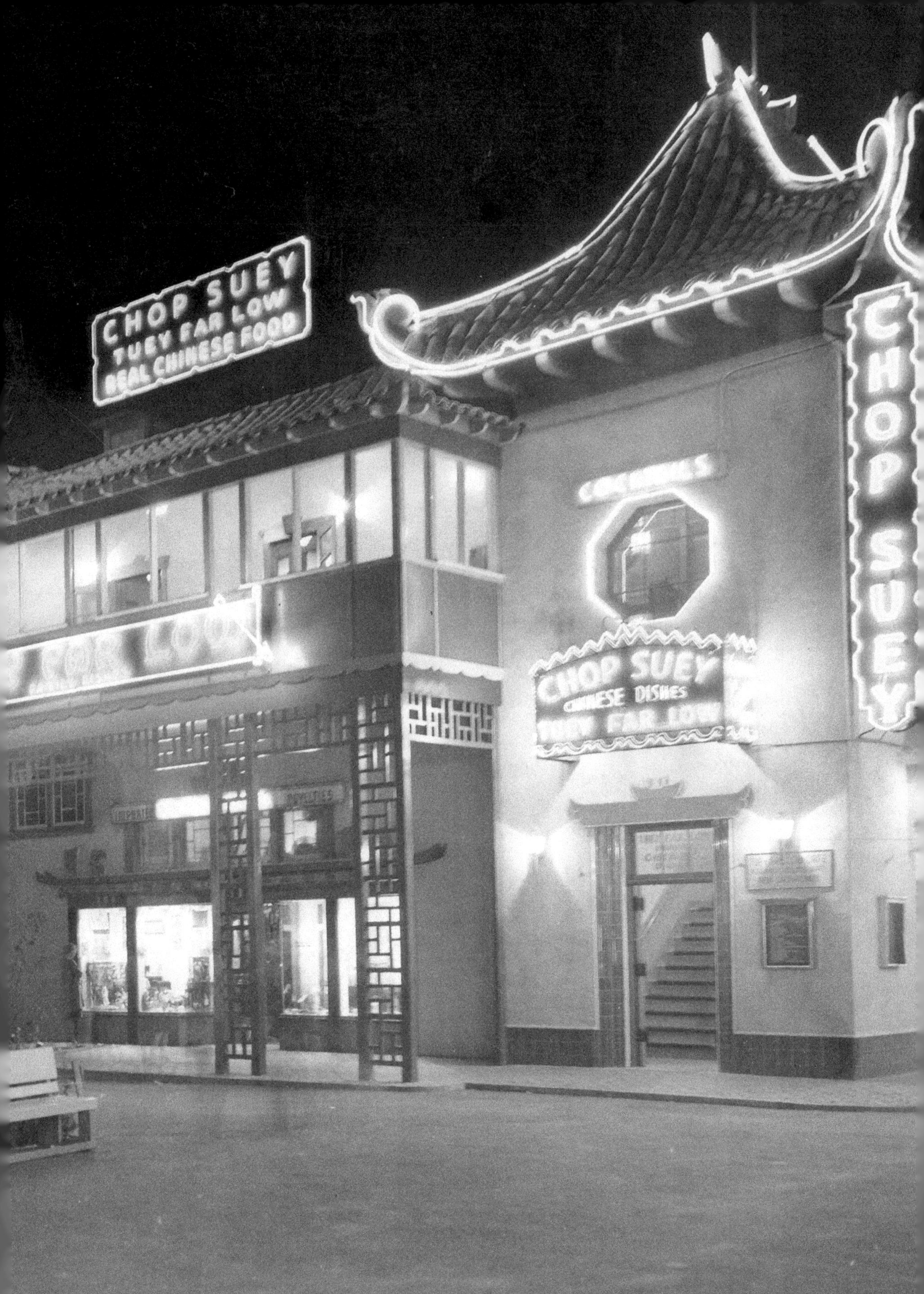
CHOP SUEY
TUEY FAR LOW
REAL CHINESE FOOD
CHOP SUEY
CHOP SUEY
CHINESE DISHES
TUEY FAR LOW

Overleaf: (Circa 1940s, Security Pacific National Bank Collection)

Opposite: In 1941, the five tiers of the Golden Pagoda restaurant were constructed in New Chinatown and illuminated top to bottom with yellow neon tubing. Its height, looming over the low-rise structures around it, was a beacon in the night. Yet it wasn't alone as its neighbors also decked out their Chinese-style rooftops with glowing ribbons of neon to make Chinatown a colorful, commercial destination.
(1948, Harry Quillen Collection)

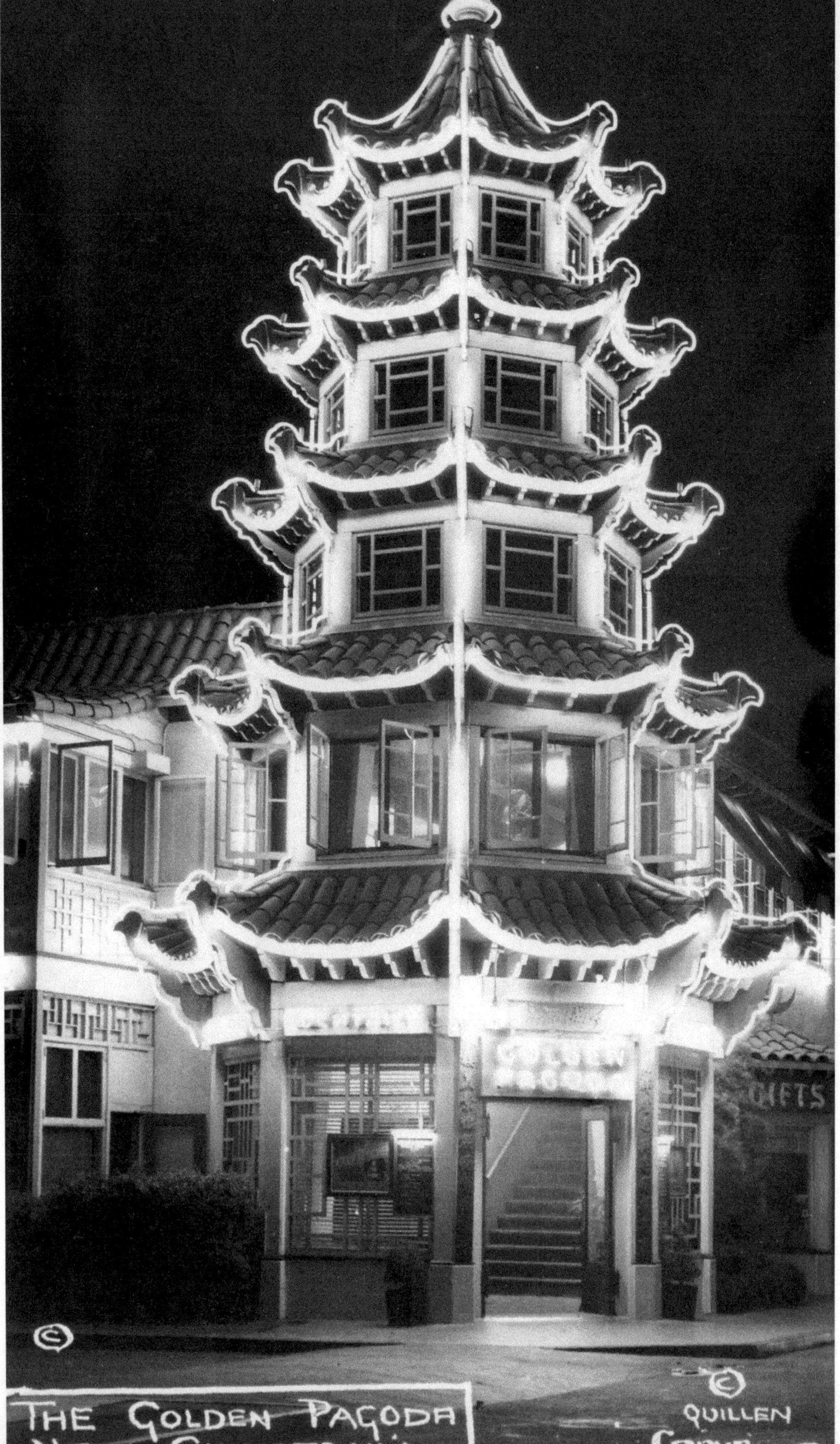
THE GOLDEN PAGODA
NEW CHINATOWN
GIFTS
QUILLEN
COPYRIGHT
1948

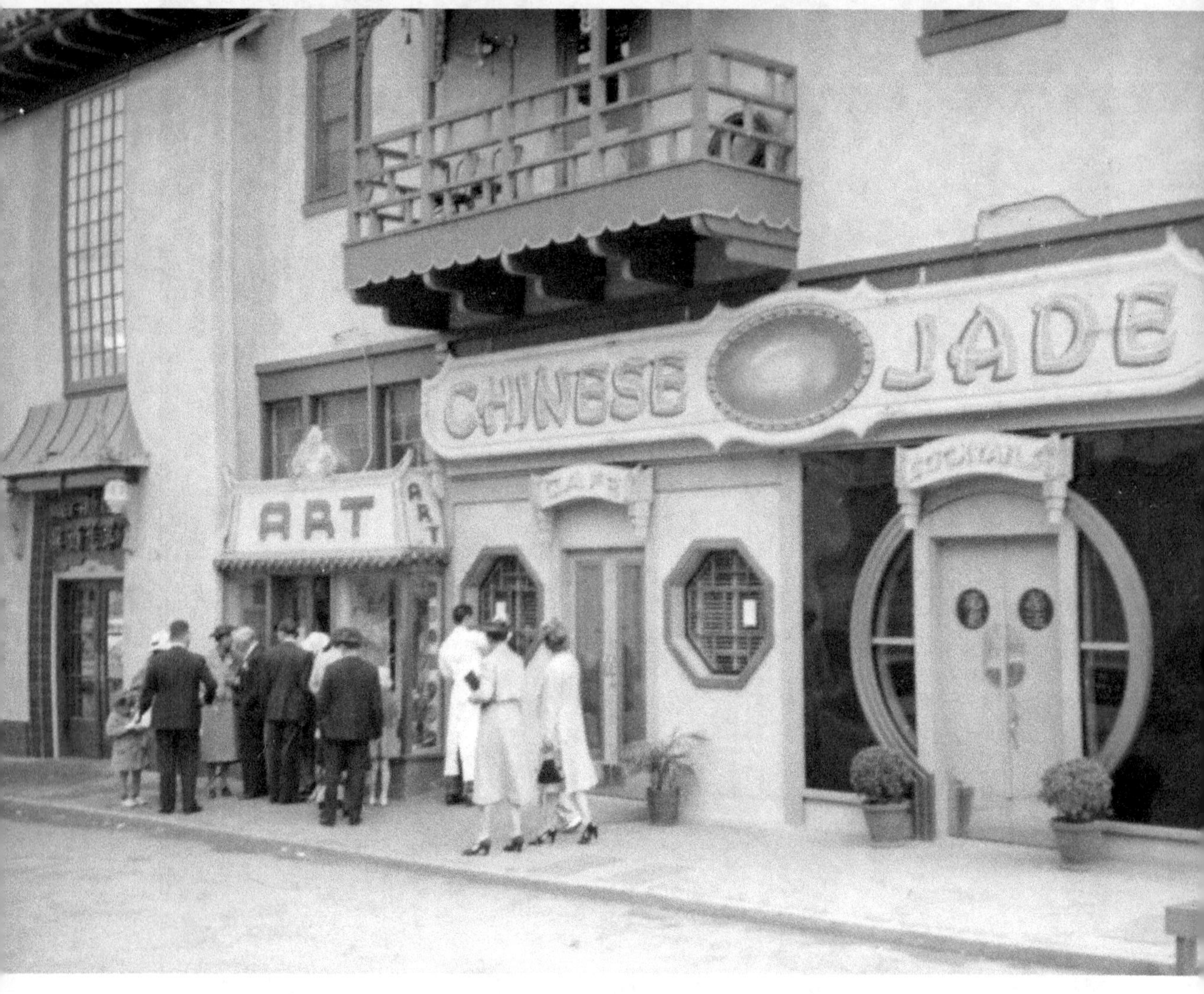

New Chinatown's Gin Ling Way held a gem of a joint in Chinese Jade which had separate entrances for its café and cocktail lounge. Much could be written about the dimensional and arching entrance signs for the eatery, but to the left is something far more important. K.G. Louie Art Supply marked its entrance with a seated neon Buddha figure which was animated to slap his belly. The creative and unique Art sign and Buddha remain in Chinatown to this day. (1939, Herman J. Schultheis Collection)

Opposite: Two women walk past the neon sign above the entry to the Soochow Cafe located at 504 N. Los Angeles Street in Old Chinatown. (1937, Herman J. Schultheis Collection)

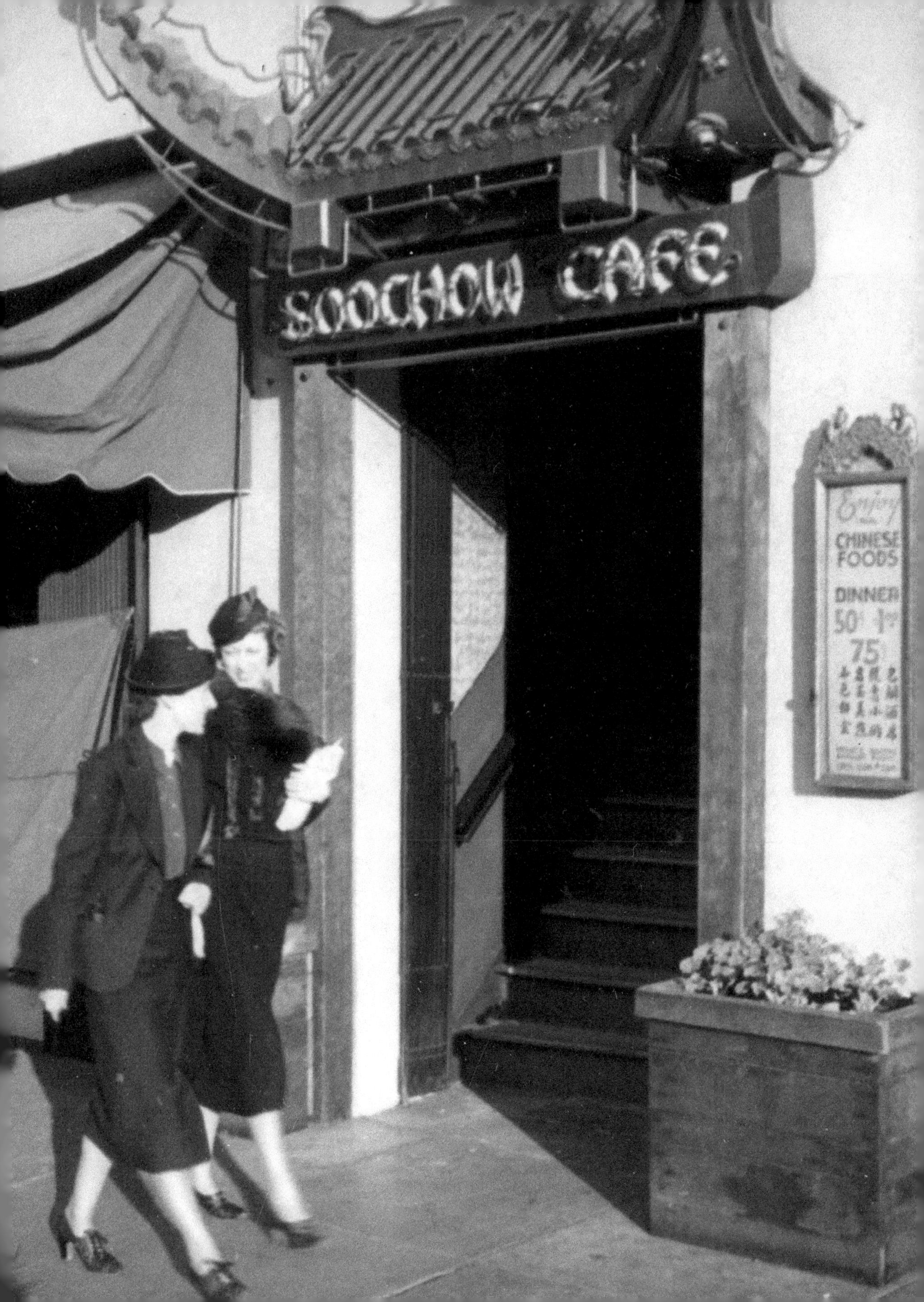
SOOCHOW CAFE
Enjoy
CHINESE FOODS
DINNER
50
75

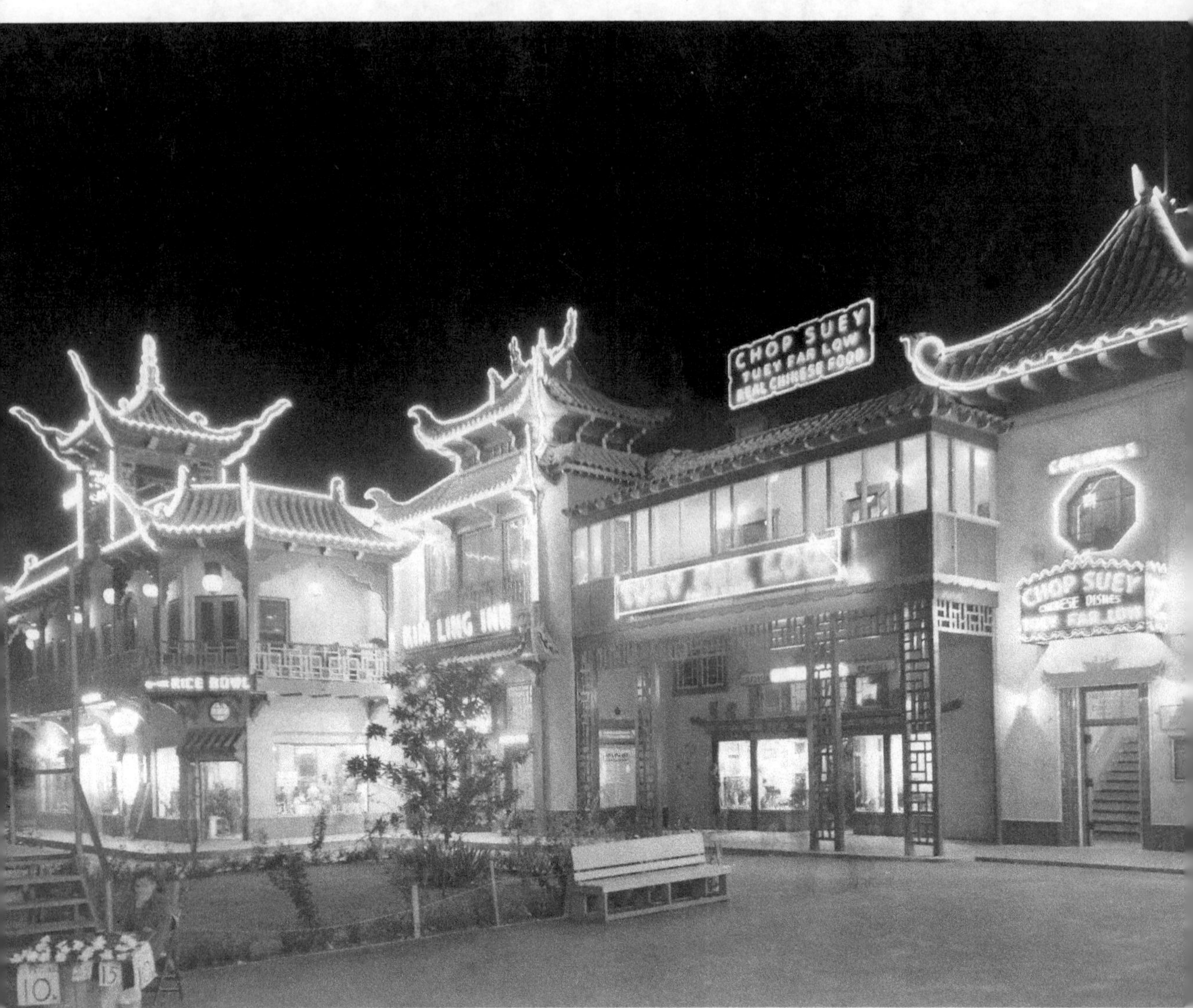

(Circa 1940s, Security Pacific National Bank Collection)

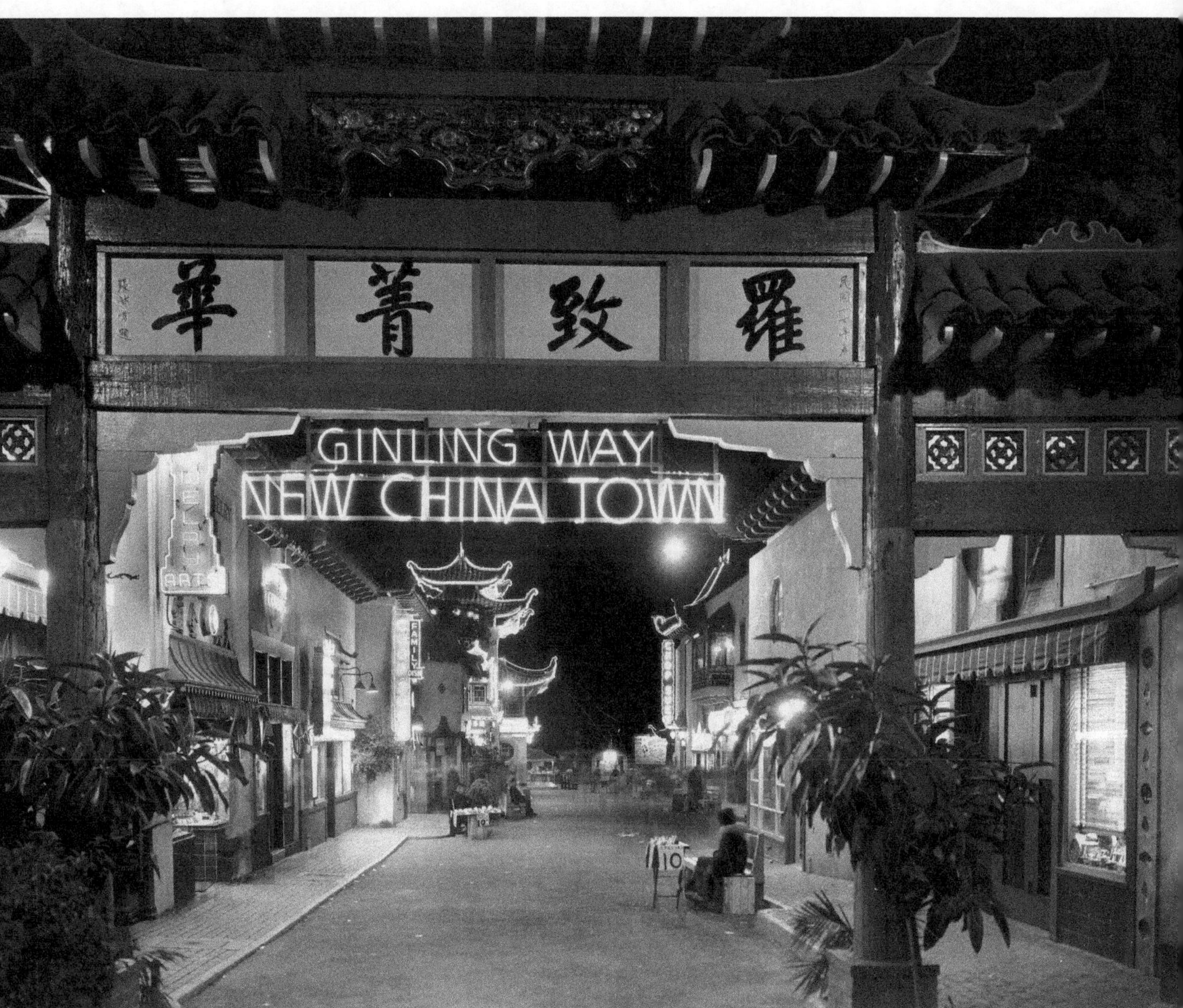

(Circa 1940s, Security Pacific National Bank Collection)

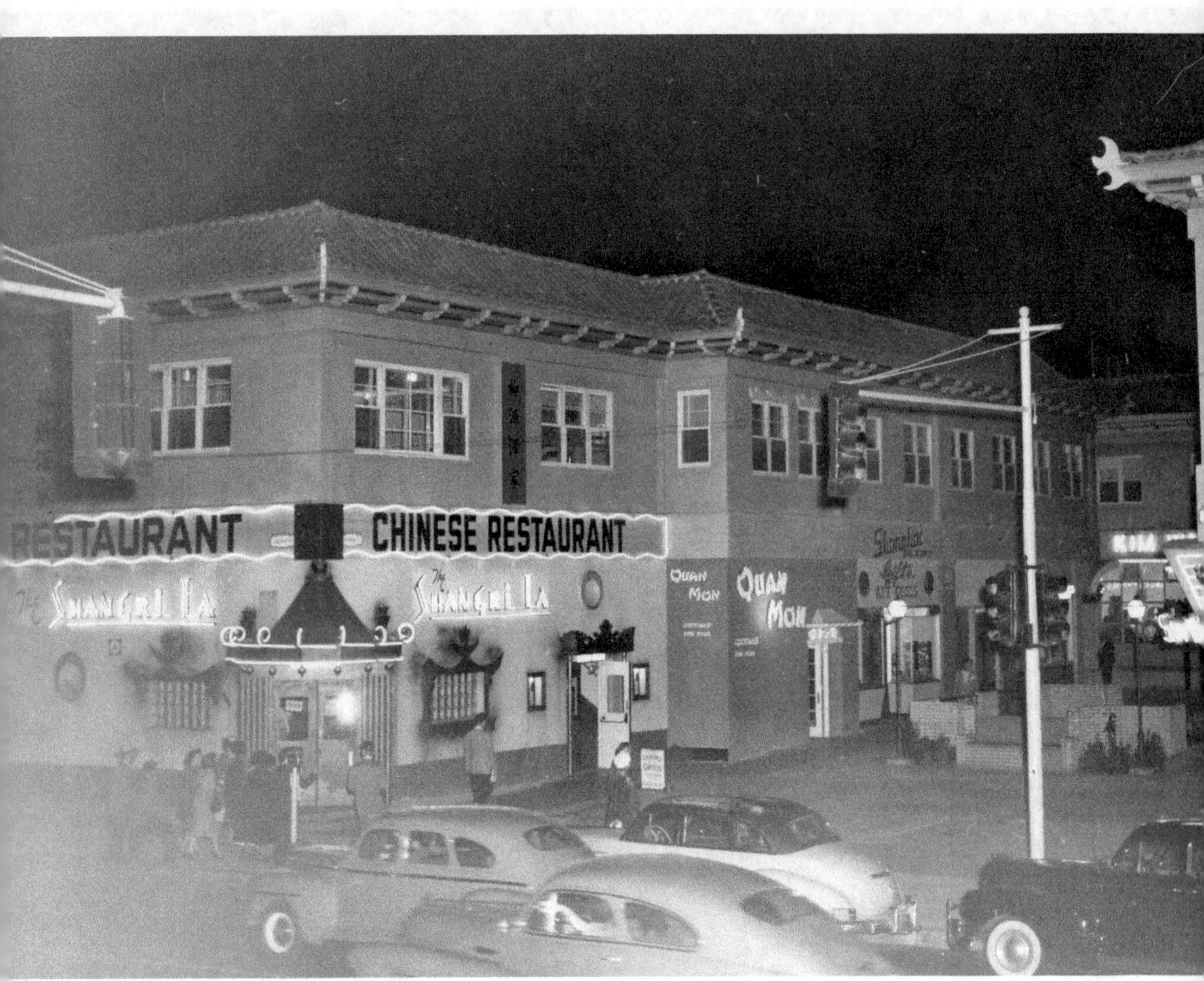

Above & opposite: (Circa 1940s, Harry Quillen Collection)

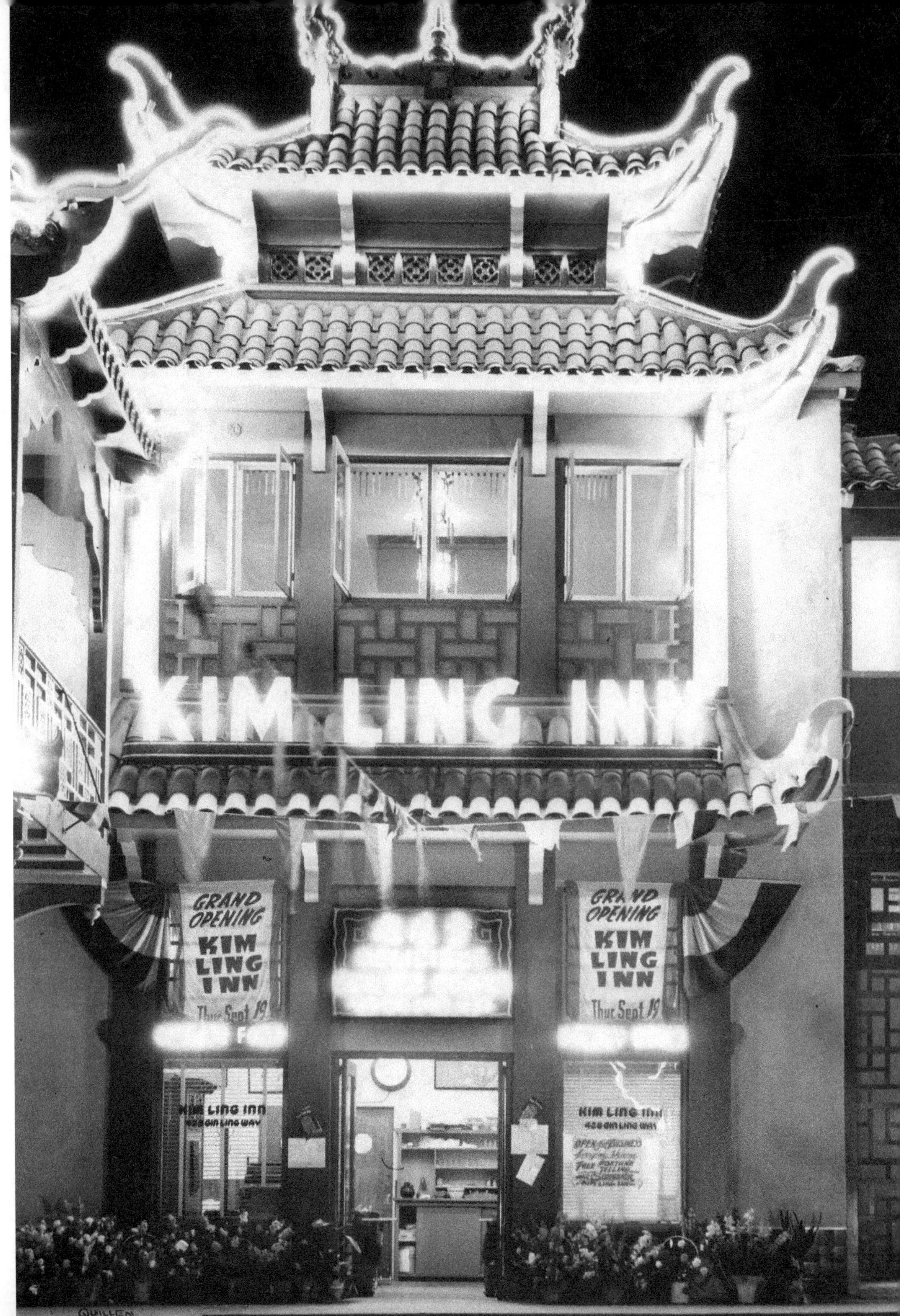
KIM LING INN
GRAND OPENING
KIM LING INN
Thur Sept 19
GRAND OPENING
KIM LING INN
Thur Sept 19
KIM LING INN
428 GIN LING WAY
KIM LING INN
428 GIN LING WAY
OPEN for BUSINESS
FREE FORTUNE TELLING
QUILLEN

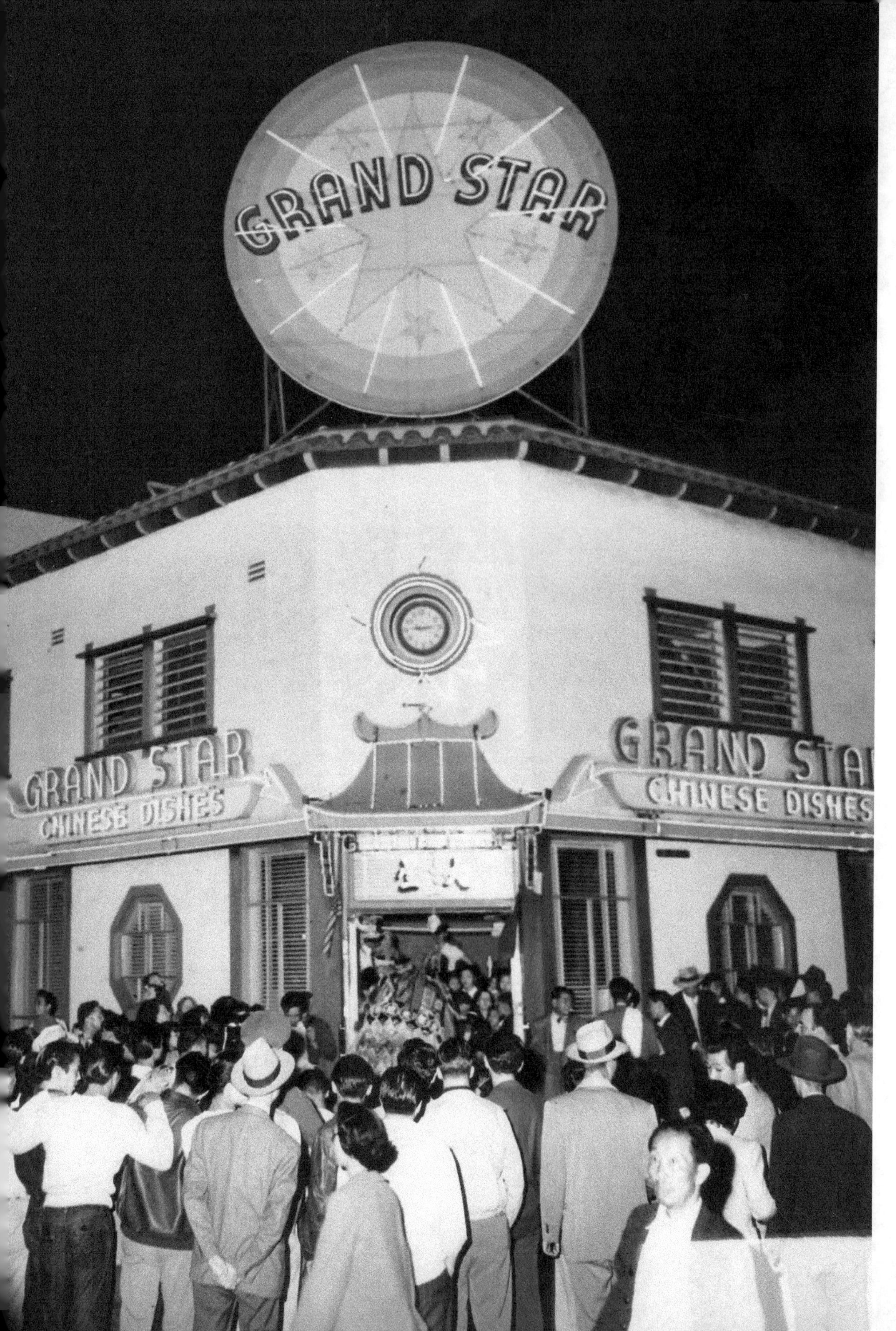
GRAND STAR
GRAND STAR
CHINESE DISHES
GRAND STAR
CHINESE DISHES

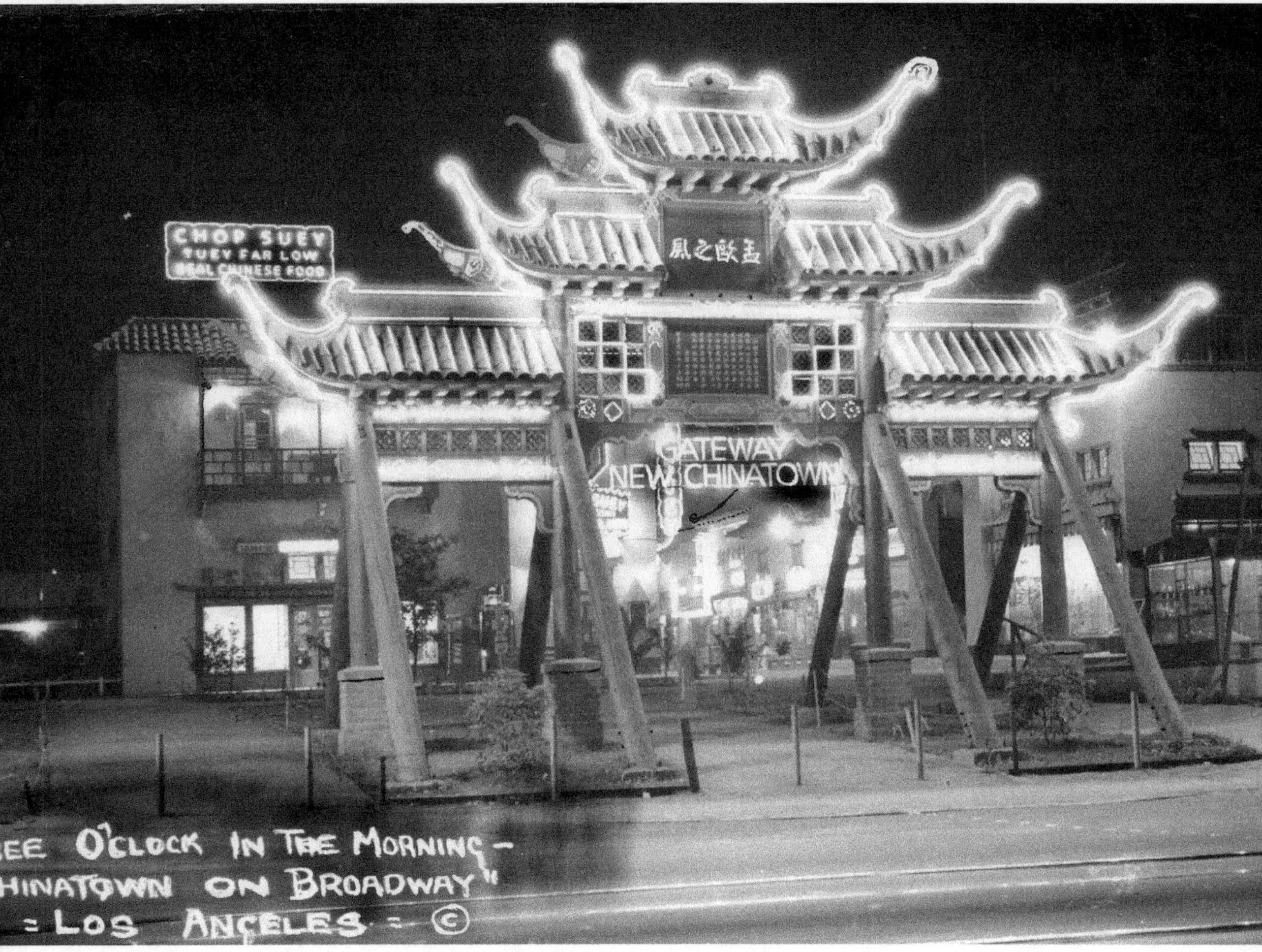

(1942, Harry Quillen Collection)

Opposite: (Circa 1940s, Harry Quillen Collection)

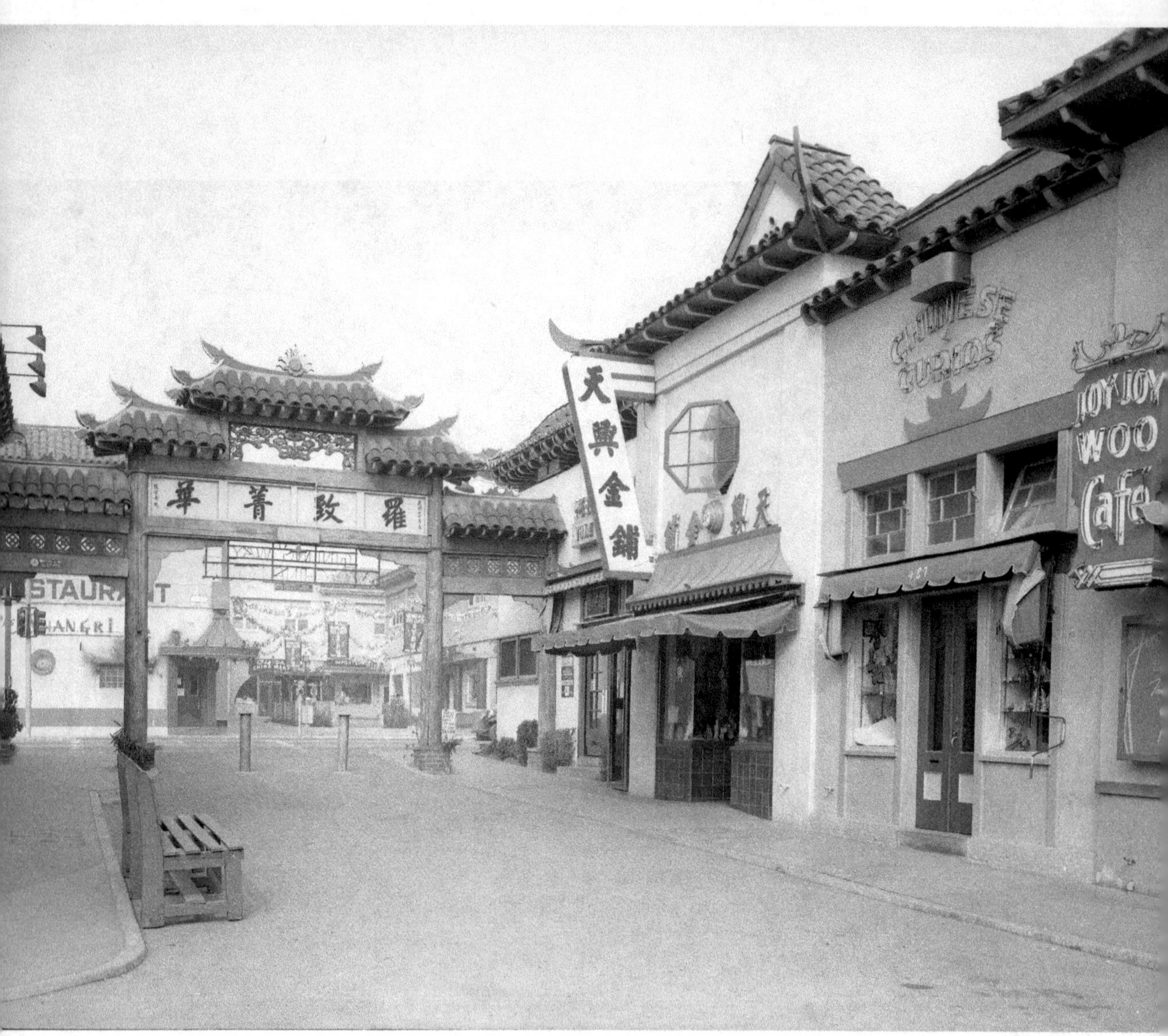

(1950, Harry Quillen Collection)

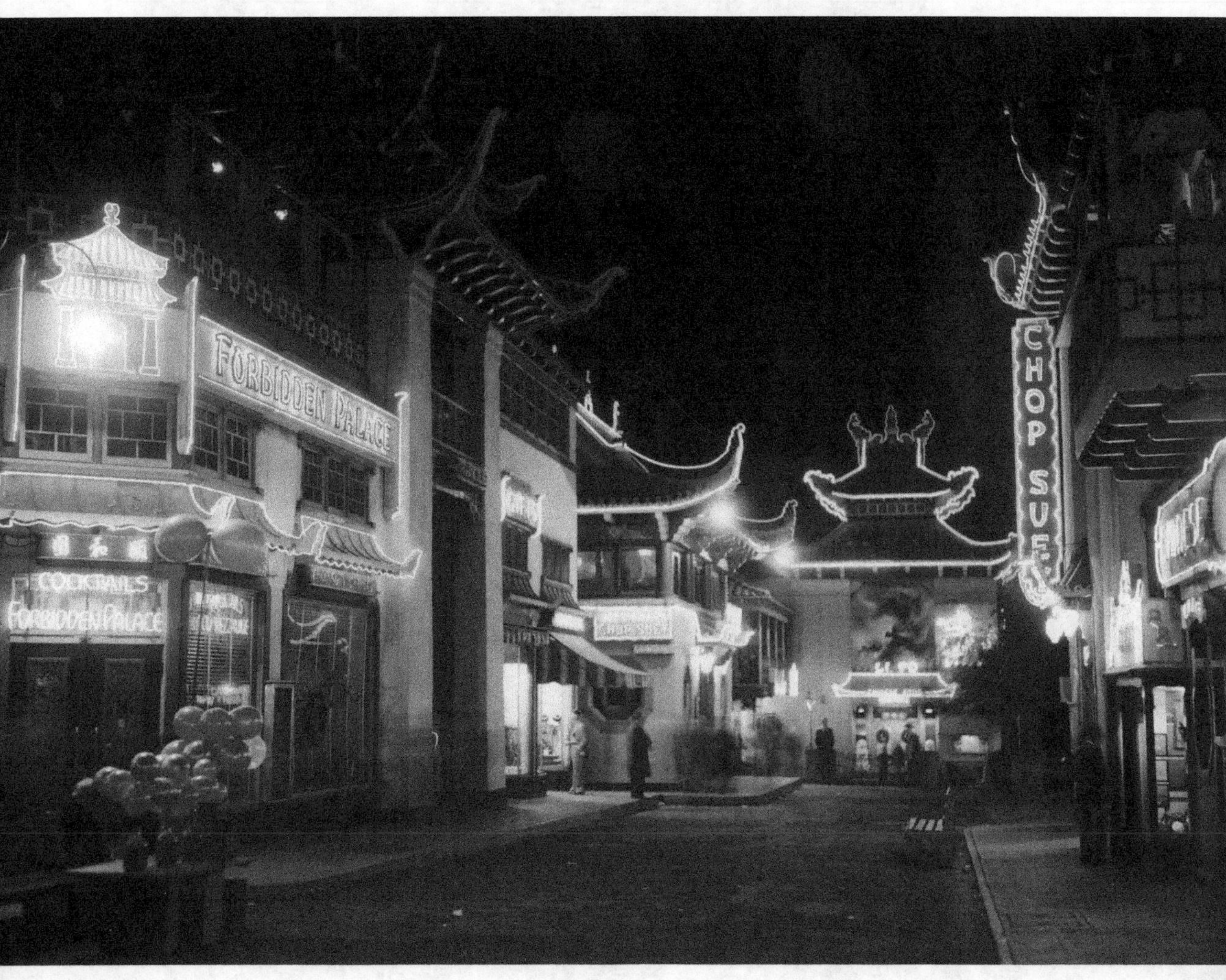

(Circa 1950s, Security Pacific National Bank Collection)

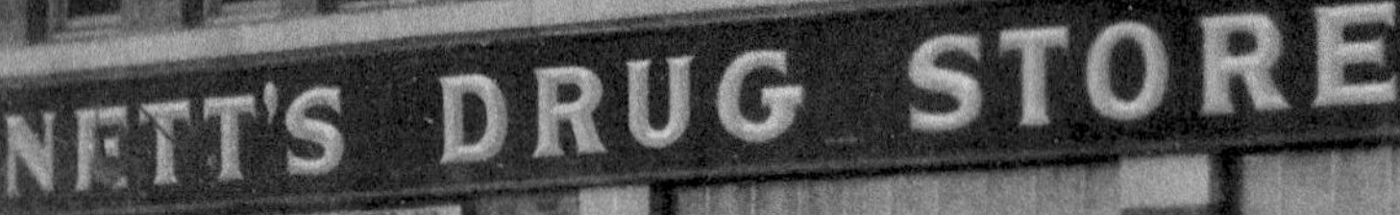
NNETT'S DRUG STORE

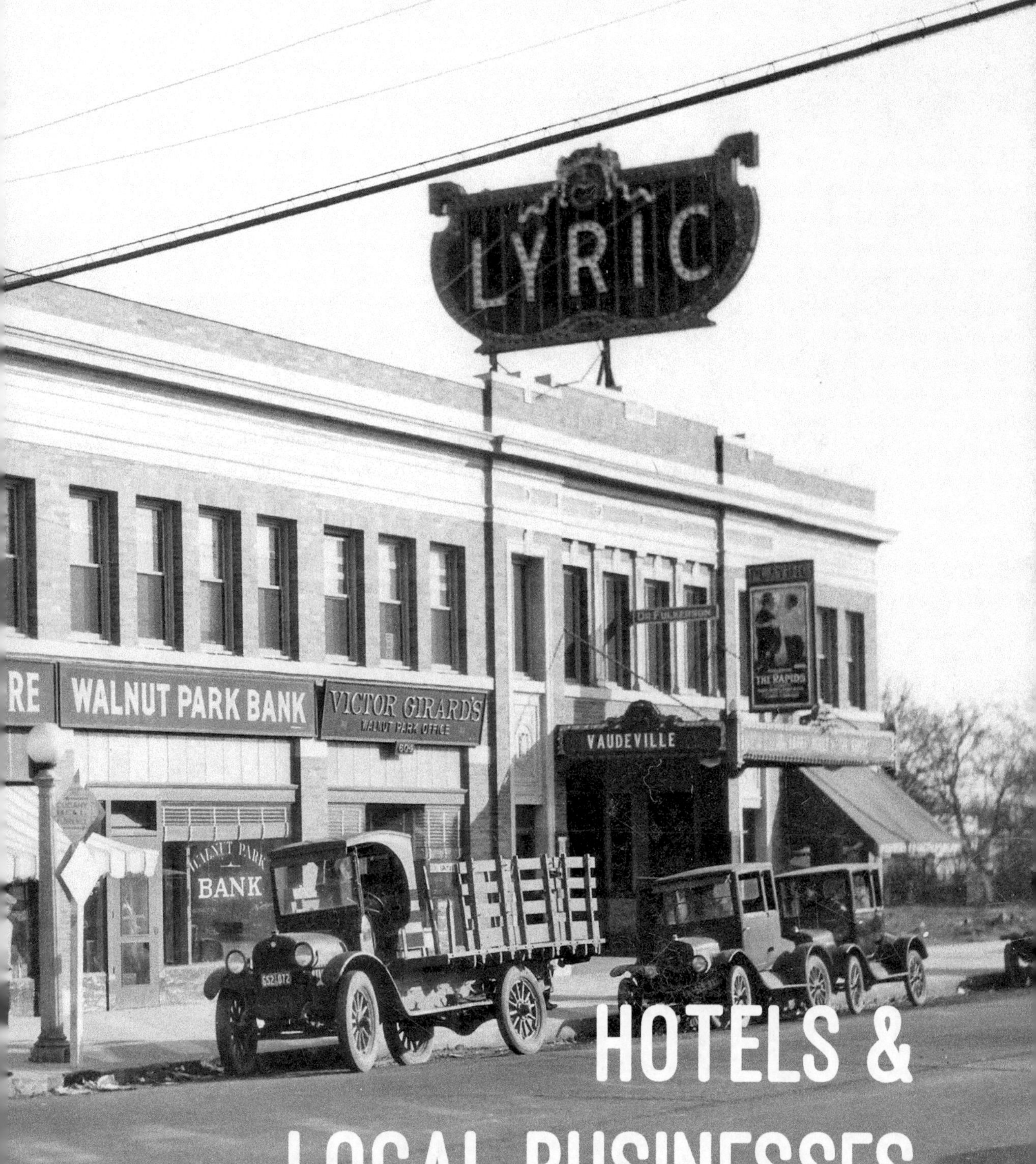

HOTELS & LOCAL BUSINESSES

Overleaf: Various signs adorn a commercial building at the intersection of Florence Avenue and Pacific Boulevard in Walnut Park. (Circa 1920s, Security Pacific National Bank Collection)

Opposite: The once grand, turn-of-the-century hotels of 5th Street welcomed passengers from the train stations east of downtown. The stations are gone, but the hotels remain as Skid Row grew around them, absorbing the grand dames into its fold. Lost are the neon vertical signs of the Baltimore Hotel and Hotel King Edward, but stalwart is the Rosslyn Hotel vertical and rooftop signs. The rooftop sign was originally illuminated with incandescent light bulbs, later restored with neon tubing in the year 2000 by the Cultural Affairs Department which recognized the sign's cultural value and rarity. (1973, Security Pacific National Bank Collection)

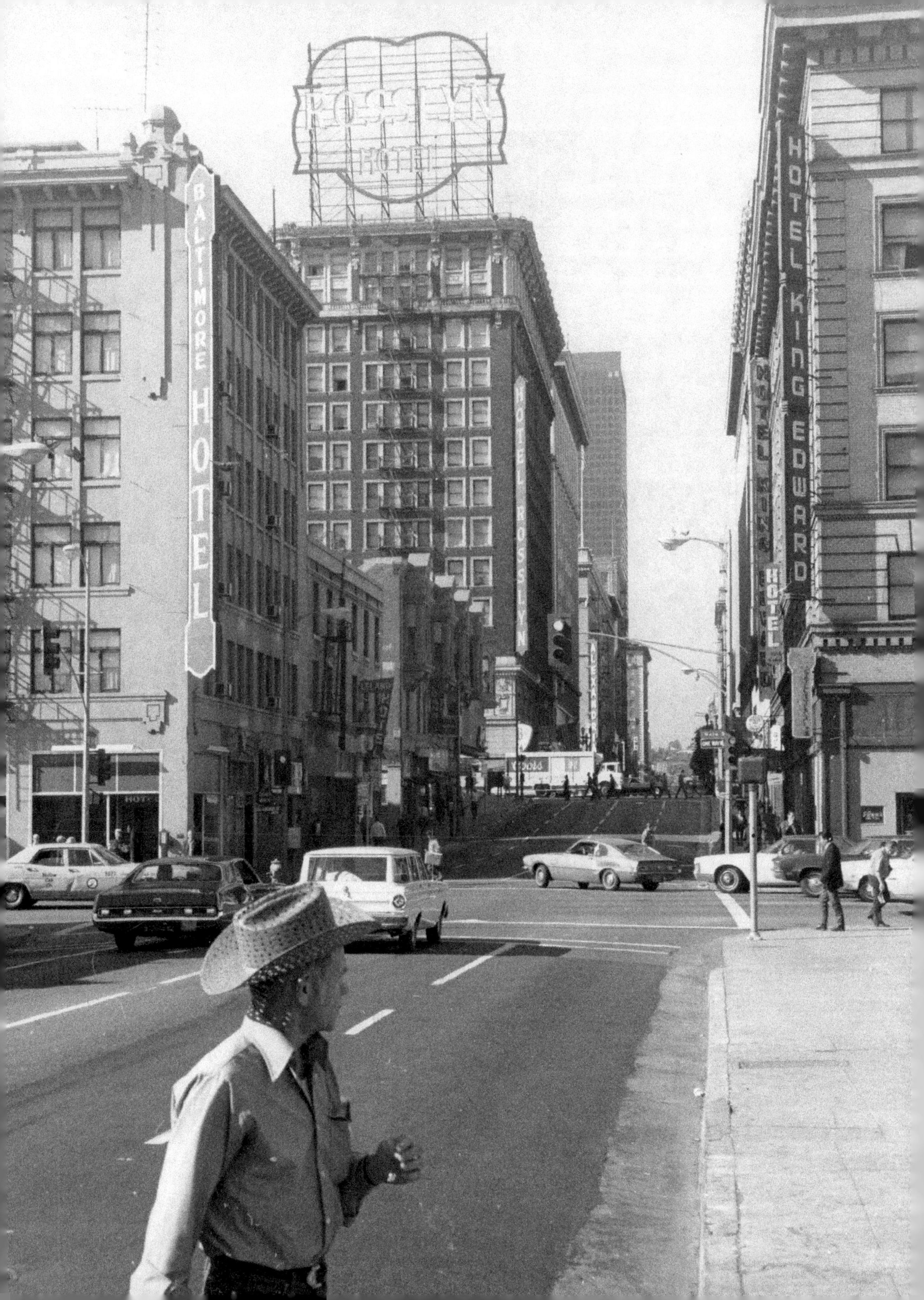

ROSSLYN
HOTEL
BALTIMORE
HOTEL
HOTEL ROSSLYN
HOTEL KING EDWARD
HOTEL

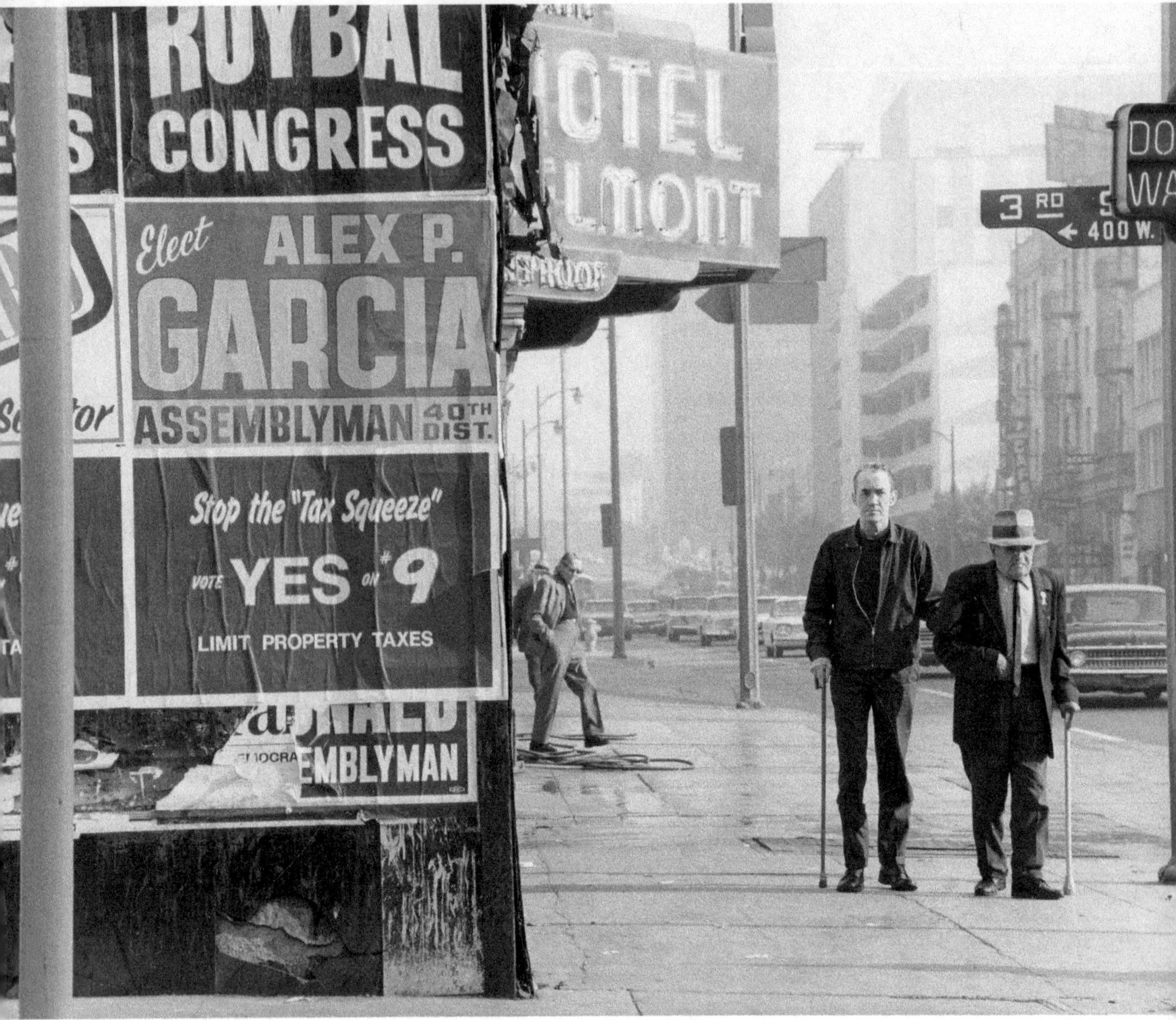

Walking past the neon marquee of the Hotel Belmont, two residents may lament that the neighborhood around 251 S. Hill had seen better days. The Art Deco, neon marquee dates to the building's conversion from a YWCA to a hotel in 1924. Don't ignore the neon Walk/Don't Walk sign, a lost design that was replaced by wordless pictogram crosswalk signs in the late 1990s. (1969, William Reagh Collection)

Opposite: A modest neon sign directs guests to the entrance of the Beverly Hills Hotel. (Circa 1937, Herman J. Schultheis Collection)

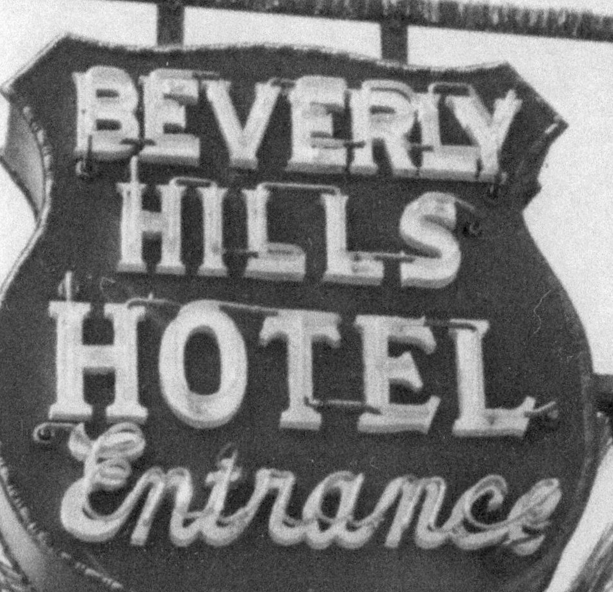
BEVERLY
HILLS
HOTEL
Entrance

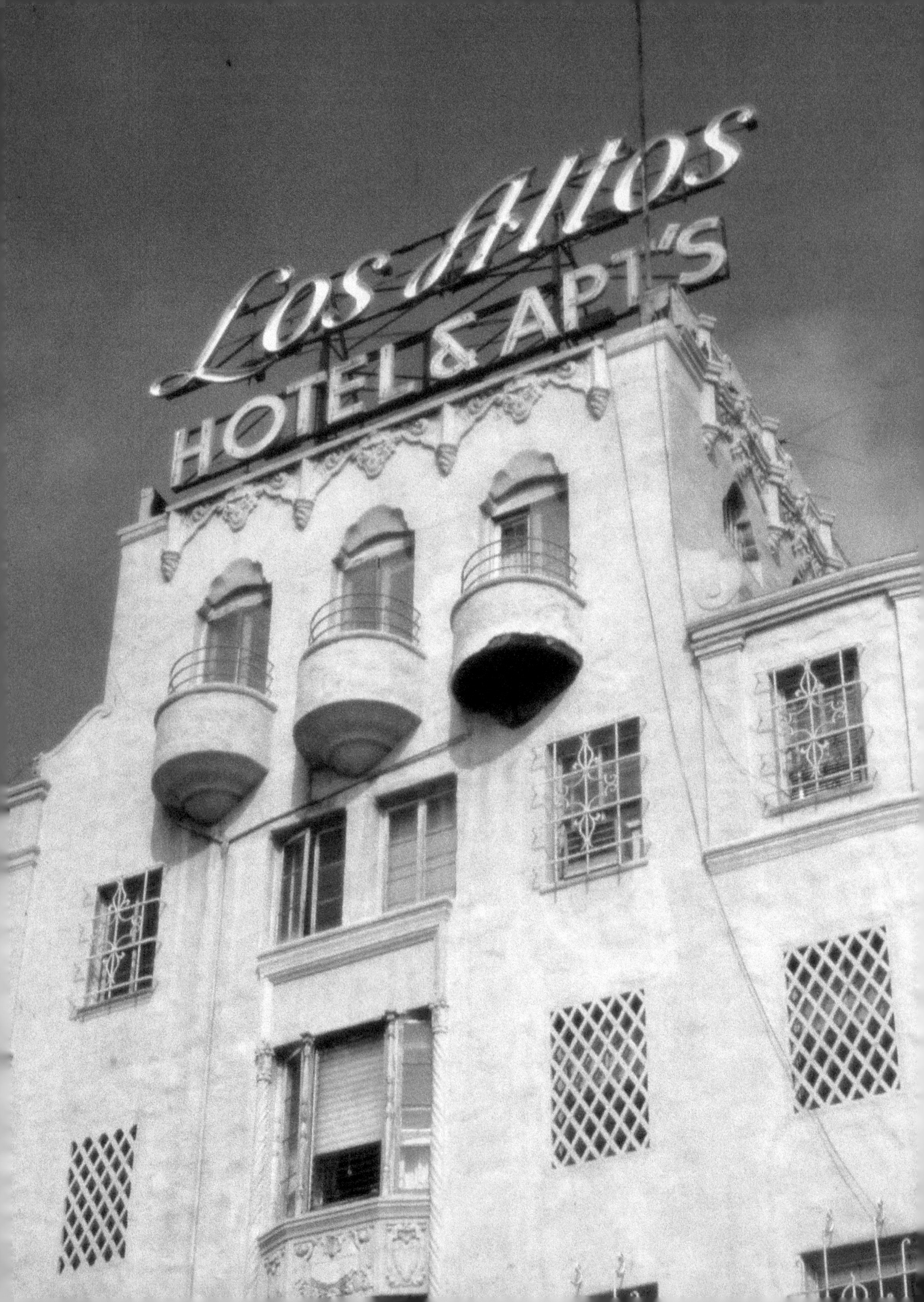
Los Altos
HOTEL & APT'S

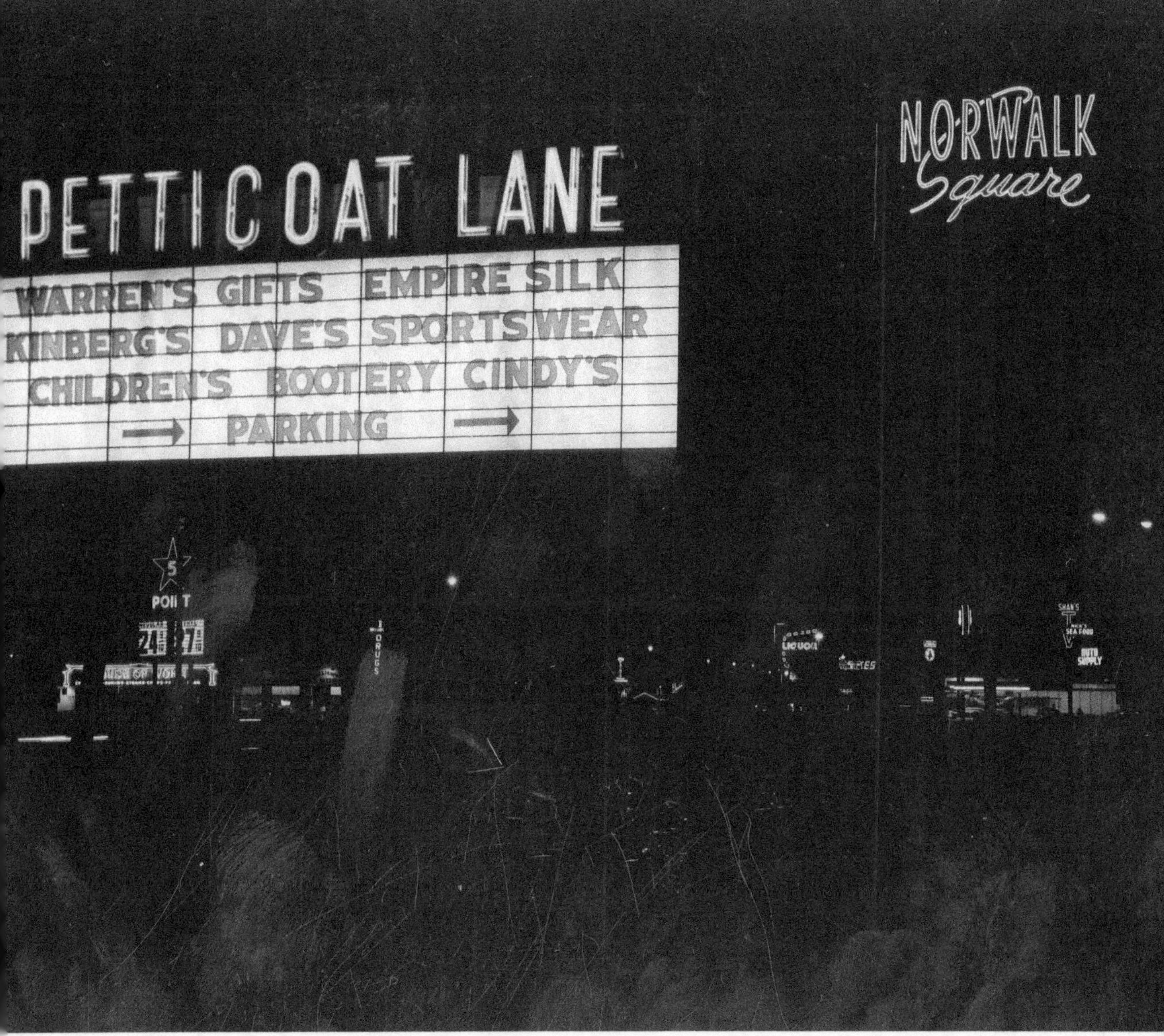

Neon illuminates the Norwalk Square Shopping Center. (1954, Ralph Morris Collection)

Opposite: The neon signage for the Los Altos Apartments on Wilshire Boulevard has been a mainstay for decades. (1978, Anne Laskey/Marlene Laskey Collection)

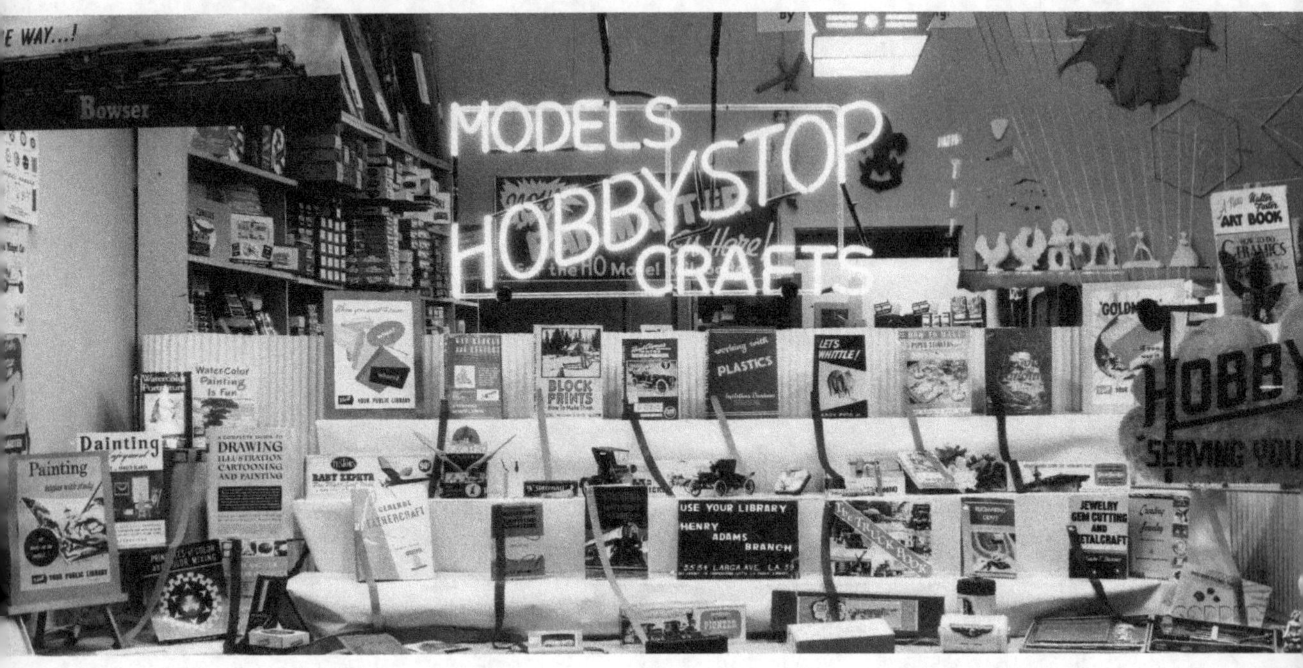

A neon sign draws customers to this shop in Atwater Village. (1950, Security Pacific National Bank Collection)

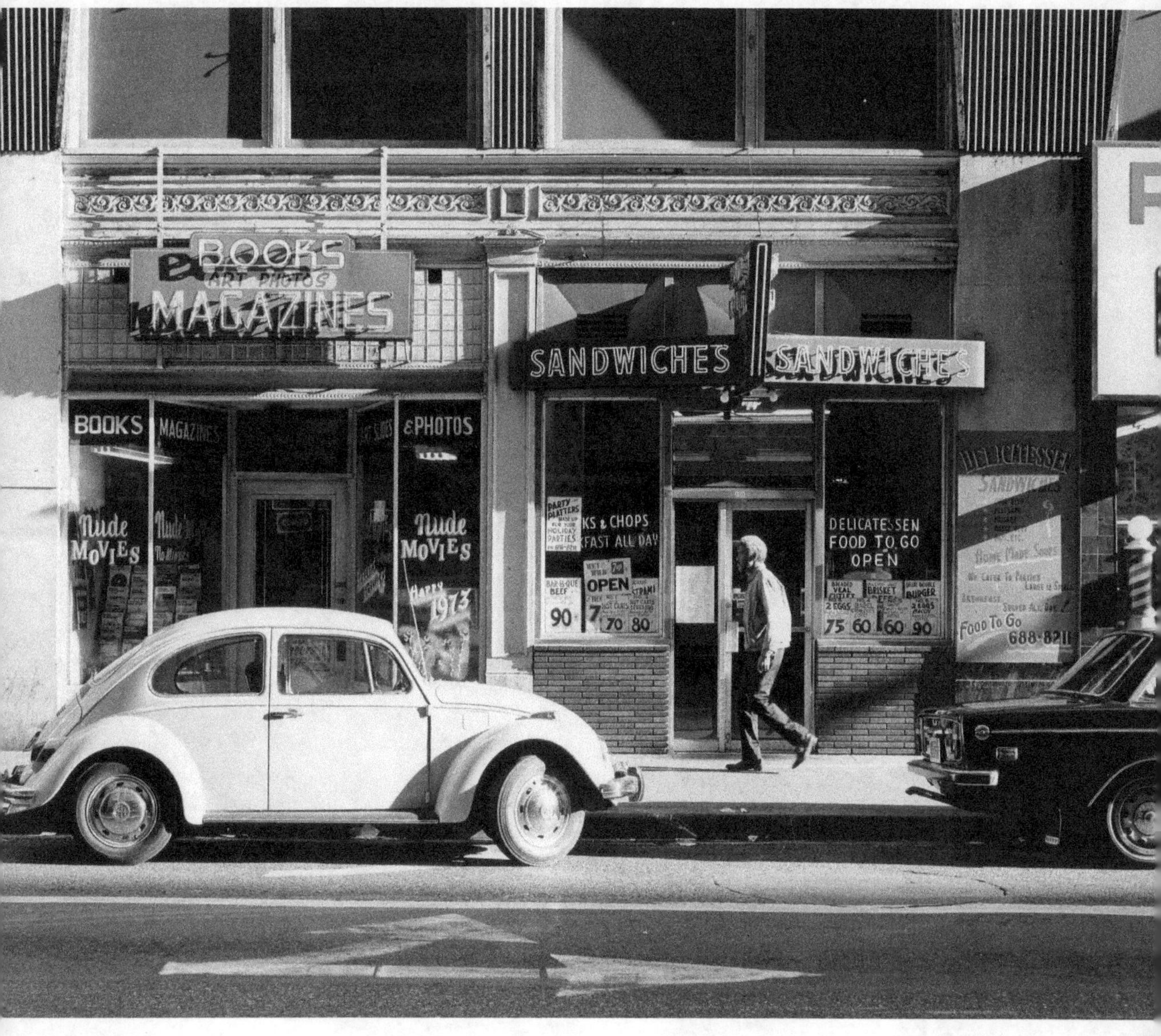

Neon signs are used to advertise an adult bookshop and the sandwich shop next door in downtown Los Angeles. (1972, William Reagh Collection)

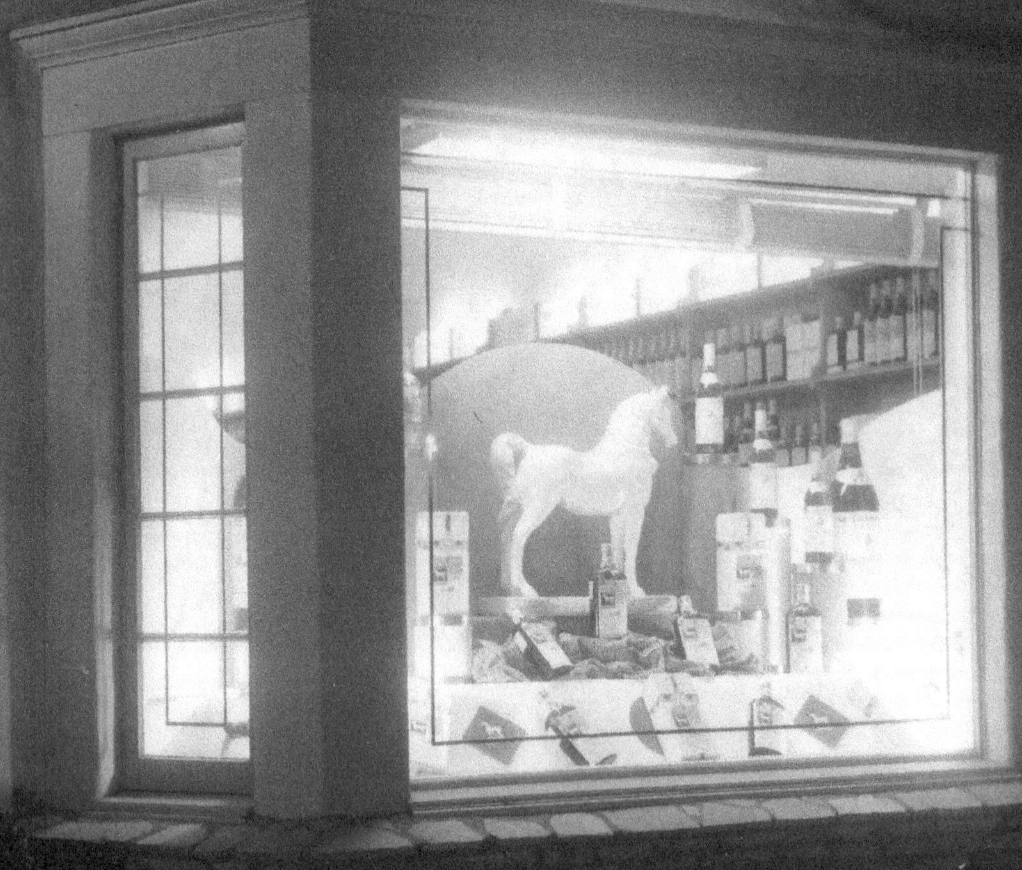
Llords
WINES & SPIRITS
124

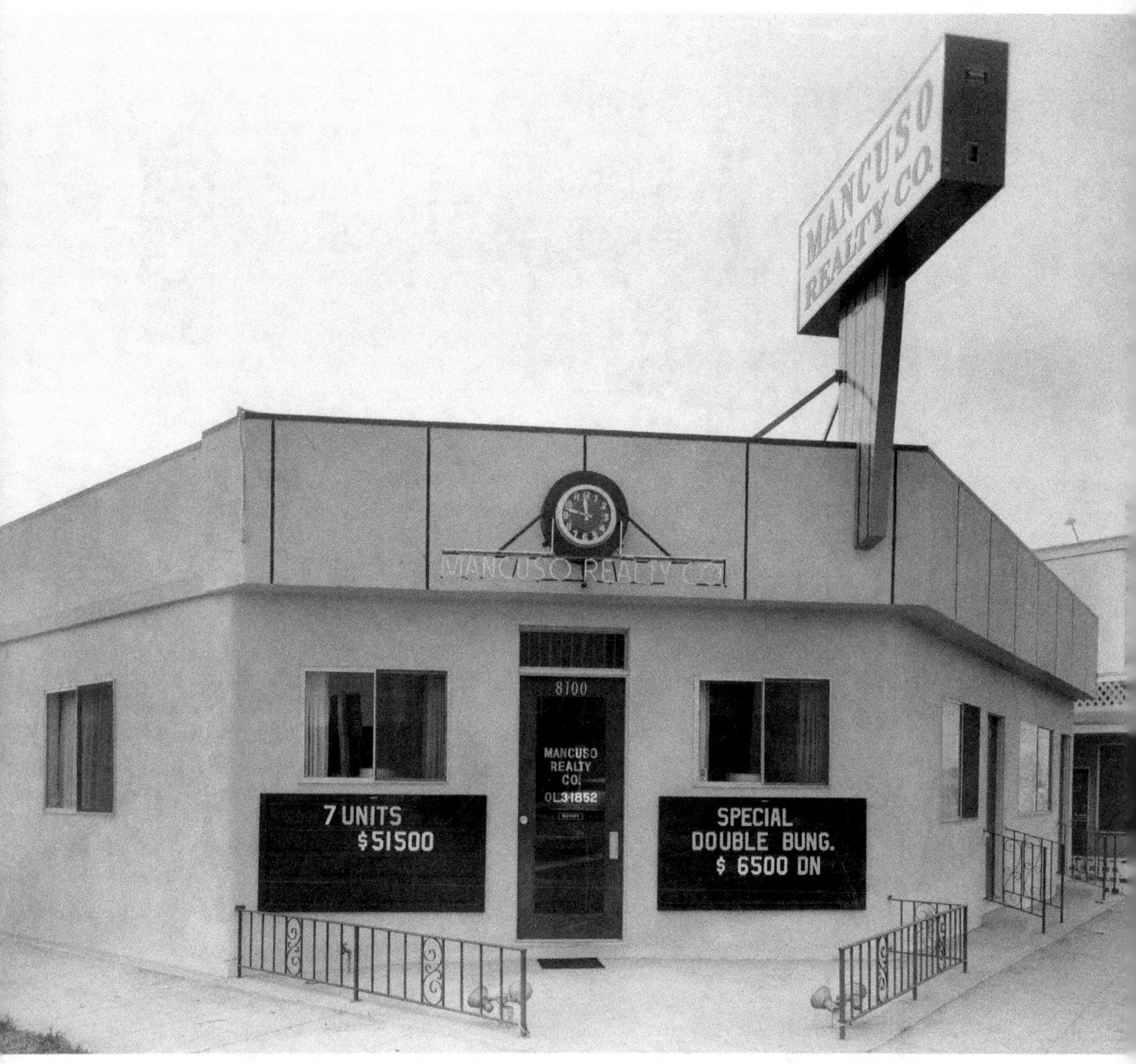

A touch of neon at the real estate office of Mancuso Realty Co. at the corner of Melrose Avenue and Crescent Heights Boulevard. (1962, Security Pacific National Bank Collection)

Opposite: Llords Wine & Spirits adds a touch of neon to a building at 9124 Sunset Boulevard. (Circa 1940s, (Security Pacific National Bank Collection)

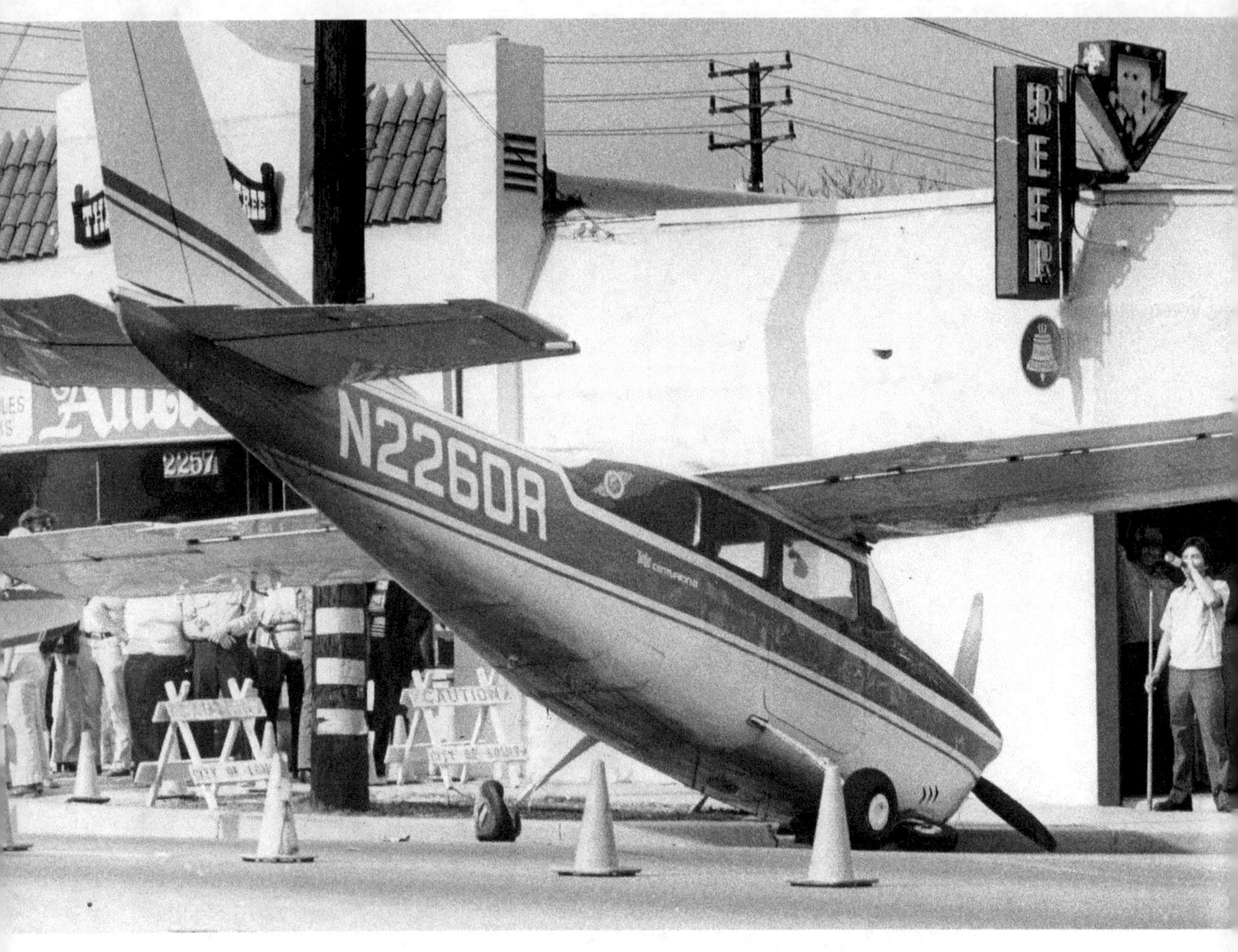

A crashed plane only slightly distracts from a neon BEER sign on Pacific Coast Highway in Lomita. (1978, Michael Haering/Los Angeles Herald Examiner Collection)

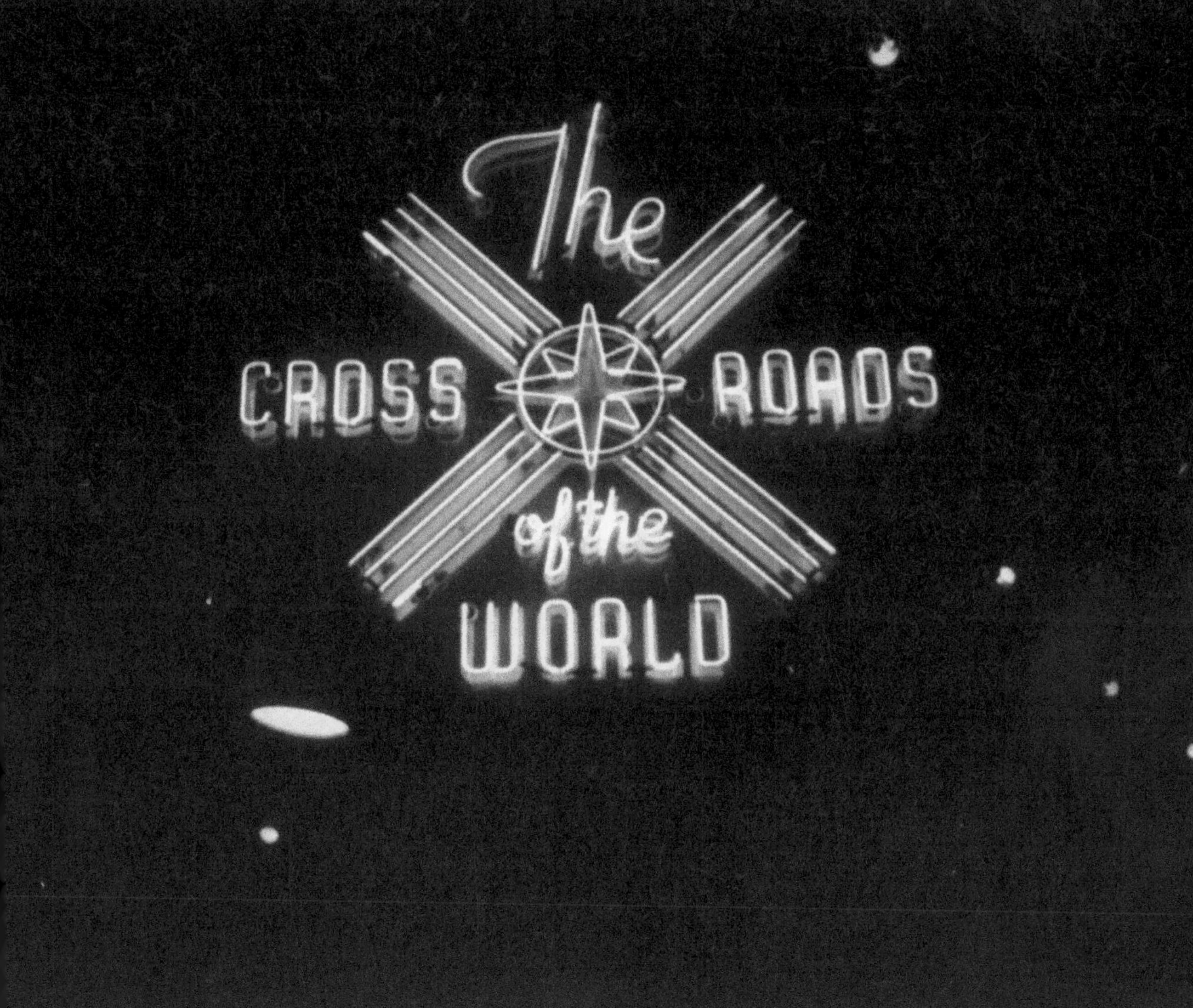

A detailed view of the sign for the historic Crossroads of the World office complex. (Circa 1937, Herman J. Schultheis Collection)

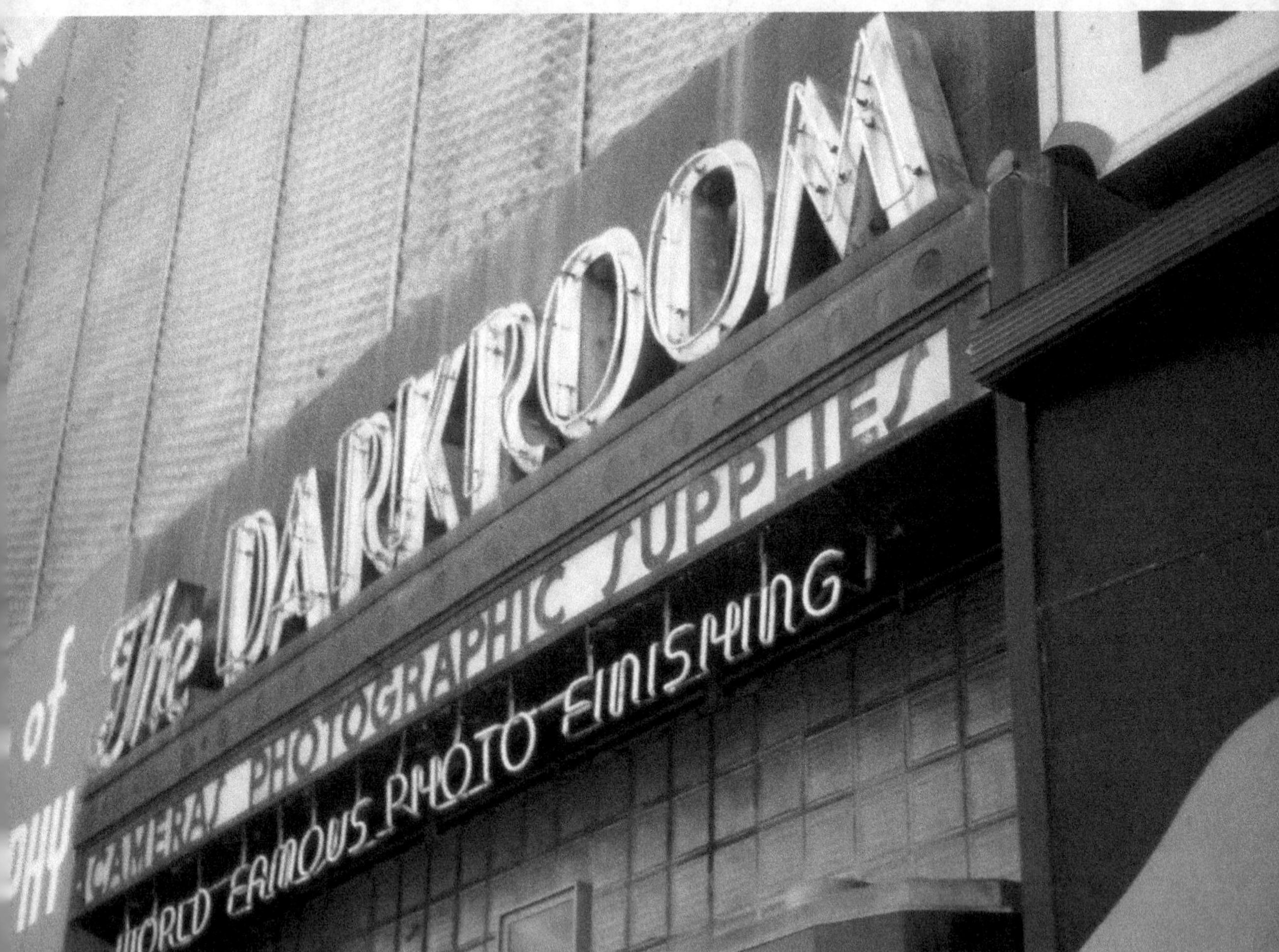

Neon signs above the entrance for the Darkroom Camera Shop, located at 5370 Wilshire Boulevard. (1978, Anne Laskey/Marlene Laskey Collection)

Opposite and pages 90-93: Small businesses on Wilshire Boulevard utilize artful neon. (1978, Anne Laskey/Marlene Laskey Collection)

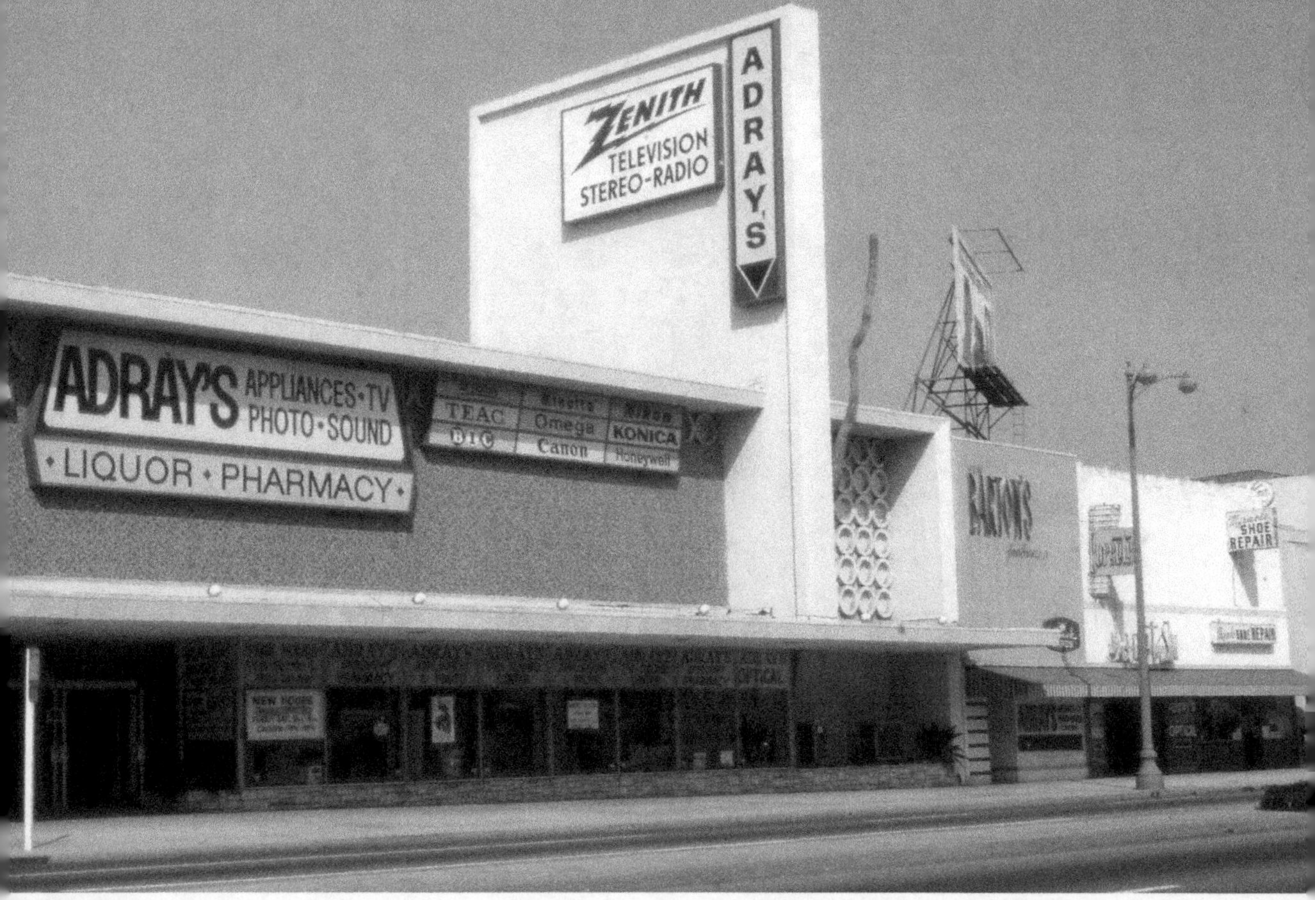

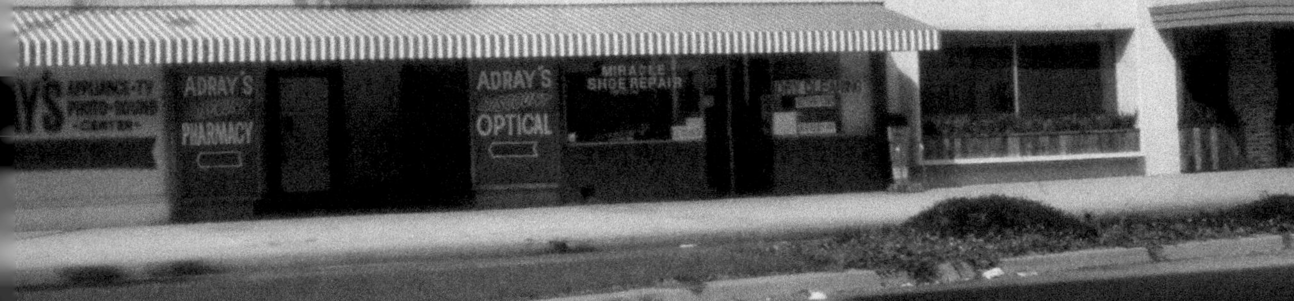
ADRAY'S
PHARMACY
ADRAY'S
OPTICAL
MIRACLE
SHOE REPAIR

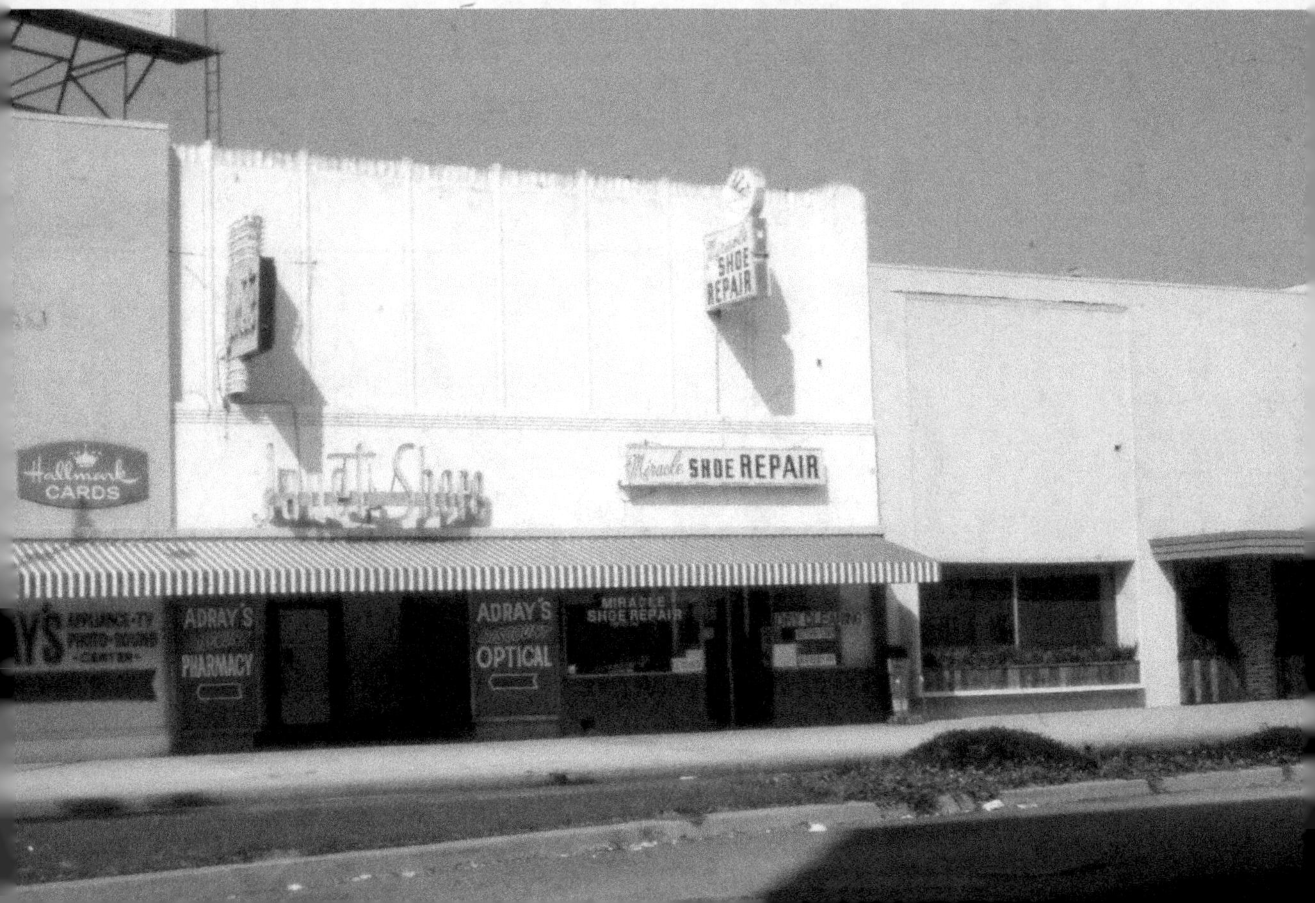

furs

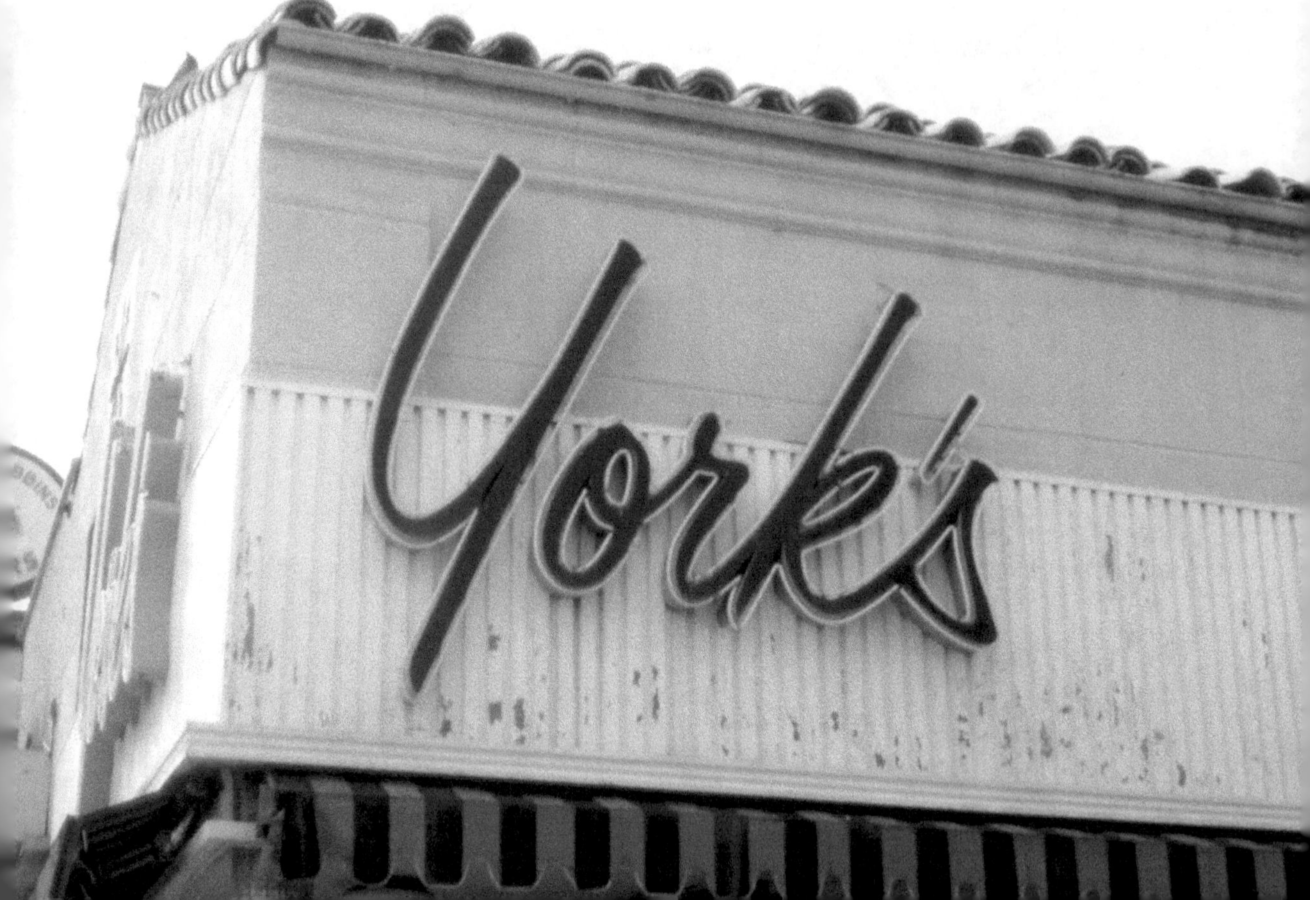
York's

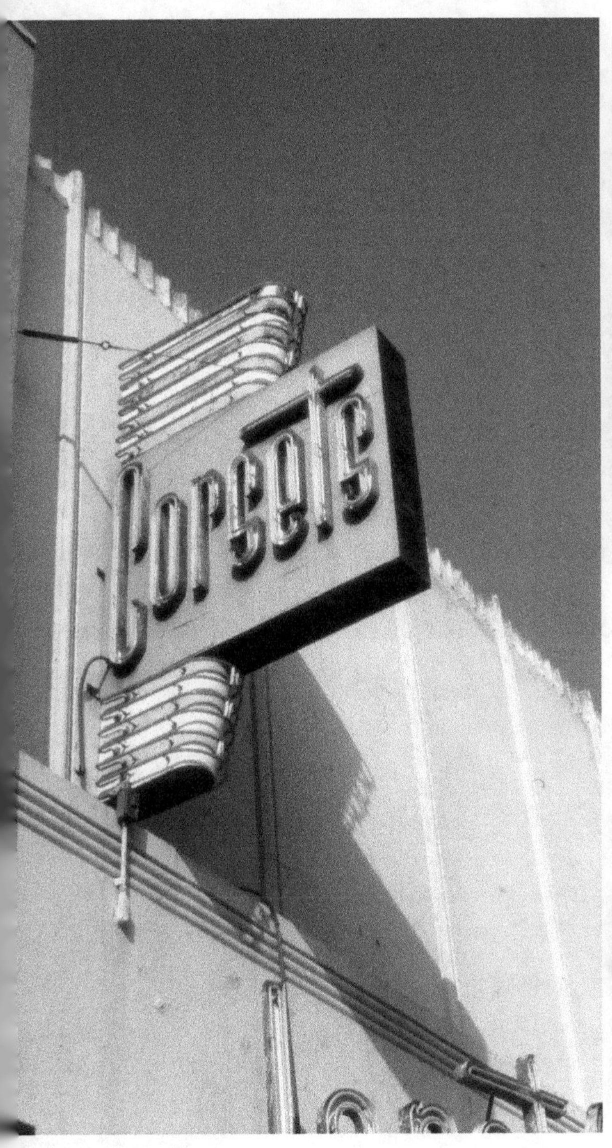
Corsets

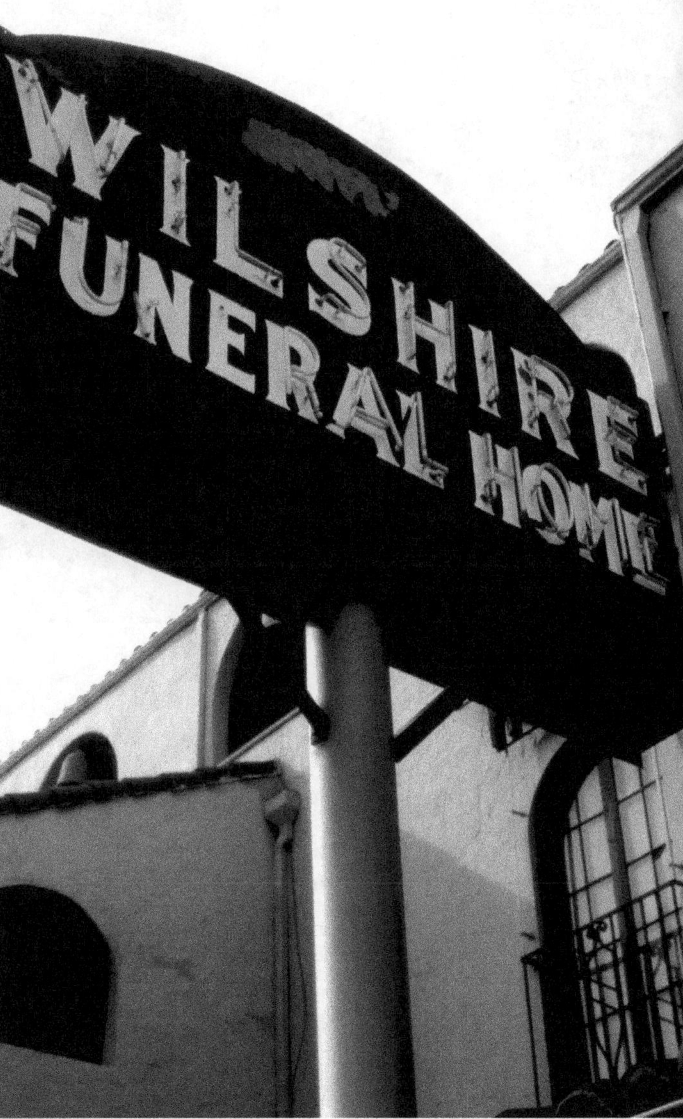
WILSHIRE
FUNERAL HOME

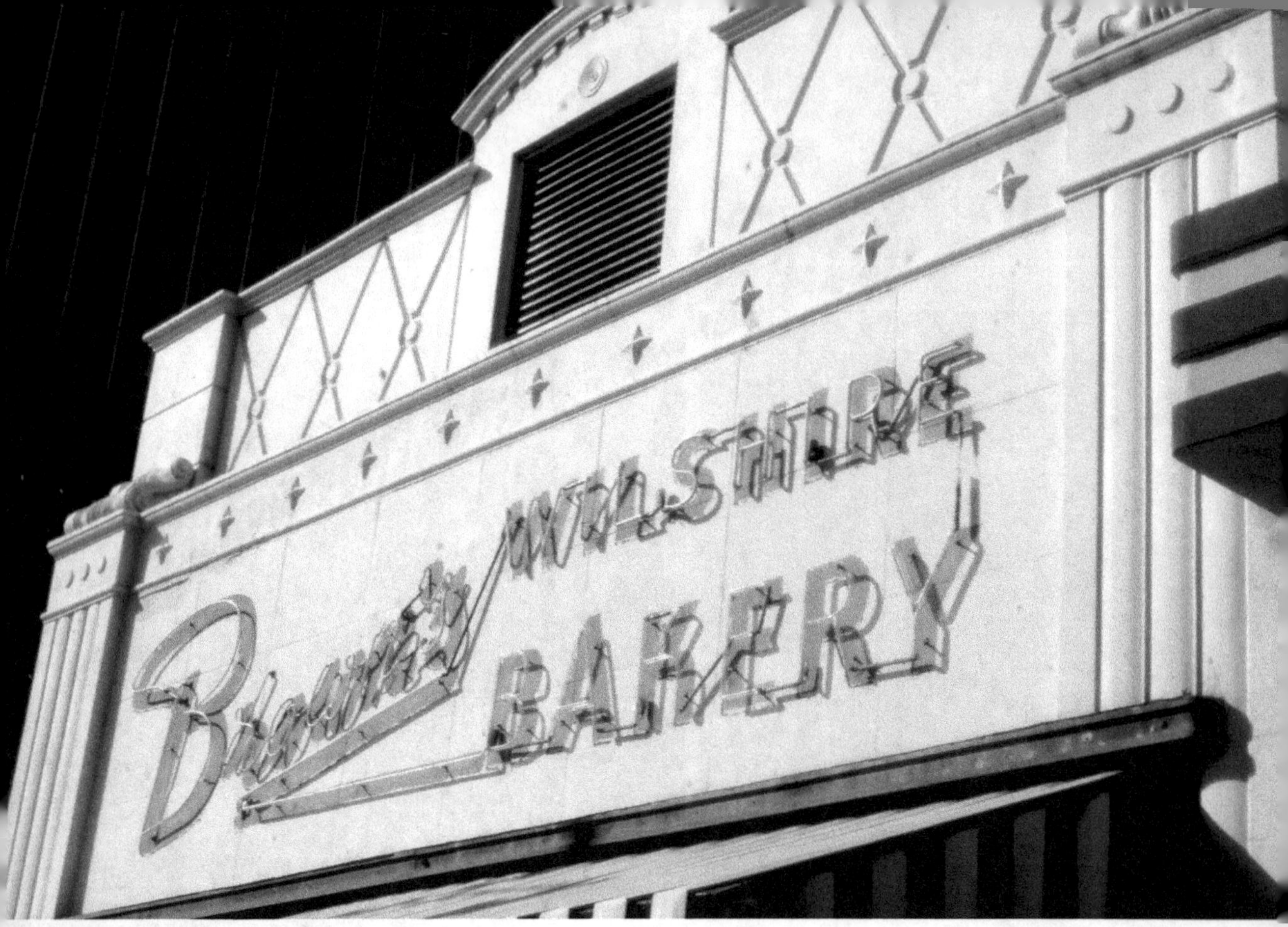

Brown's
WILSHIRE
BAKERY

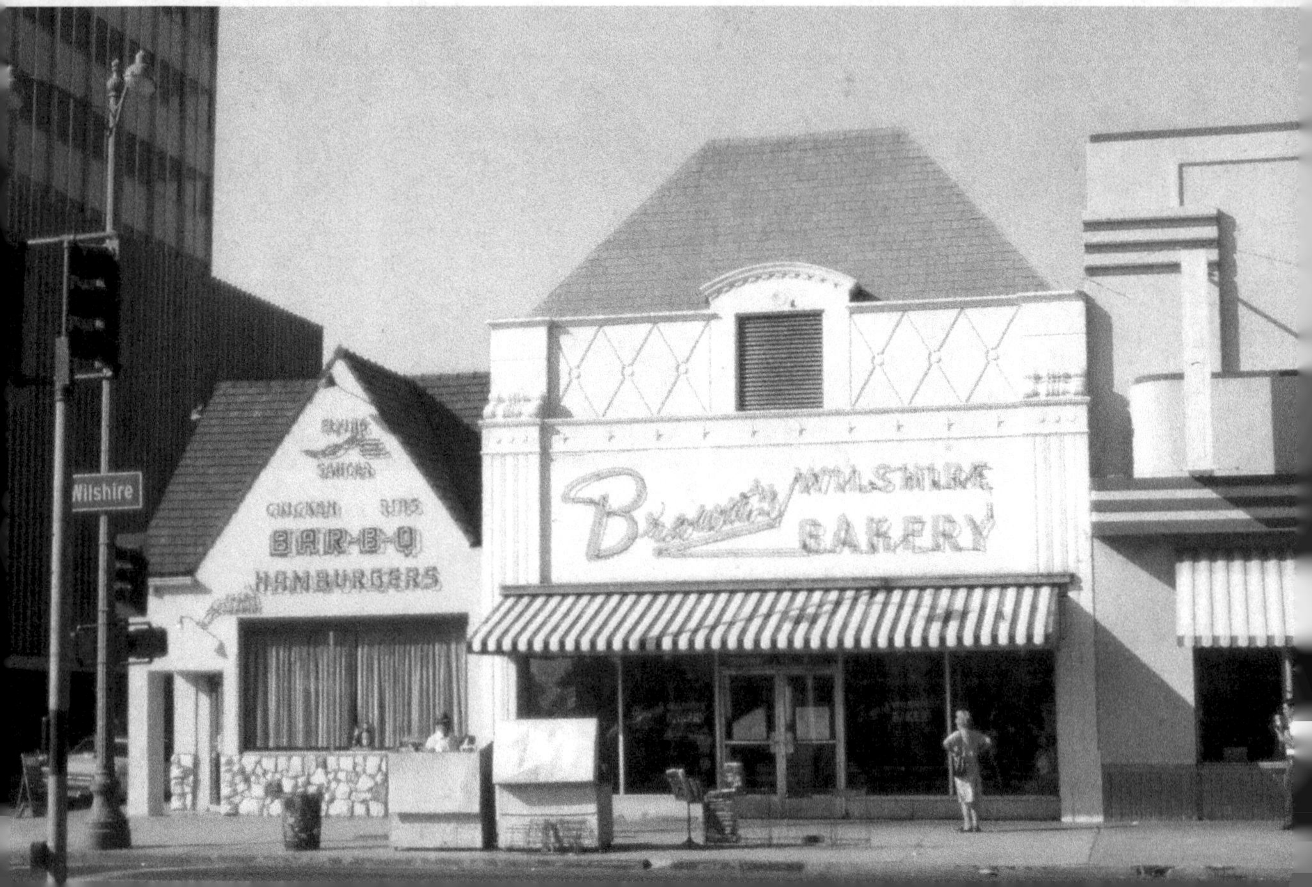

Wilshire
BAR-B-Q
HAMBURGERS
Brown's
WILSHIRE
BAKERY

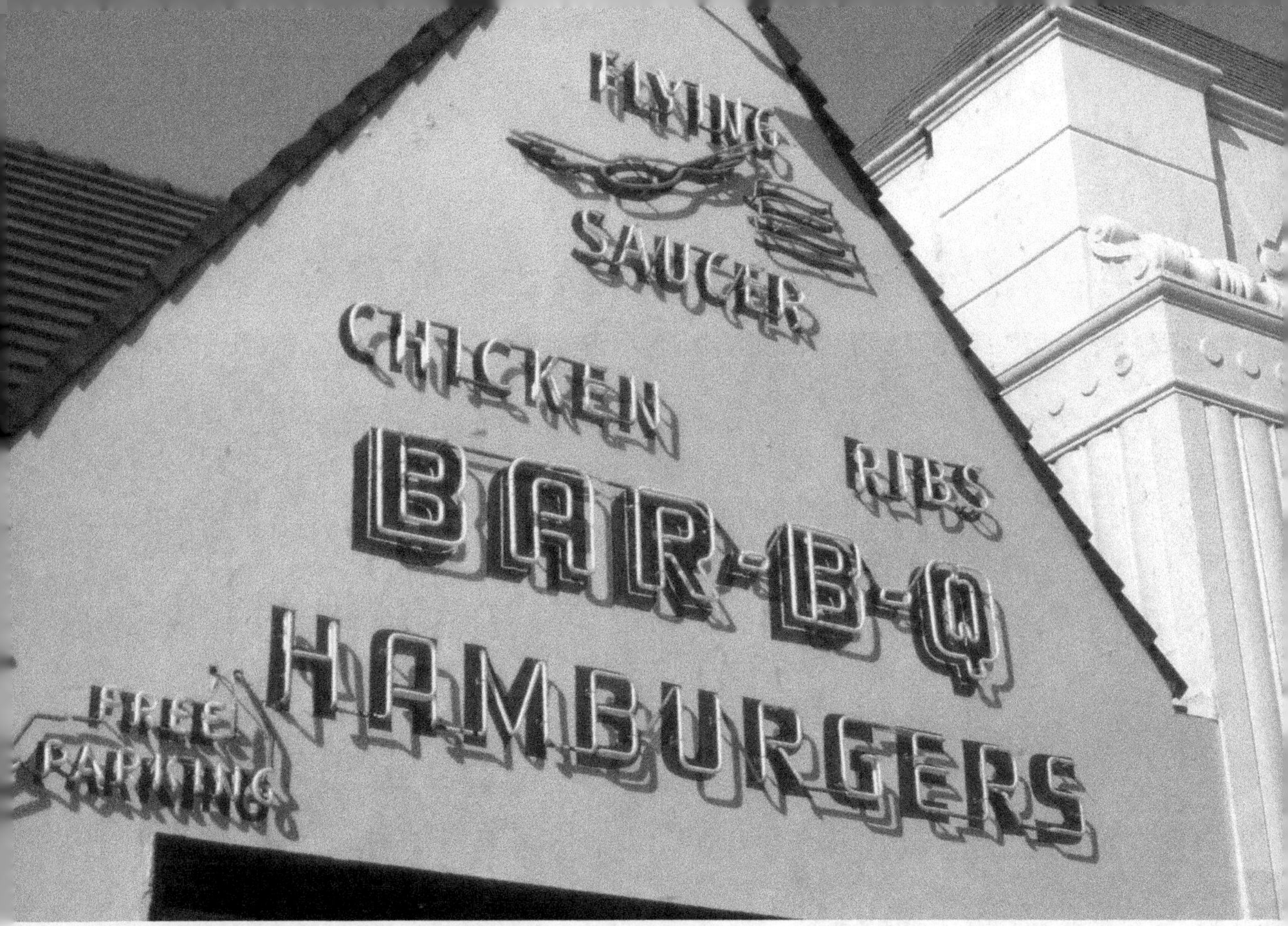

FLYING
SAUCER
CHICKEN
RIBS
BAR-B-Q
HAMBURGERS
FREE
PARKING
Shore

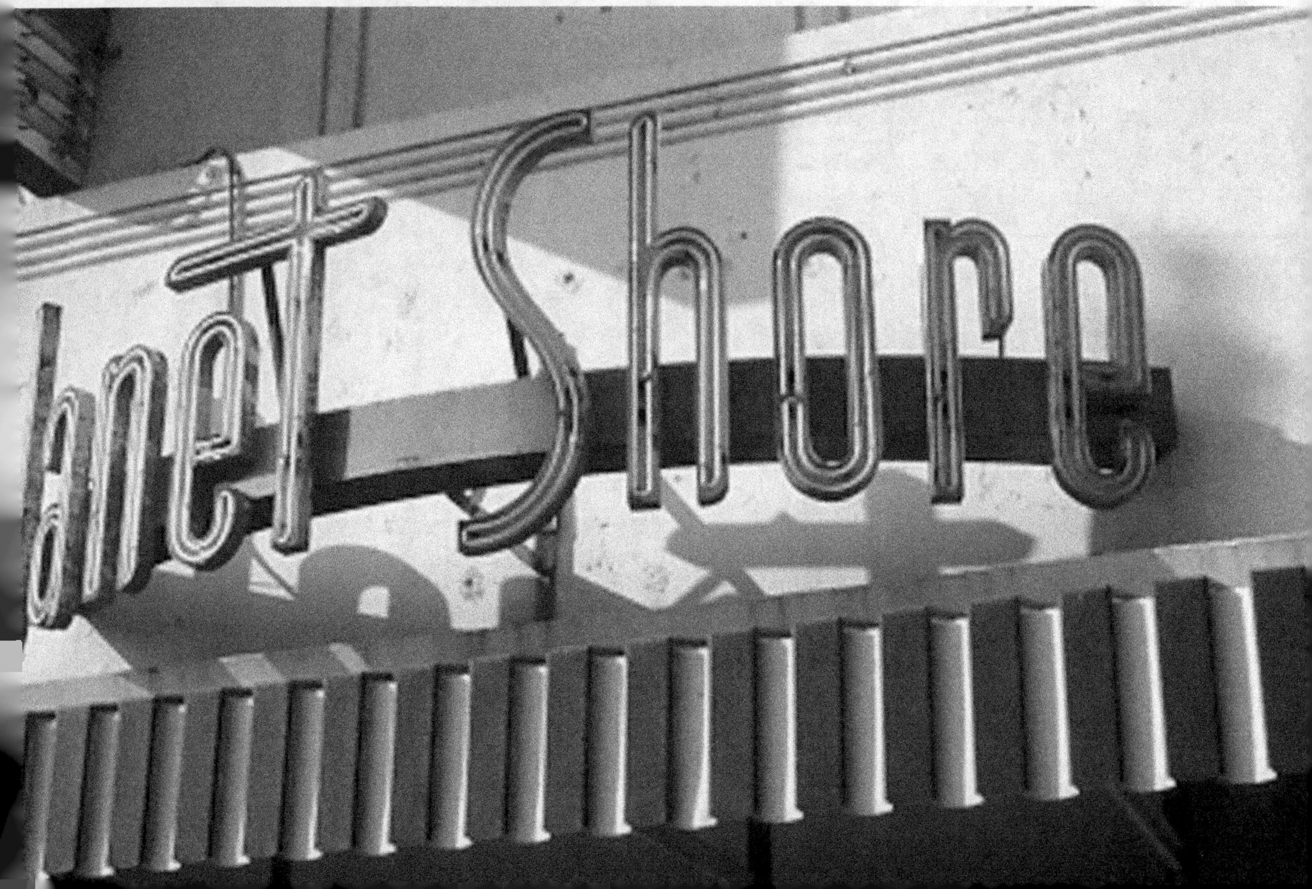

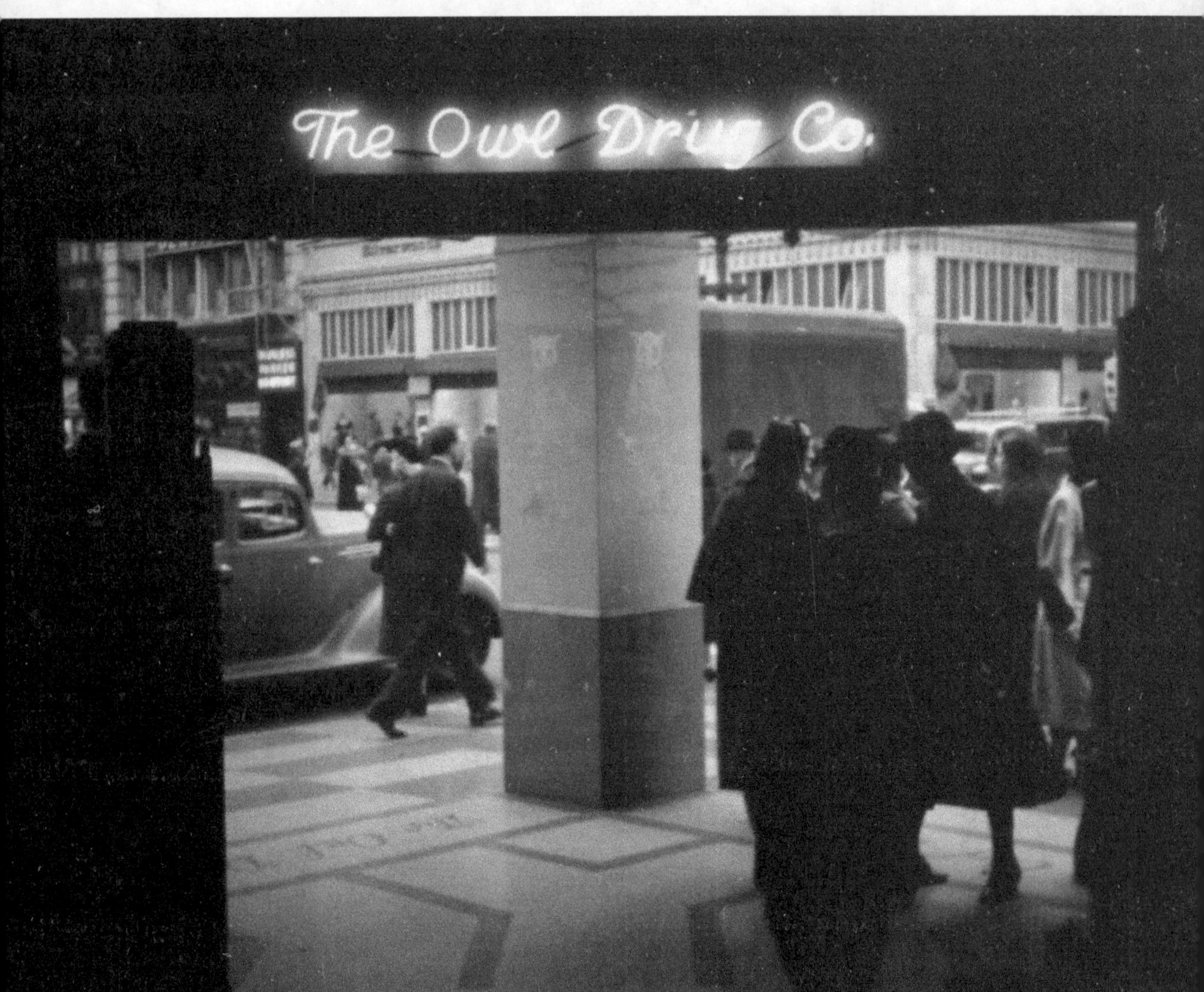
The Owl Drug Co.

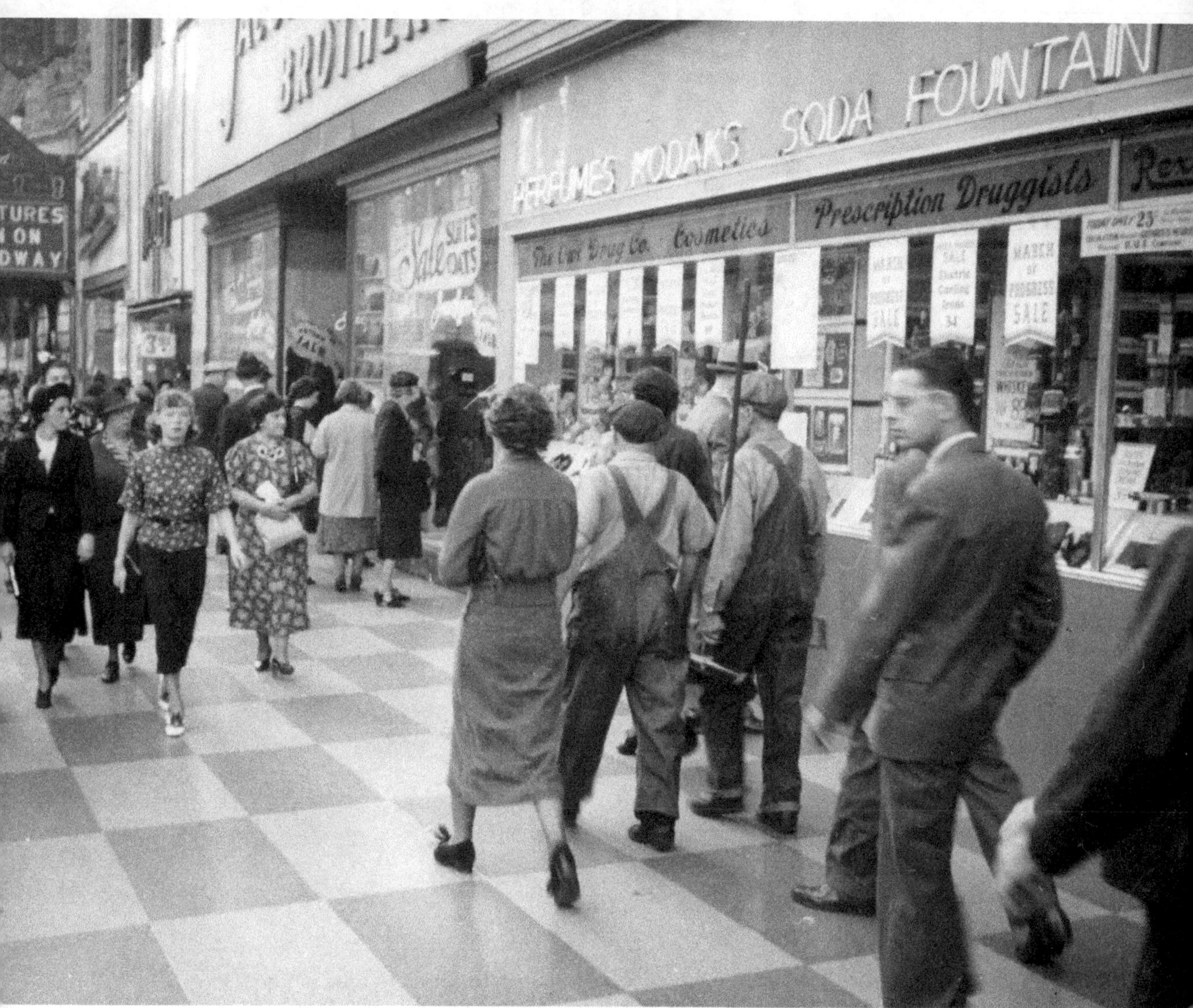

Above and opposite: At the busy intersection of 6th and Broadway, The Owl Drug Company promoted its name twice in the terrazzo sidewalk as well as figurally in the shape of an owl and pharmaceutical mortar on a marble column. Yet it's the neon that catches the eye in any environment – even if it is placed so only exiting customers may see it. (Circa 1937, Herman J. Schultheis Collection)

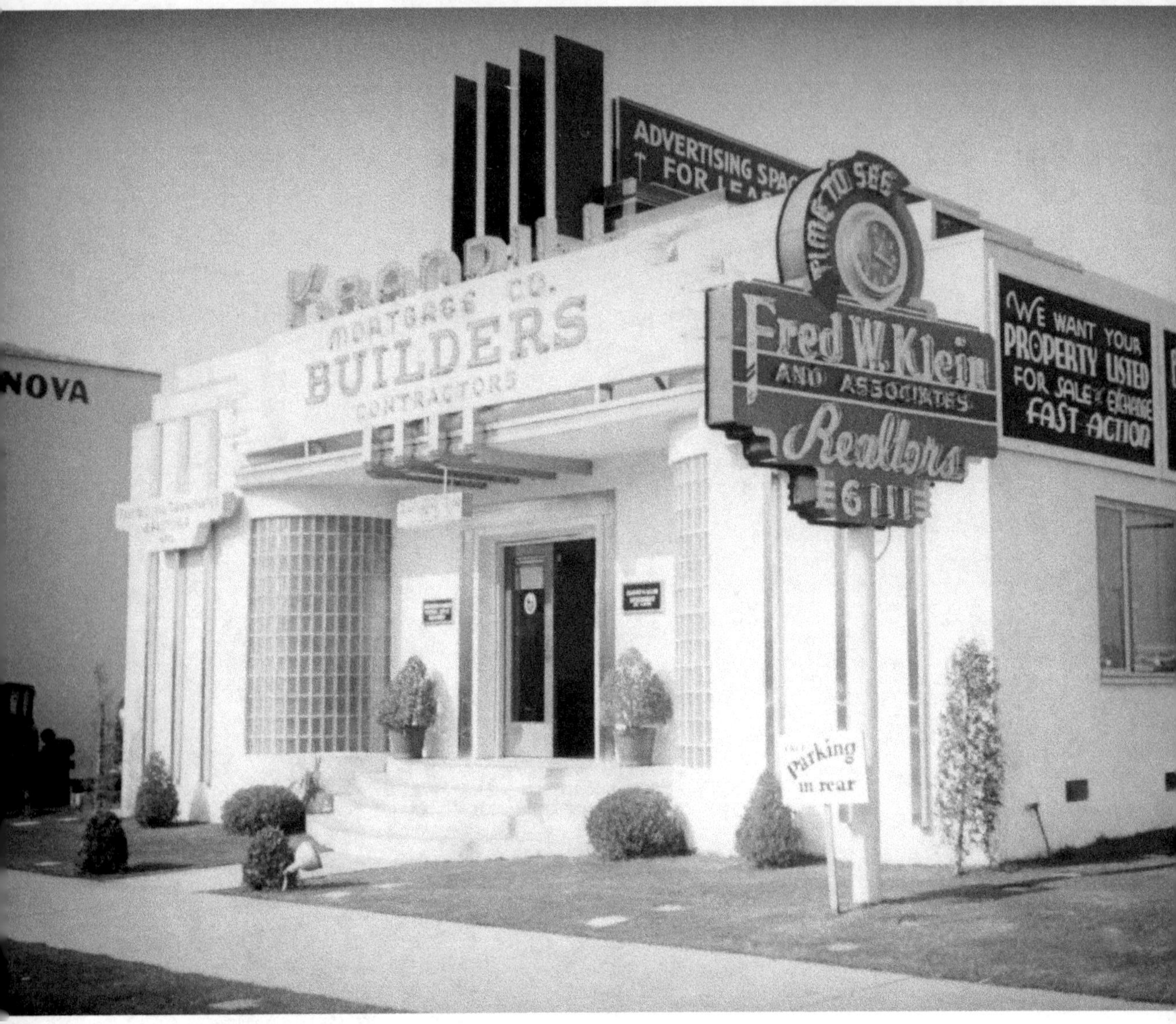

A beautiful Streamline Modern façade wasn't enough to compete for a motorist's attention along busy Wilshire Boulevard. Signage is used to compliment the building's architecture yet nearly buries it under wordy advertising murals and neon. Note Fred W. Klien's neon pole sign and clock as well as the two additional neon signs suspended in front and to the left of the front door. The building's rooftop billboard is available for lease, squeezing even more advertising onto this petite structure.
(1937, Herman J. Schultheis Collection)

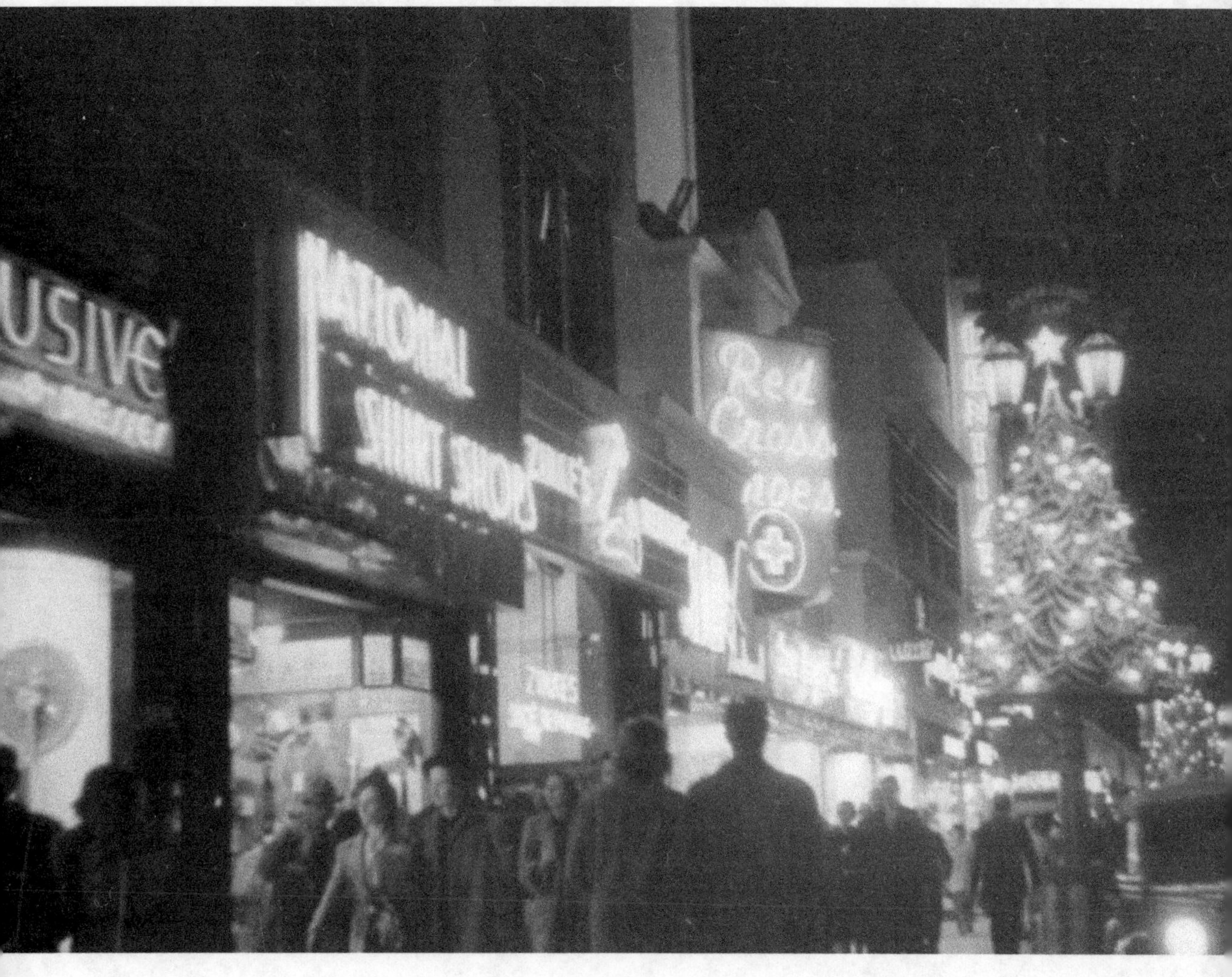

Neon adorns multiple businesses in this view of Hollywood Boulevard.
(Circa 1937, Herman J. Schultheis Collection)

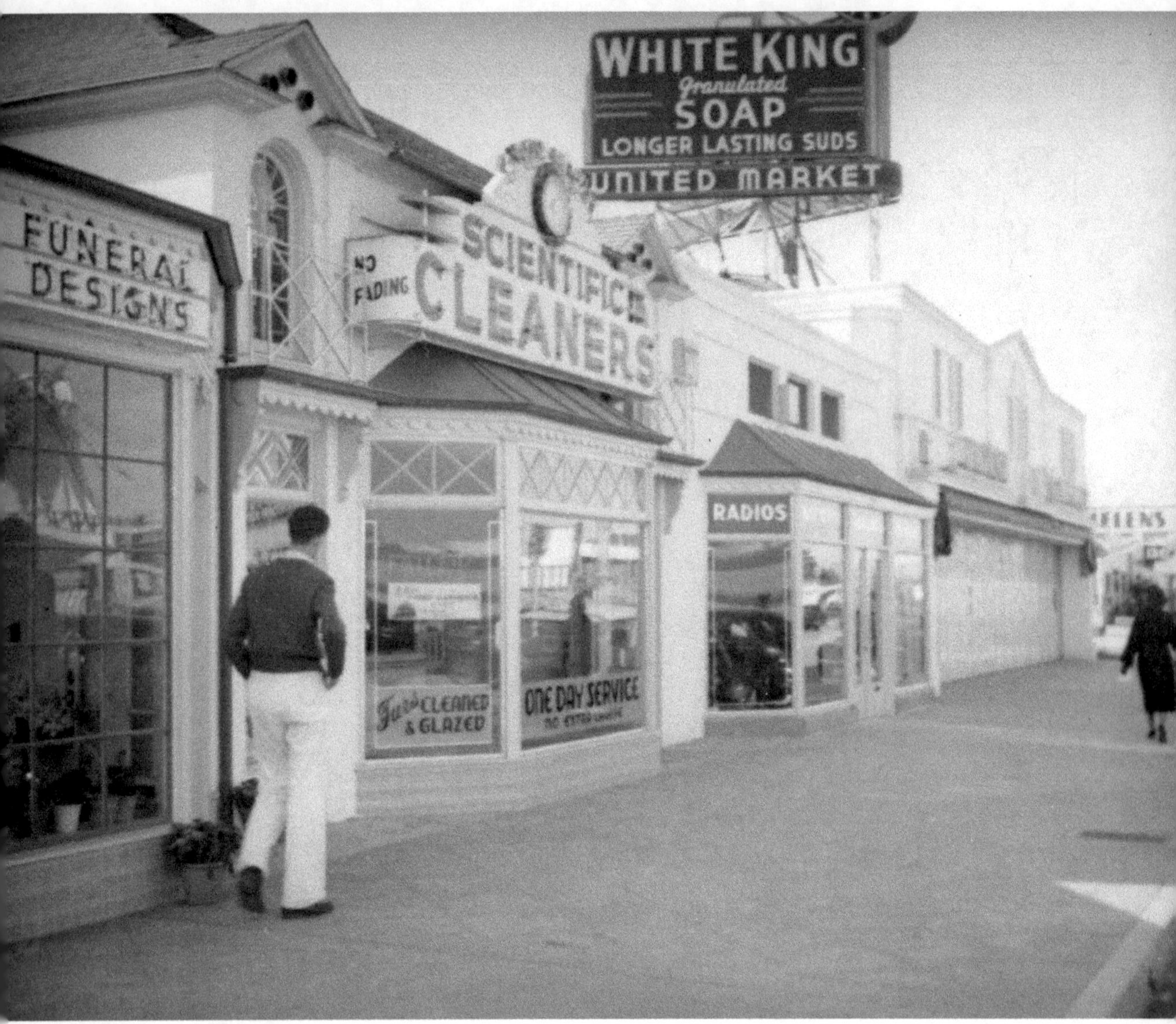
WHITE KING
Granulated
SOAP
LONGER LASTING SUDS
UNITED MARKET
FUNERAL
DESIGN'S
NO
FADING
SCIENTIFIC
CLEANERS
RADIOS
CLEANED
& GLAZED
ONE DAY SERVICE

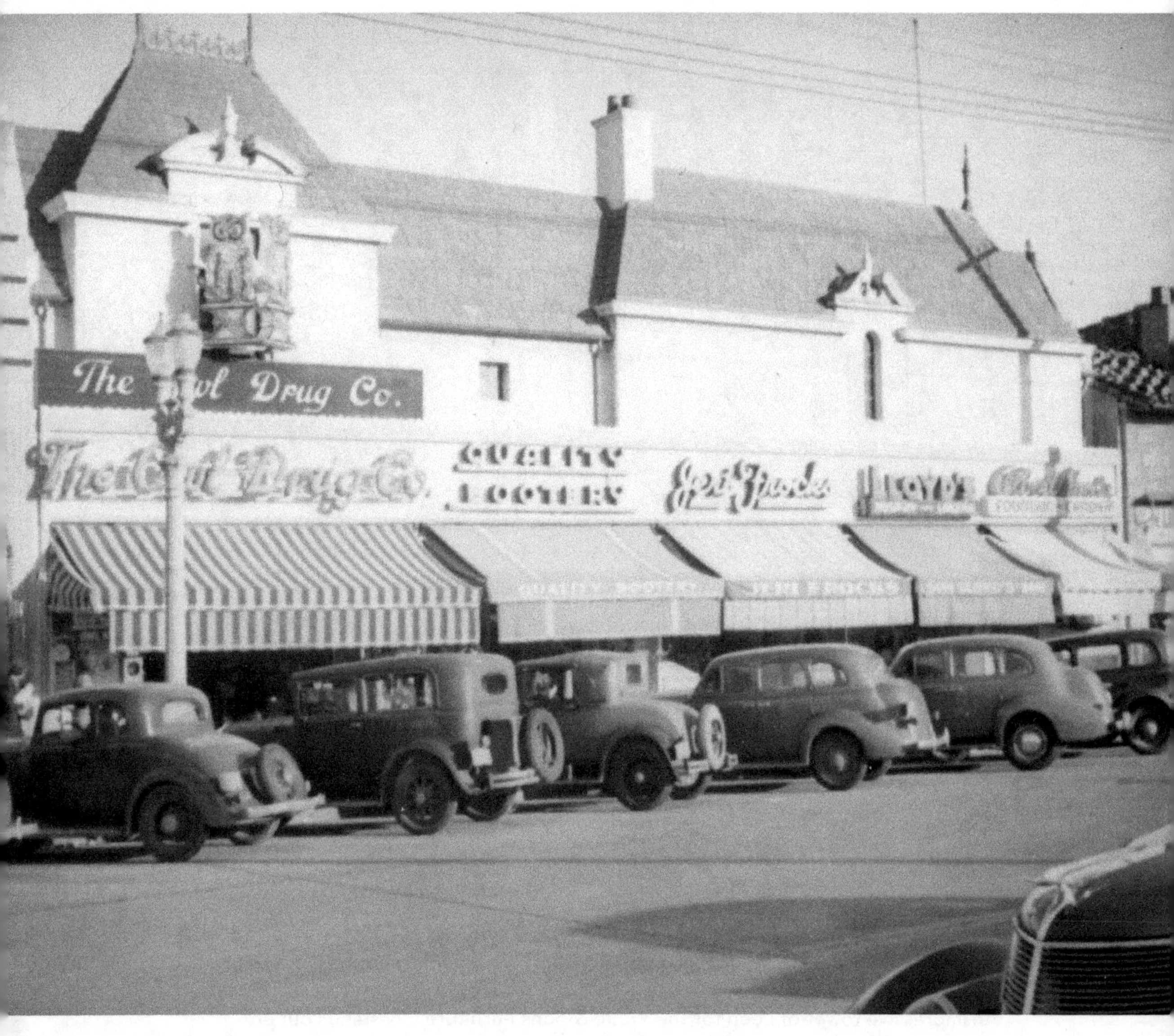

Above and opposite: Neon is well represented on this stretches of Crenshaw Boulevard in Leimert Park and Hyde Park. (Circa 1938, Herman J. Schultheis Collection)

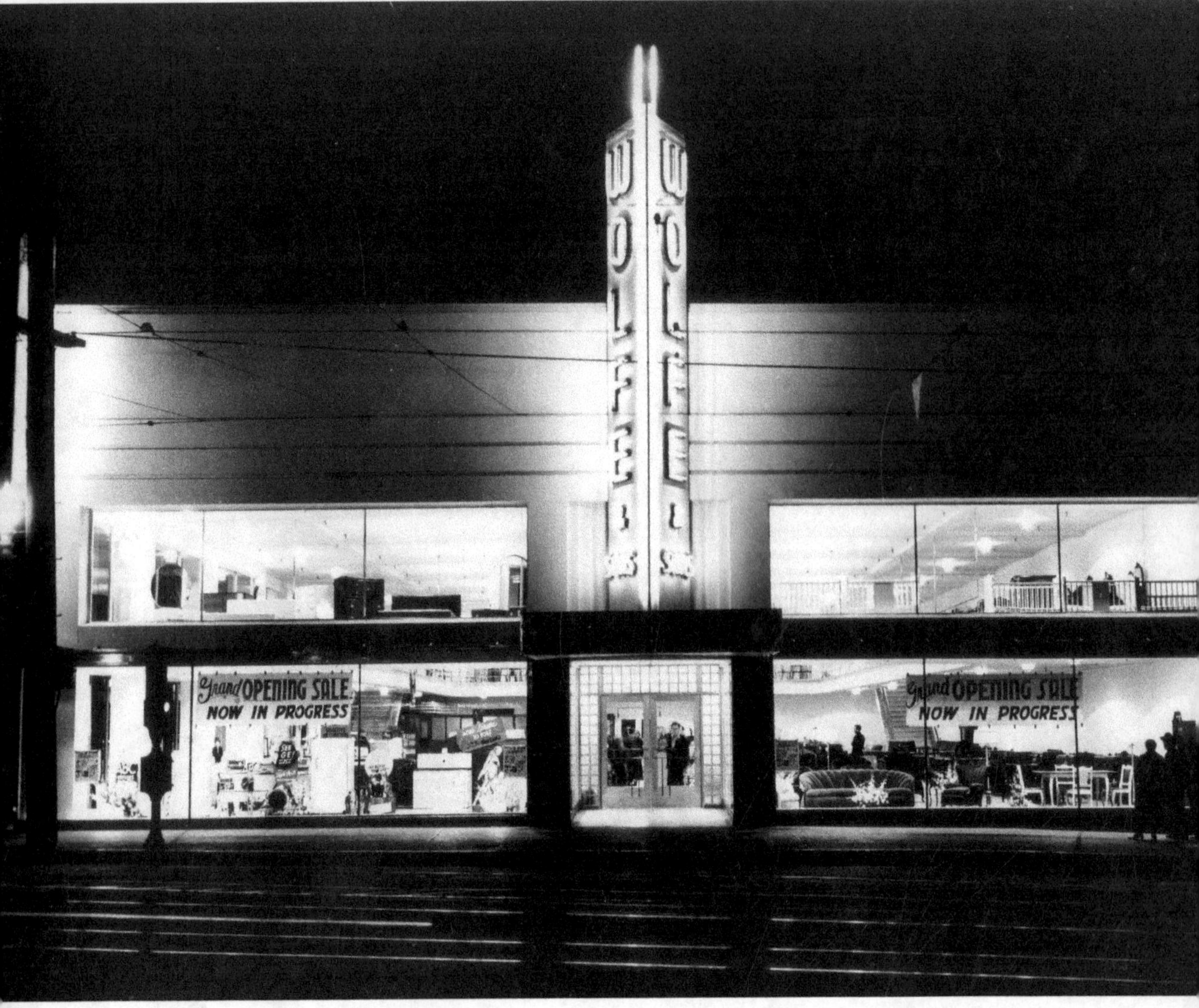

An impressive tower of neon for the Wolfe & Sons Furniture Co. stands out on Broadway in the Lincoln Heights neighborhood. (Circa 1948, Shades of L.A. Collection)

Opposite: To celebrate the 44th anniversary of Kay Jewelers, the staff of the Burbank location at 139 San Fernando Road gather beneath their verbose neon marquee for a photoshoot. An overabundance of signage is not uncommon for a store in the 1950s. Within the next few years, a city-beautiful movement would begin to sweep the nation to ban many types of commercial and public advertising from such crowded visual displays, neon included. (1959, Valley Times Collection)

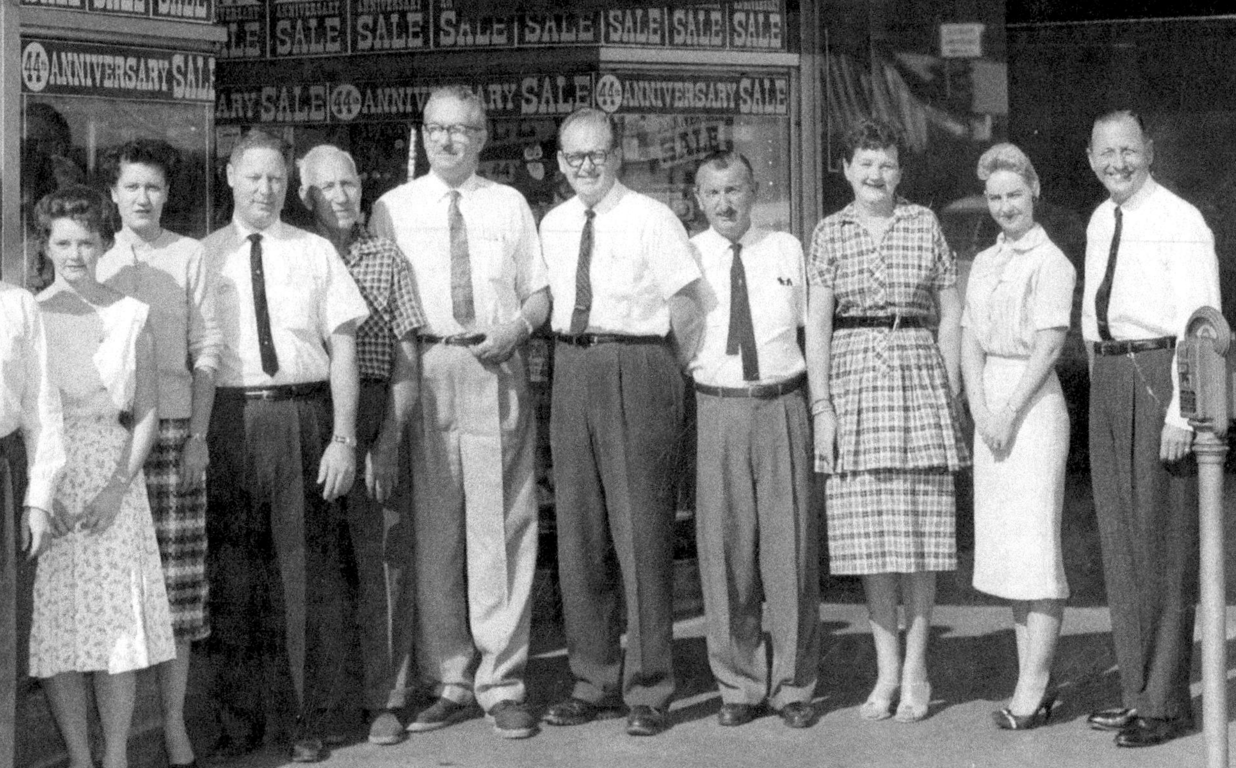
AMERICA'S LARGEST CREDIT JEWELERS
135 STORES · COAST TO COAST
Kay JEWELERS
DIAMONDS
On Credit
44th ANNIVERSARY SALE
EYES EXAMINED
DR. LIONEL LEWIS
OPTOMETRIST
GLASSES ON CREDIT

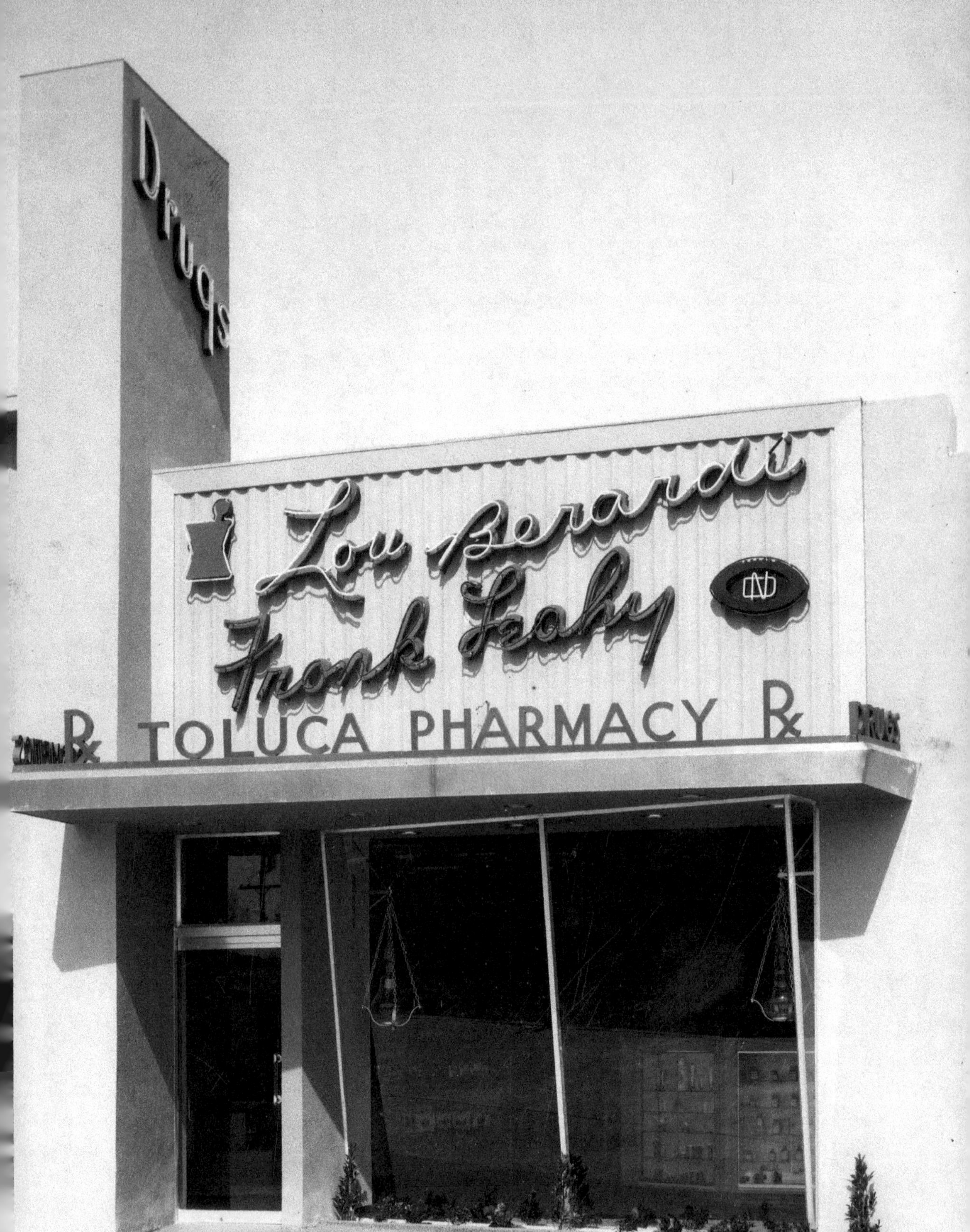
Drugs
Lou Berardi
Frank Leahy
℞ TOLUCA PHARMACY ℞
DRUGS

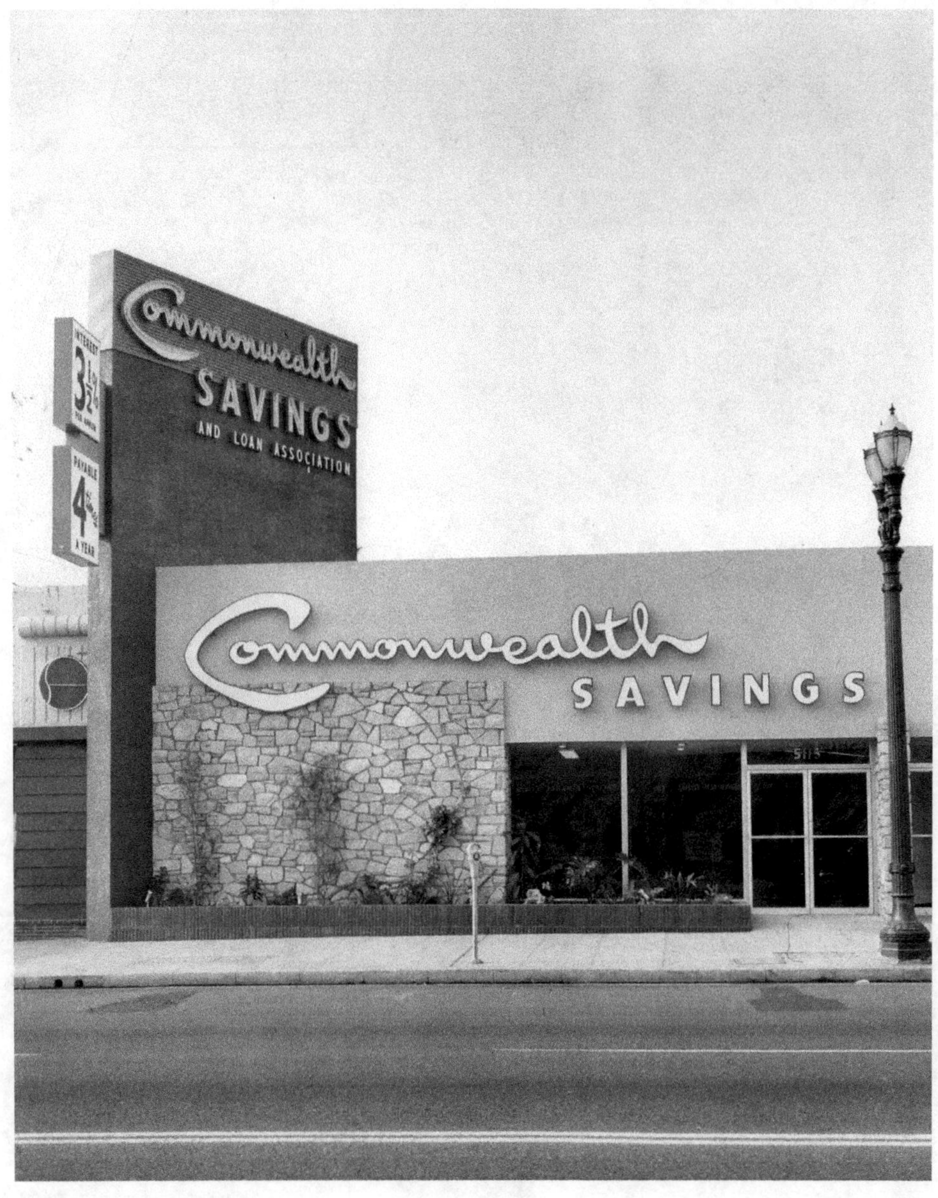

The newly constructed Commonwealth Loan building proudly displays neon on Lankershim Boulevard in North Hollywood. (1954, Valley Times Collection)

Opposite: A Toluca Lake Pharmacy shows examples of both neon fonts and shapes. (1956, Valley Times Collection)

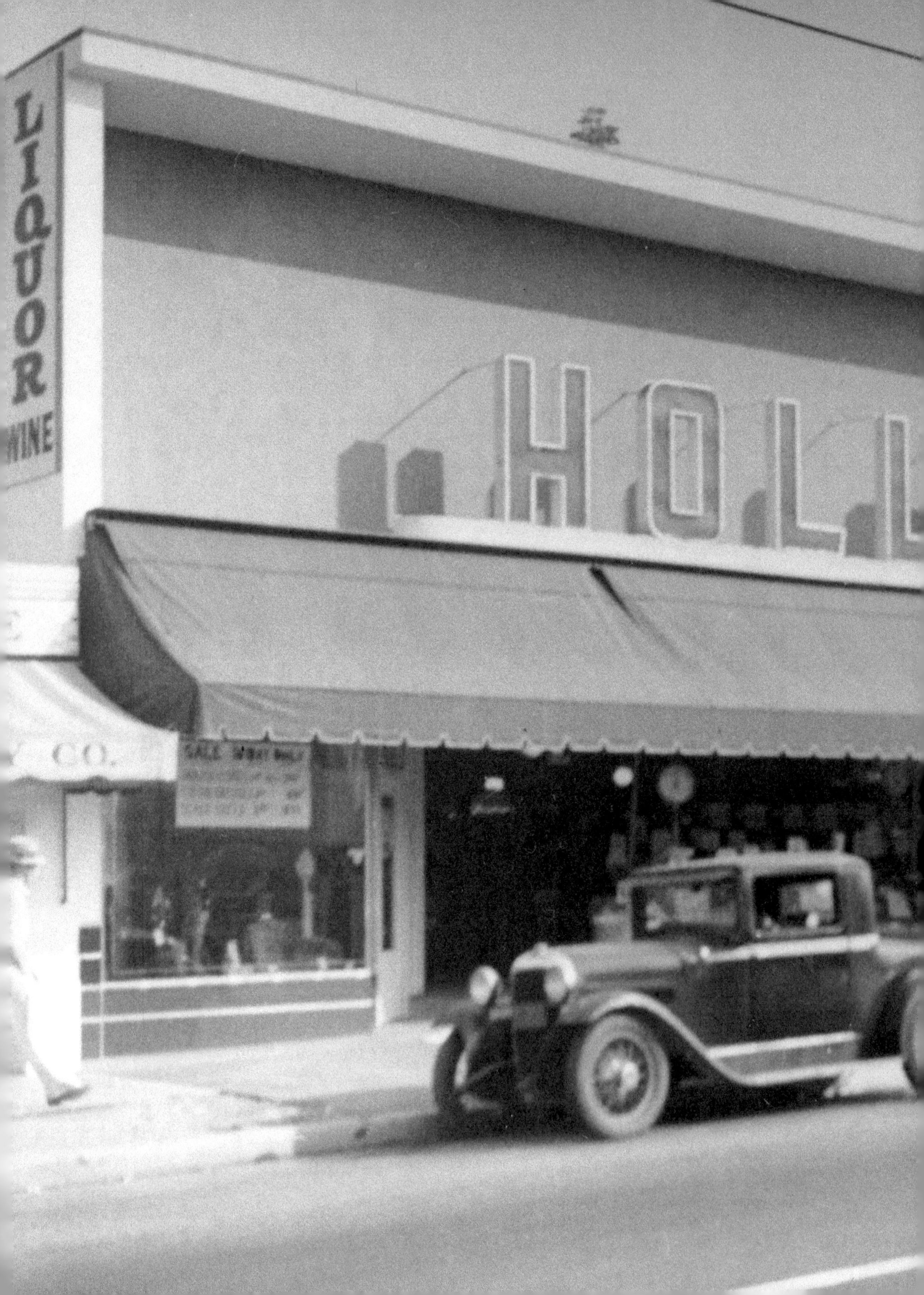
LIQUOR
WINE
HOLL
CO.

MARKETS

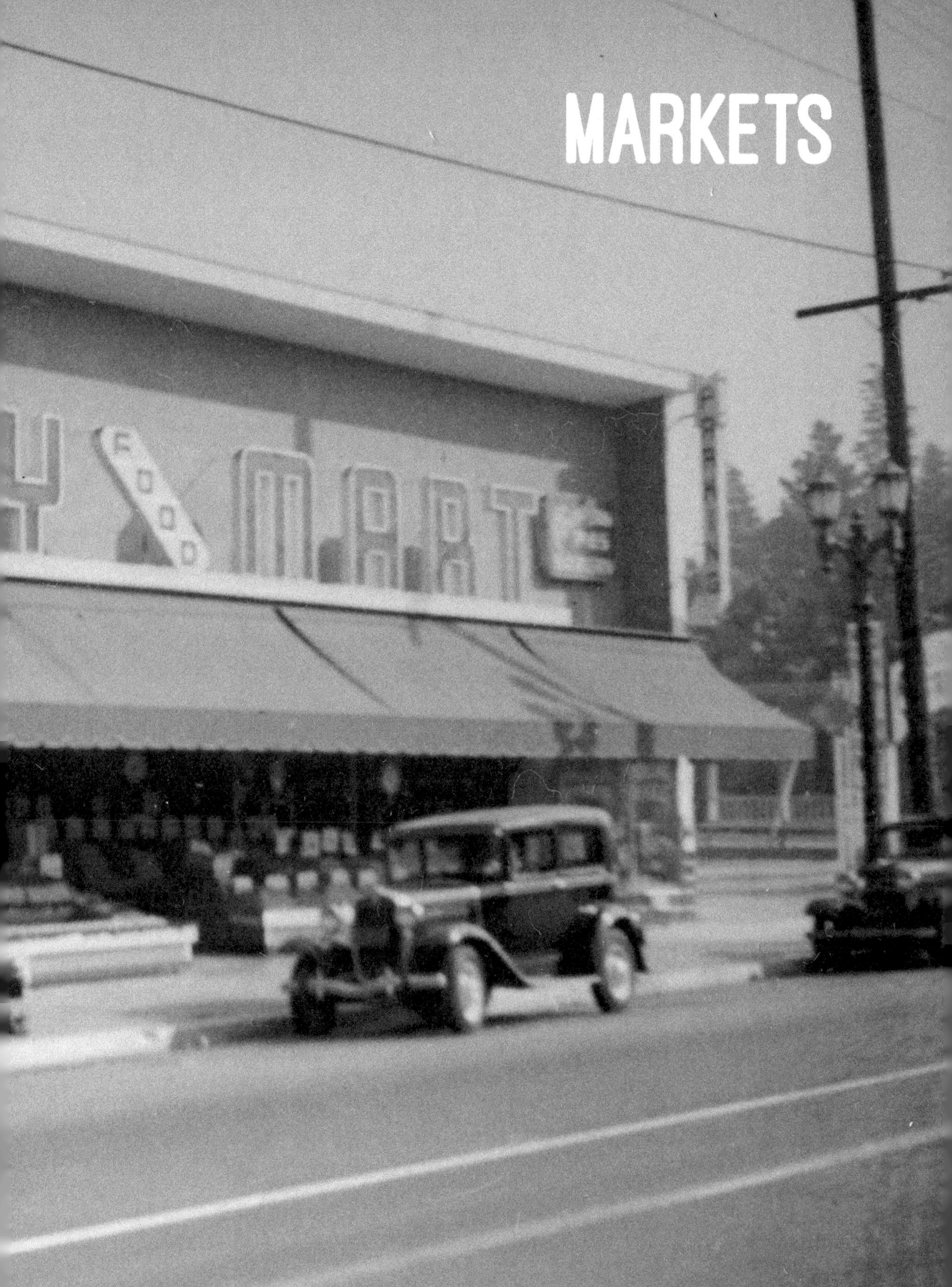

Overleaf: Day view of Holly Food Mart sign, on Hollywood Boulevard, east of Gower Street. (Circa 1937, Herman J. Schultheis Collection)

Opposite: A vertical neon sign is visible in this view of the Los Angeles Produce Terminal Market. (1961, Larry Leach/Valley Times Collection)

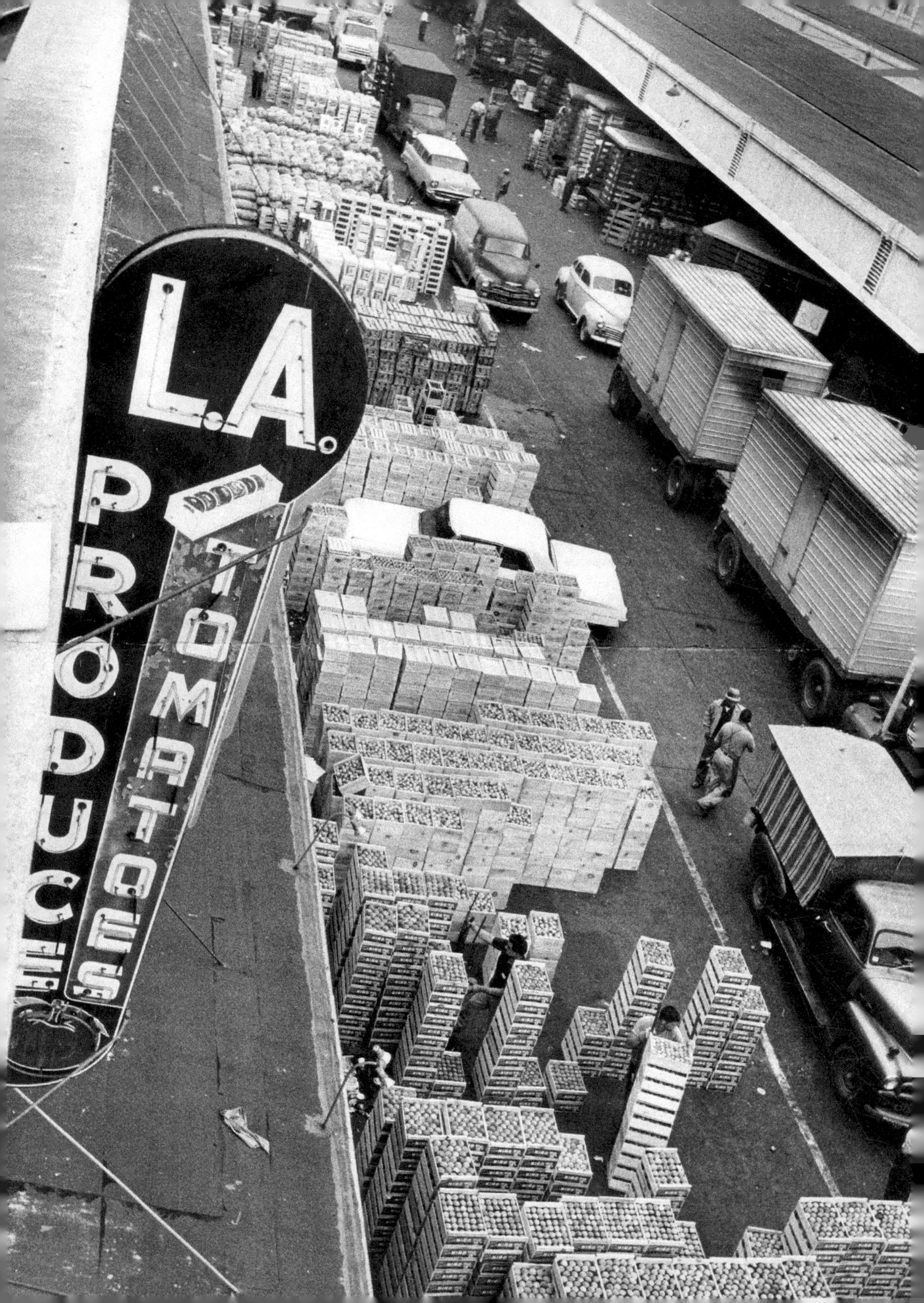
L.A.
PRODUCE
TOMATOES

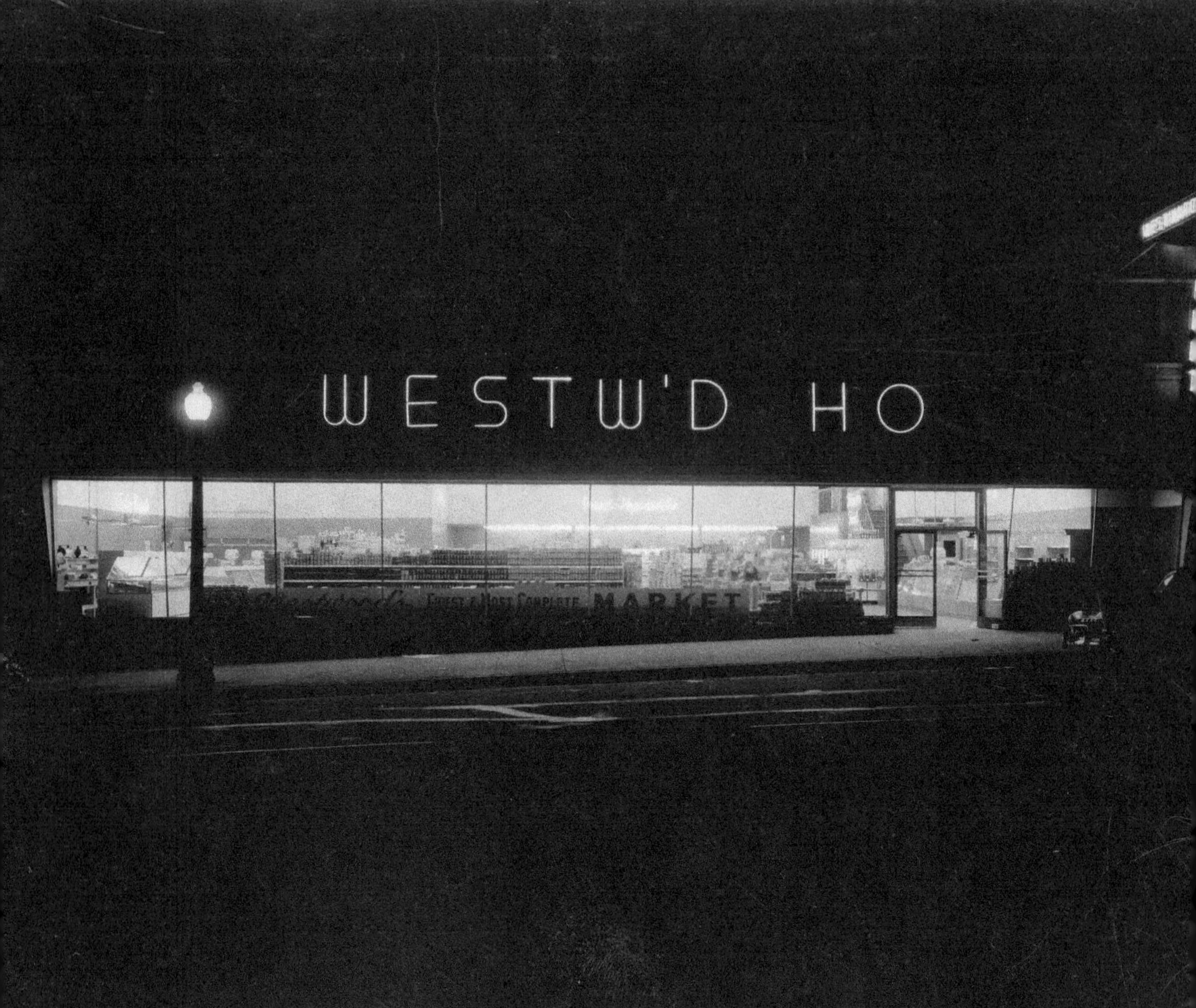

Westward Ho's simple neon stands out at night in Westwood Village.
(Circa 1950s, Ralph Morris Collection)

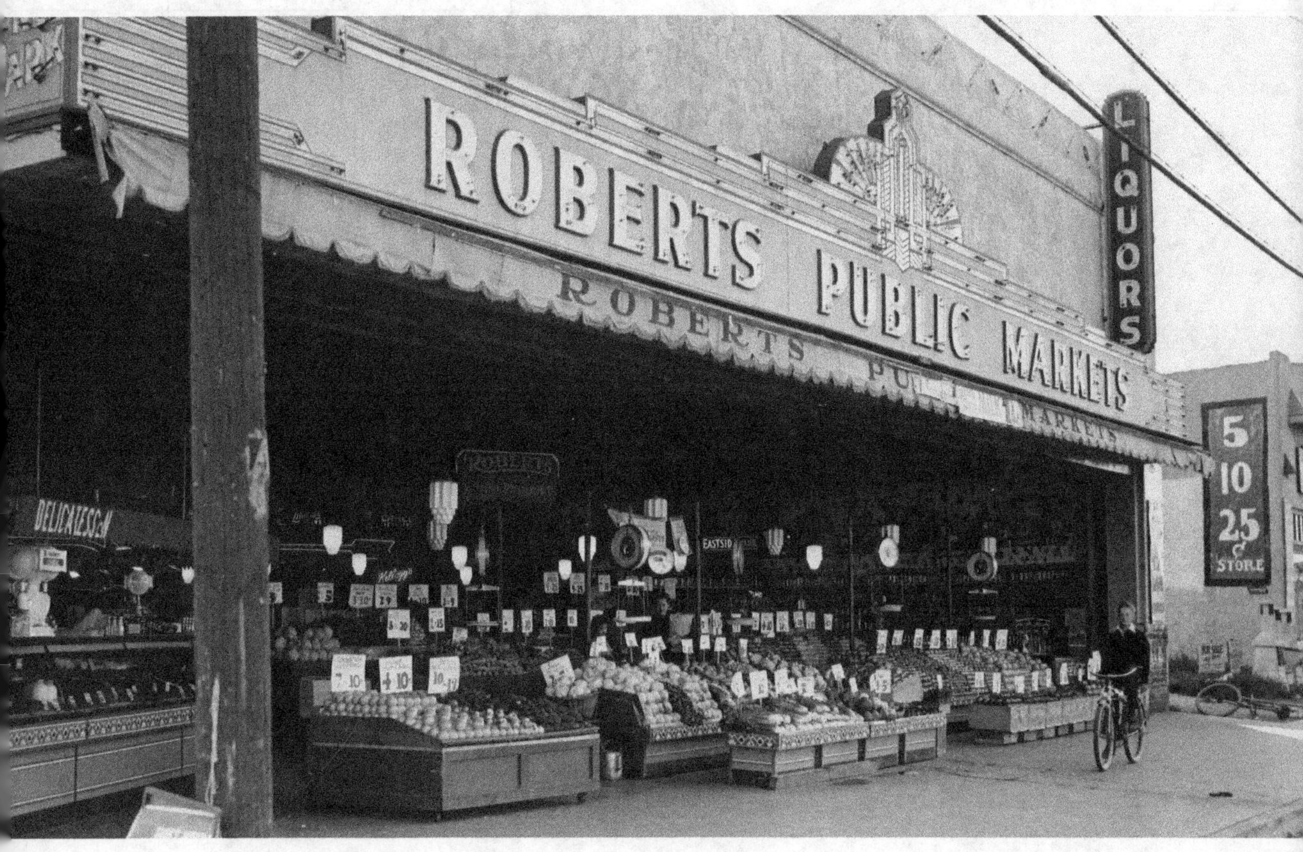

Neon with an Art Deco influence graces the front of Roberts Public Market on Adams Boulevard near Hauser Boulevard. (1941, Security Pacific National Bank Collection)

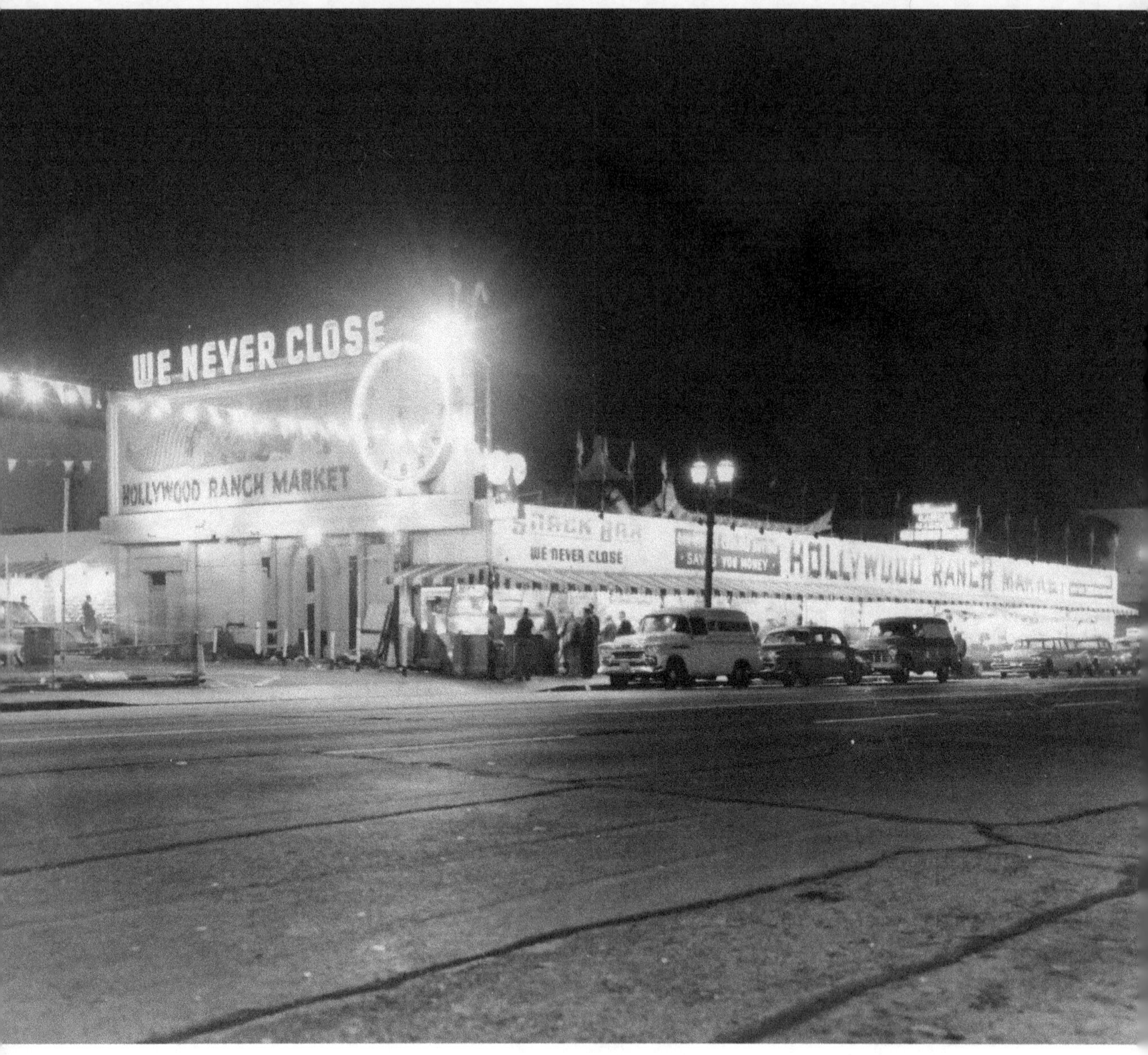
WE NEVER CLOSE
HOLLYWOOD RANCH MARKET
WE NEVER CLOSE
HOLLYWOOD RANCH

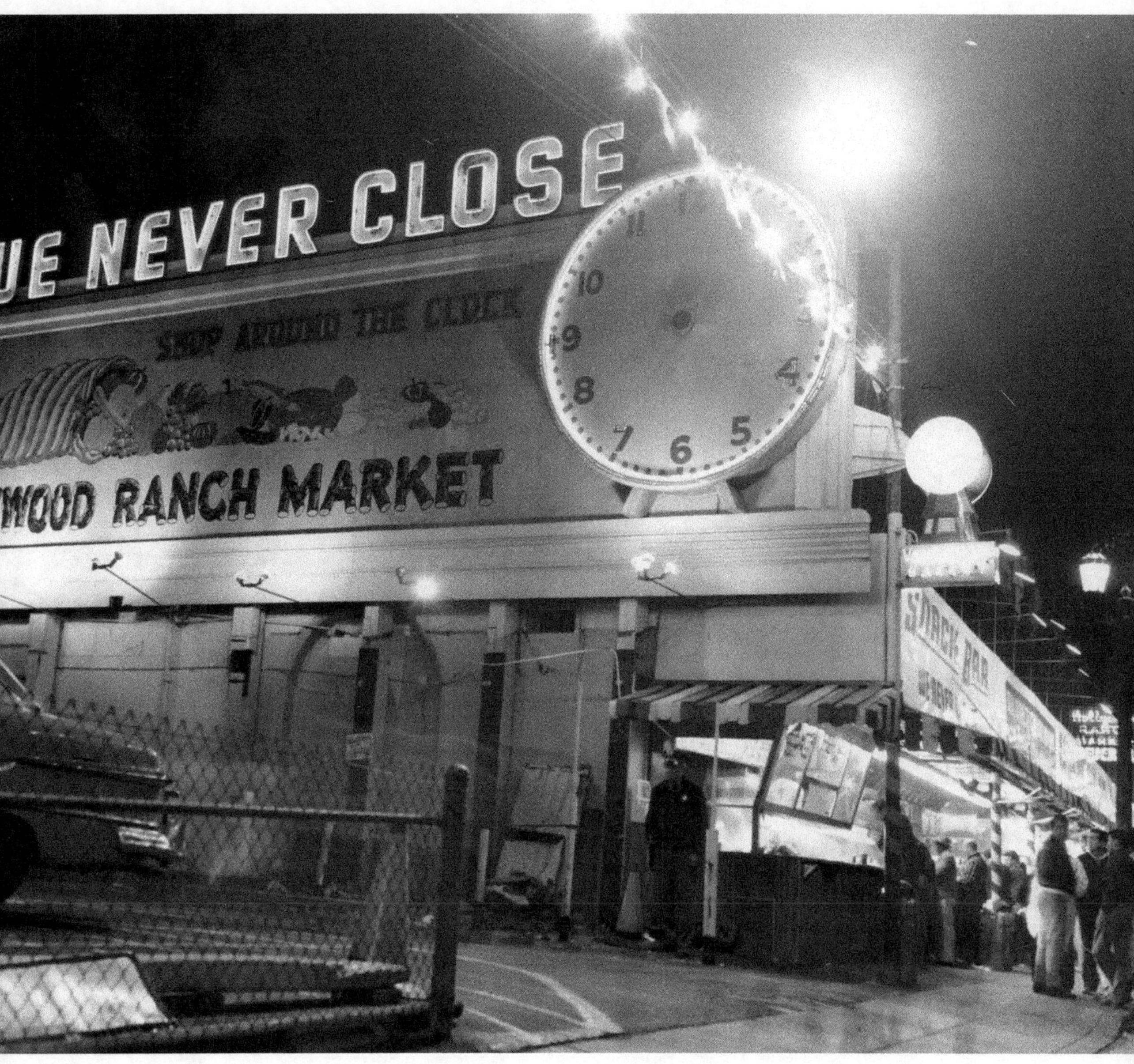

Above and opposite: Neon is used to proclaim that the Hollywood Ranch Market never closes. (1961, Security Pacific National Bank Collection)

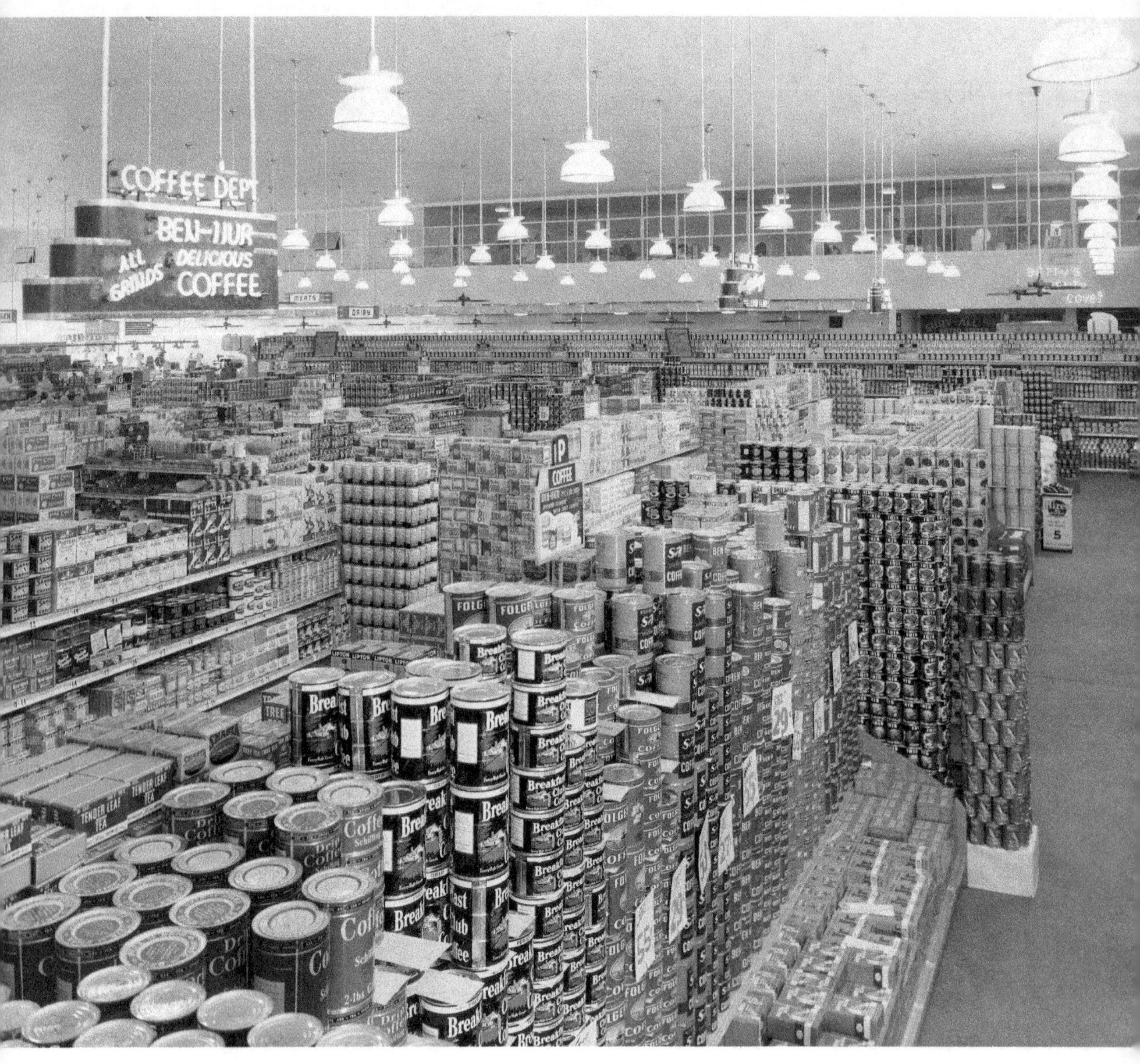

In the vast aisles of Los Angeles' new grocery stores, Ben-Hur Coffee seems to have cornered the market (pun intended) in the coffee aisle. Other streamlined neon signs promote other sections of the store, but it's "Betty's Beauty Cove" in the background that certainly catches the eye. (1942, Security Pacific National Bank Collection)

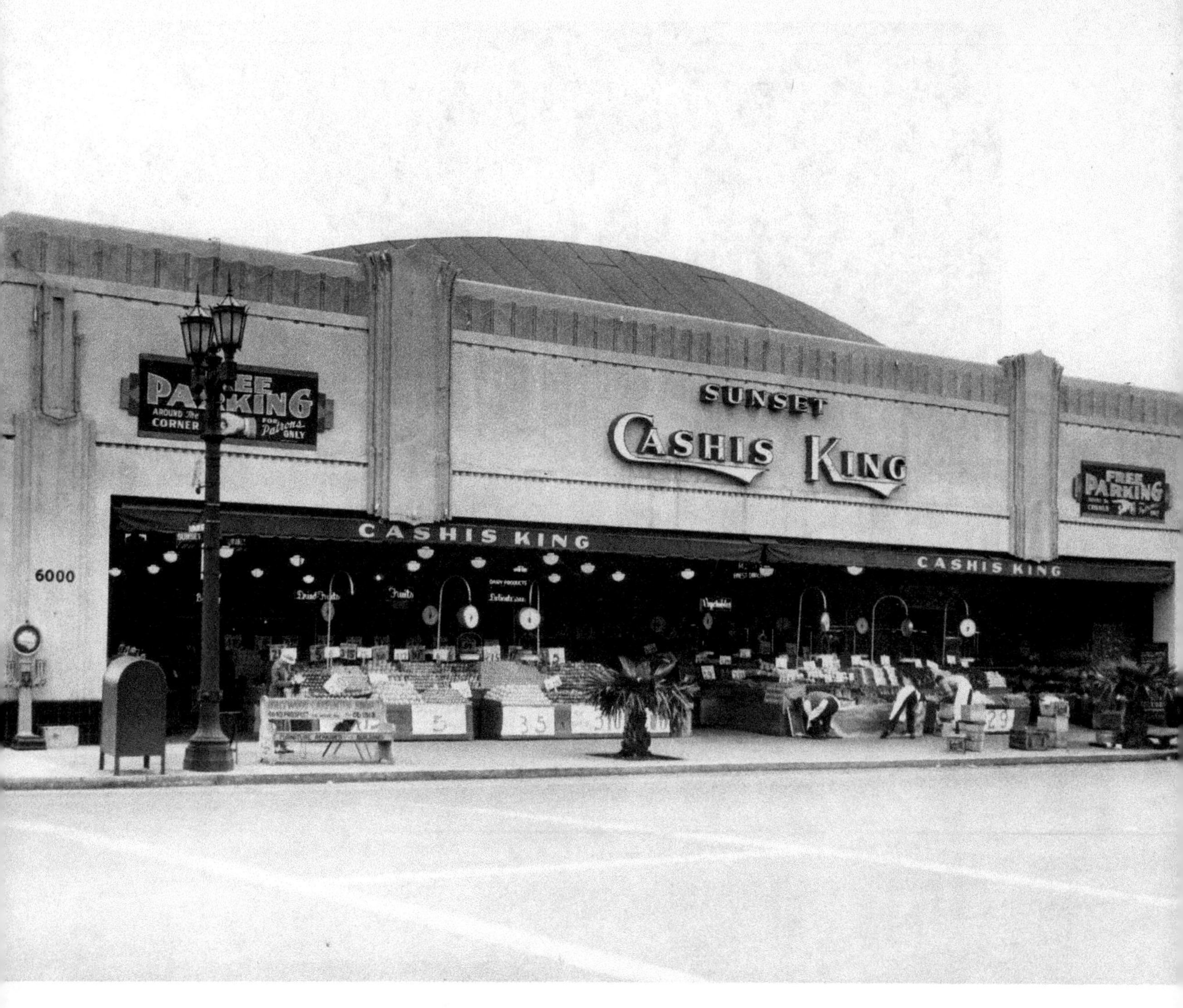

The Cashis King Market at 6000 Sunset Boulevard shows off neon inside and out. (Circa 1930s, Security Pacific National Bank Collection)

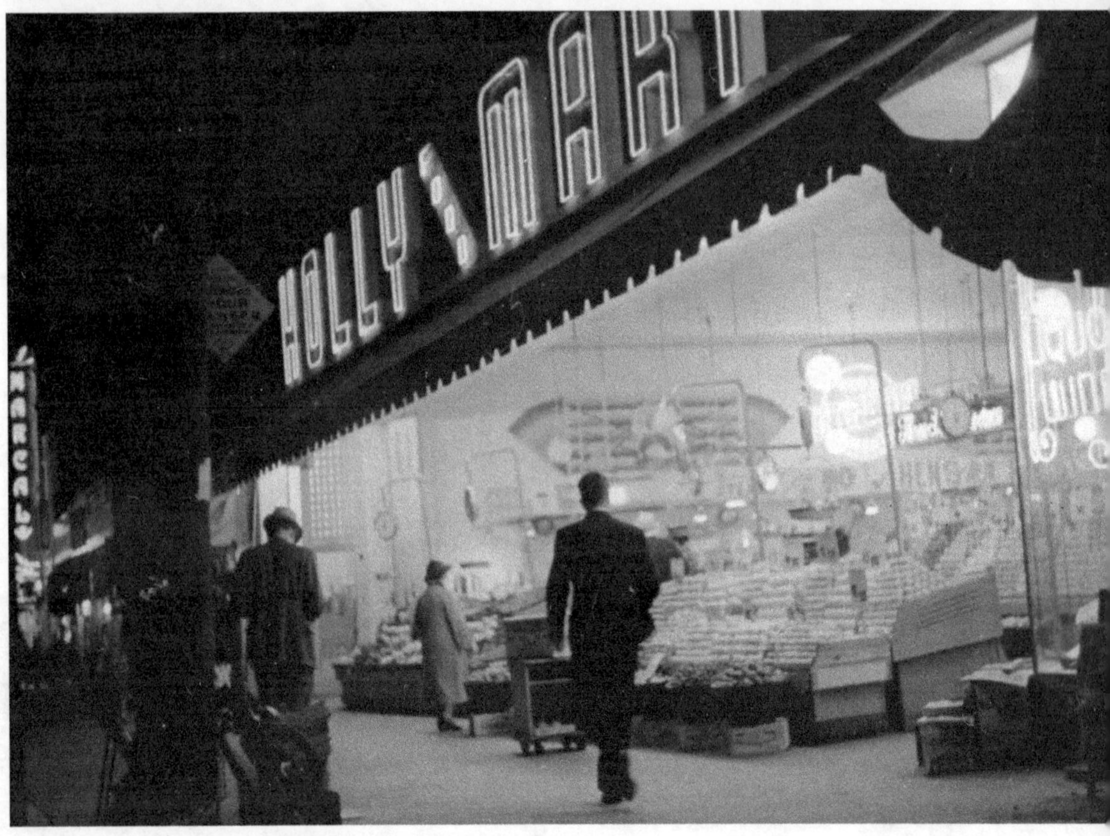

Grocery shopping was convenient at any time thanks to inviting illumination in the form of neon signs and brightly lit aisles. Suspended neon tubing for "Liquors Wines," at right, brought attention to a window display without obscuring the contents of the window with opaque signage. The neon vertical sign for the short-lived Marcal Theatre is down the street at 6025 Hollywood Boulevard. (Circa 1937, Herman J. Schultheis Collection)

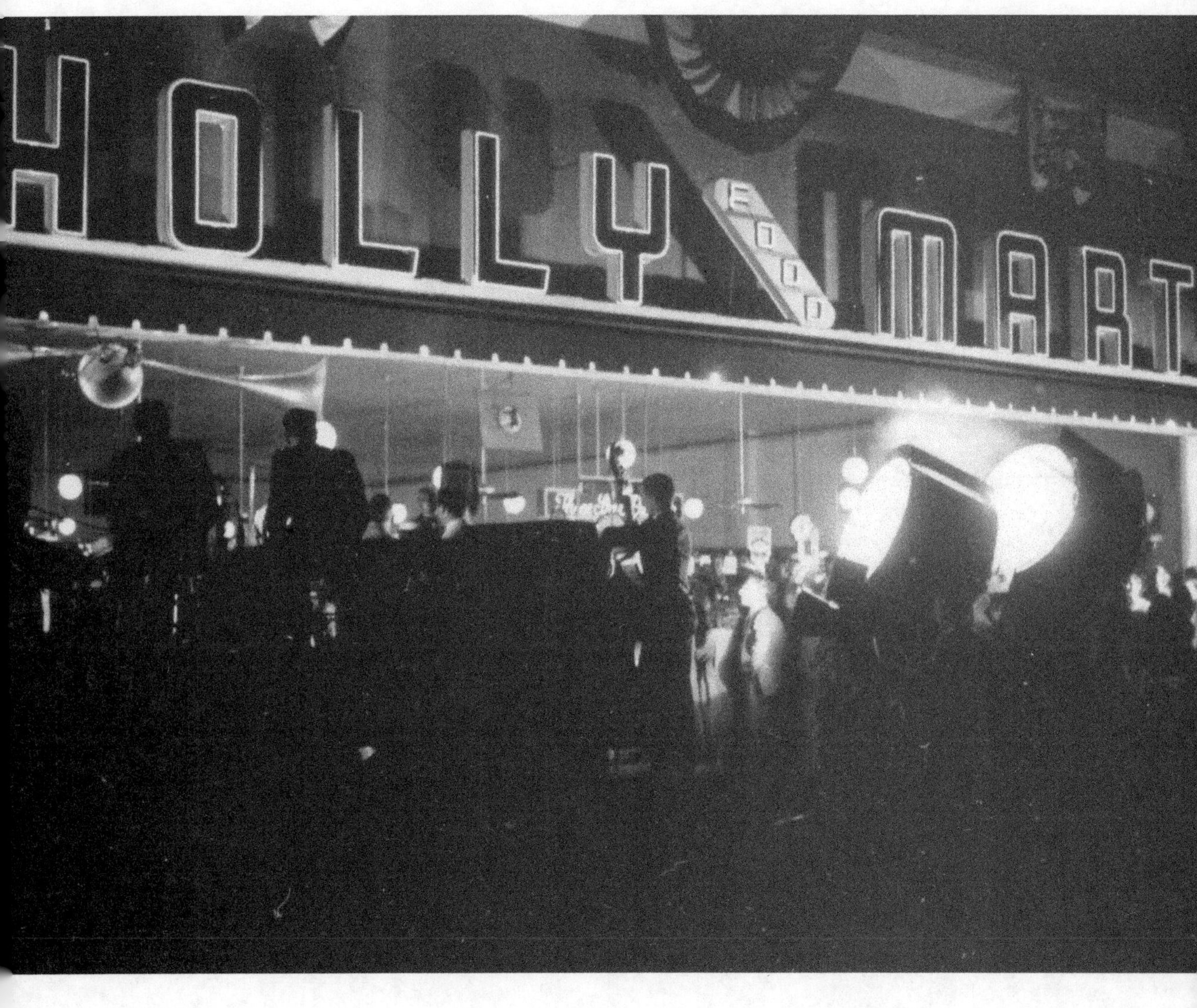

Detail of the neon at the Holly Food Mart on its opening night. (Circa 1937, Herman J. Schultheis Collection)

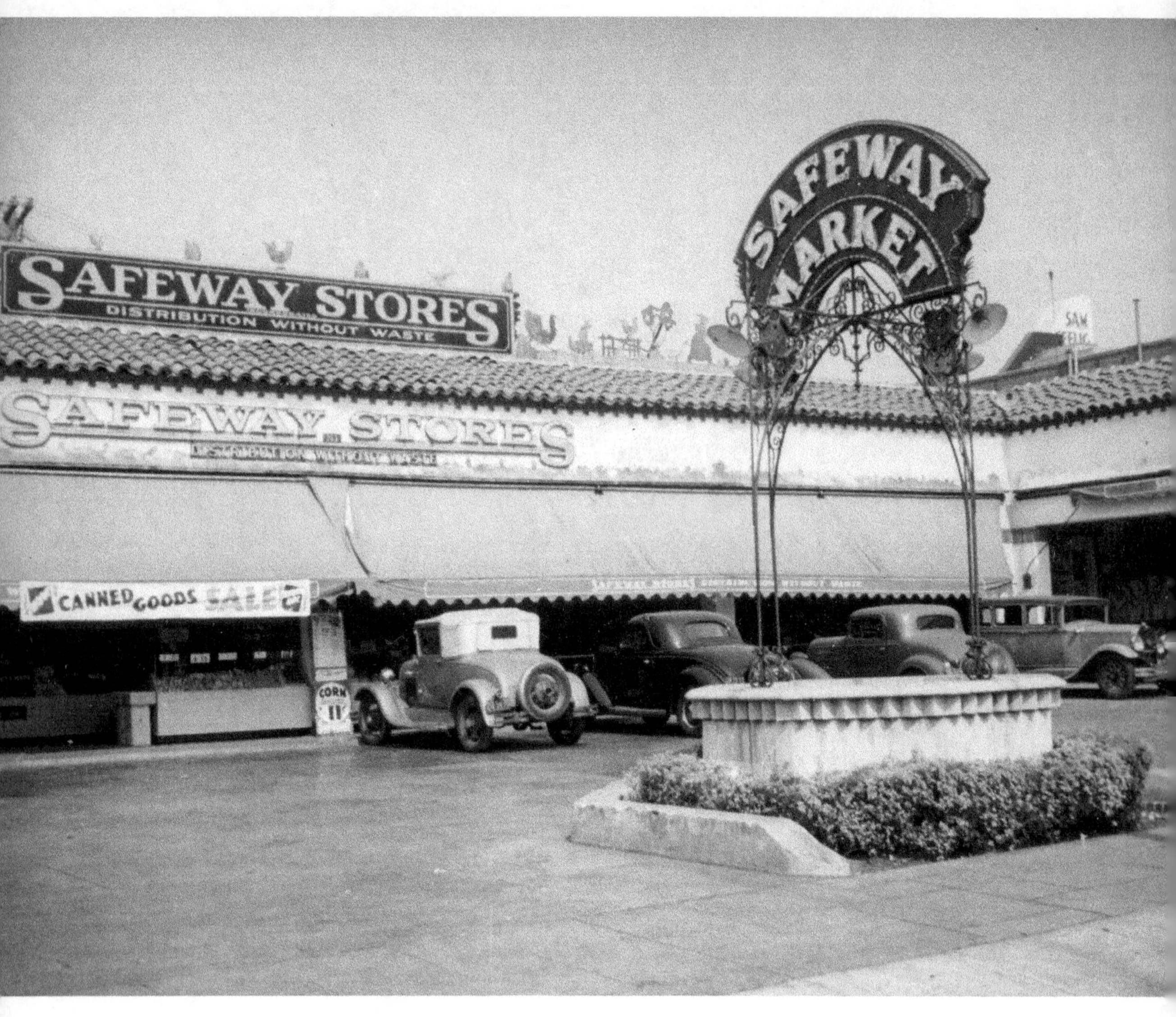

Neon lures motorists to the Safeway Market on Sunset Boulevard near Western Avenue. (Circa 1937, Herman J. Schultheis Collection)

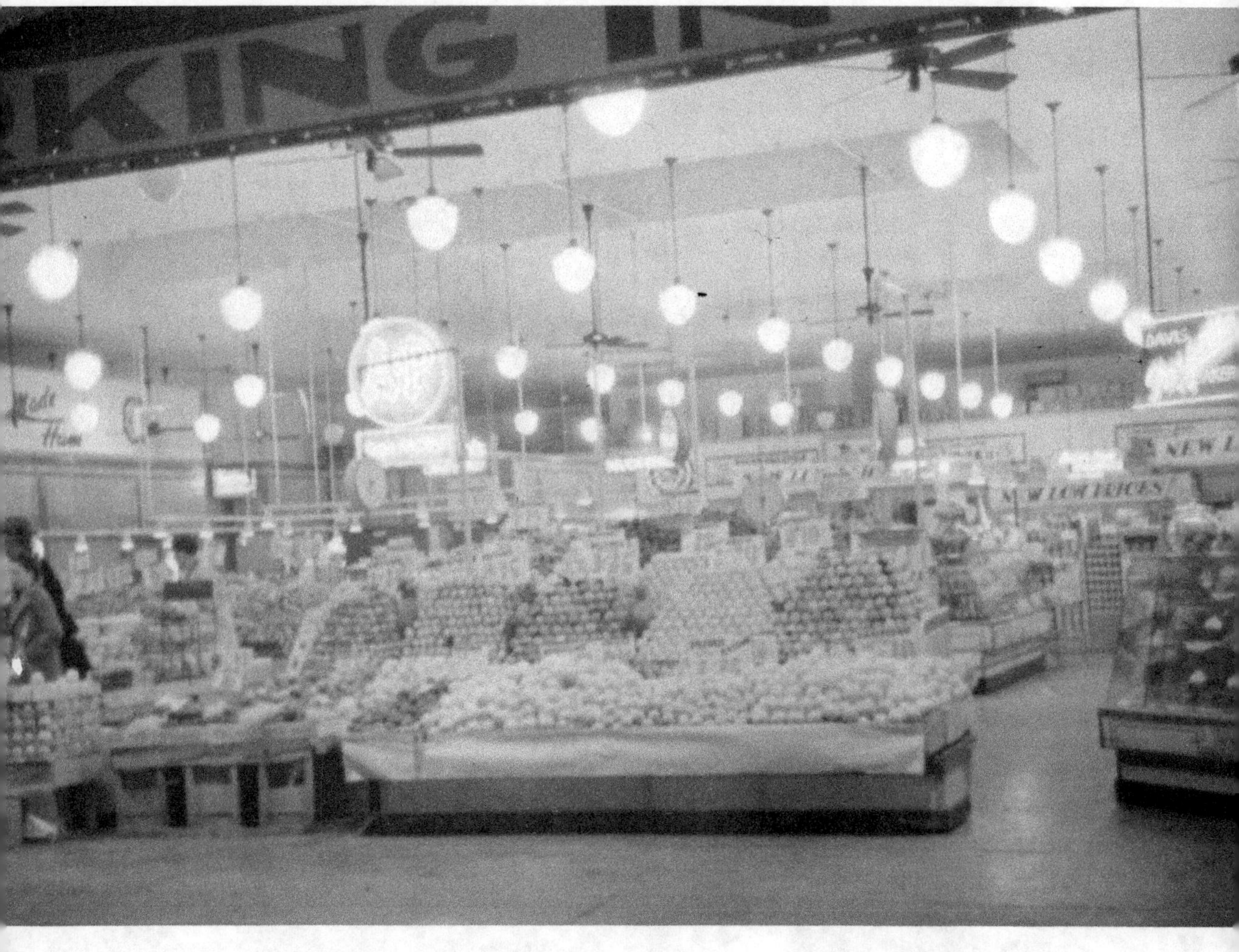

Interior view of the brightly lit Great Atlantic & Pacific Tea Company (A&P) shows many examples of neon signage. (Circa 1937, Herman J. Schultheis Collection)

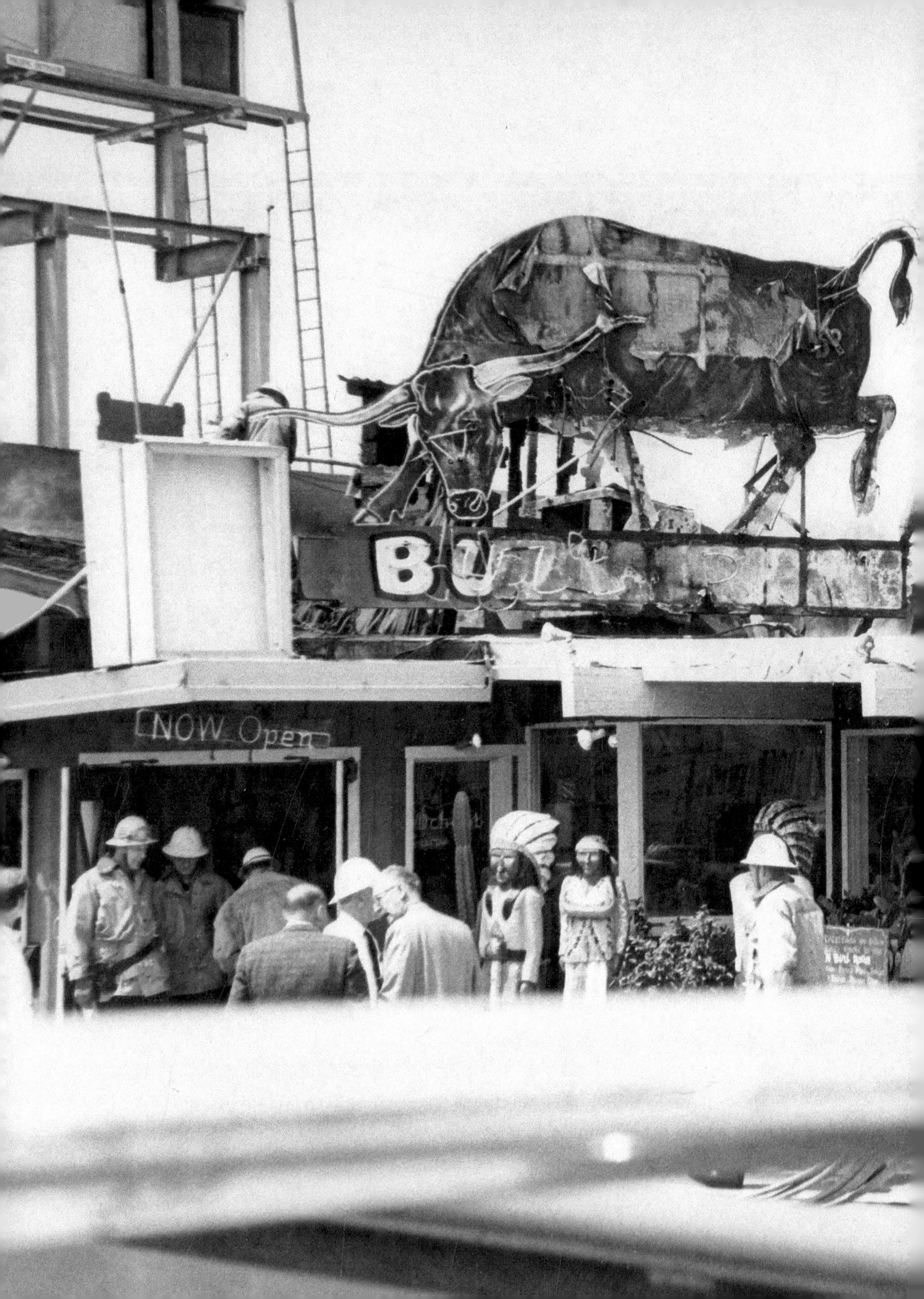
BU
NOW Open

NIGHTCLUBS & BARS

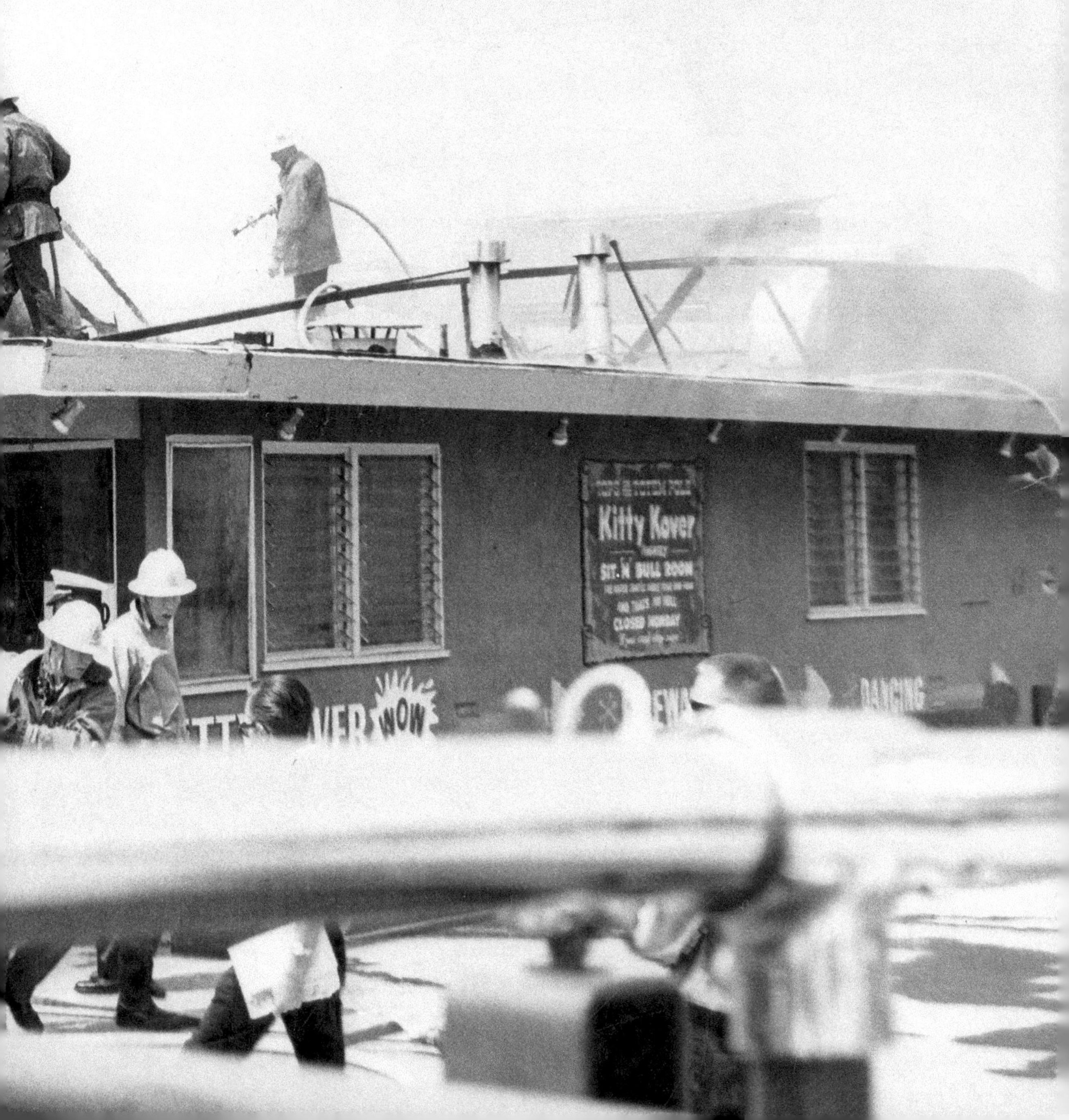

Overleaf: Urban decay claimed many a neon sign in the 1960s and 70s, but the animated Bull Pen neon sign succumbed to a kitchen fire. Formerly located in Sherman Oaks at 14649 Ventura Boulevard, the 24-hour eatery was famous for its bucking bull neon sign and cocktails served in the Sit'n Bull Room. (1964, Jeff Robbins/Valley Times Collection)

Opposite: Lionel Hampton poses in front of the duel neon signs for Club Alabam on Central Avenue, the heart of the Los Angeles jazz scene. (Circa 1953, Shades of L.A. Collection)

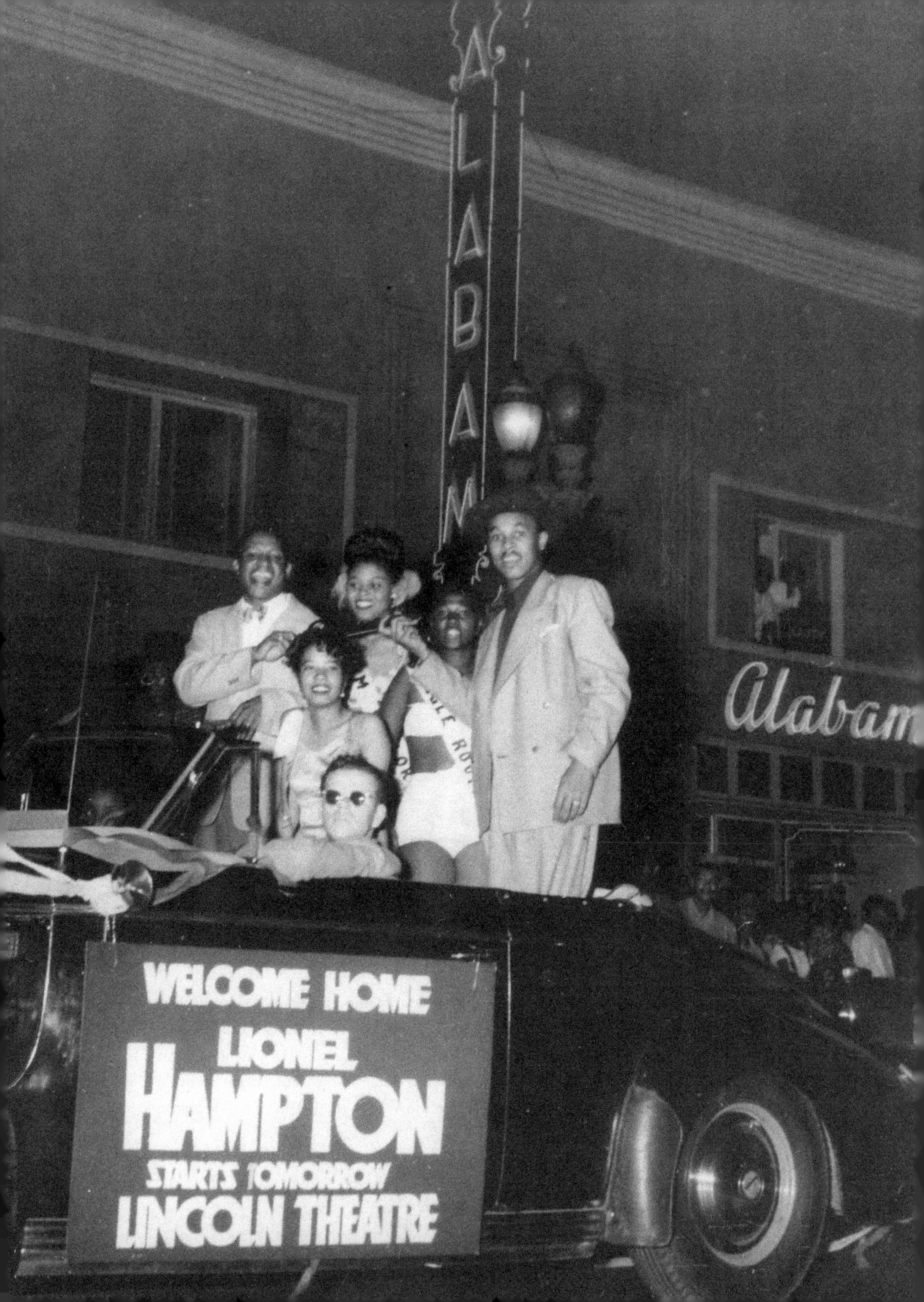

ALABAM
Alabam
WELCOME HOME
LIONEL
HAMPTON
STARTS TOMORROW
LINCOLN THEATRE

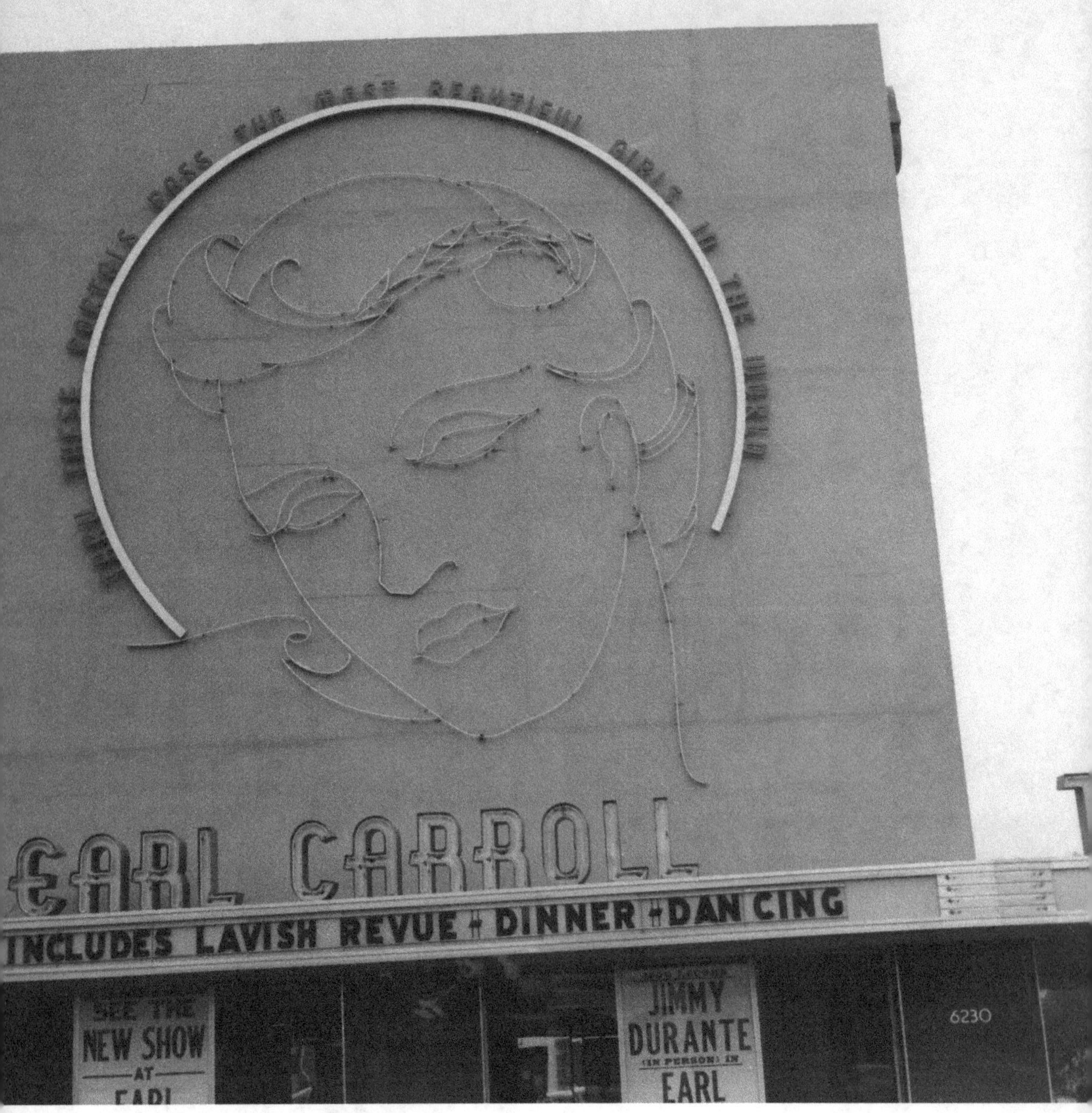

Above and opposite: Rare photos capture the famous neon portrait of showgirl Beryl Wallace who graced the exterior of the Earl Carroll Theatre on Sunset Boulevard. With scaffolding and a few stray wires, it appears the sign is undergoing installation. Its trademark lettering would soon be installed to become the showgirl's halo: Thru These Portals Pass the Most Beautiful Girls in the World. (1938, Herman J. Schultheis Collection, 1940 Ansel Adams Collection)

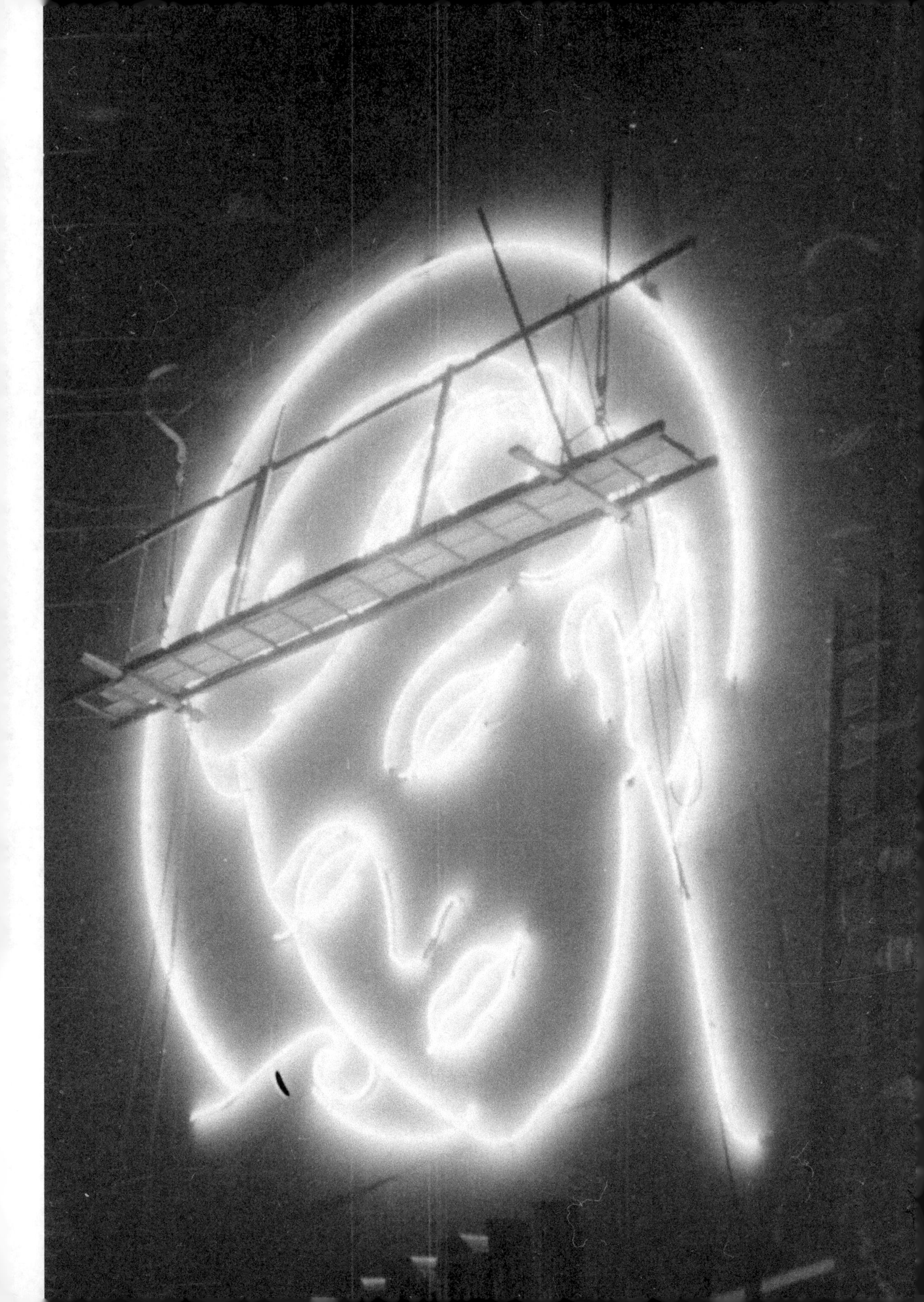

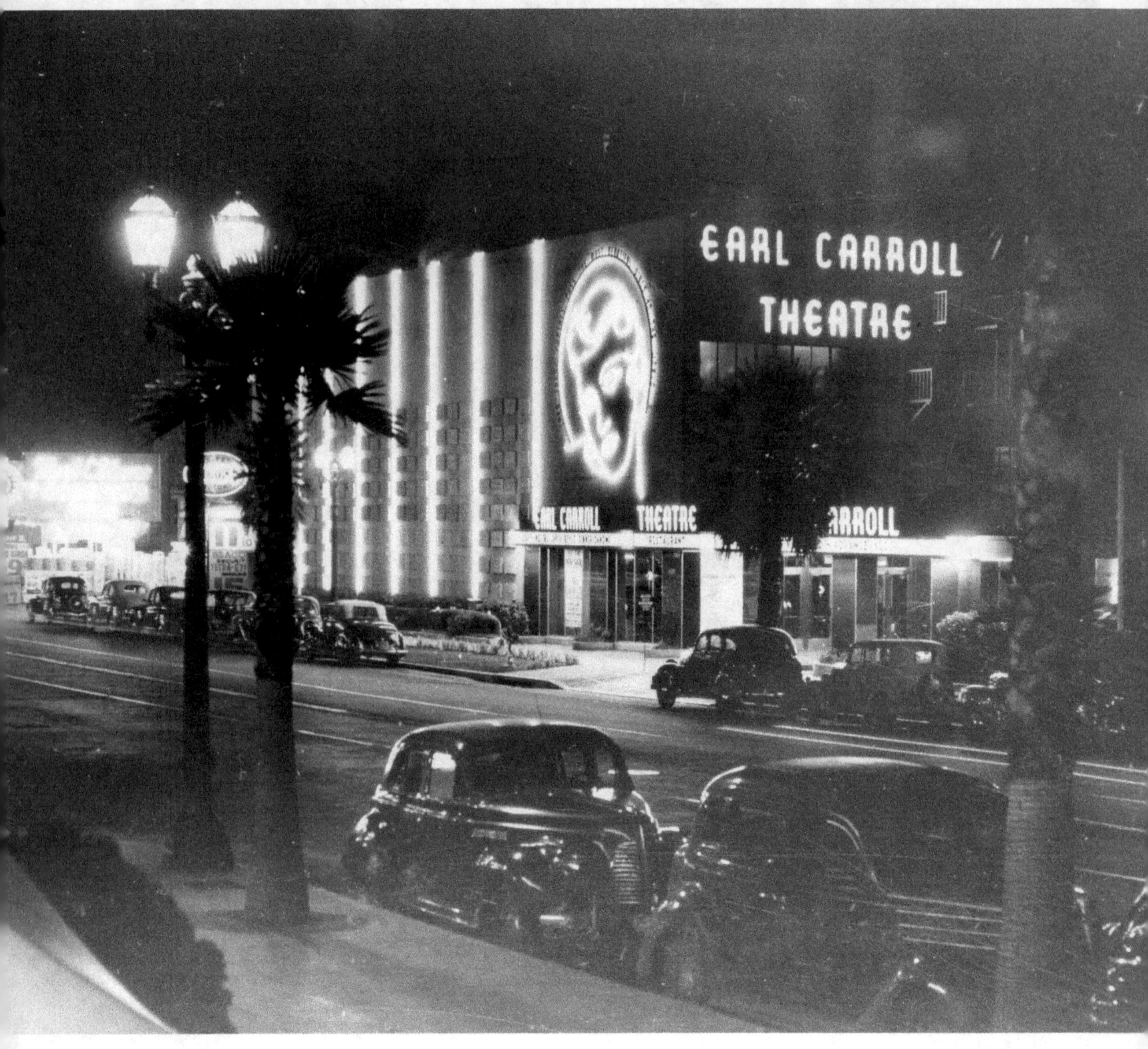

Long view of the neon-clad Earl Carroll Theatre on Sunset Boulevard. (Circa 1940s, Security Pacific National Bank Collection)

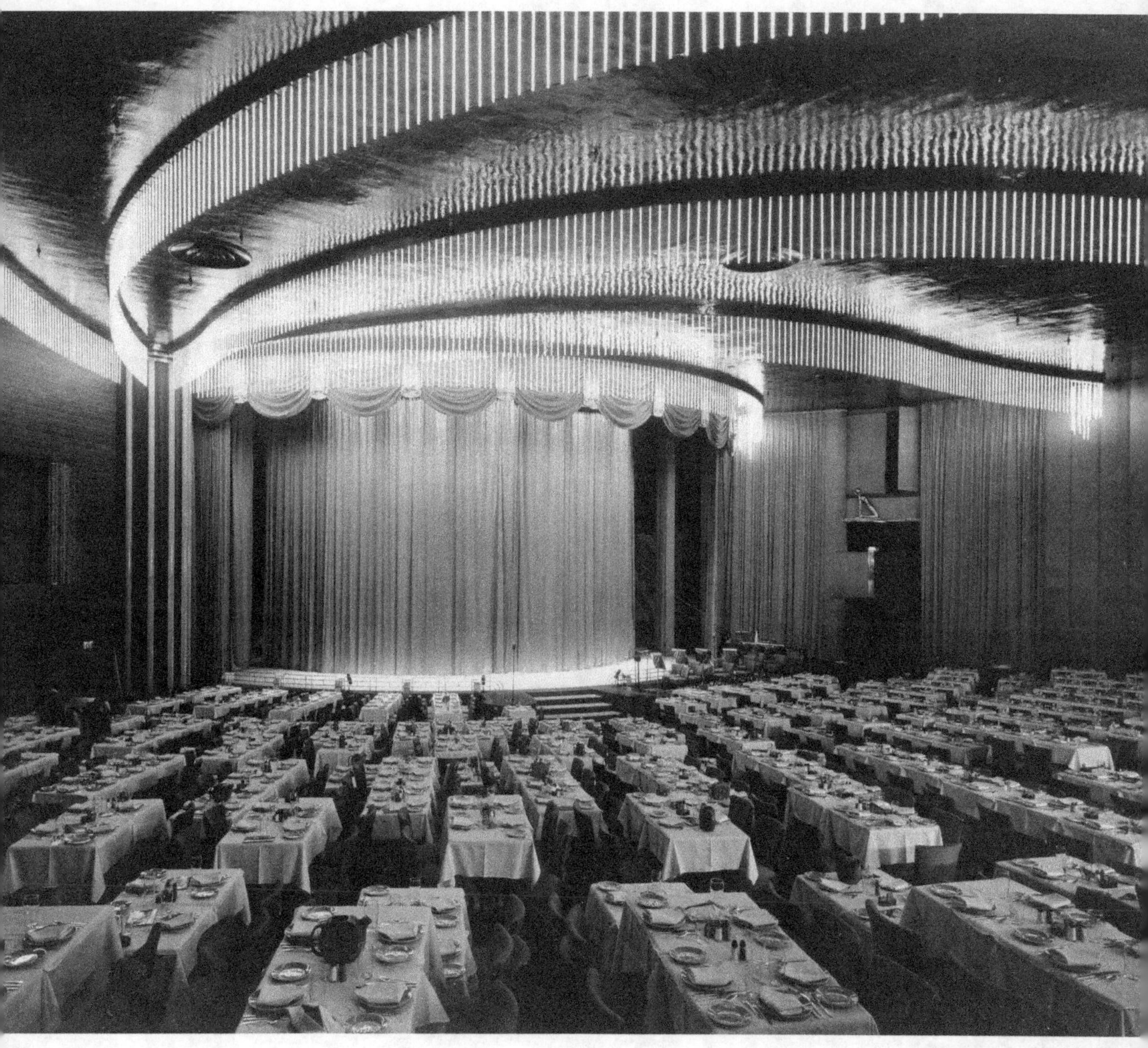

An impressive amount of neon illuminates the interior of the Earl Carroll Theatre. (Circa 1938, Security Pacific National Bank Collection)

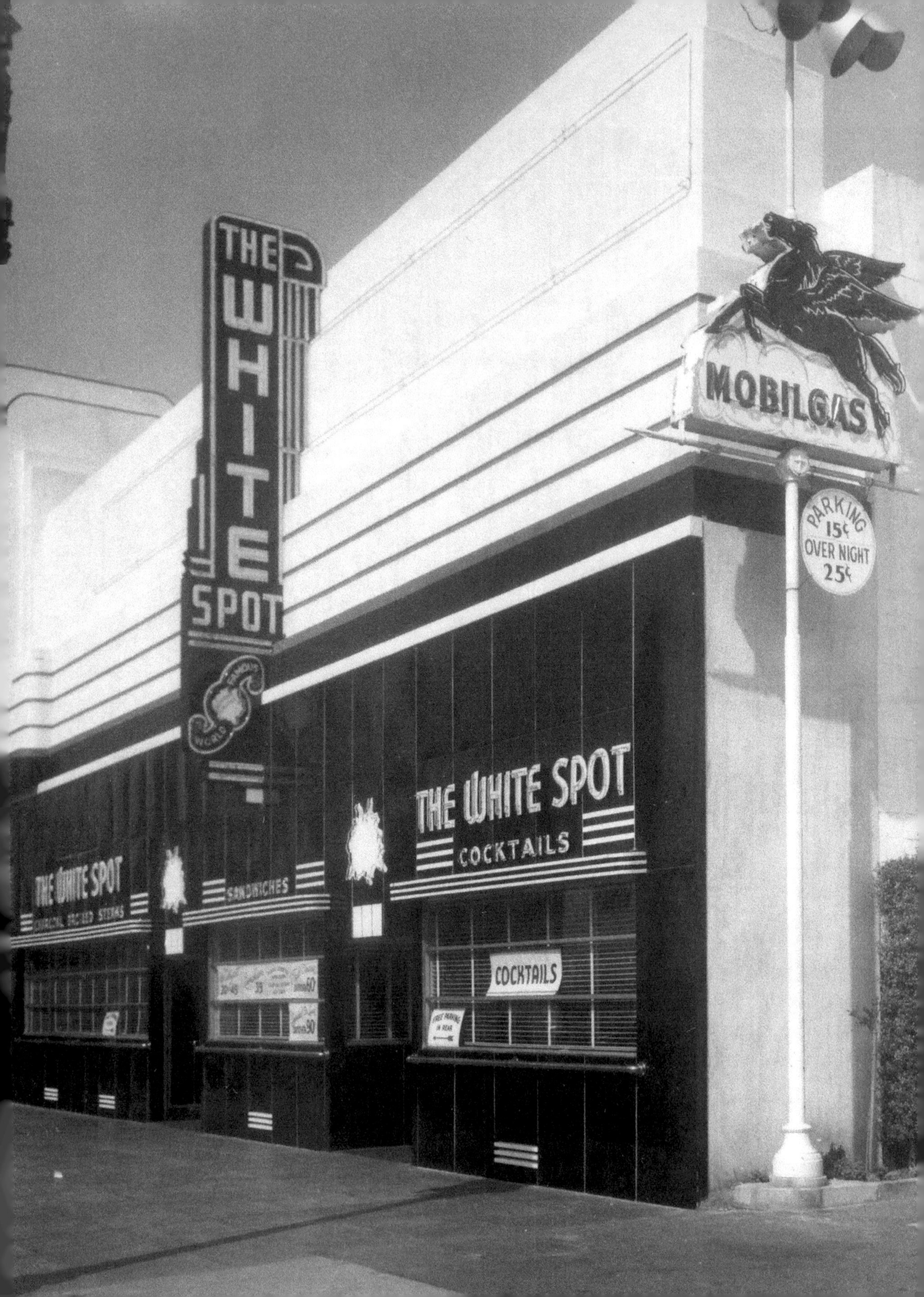
THE WHITE SPOT
MOBILGAS
PARKING 15¢
OVER NIGHT 25¢
THE WHITE SPOT
COCKTAILS
THE WHITE SPOT
SANDWICHES
COCKTAILS

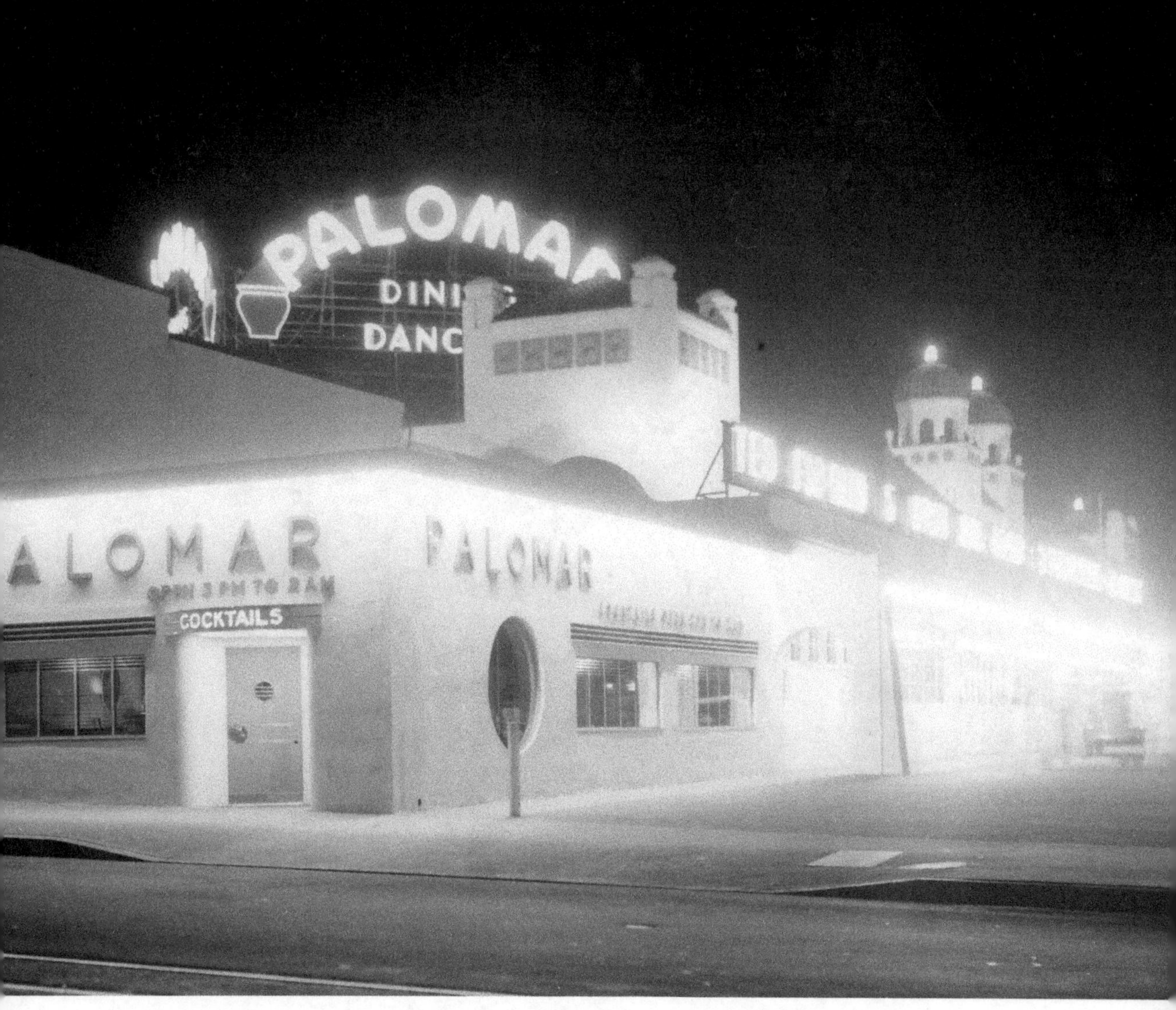

With an enormous and enticing dancefloor that could accommodate 4,000 couples, the luminous Palomar Ballroom made a splash when it debuted on Vermont Avenue. The names of its big band performers such as Benny Goodman, Tommy Dorsey, Glenn Miller, and Artie Shaw were illuminated in neon tubing for long engagements. Its fame lasted longer than the venue as it burned down in 1939 after only 14 years of use. (Circa 1930s, Security Pacific National Bank Collection)

Opposite: The neon signs for the White Spot restaurant on Wilshire Boulevard are joined by a sign for Mobilgas. (Circa 1930s, Security Pacific National Bank Collection)

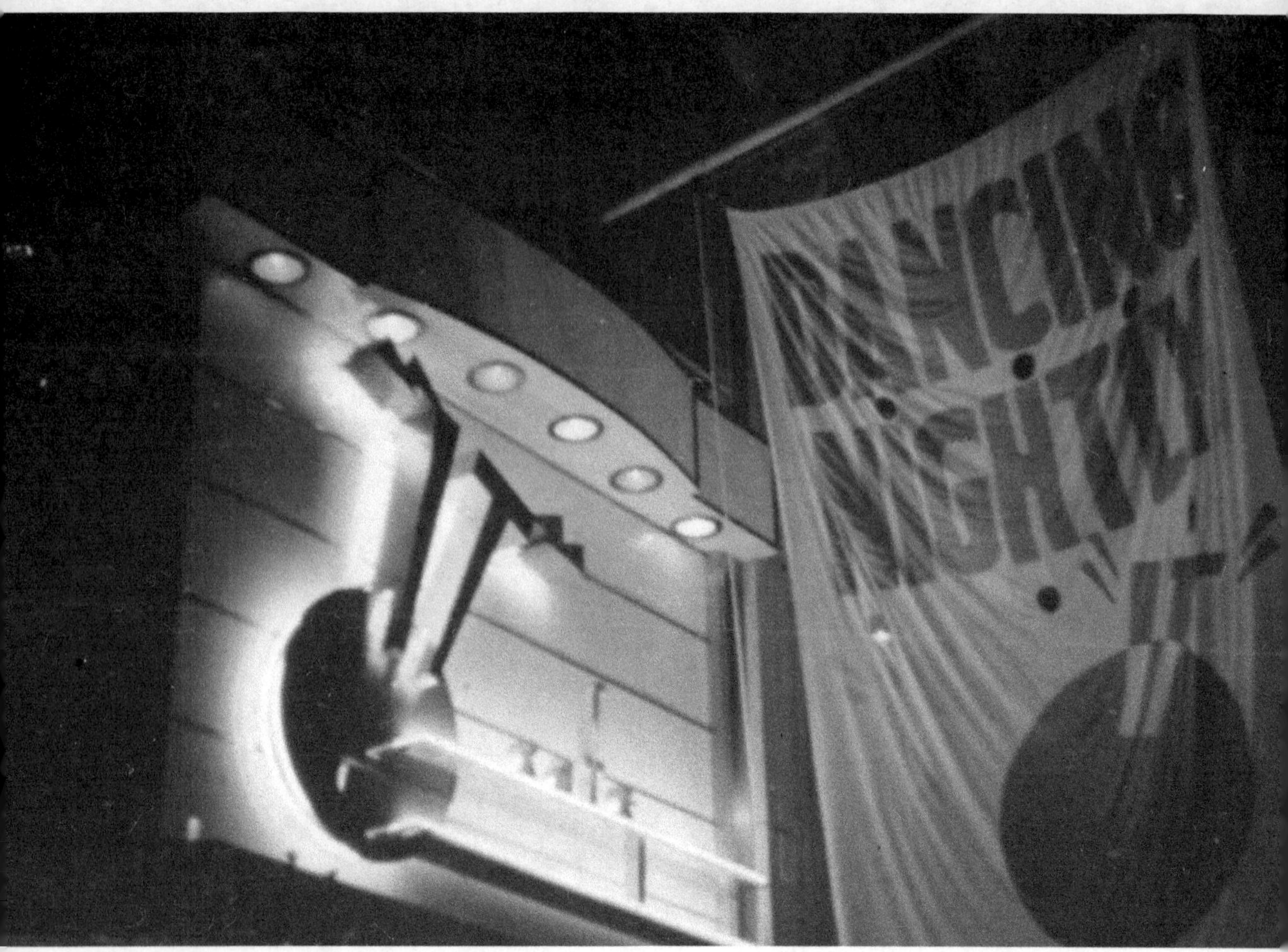

The neon sign for Clara Bow's It Cafe, located on the ground floor of the Hollywood Plaza Hotel bears an almost abstract design. (Circa 1937, Herman J. Schultheis Collection)

Opposite: Two women bypass Al Levy's Tavern on Vine Street in Hollywood despite the neon sign boasting of air conditioning. (Circa 1937, Herman J. Schultheis Collection)

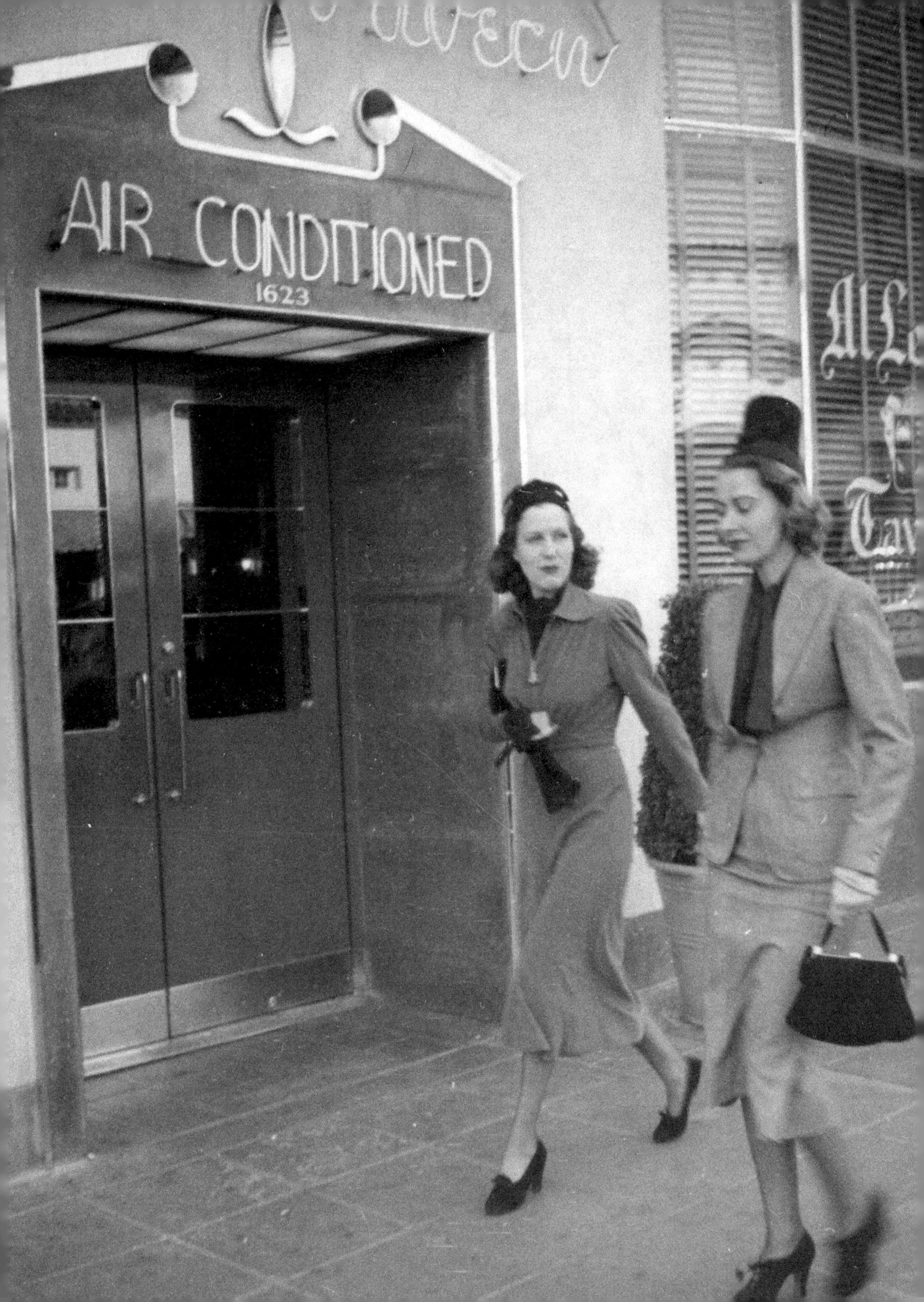

AIR CONDITIONED
1623

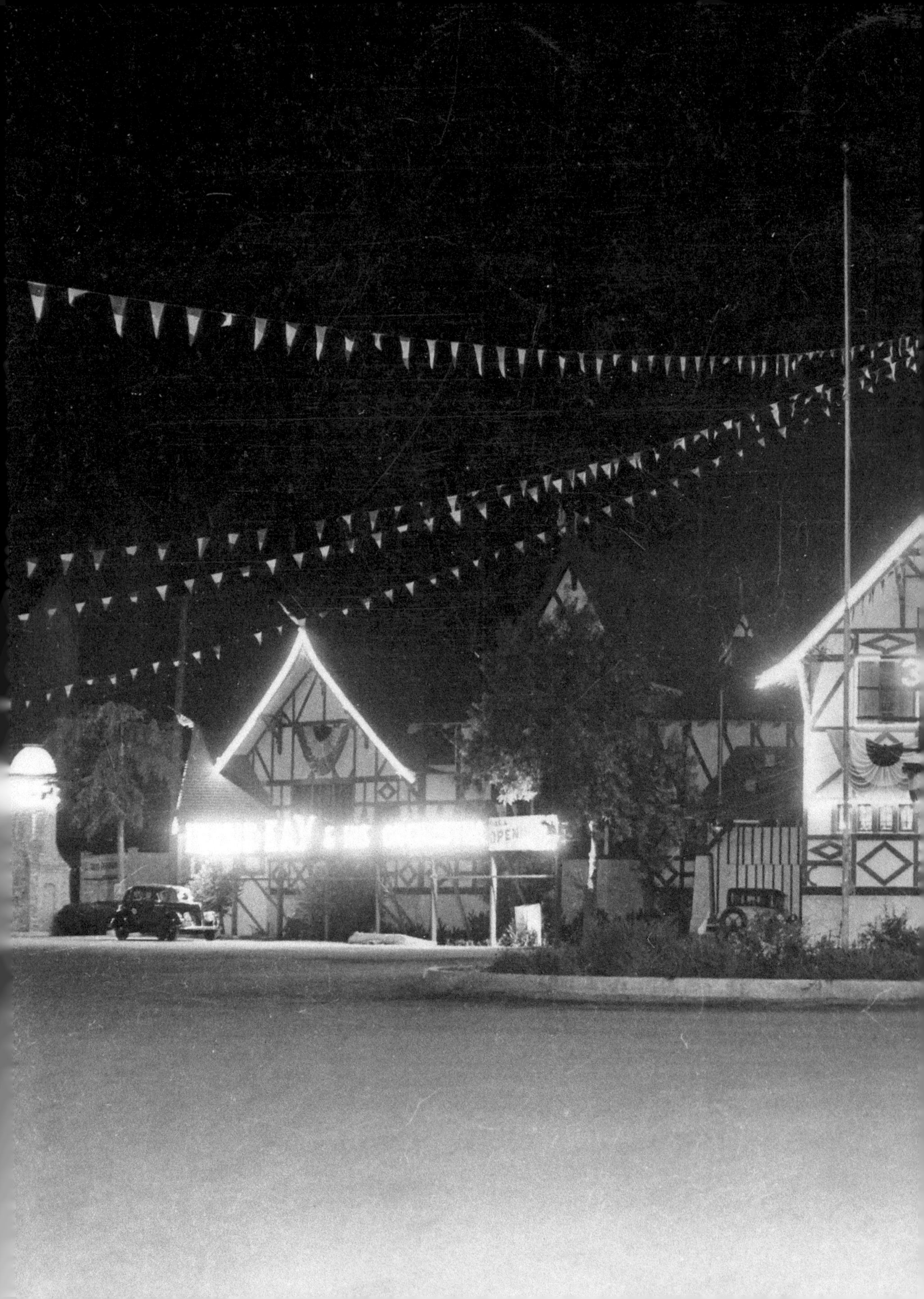
OPEN

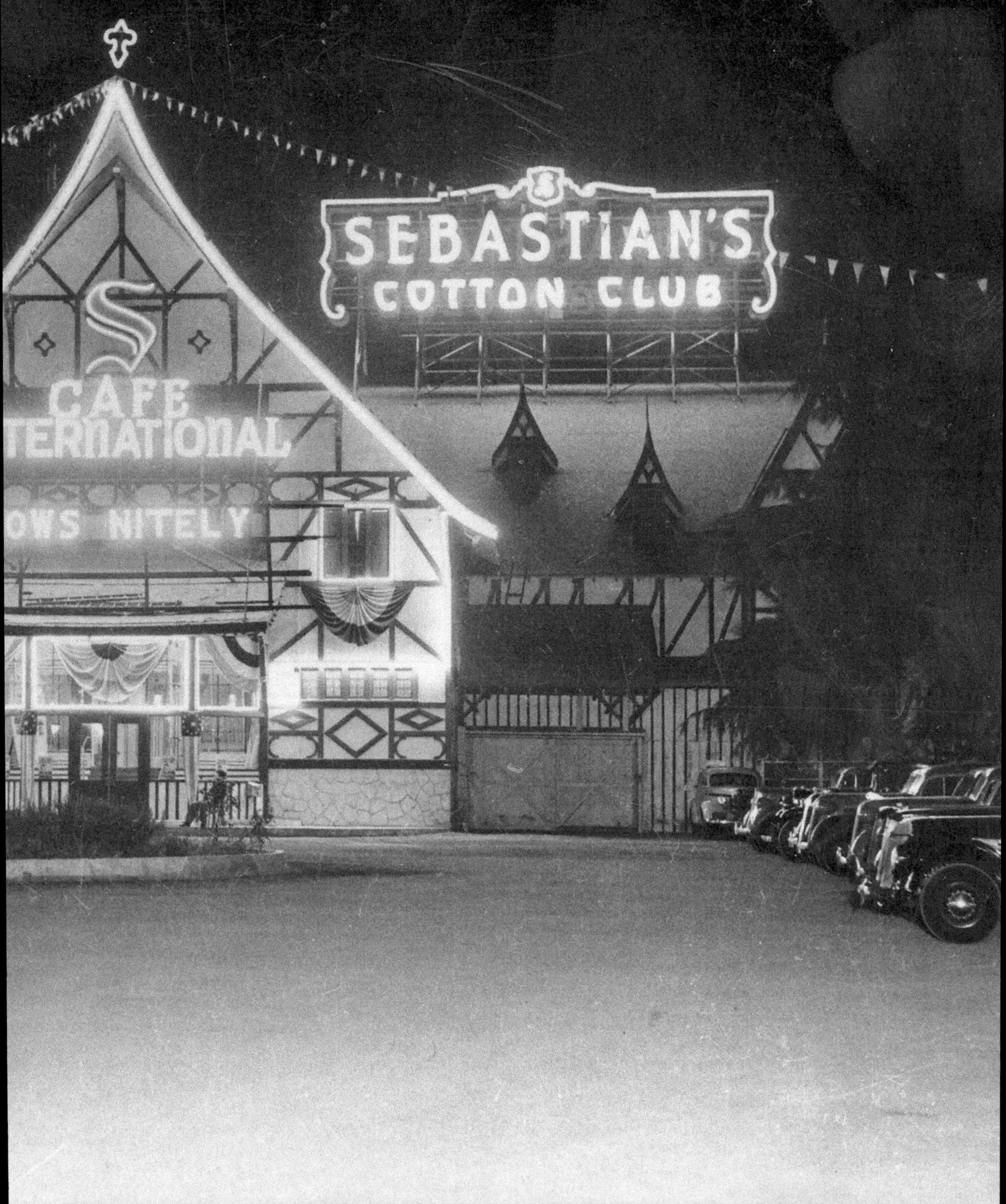

SEBASTIAN'S
COTTON CLUB
CAFE
[IN]TERNATIONAL
[SH]OWS NITELY

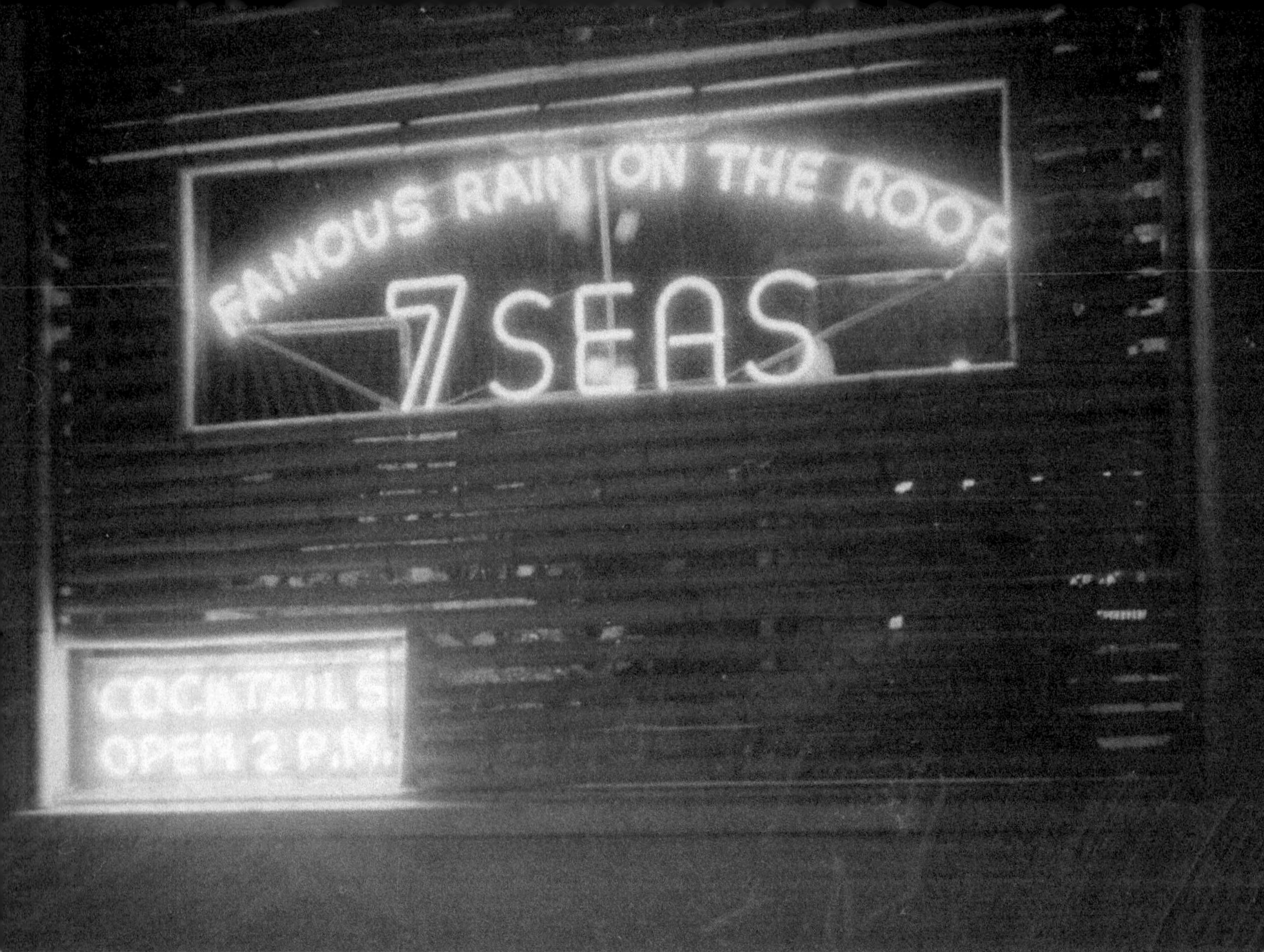

Neon burns brightly for the Seven Seas Restaurant on Hollywood Boulevard, where the sophisticated dine in an exotic Tahitian atmosphere amidst tropical thunder, lightning and the famous "Rain on the Roof." (Circa 1940, Herman J. Schultheis Collection)

Opposite: A neon canopy sign decorates the entrance to Rene & Jean French Table d'Hote restaurant, located at 639 S. Olive Street. (Circa 1930s, Security Pacific National Bank Collection)

Overleaf: Frank Sebastian ran the famed Cotton Club café and showplace which replaced the Green Mill nightclub in 1926 at National and Washington in Culver City. Just outside of the city limits of Los Angeles, the venue stretched the boundaries of Prohibition and featured numerous African American orchestras and headliners such as Cab Calloway, Duke Ellington, Leon Herriford, Fats Waller, and Louis Armstrong. With a neon rooftop sign and numerous fascia signs, the venue was a beacon in the night. (Circa 1930, Security Pacific National Bank Collection)

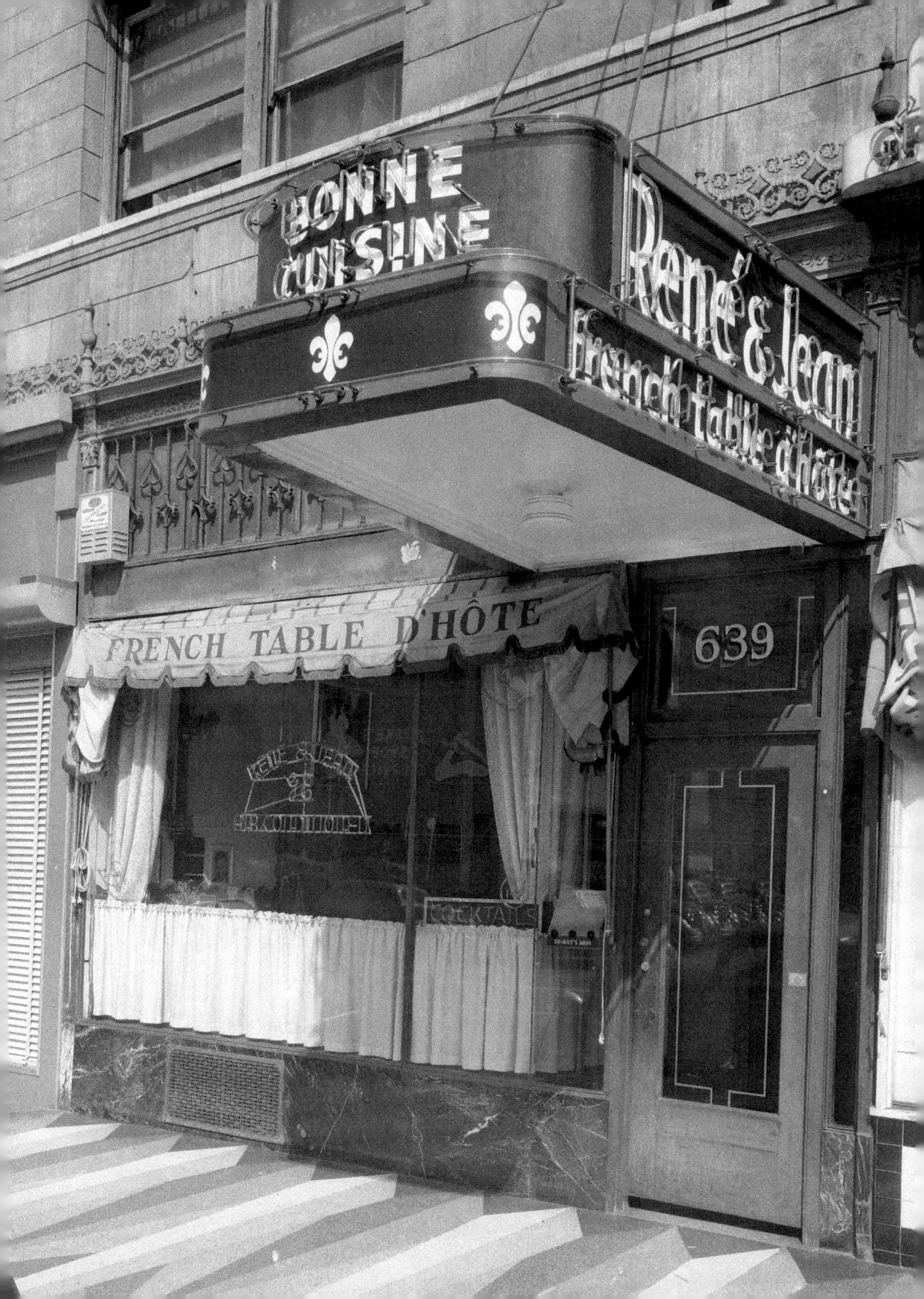
BONNE
CUISINE
René & Jean
French table d'hôte
639
FRENCH TABLE D'HÔTE
COCKTAILS

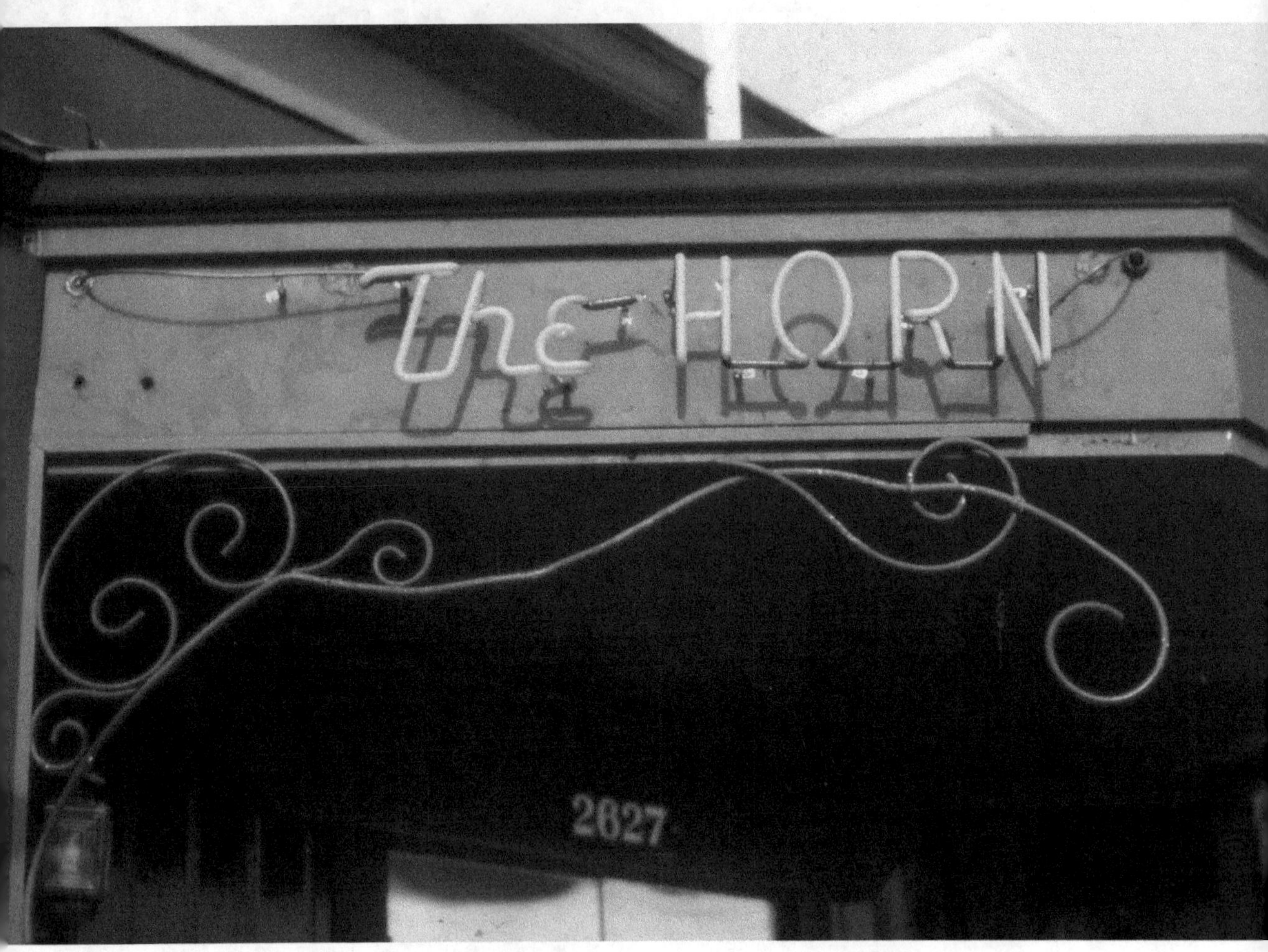

A simple neon sign marks the location of The Horn nightclub, location in Santa Monica on Wilshire Boulevard. (1979, Anne Laskey/Marlene Laskey Collection)

Opposite: Multiple neon signs adorn the Gayway Café on Main Street. (1948, Los Angeles Herald Examiner Collection)

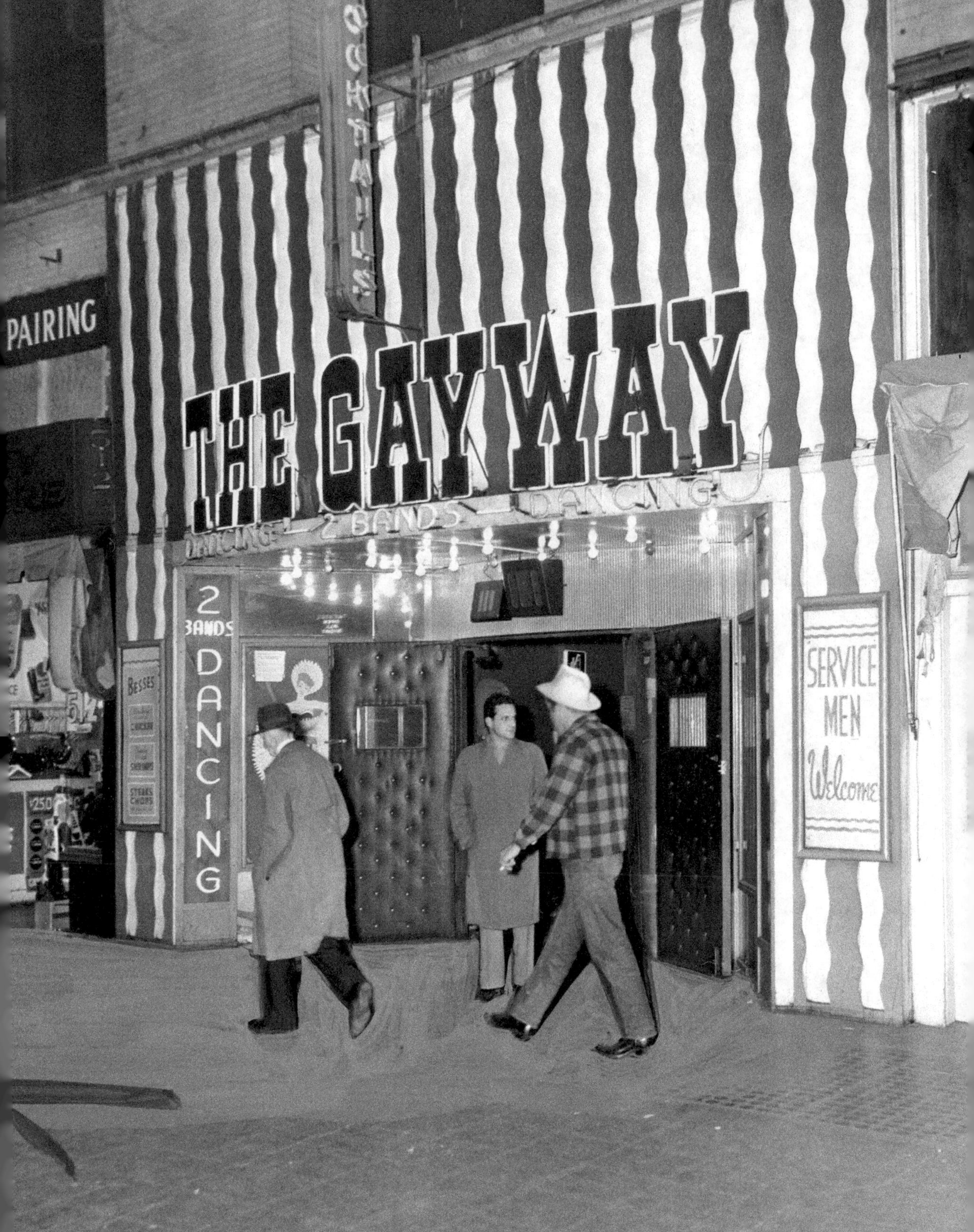

PAIRING
THE GAYWAY
DANCING 2 BANDS DANCING
2 BANDS DANCING
SERVICE MEN Welcome

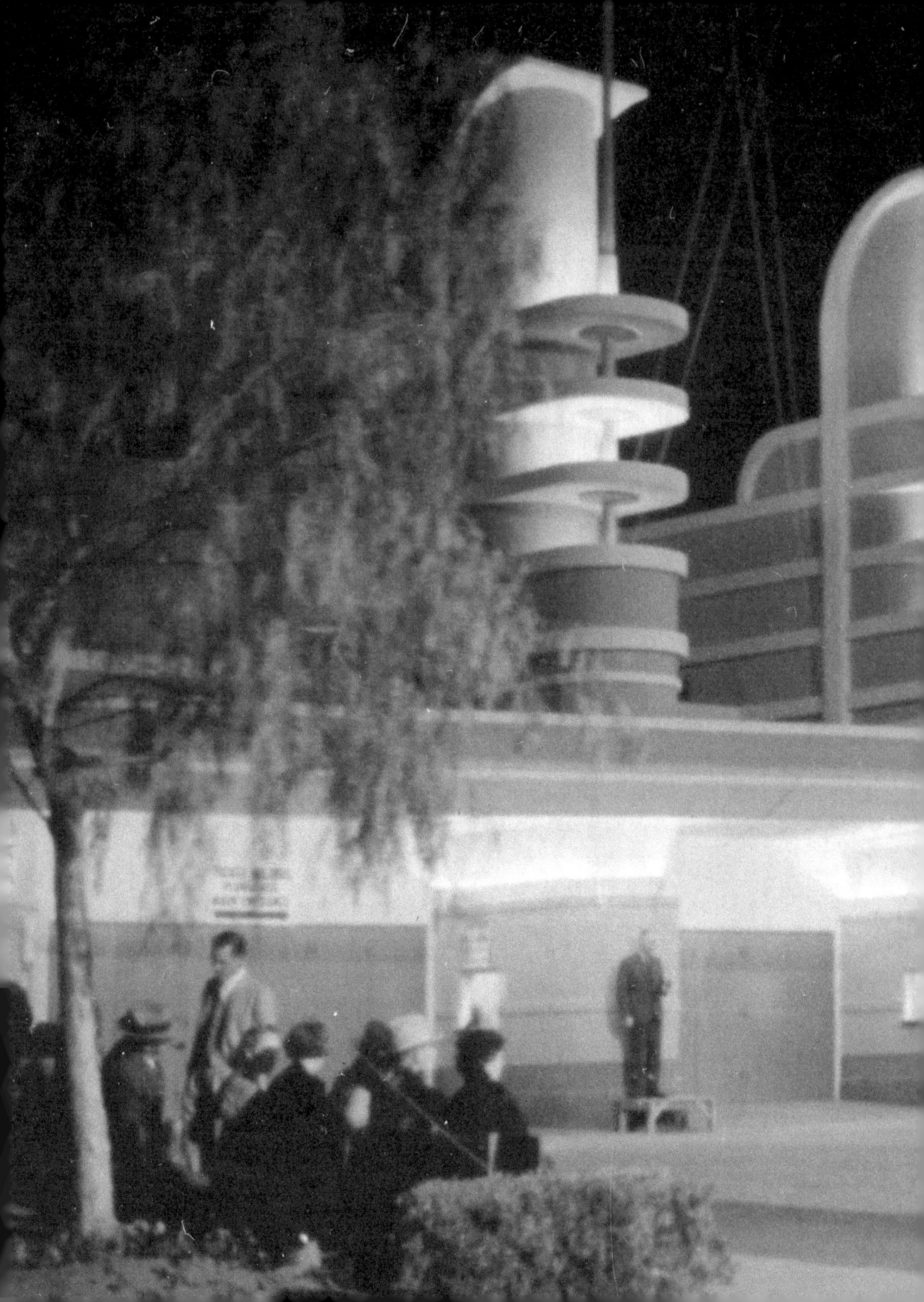

PLACES OF LEISURE/ AMUSEMENT

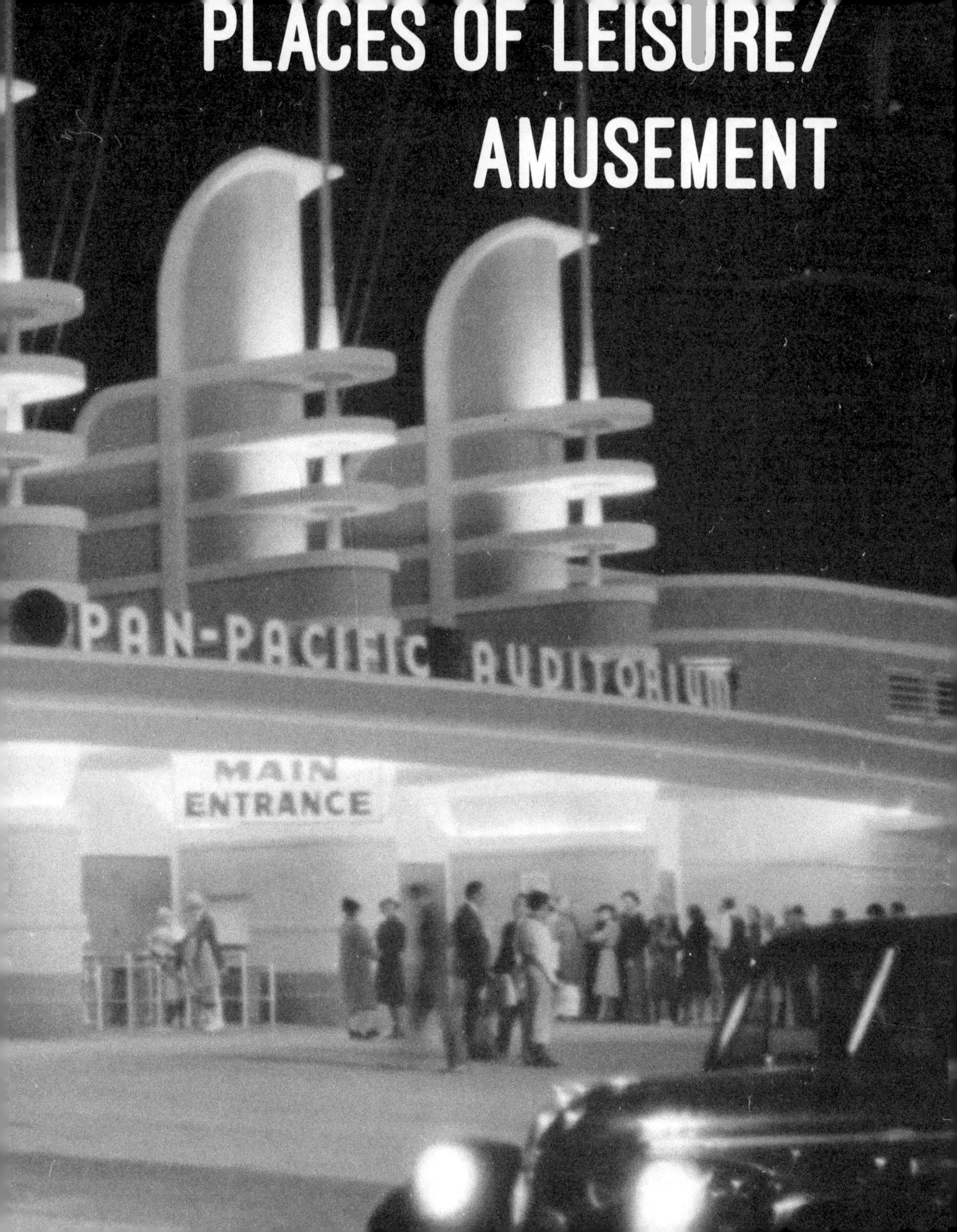

Overleaf: Neon is used to illuminate the main entrance of the Pan Pacific Auditorium. (Circa 1937, Herman J. Schultheis Collection)

A snapping neon sign invites people to drop into Lincoln Park's Alligator Farm. (Circa 1939, Herman J. Schultheis Collection)

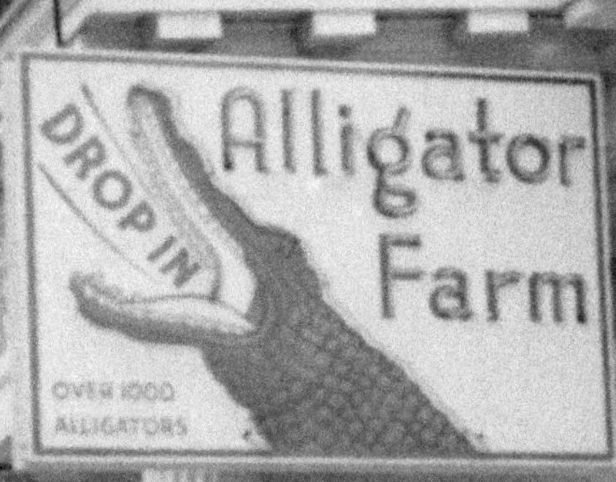
DROP IN
Alligator
Farm
OVER 1000
ALLIGATORS

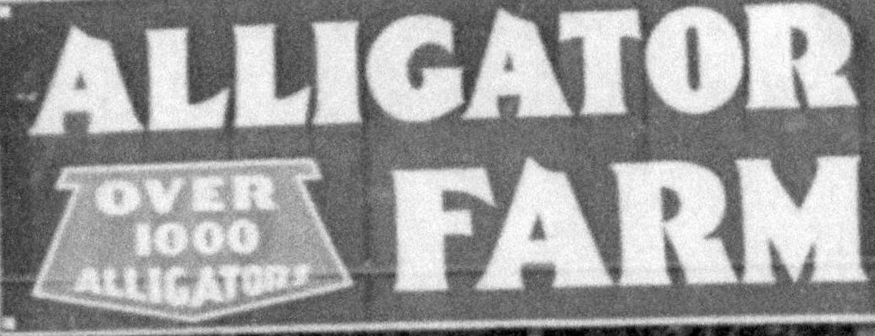
ALLIGATOR
FARM
OVER
1000
ALLIGATORS

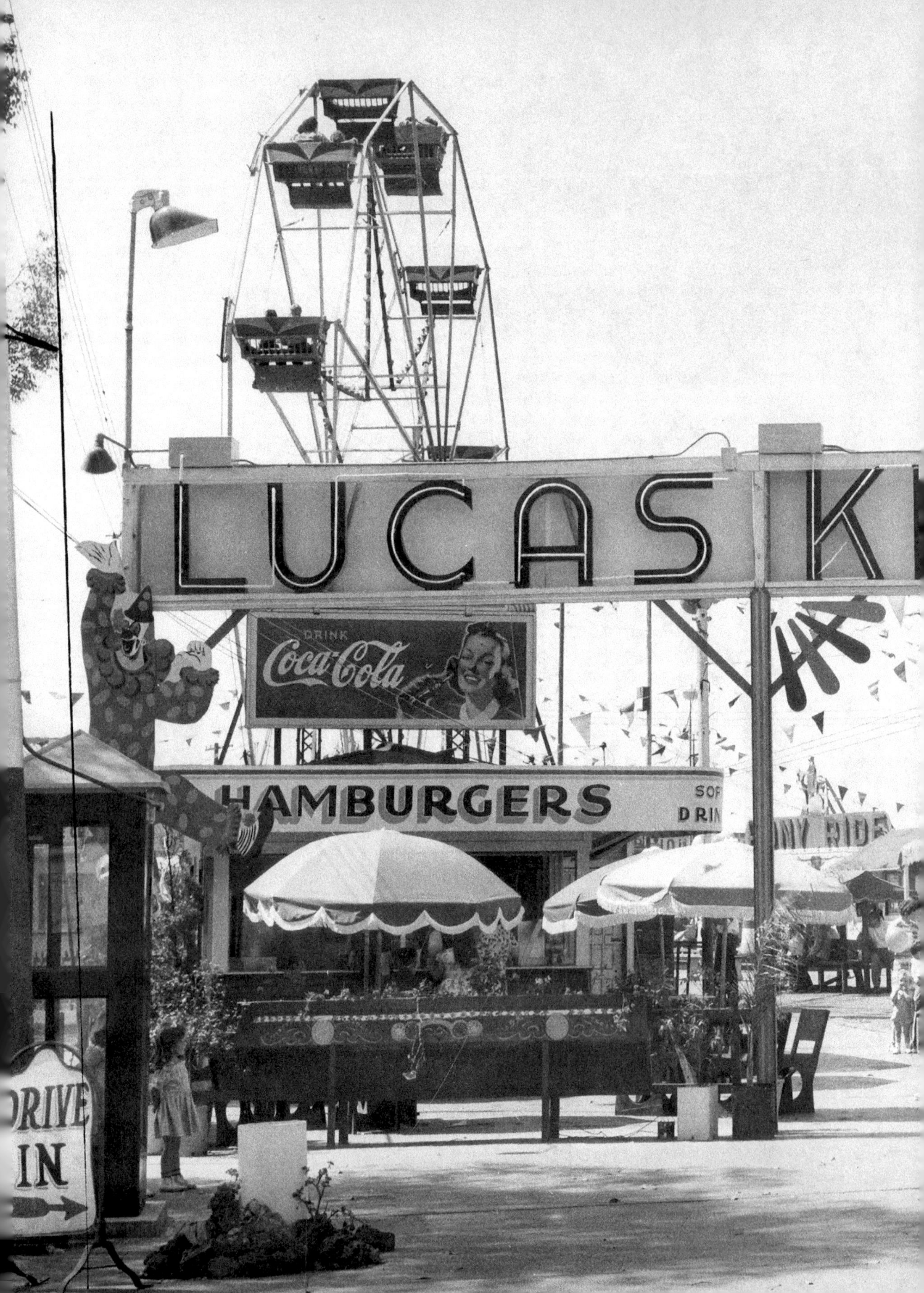
LUCAS K
DRINK
Coca-Cola
HAMBURGERS
DRIVE
IN

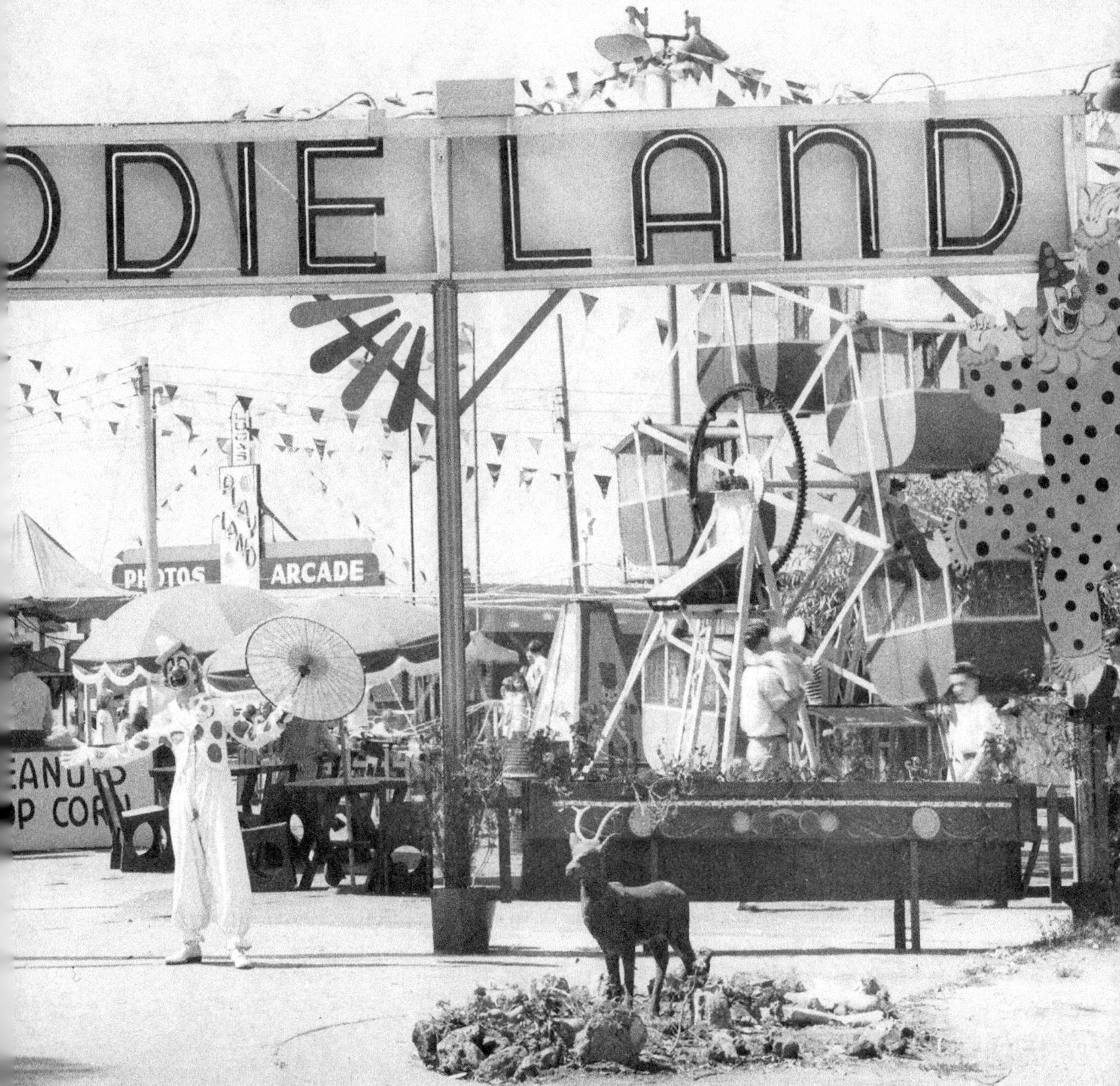
ODIELAND
PLAY LAND
PHOTOS
ARCADE

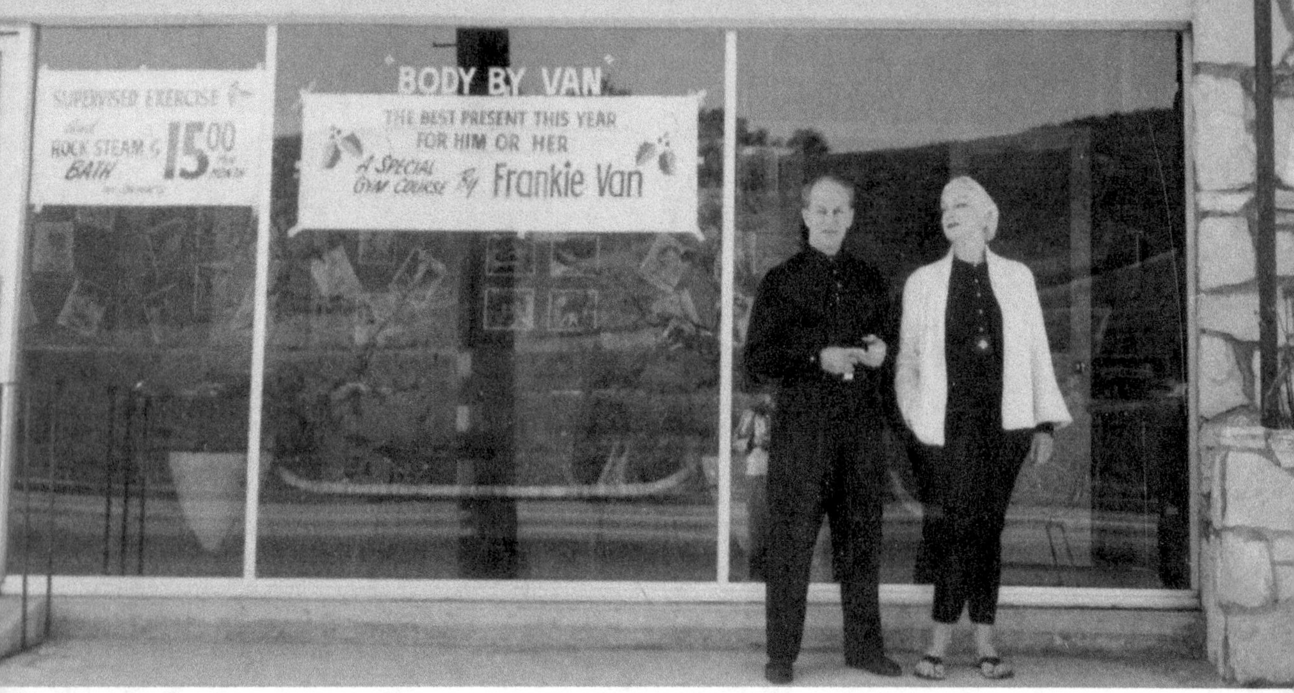

Frankie Van, owner of Frankie Van's Health Club at 3717 N. Cahuenga Boulevard poses with modern dancer Ruth St. Denis under the establishment's simple neon sign. (1962, Valley Times Collection)

Opposite: The Hollywood Recreation Center bowling alley on Vine Street takes full advantage of the glories of neon. (1938, Herman J. Schultheis Collection)

Overleaf: As if the clown and Ferris Wheel weren't enough, neon is also used drive traffic into Lucan Kiddie Land on Riverside Drive in Silver Lake. (Circa 1945, Security Pacific National Bank Collection)

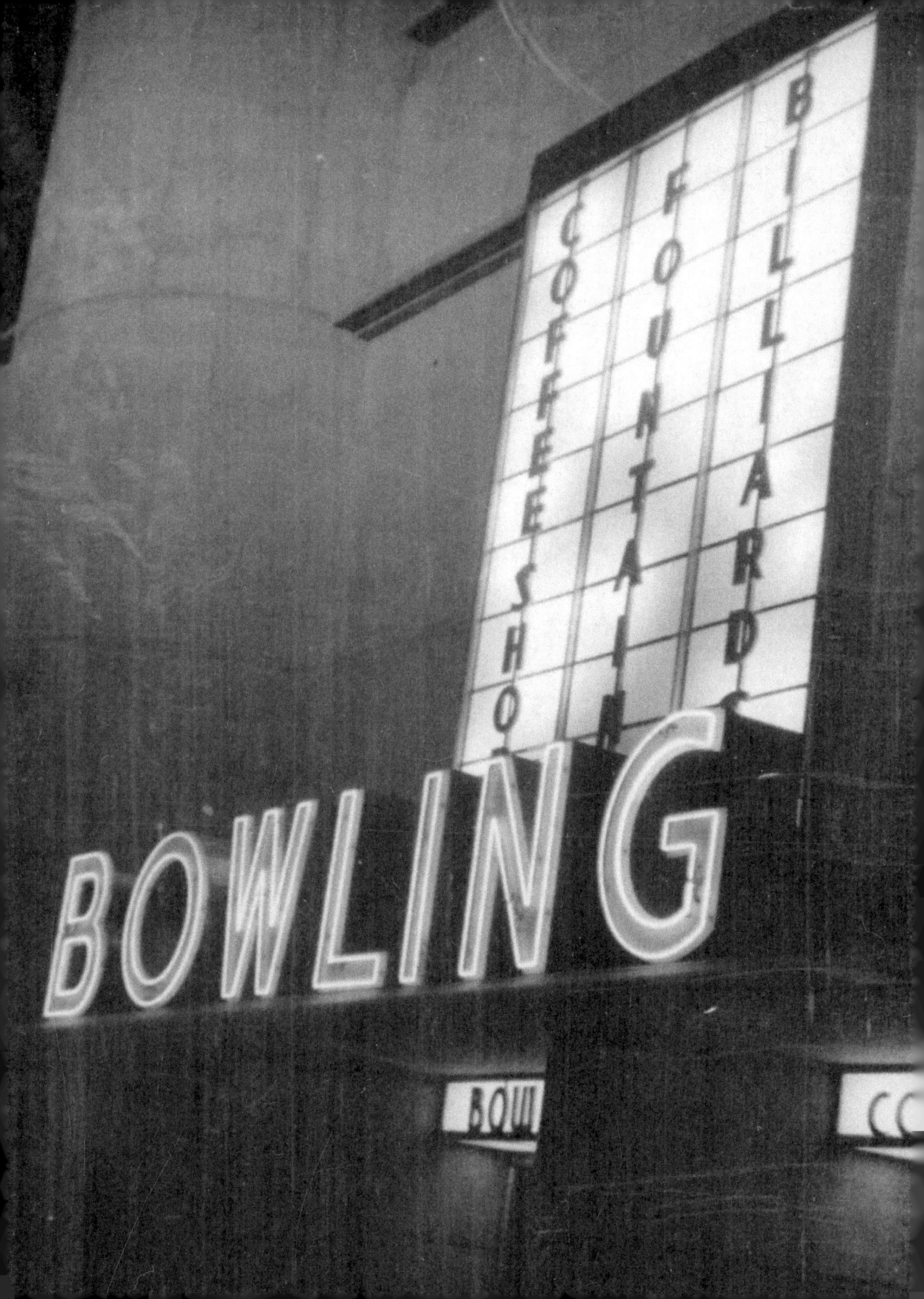

COFFEE SHO
FOUNTAI
BILLIARD
BOWLING

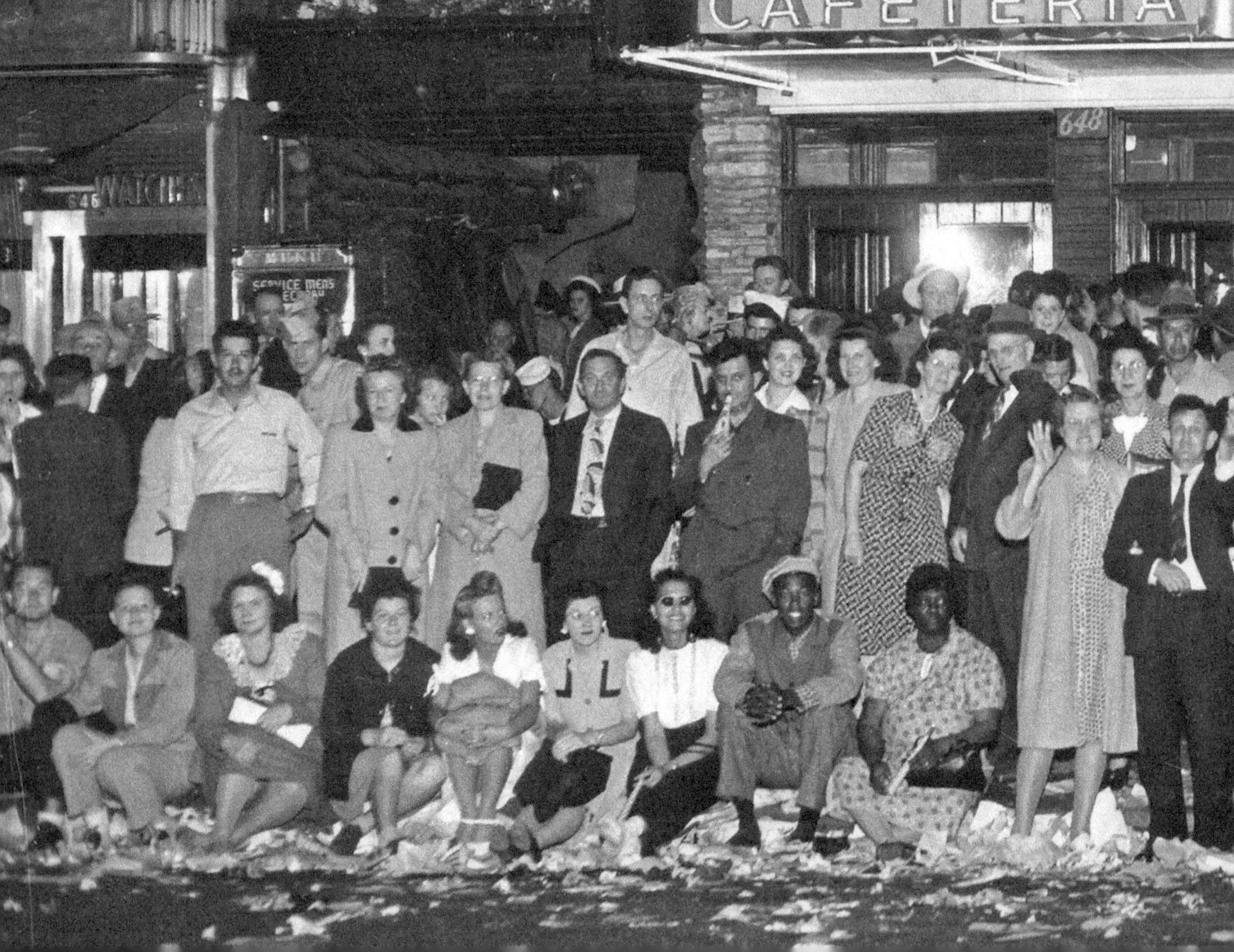
WORLD'S LARGEST
CLIFTON
BROOKDALE
CAFETERIA
648
646
SERVICE MENS

RESTAURANTS

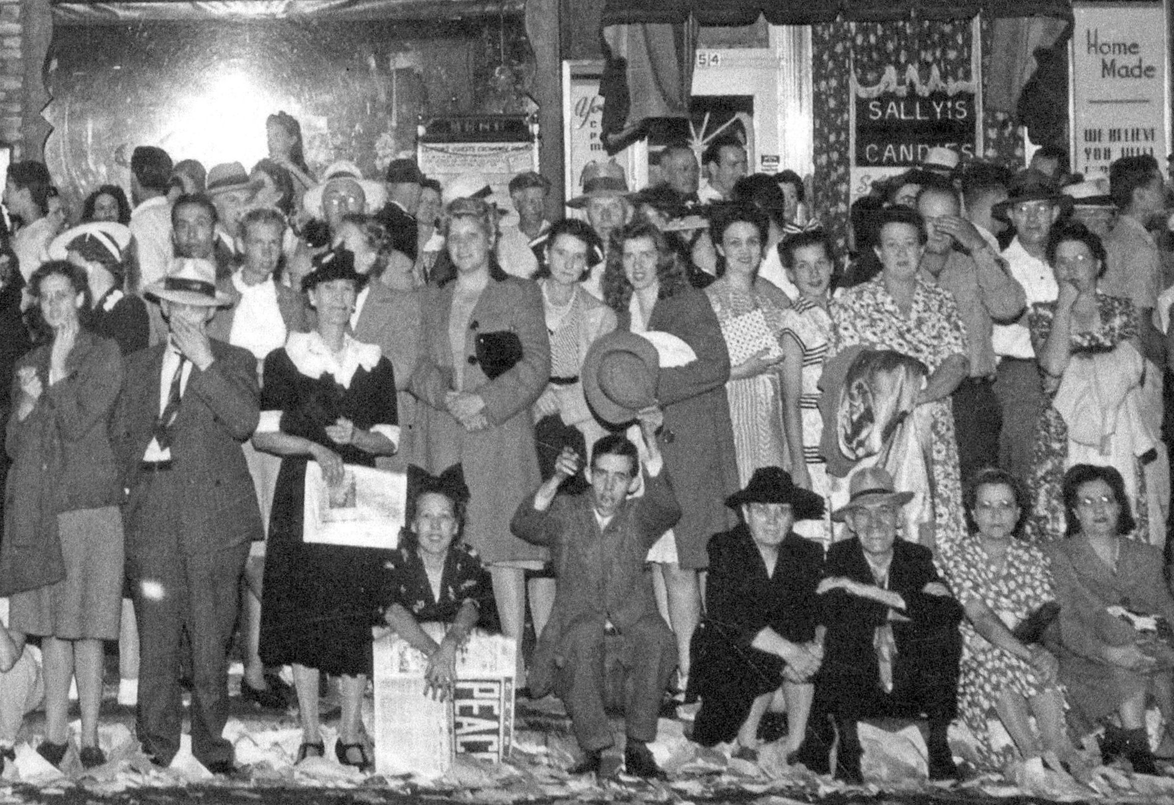

Overleaf: A group of Angelinos gather under the neon of Clifton's Cafeteria to participate in V-J Day celebrations. (1945, Security Pacific National Bank Collection)

Opposite and pages 148-149: Lost from the LA landscape, but not its memory, are the many neon palm trees and neon lilies that illuminated the interior dining rooms at Clifton's South Seas Cafeteria. Once located at 618 South Olive, the fanciful façade was covered in faux rockwork, neon flowers, and a functioning waterfall. Inside, diners ate within a wonderland of tropical bamboo huts and neon flora as simulated rainfall cascaded nearby. Such three-dimensional displays of neon were rare – outside of a Busby Berkeley movie. (1945, Lucille Stewart Collection)

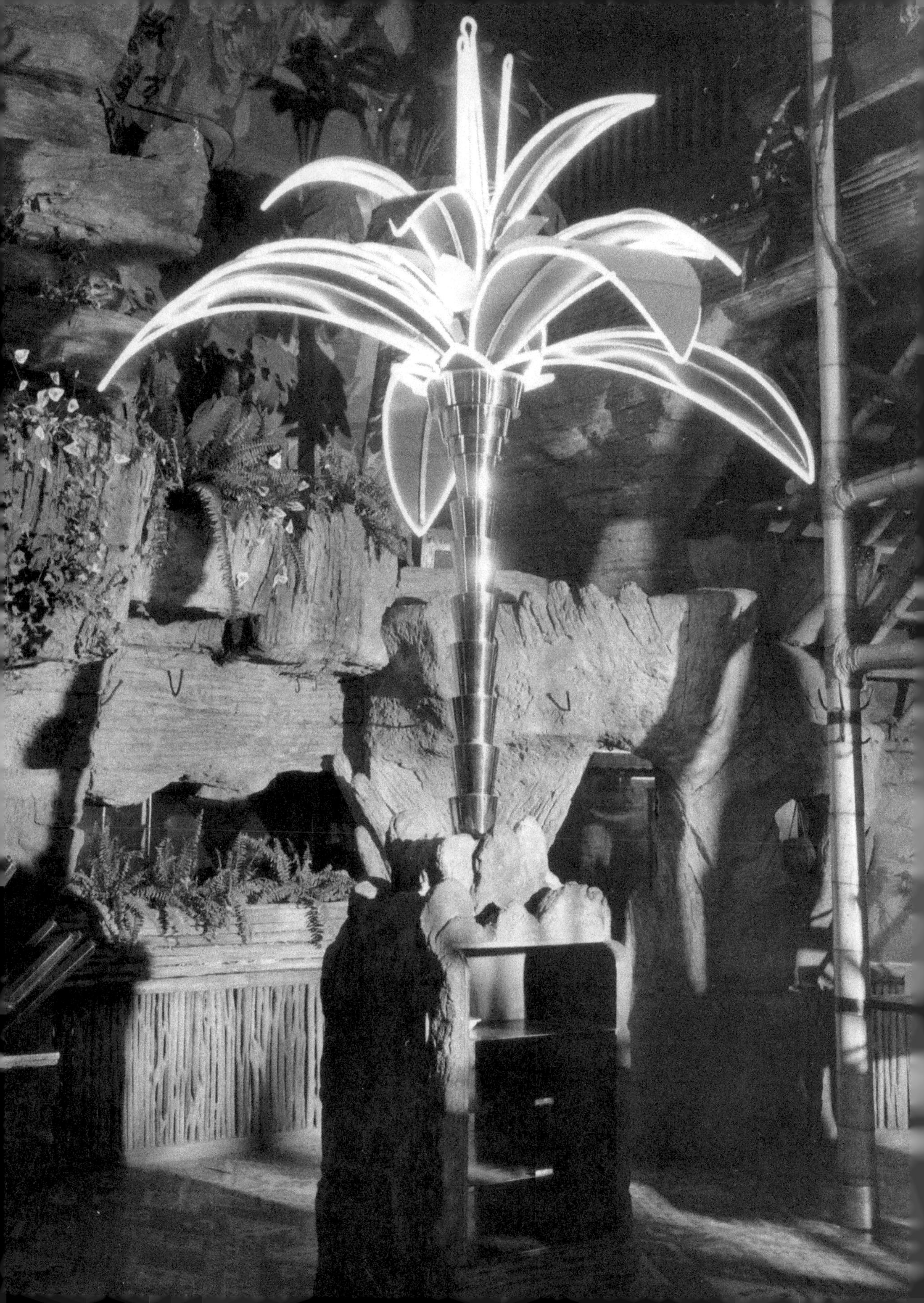

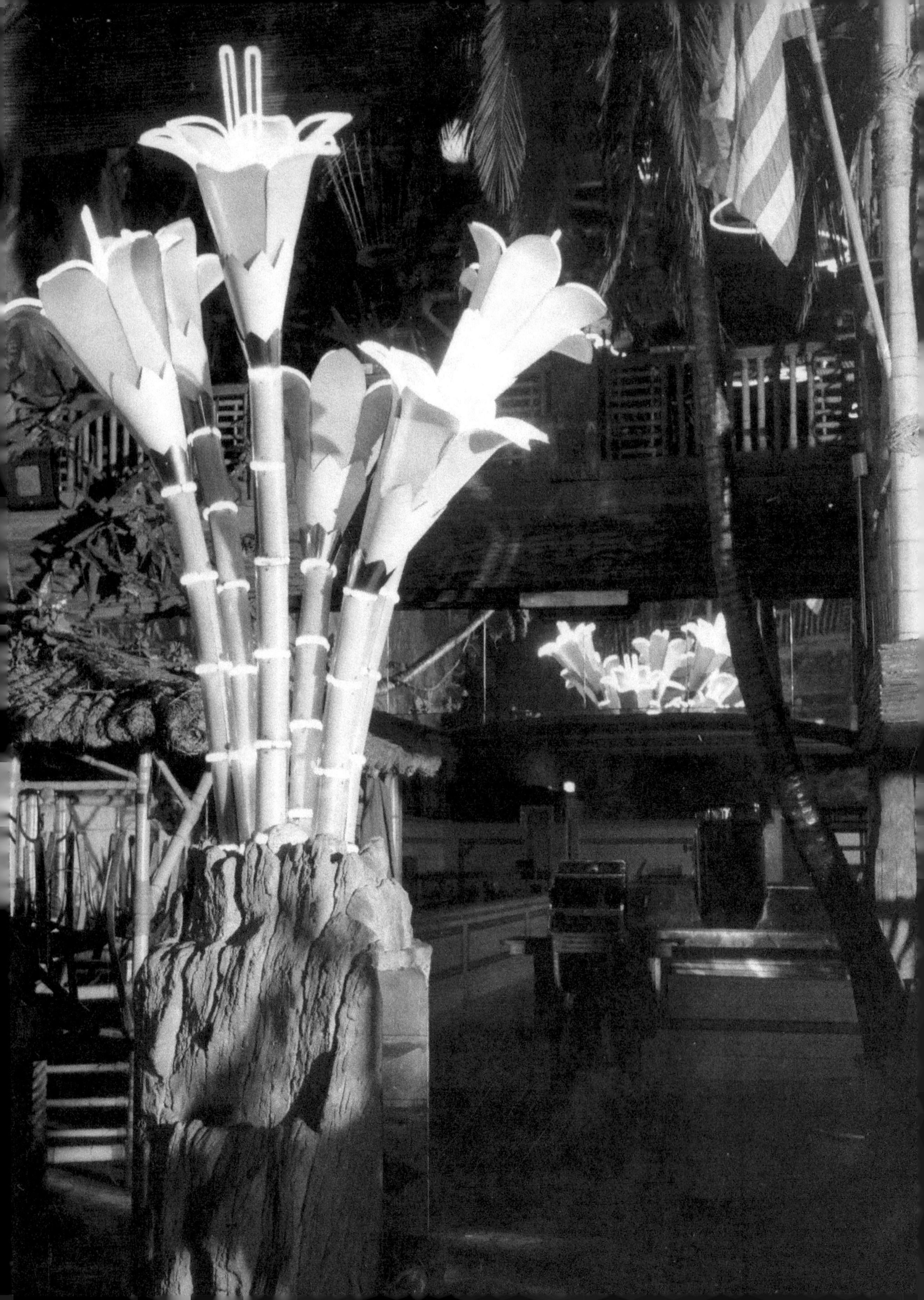

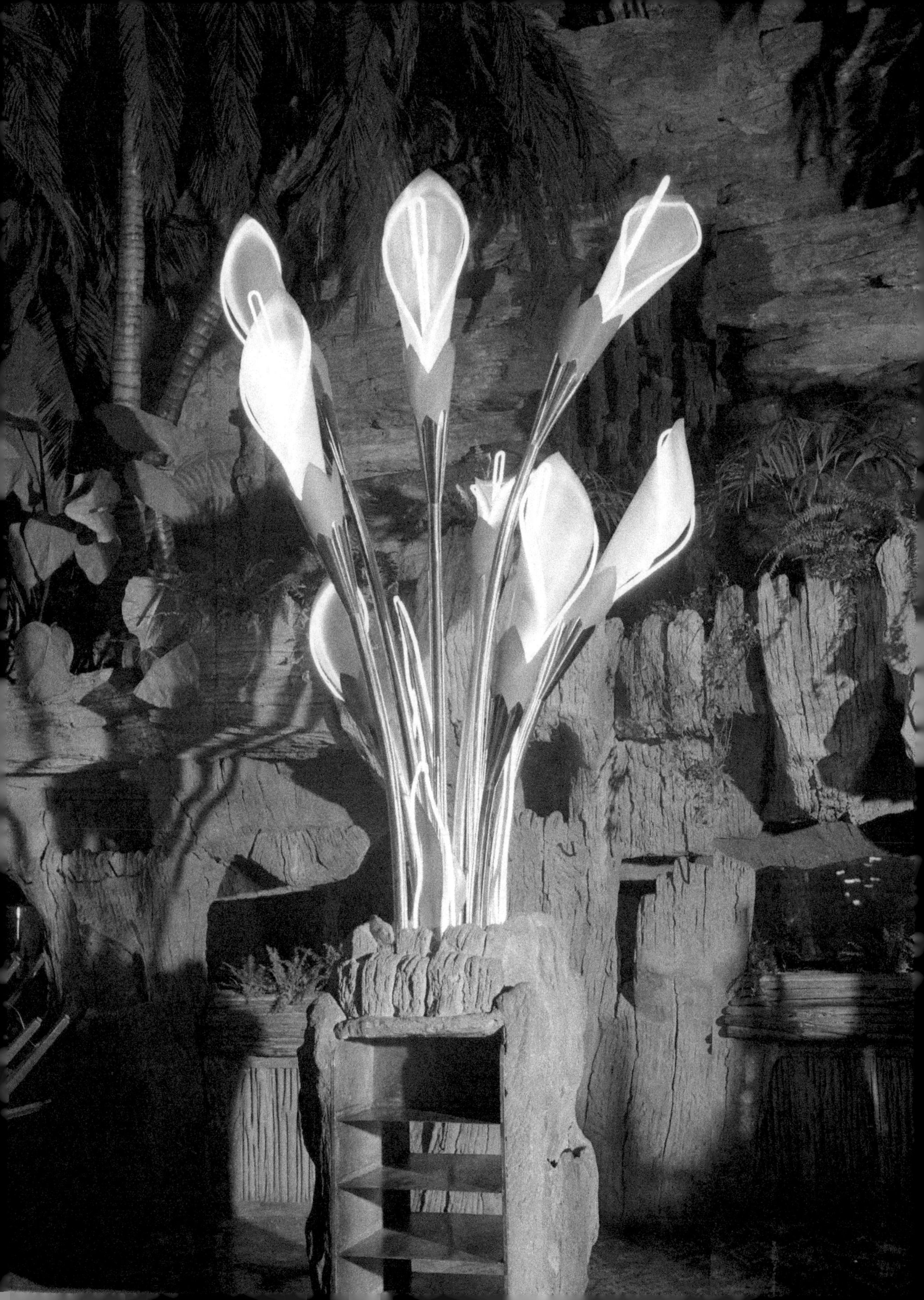

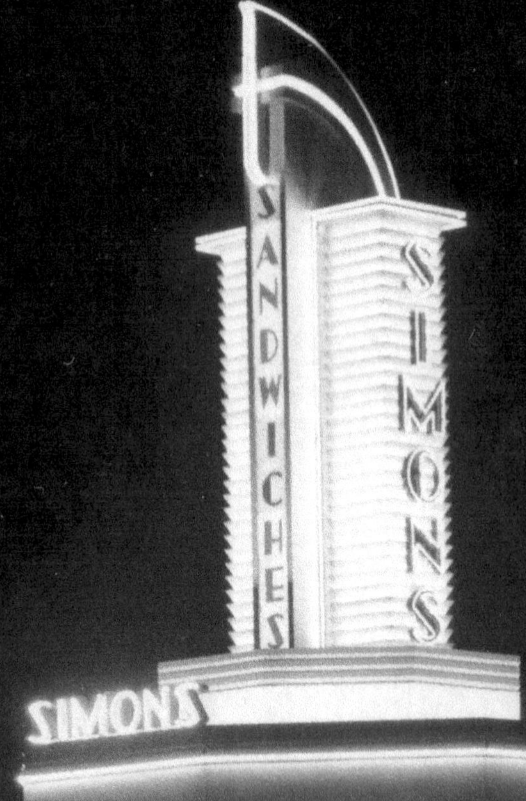
SANDWICHES
SIMONS
SIMONS
FOUNTAIN
HAMBURGERS
BARBECUE

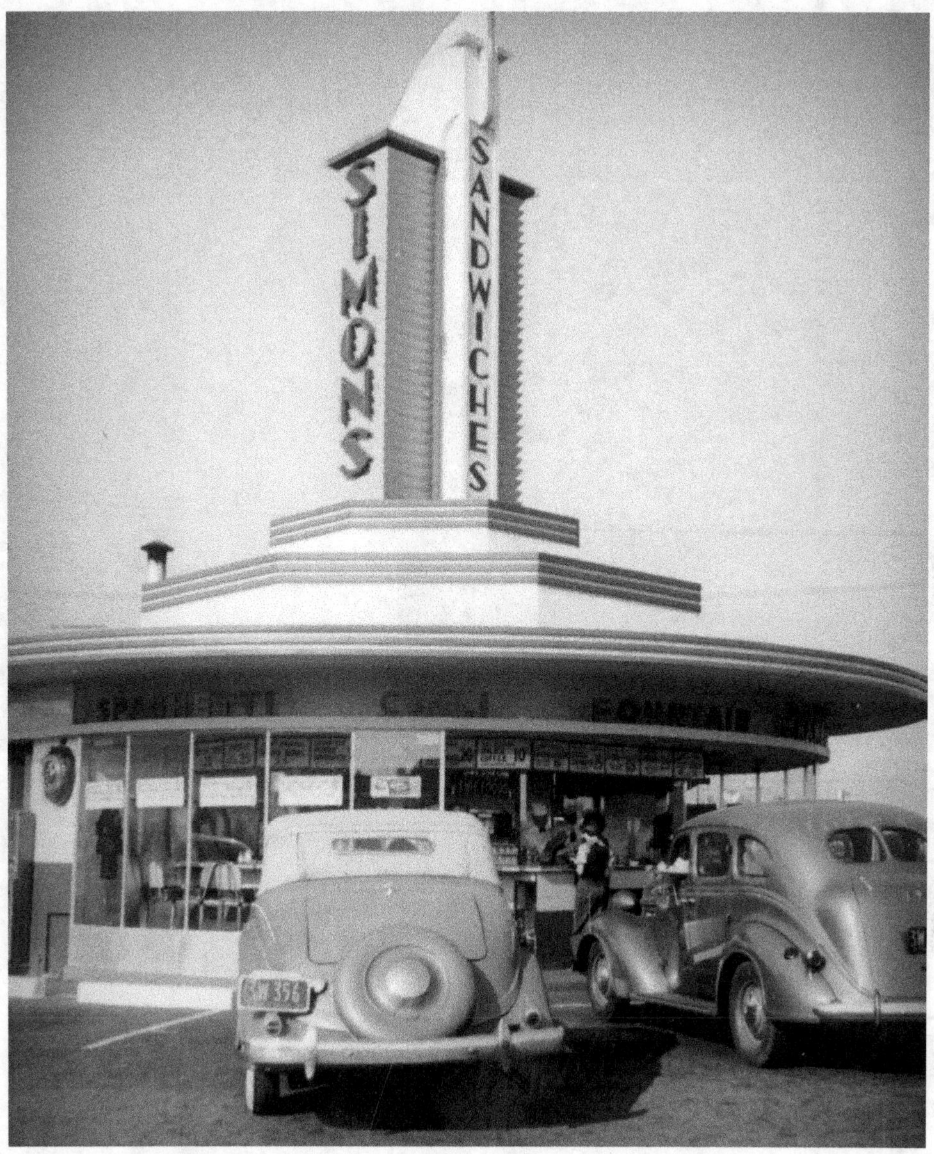

Above, opposite, and page 152: The bright neon pylons of the city's many drive-ins marked intersection upon intersection. At the Simon's Drive-In at Wilshire and Hoover, the eatery directed motorists to pull up for a quick bite with signs advertising sandwiches, hamburgers, and barbecue. Many other architects copied the circular shape and the eye-catching vertical pylon of the Wayne McAllister building and spread the inspiring design nationwide. (Circa 1930s, Security Pacific National Bank Collection and Herman J. Schultheis Collection)

SIMONS
INER
ANT ADS
HAMBURGERS
BARBECUE

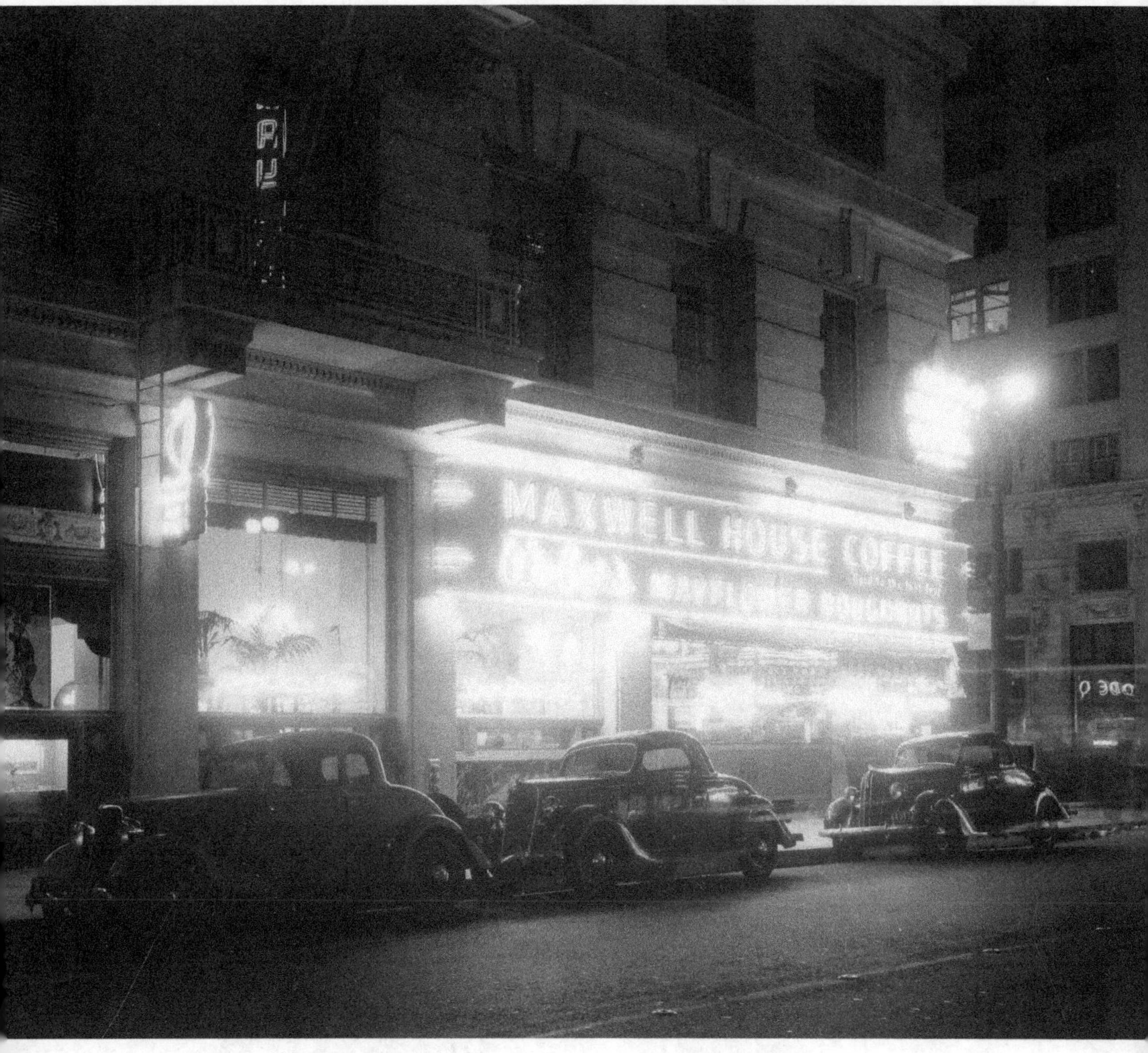

Neon is used to great effect by the Mayflower Shop on the ground floor of the Merritt Building at 8th Street and Broadway. (Circa 1937, Security Pacific National Bank Collection)

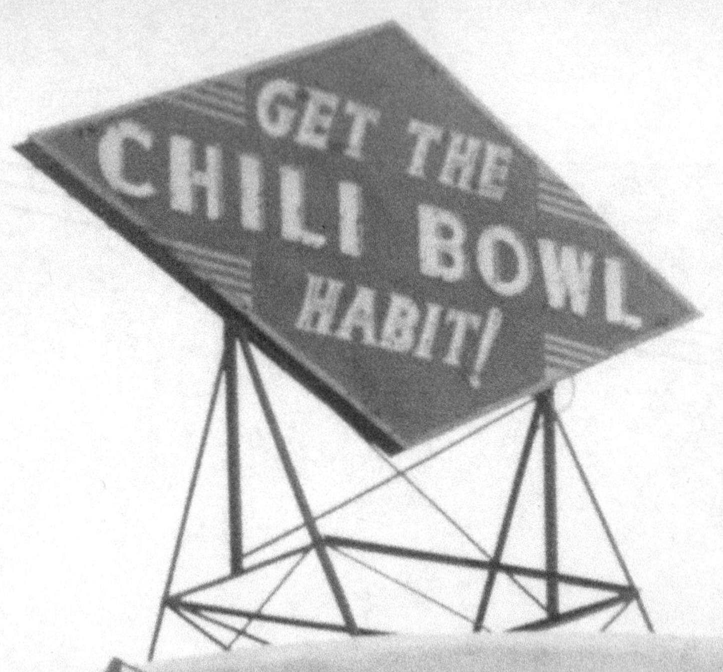
GET THE
CHILI BOWL
HABIT!

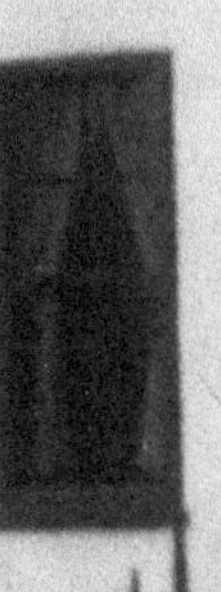
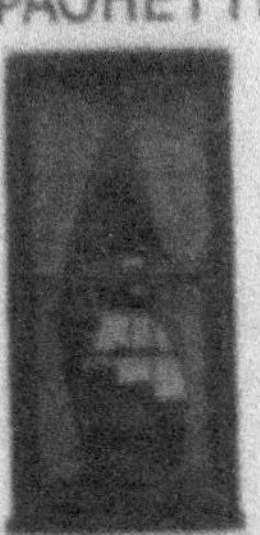
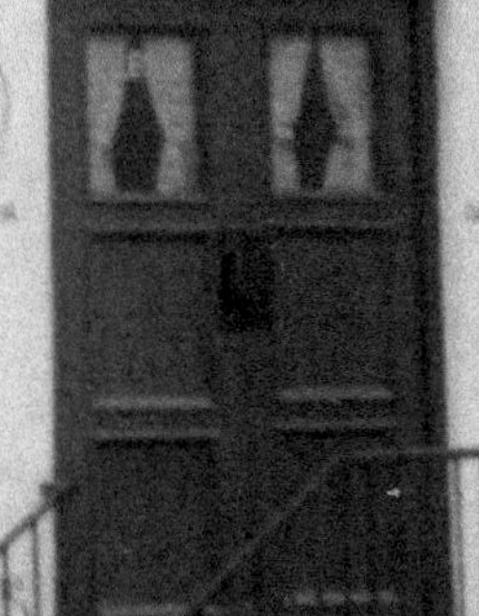

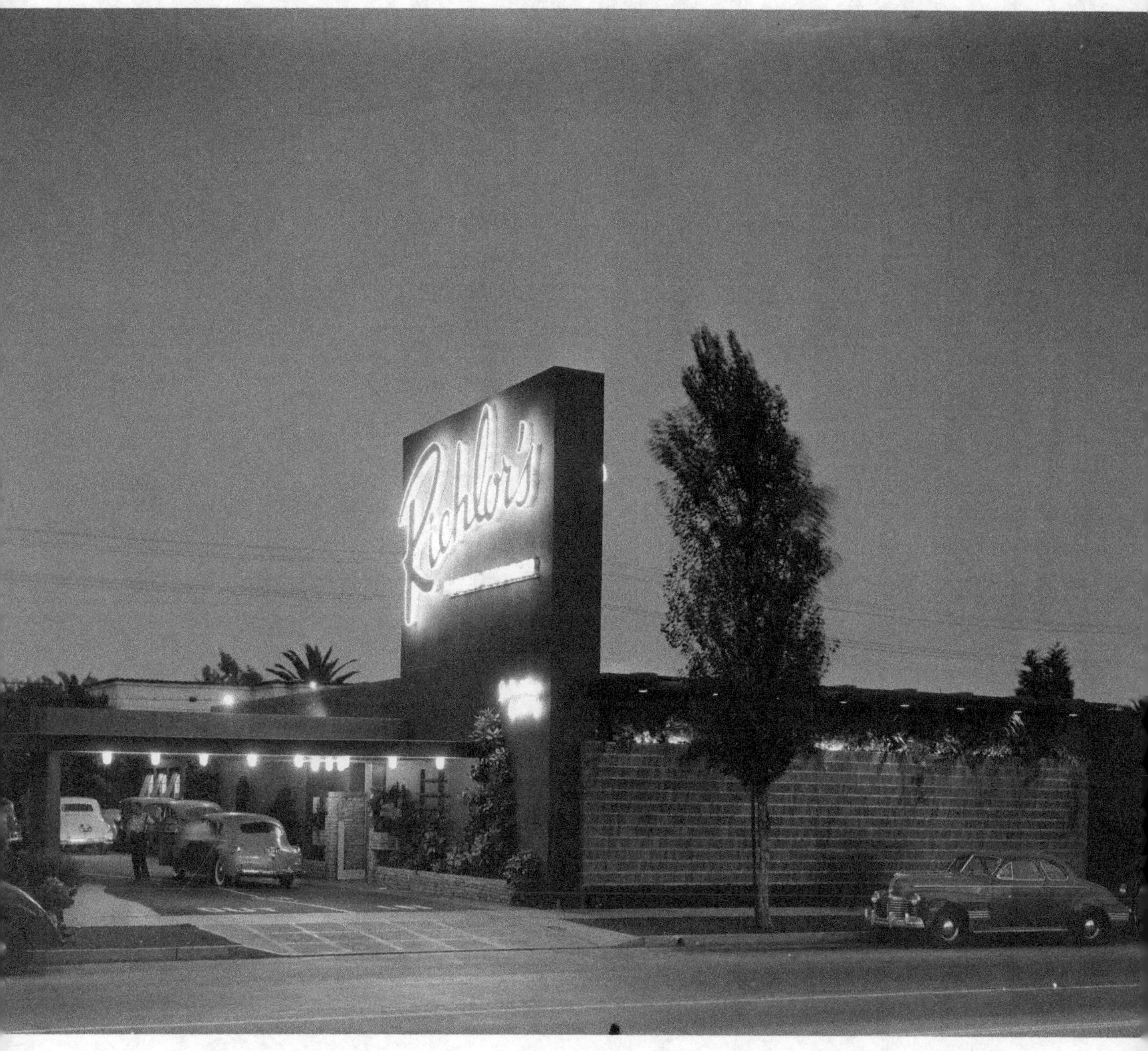

The neon sign at Richlor's helps to light up Restaurant Row on La Cienega in Beverly Hills. (Circa 1940s, Security Pacific National Bank Collection)

Opposite: As if the building shaped like a chili bowl weren't enough, the neon sign atop this restaurant encourages travelers along Wilshire Boulevard to "Get the Chili Bowl Habit!" (Circa 1937, Herman Schultheis Collection)

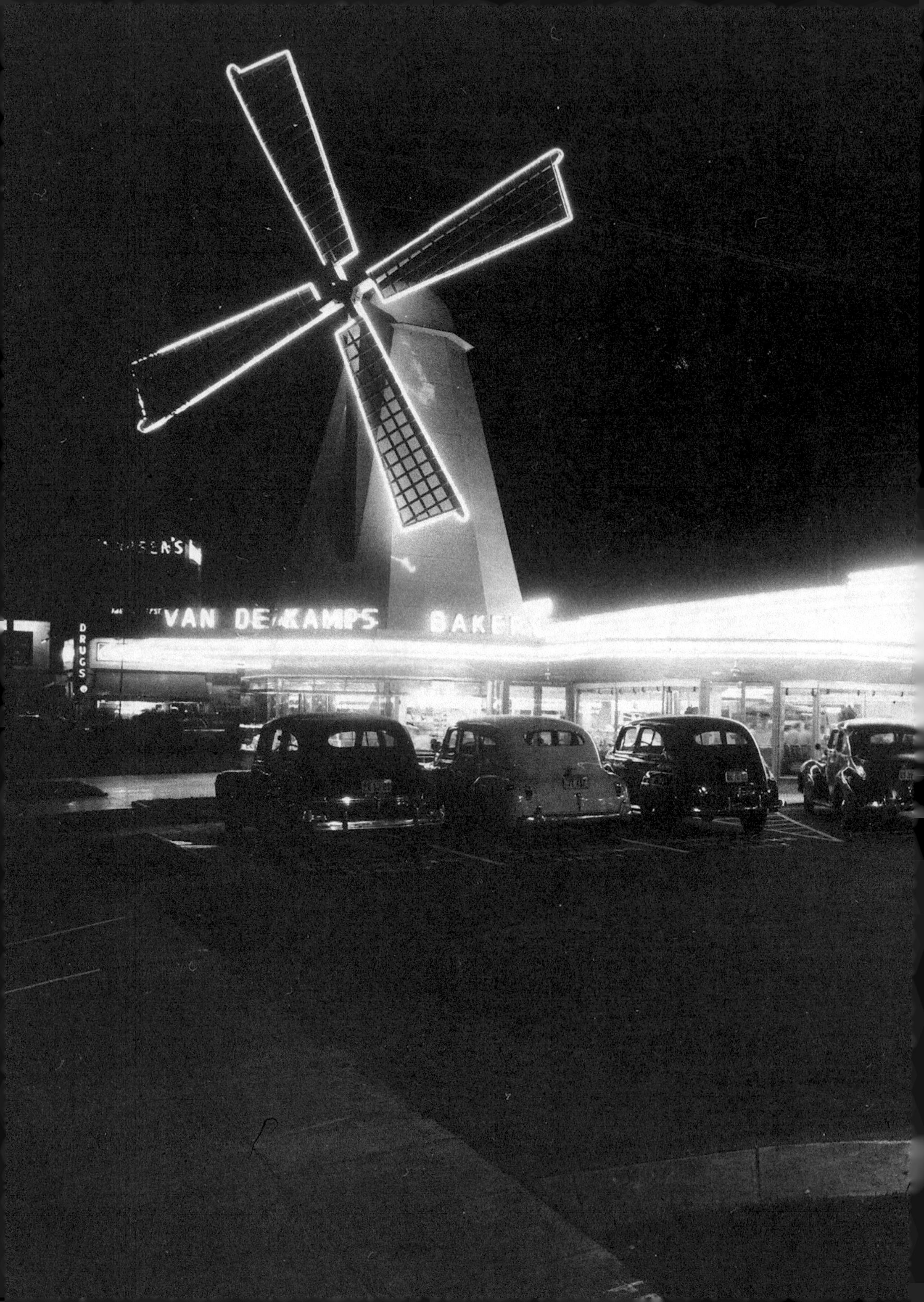

VAN DE KAMPS
DRUGS

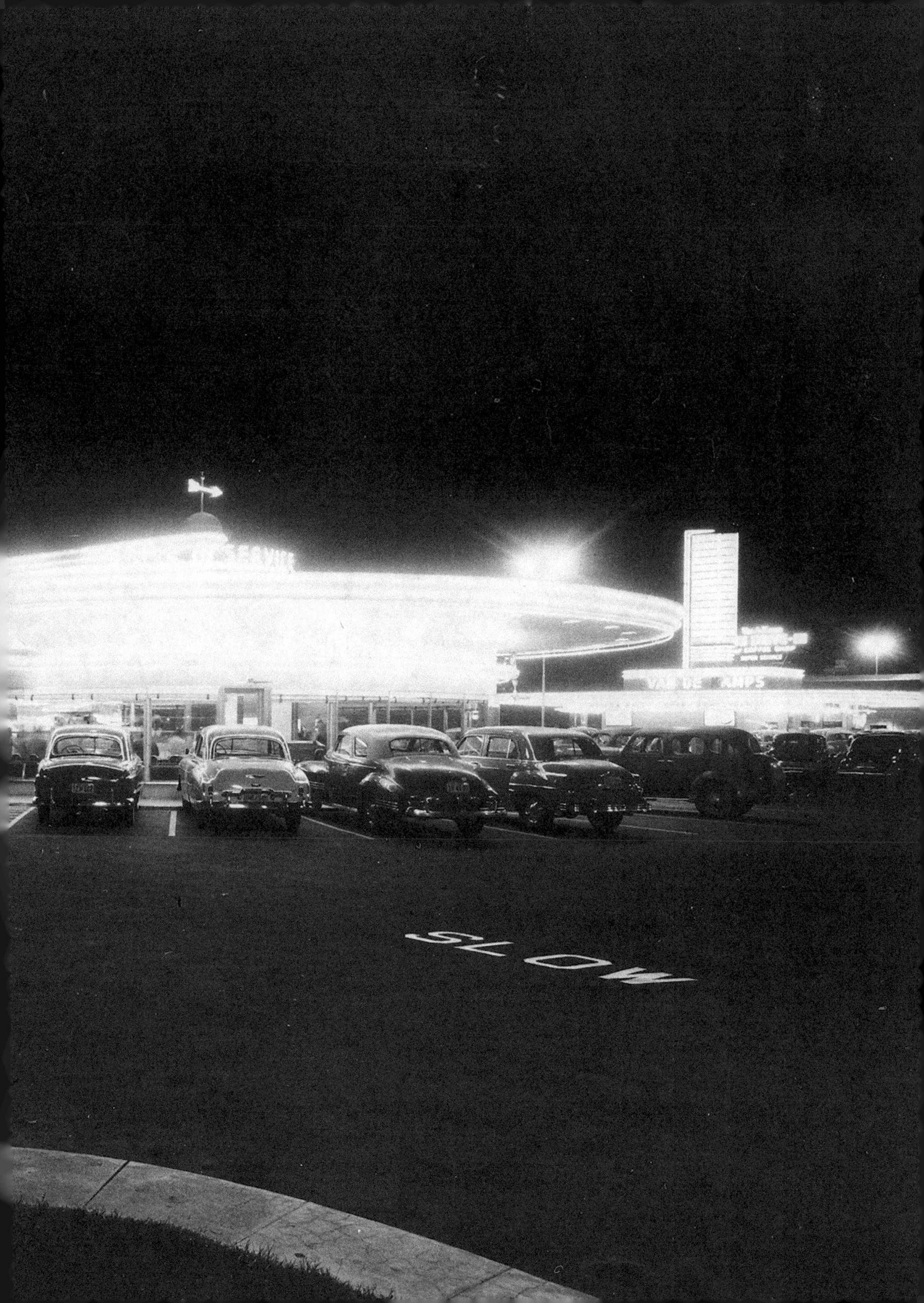
SLOW

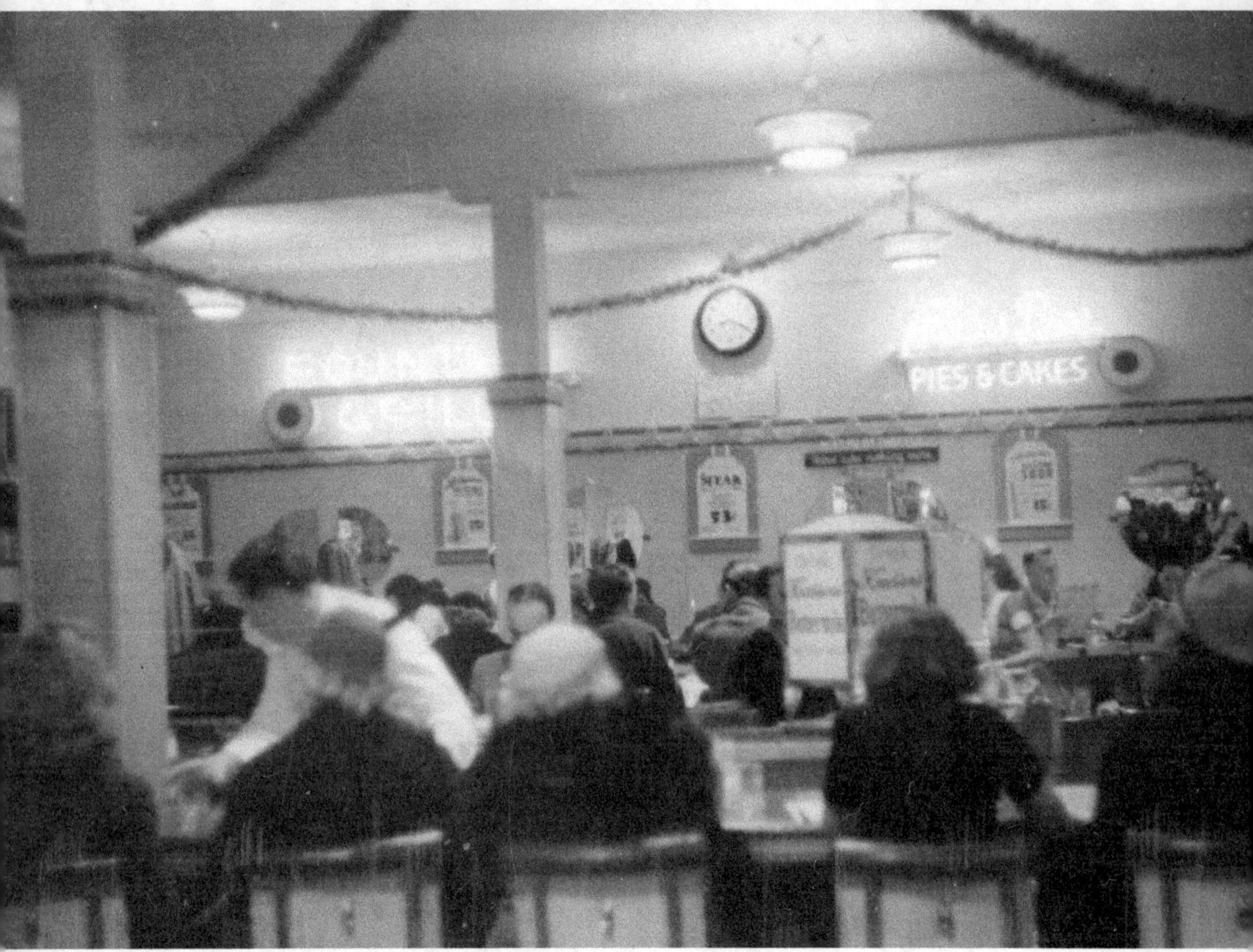

An unidentified lunch counter uses interior neon to advertise some of its menu items. (Circa 1938, Herman J. Schultheis Collection)

Opposite: A neon mouse points to what is presumably a Mexican restaurant on Figueroa Street. (Circa 1937, Herman J. Schultheis Collection)

Overleaf: Neon lights up the night sky in Atwater Village on this Wayne McAllister-designed Van de Kamp's Bakery and Coffee Shop with Drive-In. (Circa 1954, Ralph Morris Collection)

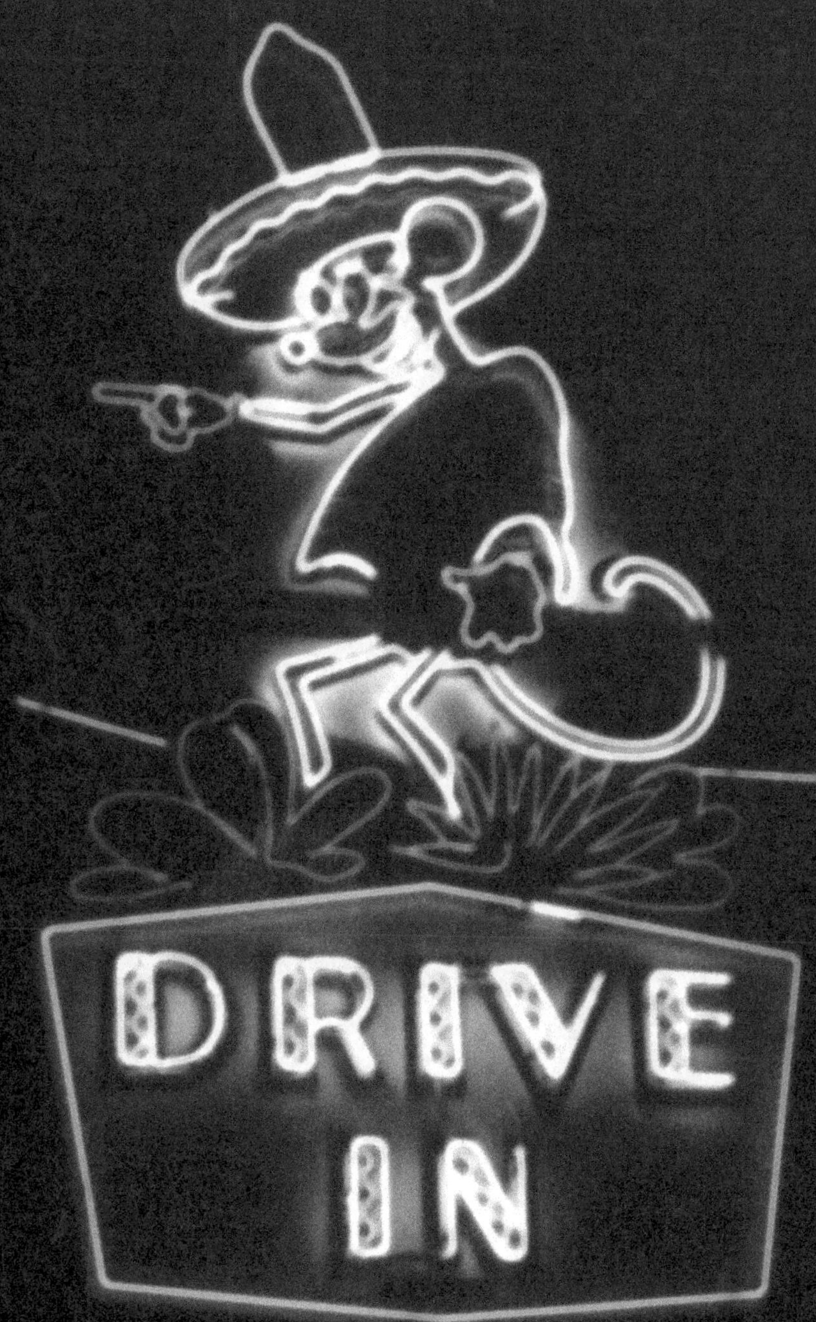
DRIVE
IN

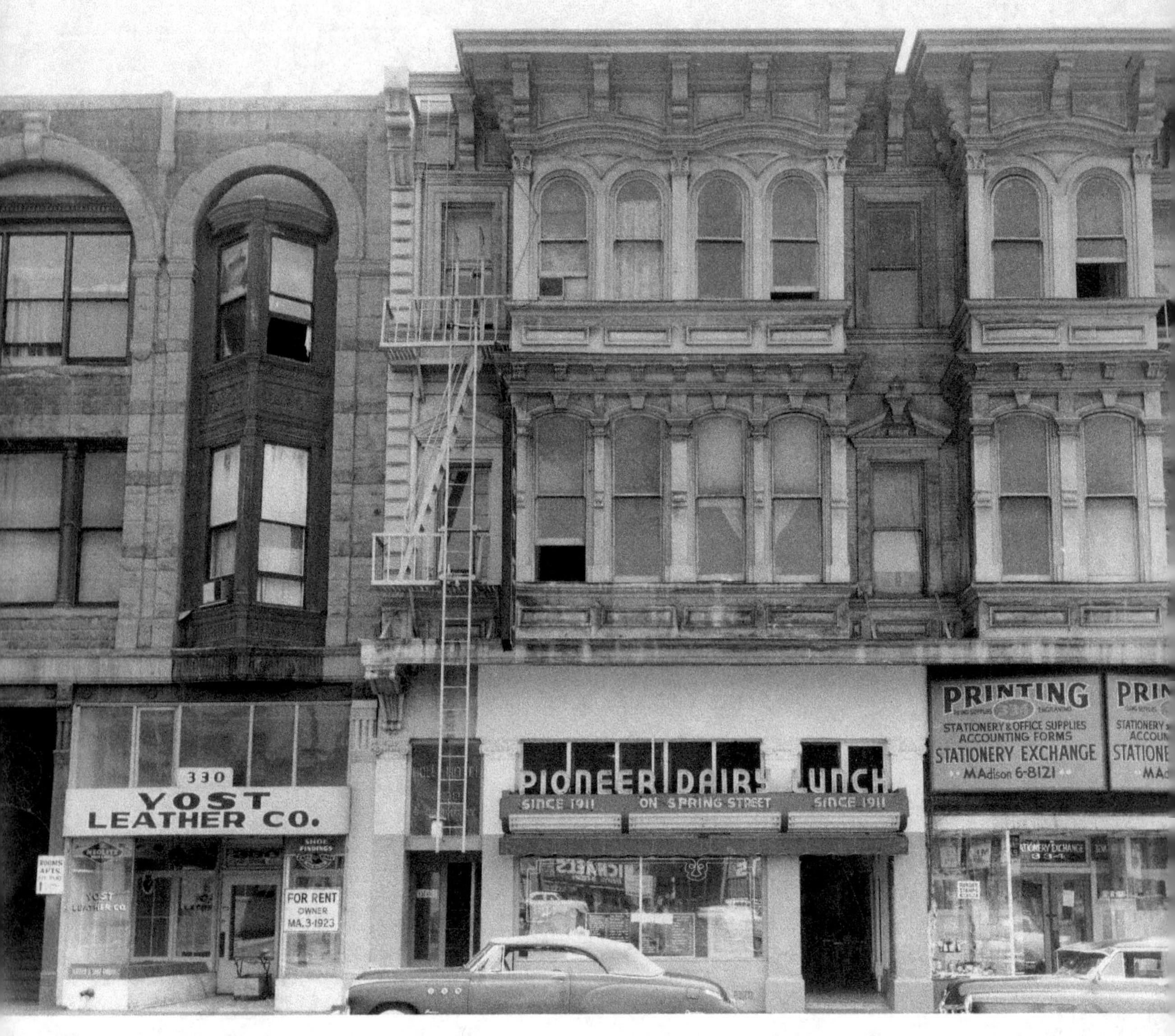

A modest lunch counter on Spring Street sports neon signage. (Circa 1955, William Reagh Collection)

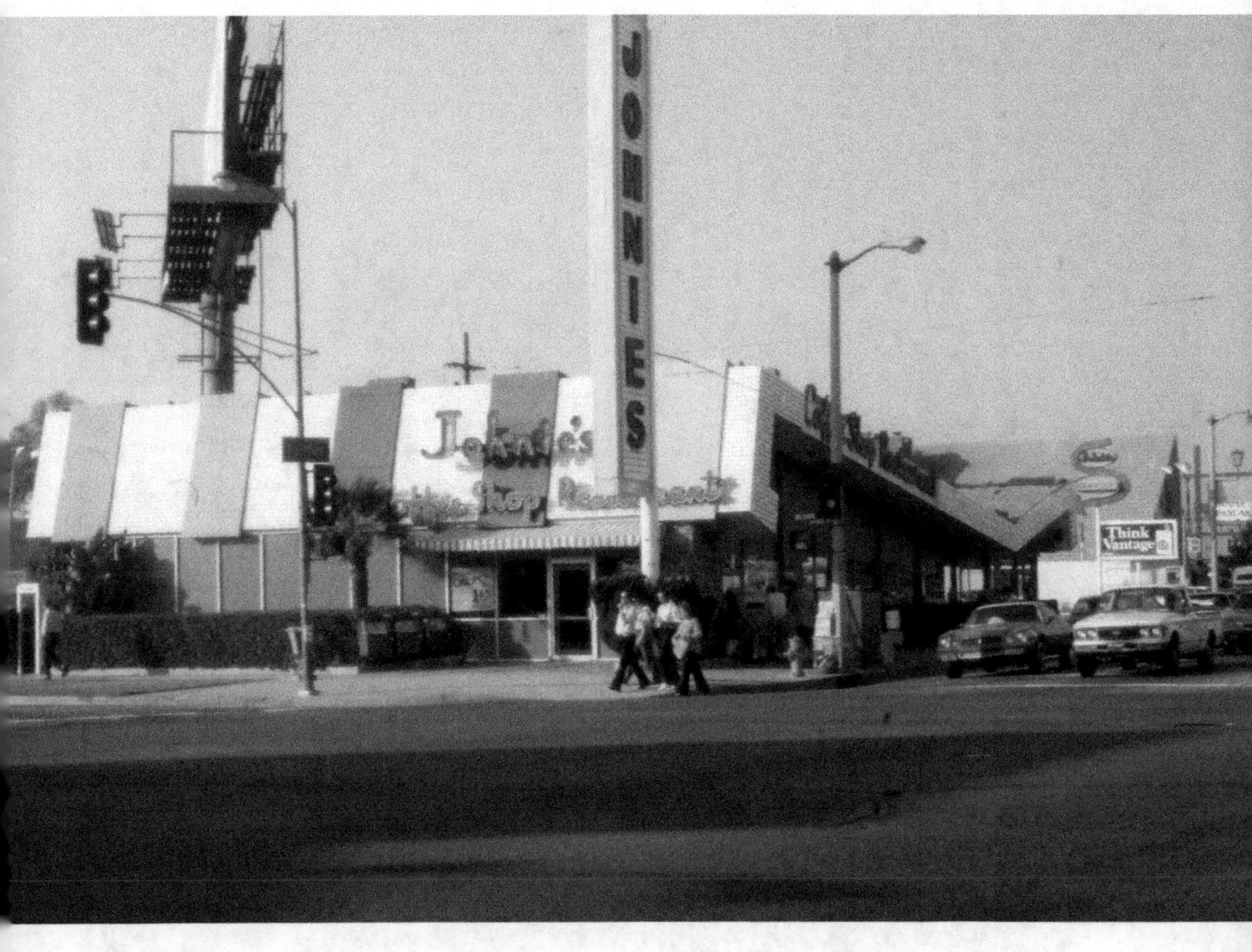

Johnnie's Coffee Shop on Wilshire Boulevard at Fairfax Avenue effectively uses neon to complement the Googie architecture. (1978, Anne Laskey/Marlene Laskey Collection)

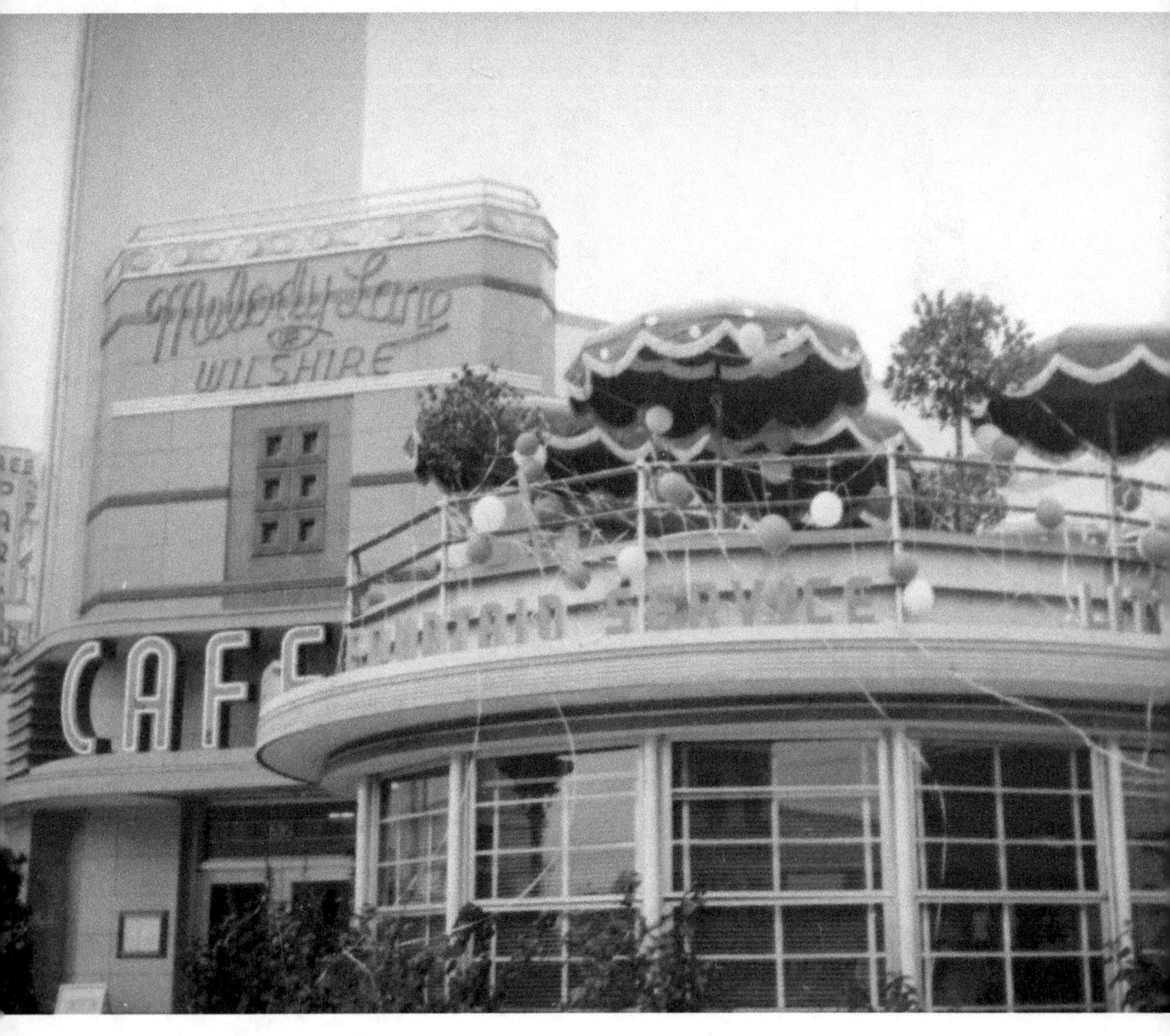

Varying fonts are used for the neon signs at Melody Lane on Hollywood Boulevard, near Detroit Street. (Circa 1938, Herman J. Schultheis Collection)

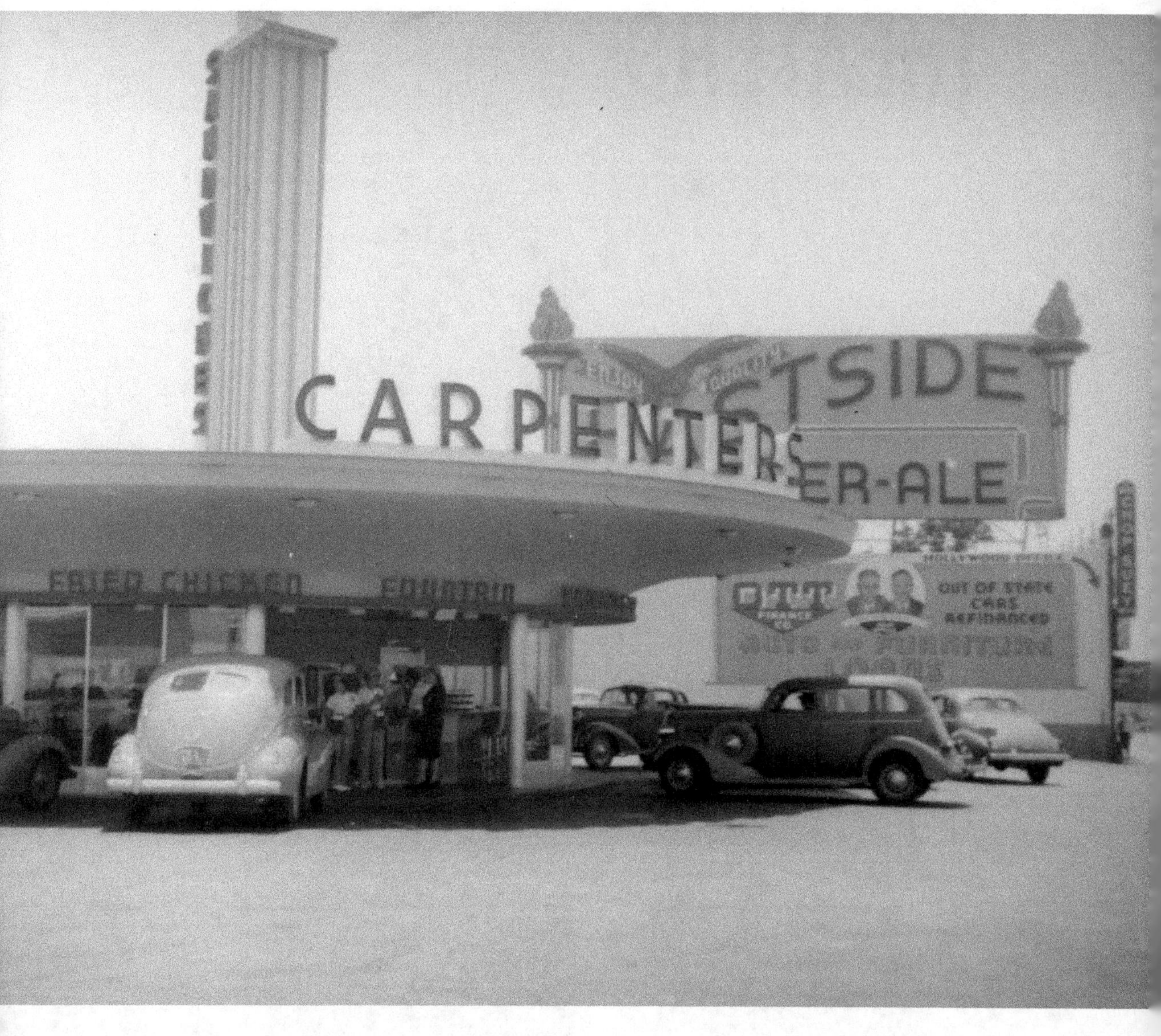

Carpenters Drive-In on Sunset Boulevard near Vine Street takes full advantage of neon on its circular structure. (Circa 1939, Herman J. Schultheis Collection)

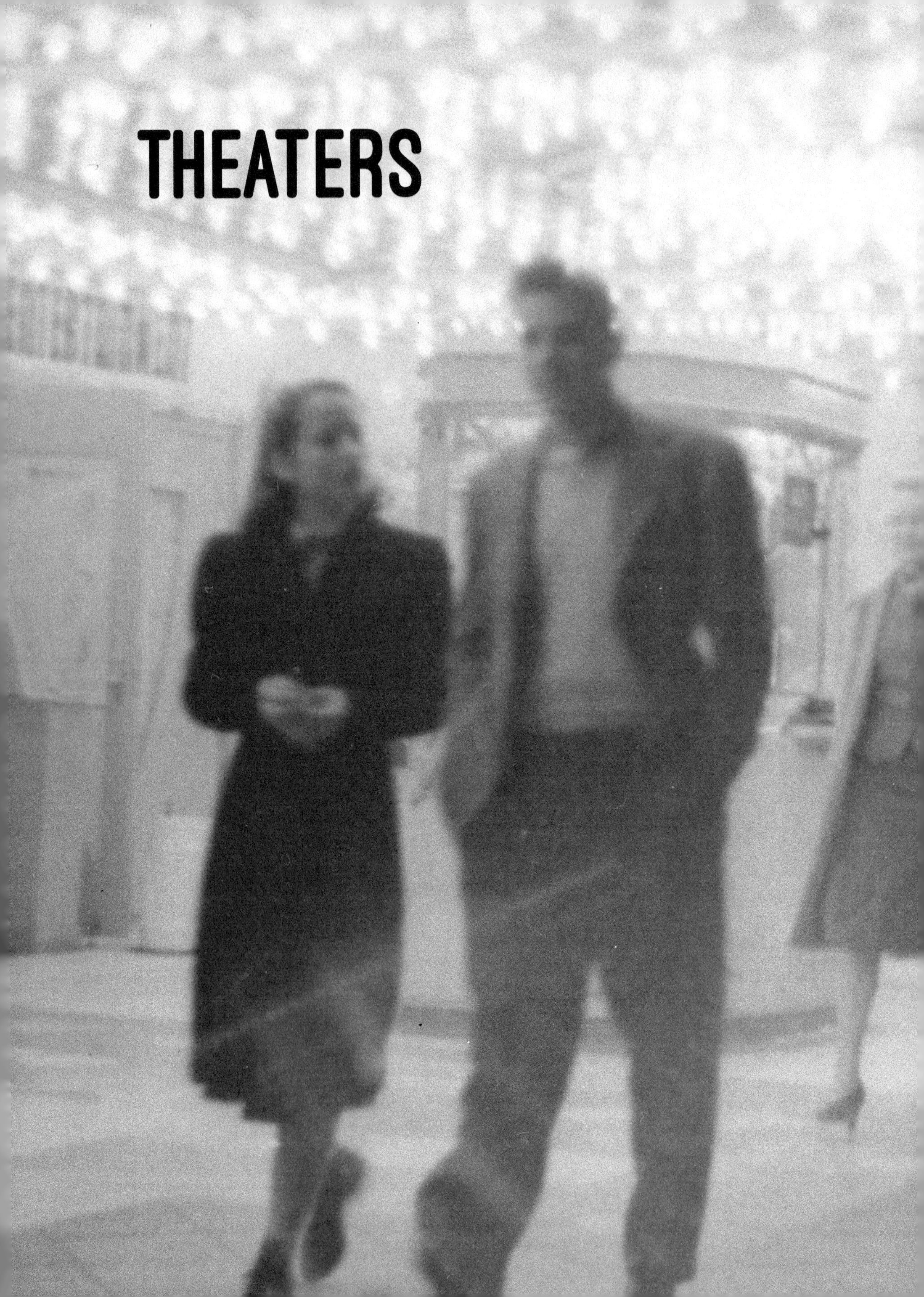

THEATERS

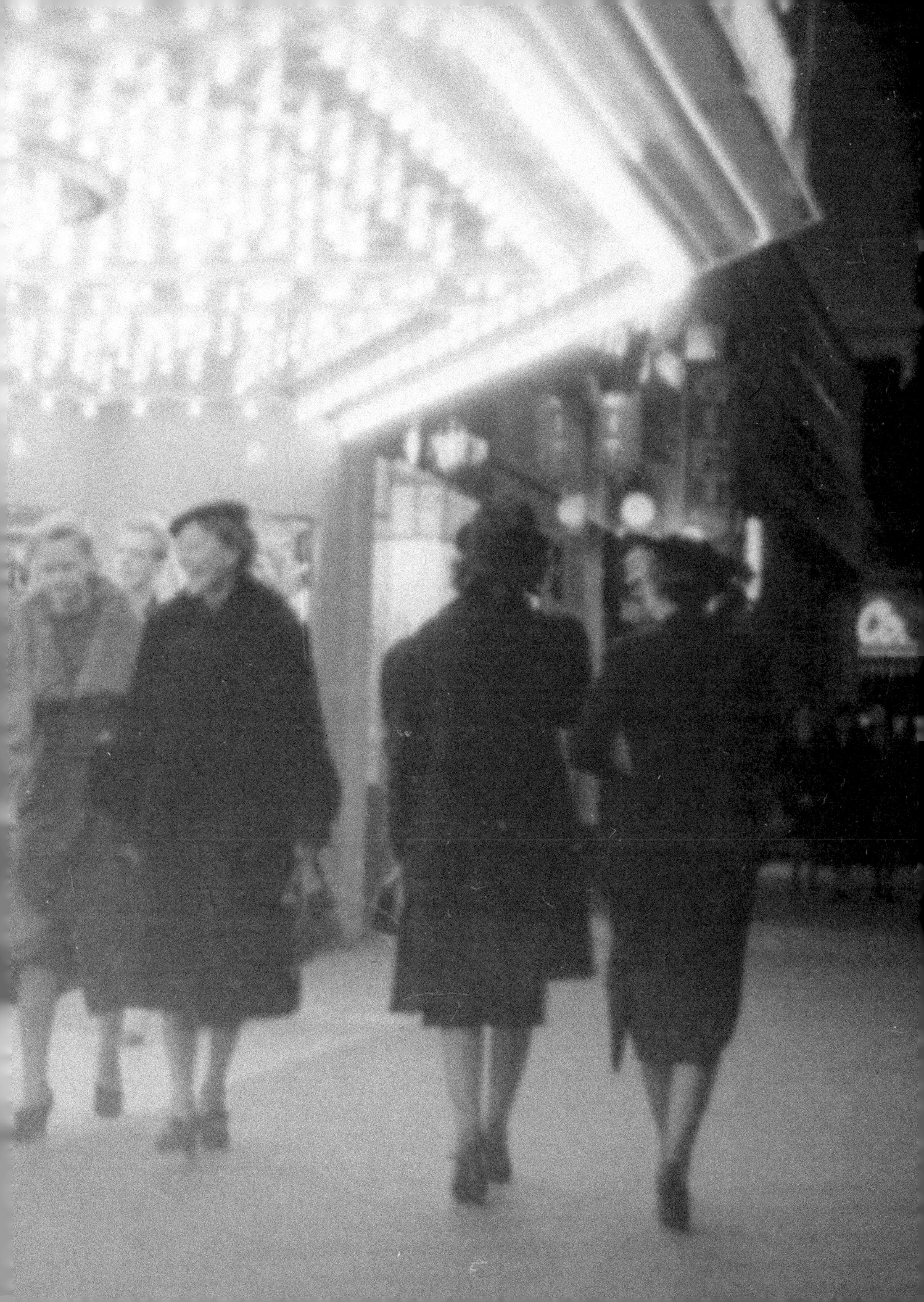

Overleaf, opposite, and page 168: The 1920s ushered in Hollywood Boulevard as an entertainment district with high profile theaters bearing the name "Grauman" along with smaller venues like the Hollywood Theatre. No matter what the capacity, all the theaters took full advantage of neon. (1938, Security Pacific National Bank Collection and Herman J. Schultheis Collection)

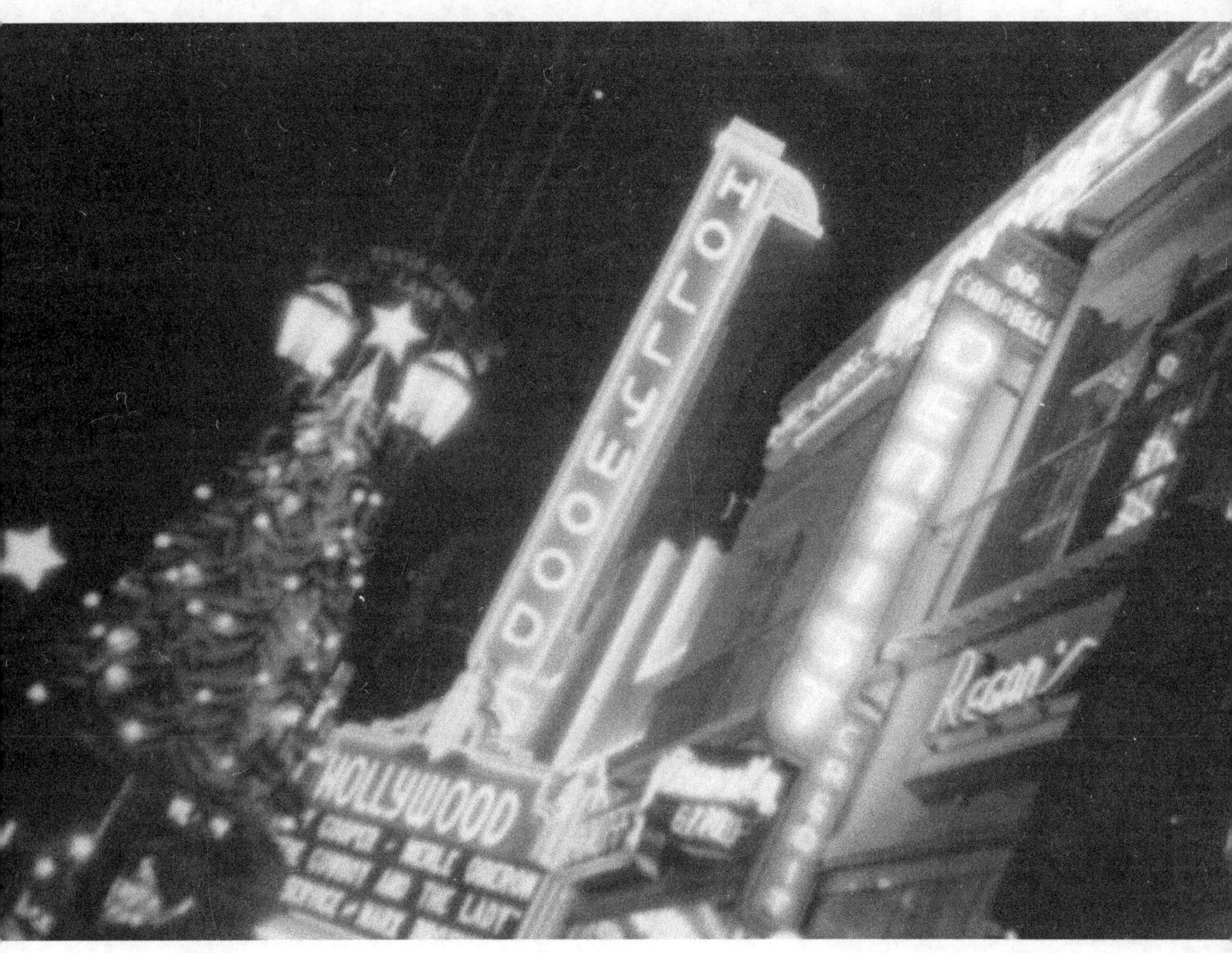
HOLLYWOOD

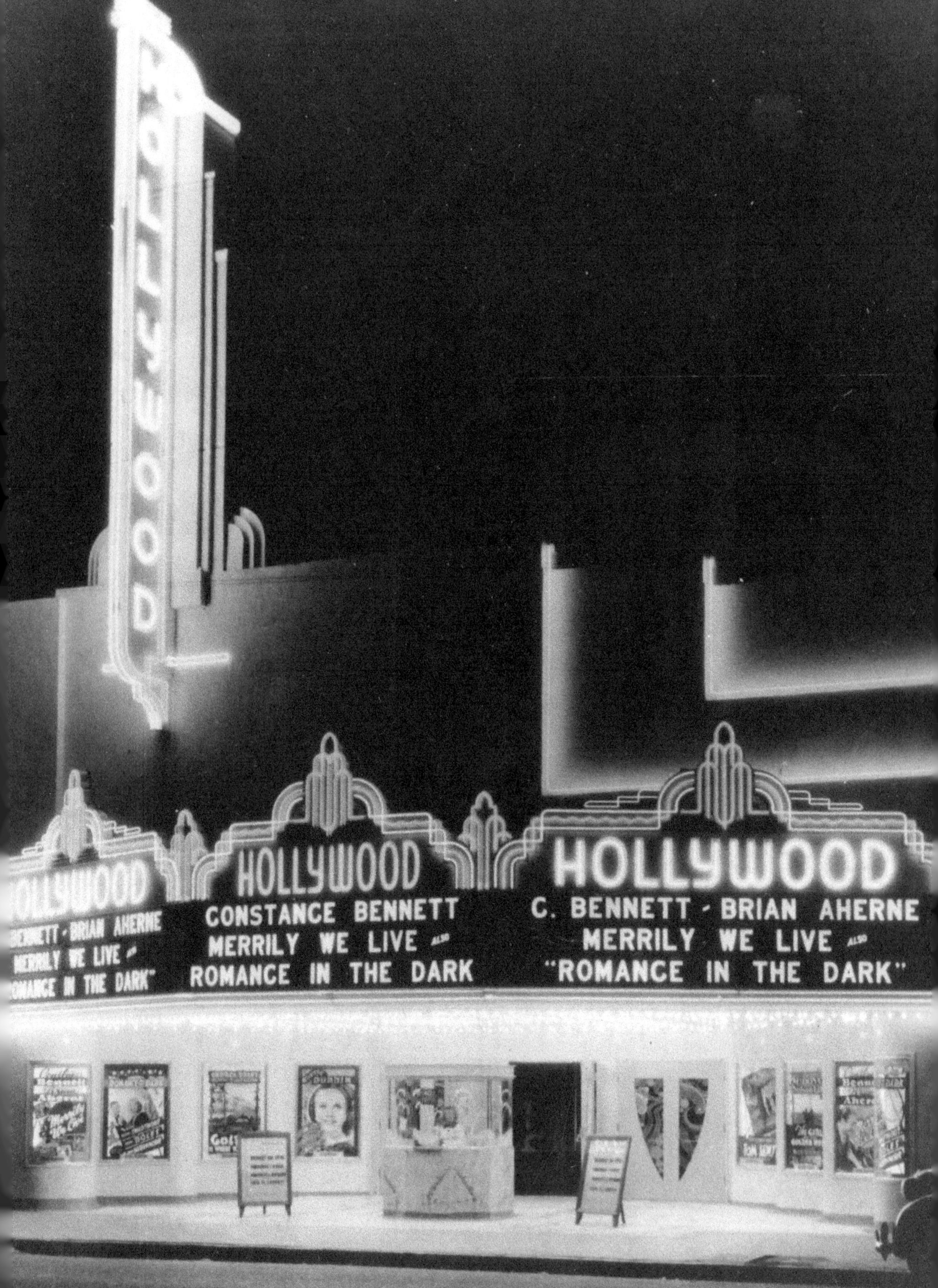
HOLLYWOOD
CONSTANCE BENNETT
MERRILY WE LIVE ALSO
ROMANCE IN THE DARK
HOLLYWOOD
C. BENNETT - BRIAN AHERNE
MERRILY WE LIVE ALSO
"ROMANCE IN THE DARK"

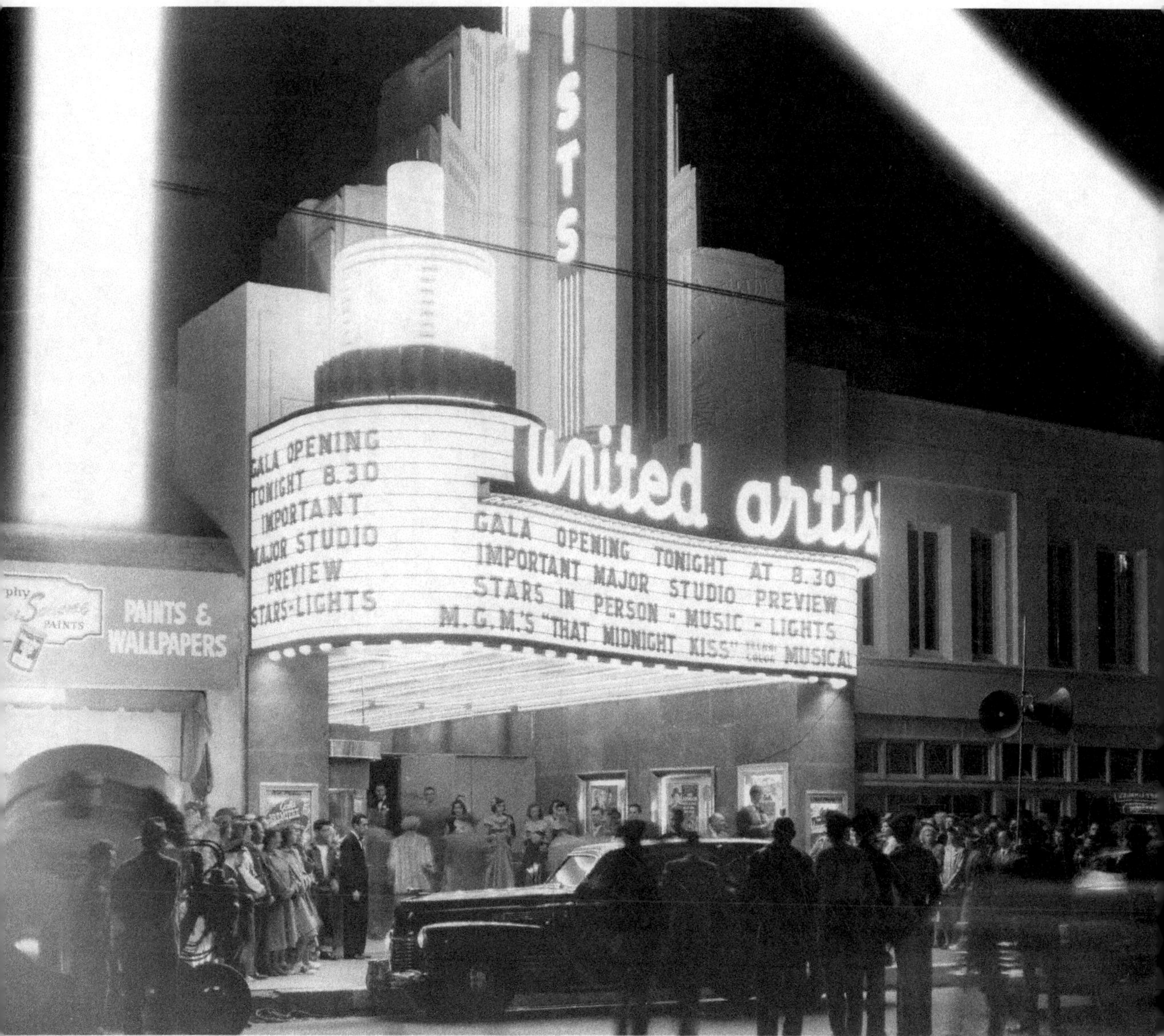

Mario Lanza's *That Midnight Kiss* made a Klieg-light splash at the United Artists Theatre in Inglewood, but it's the curvaceous marquee that catches the eye. Its undulating fascia glowed from within and was topped with curving, cursive "United Artists" lettering. More daring is the spinning wedding cake of neon at the peak of the marque that twirled the letters U and A into a blur in this long-exposure photo. Such spinning neon designs were an expensive rarity. (1949, Security Pacific National Bank Collection)

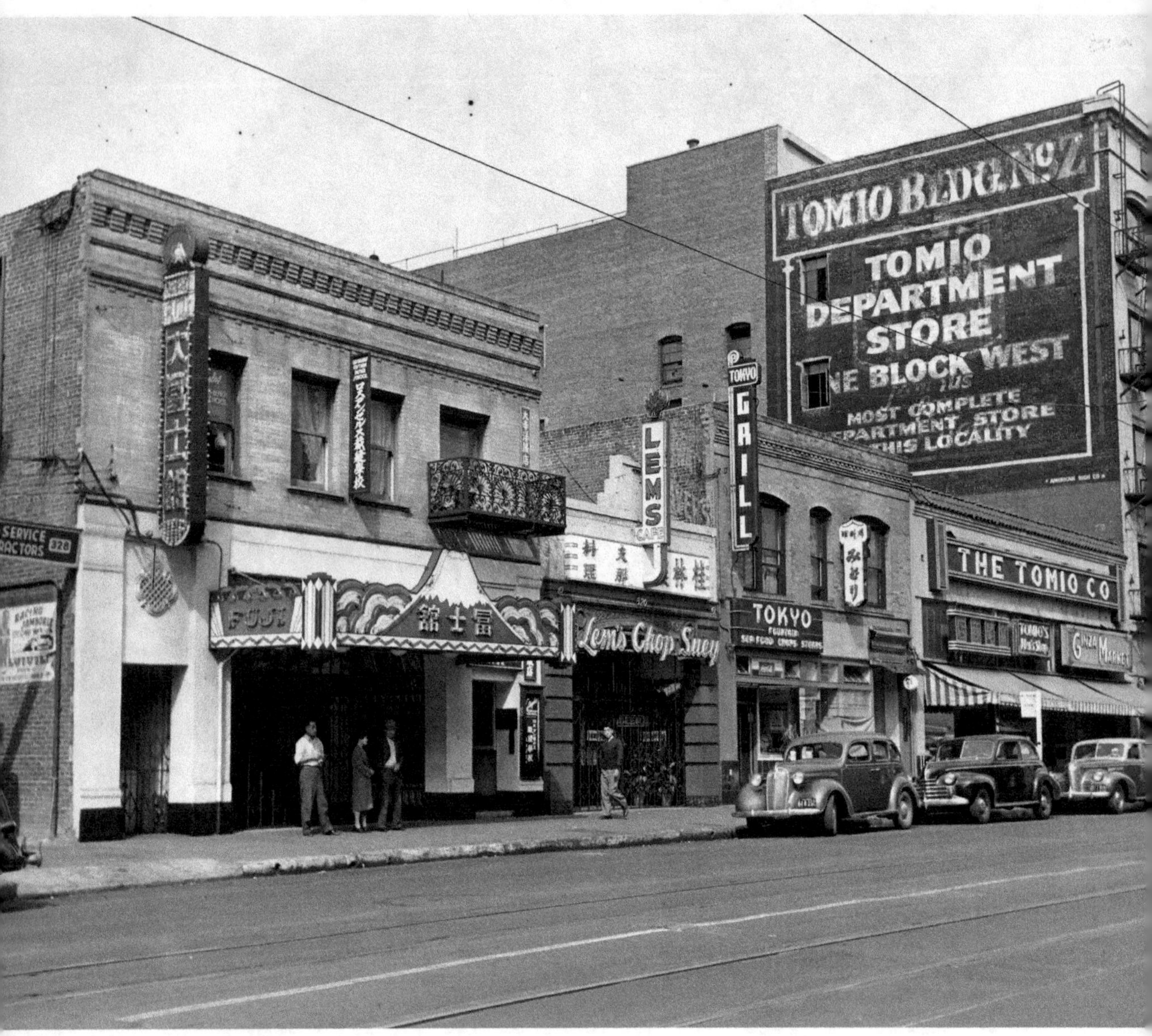

The modest Fuji Kan Theatre on 1st Street is adorned with neon Japanese characters, while additional buildings utilize neon to advertise Little Tokyo businesses. (1941, Los Angeles Herald Examiner Collection)

Opposite: The neon marquee and blade sign of the Pantages Theatre stands out in Hollywood. (Circa 1930, Ralph Morris Collection)

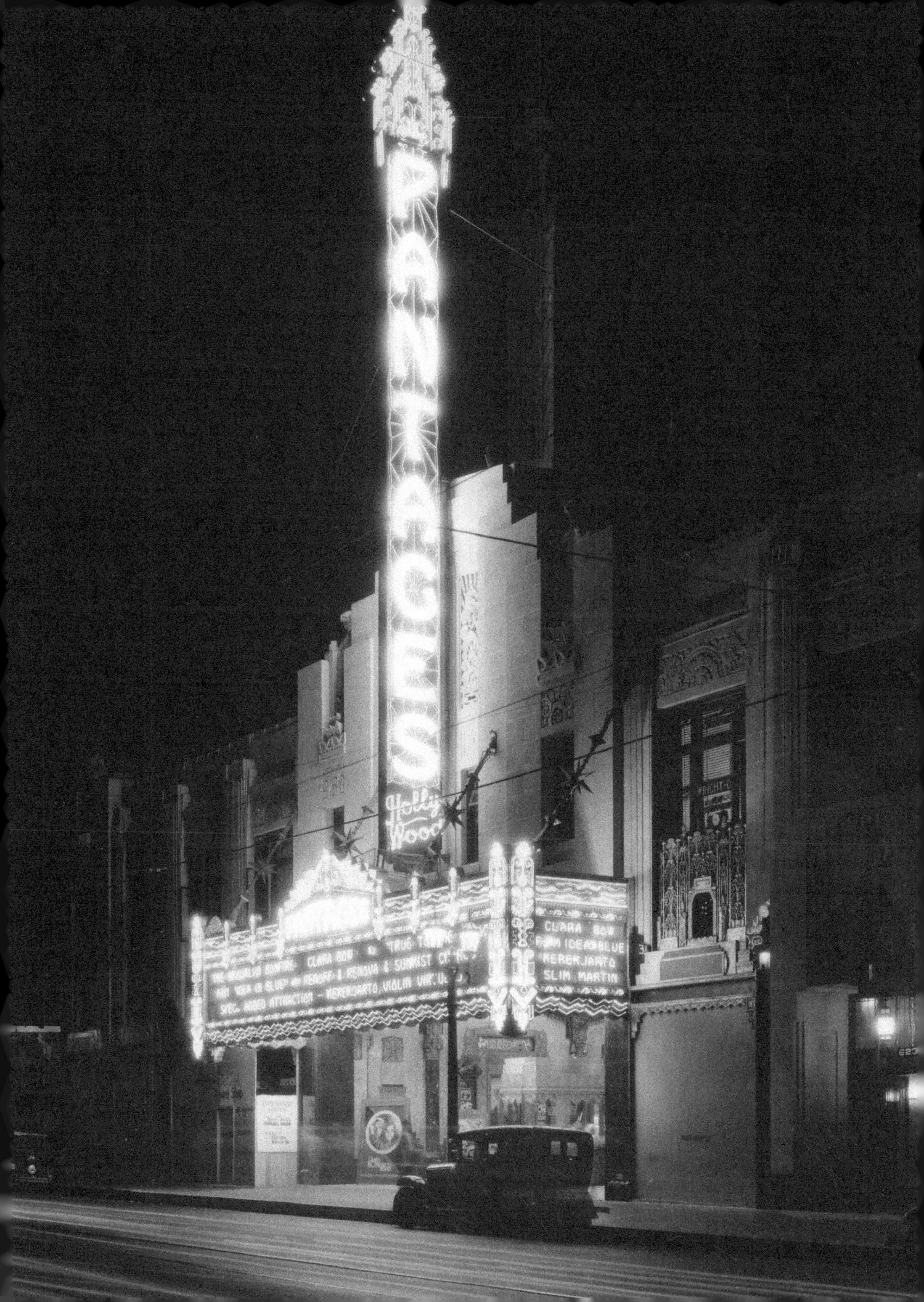
PANTAGES
Hollywood
CLARA BOW
SLIM MARTIN

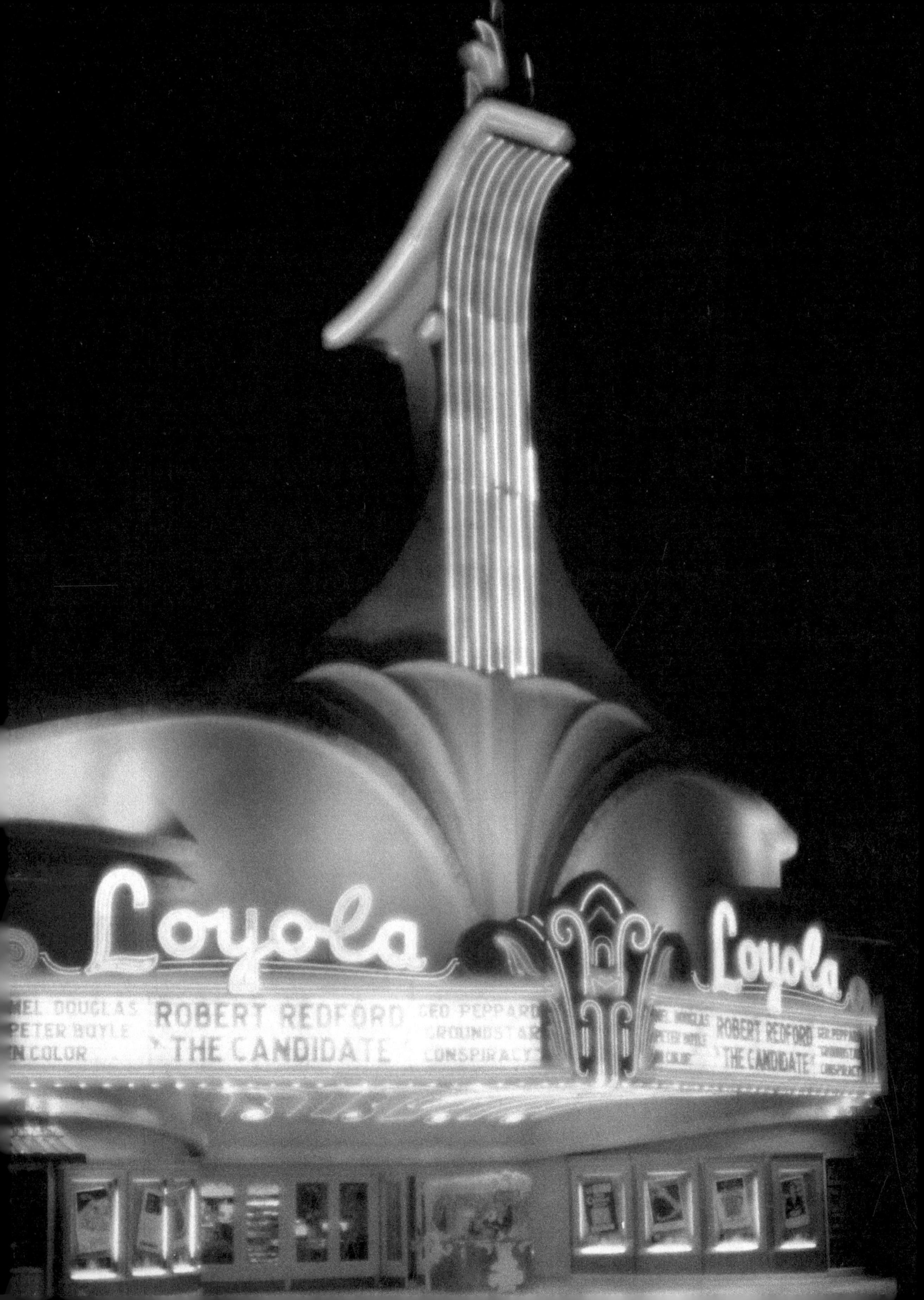

Loyola
ROBERT REDFORD
"THE CANDIDATE"
PETER BOYLE
IN COLOR
GEO PEPPARD
CONSPIRACY
Loyola
ROBERT REDFORD
"THE CANDIDATE"

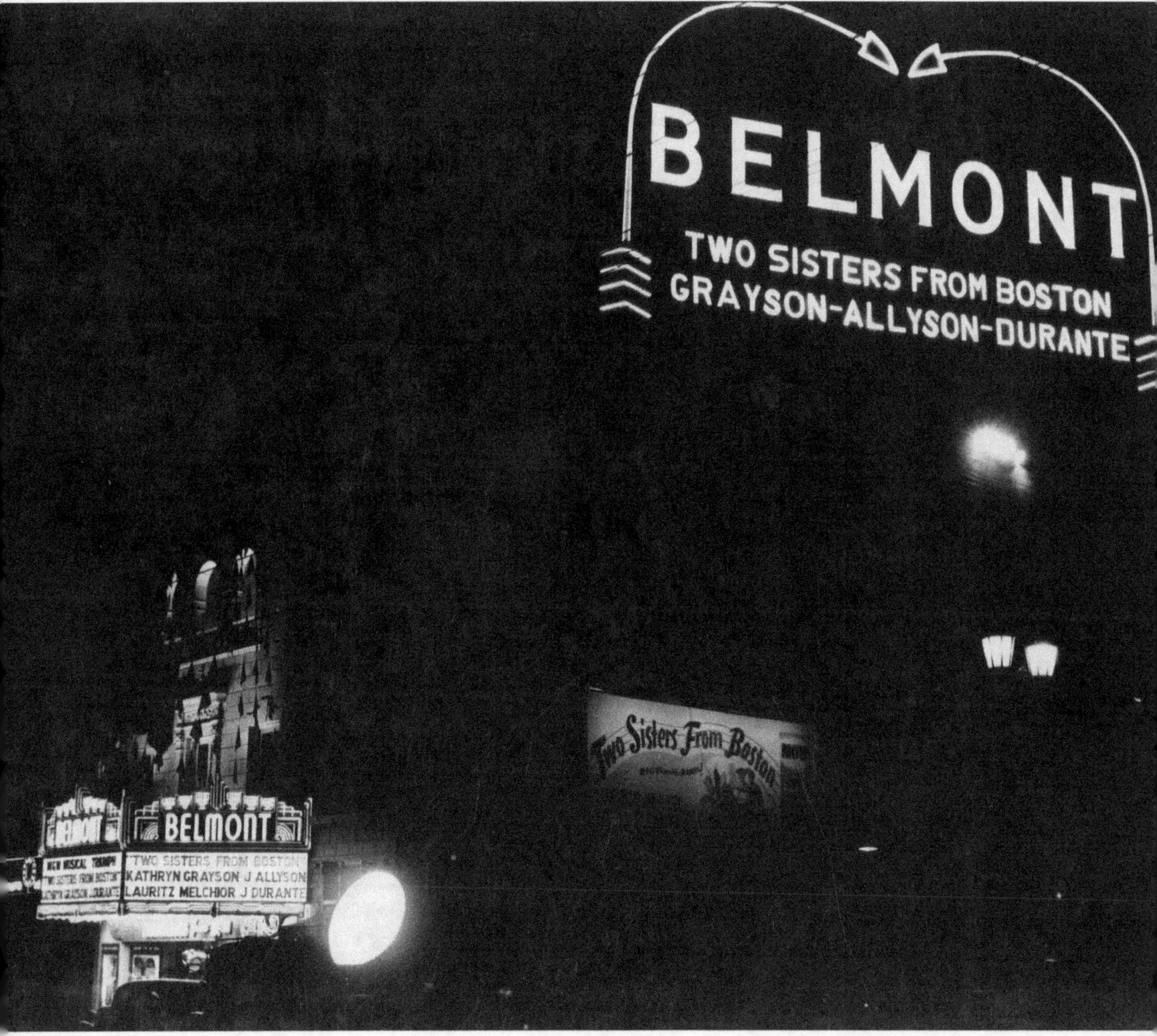

An impressive roof-top sign shines above the Fox Belmont Theatre on Vermont Avenue near Beverly Boulevard. (1946, Los Angeles Public Library Collection)

Opposite: A brilliant tower of neon compliments the marquee at the Loyola Theatre on Sepulveda Boulevard in the Westchester neighborhood. (1972, Security Pacific National Bank Collection)

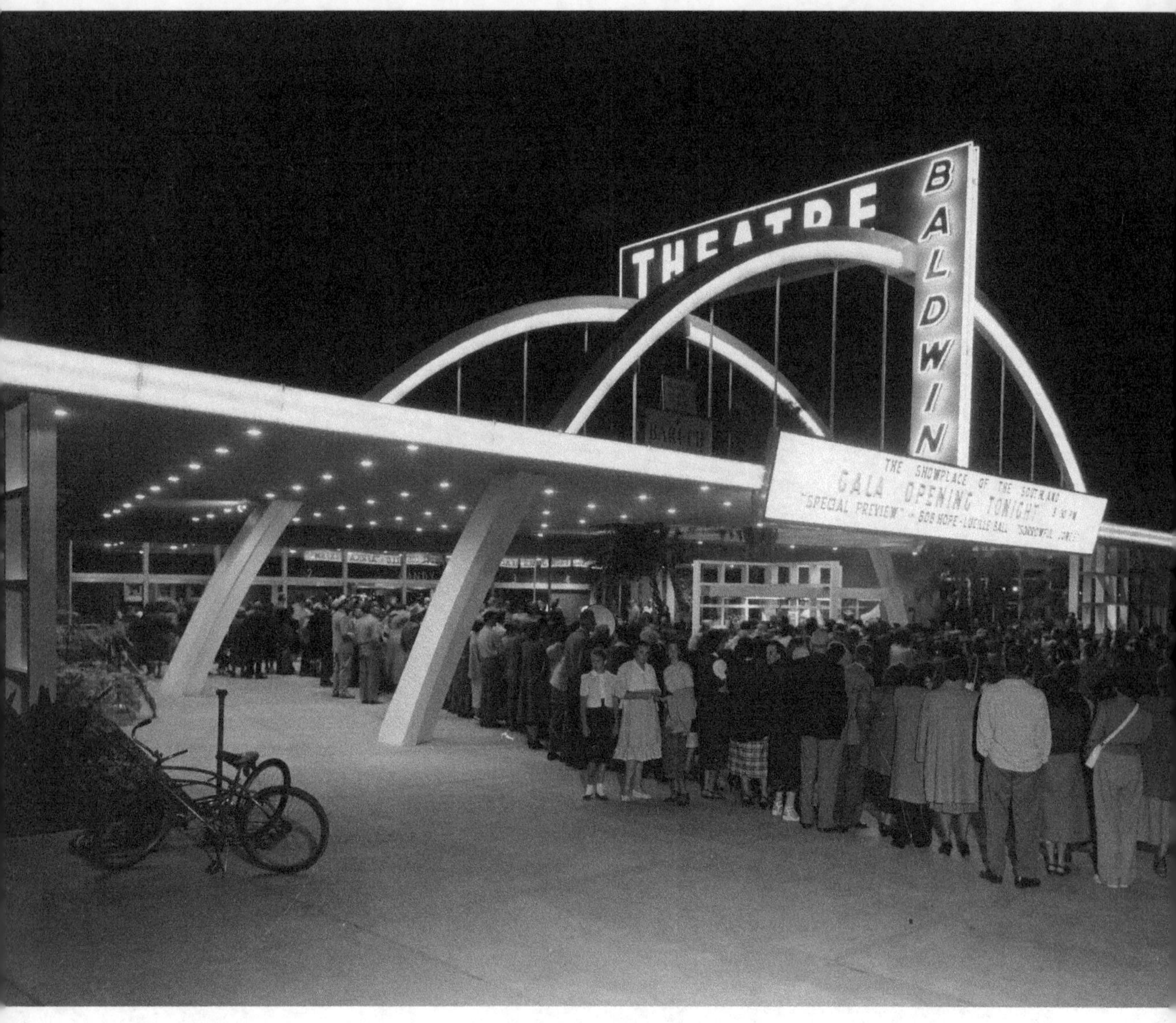

Neon beckons moviegoers into the Baldwin Theatre on La Brea Avenue, south of Rodeo Road. (1949, Ralph Morris Collection)

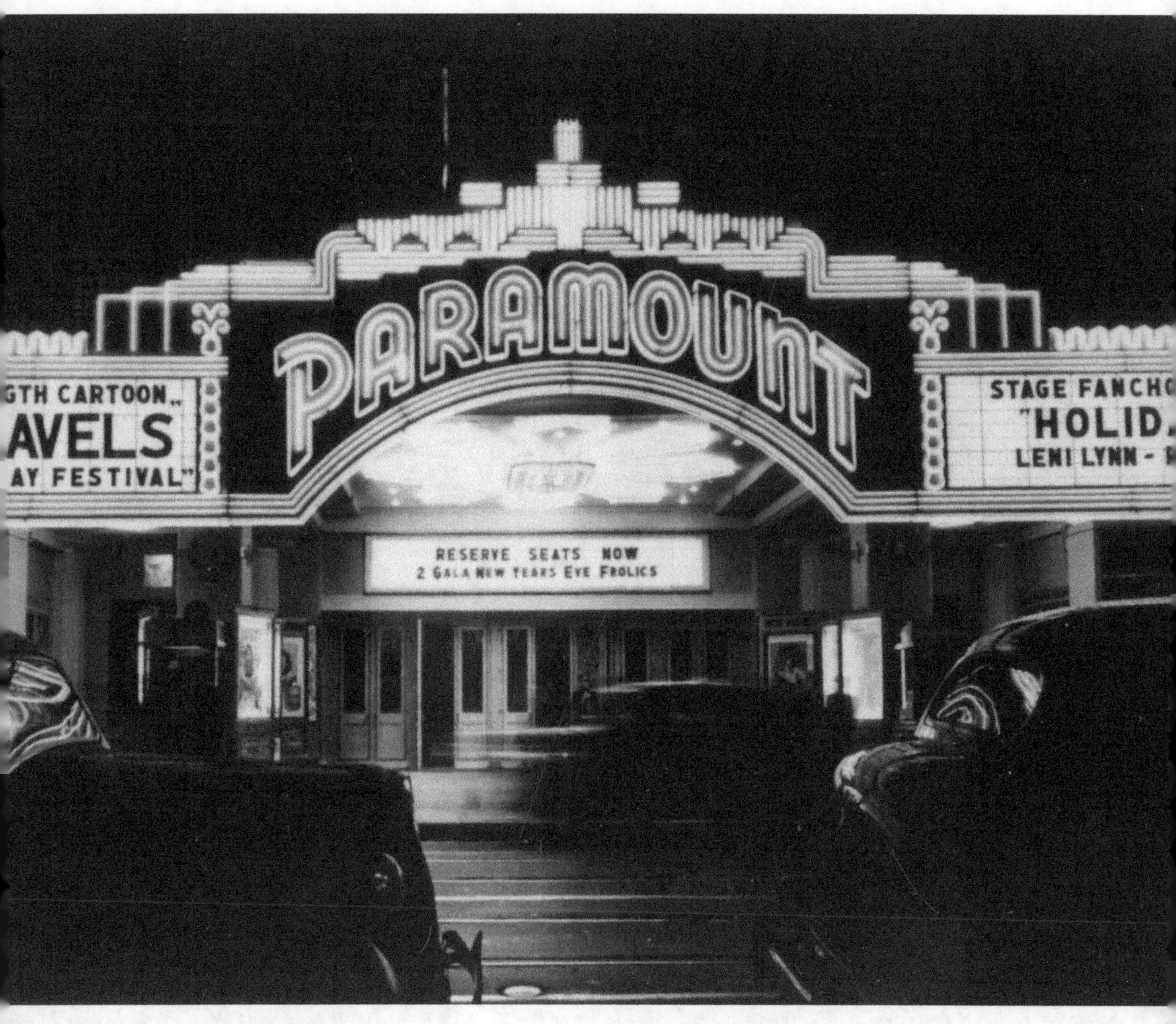

Close-up view of the neon marquee at the Paramount Theatre in Downtown Los Angeles. (1939, Los Angeles Public Library Collection)

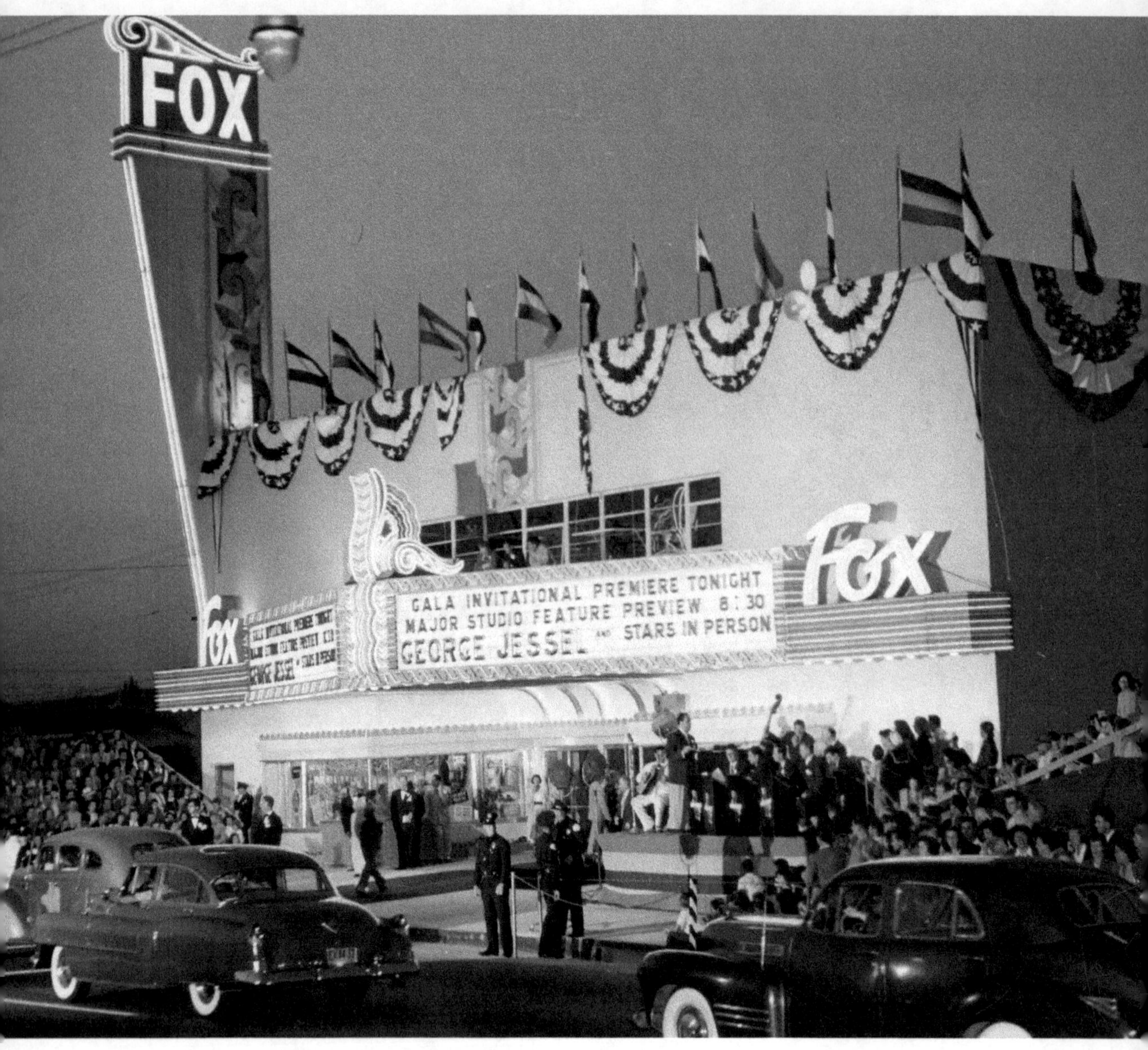
FOX
Fox
GALA INVITATIONAL PREMIERE TONIGHT
MAJOR STUDIO FEATURE PREVIEW 8:30
GEORGE JESSEL AND STARS IN PERSON
Fox

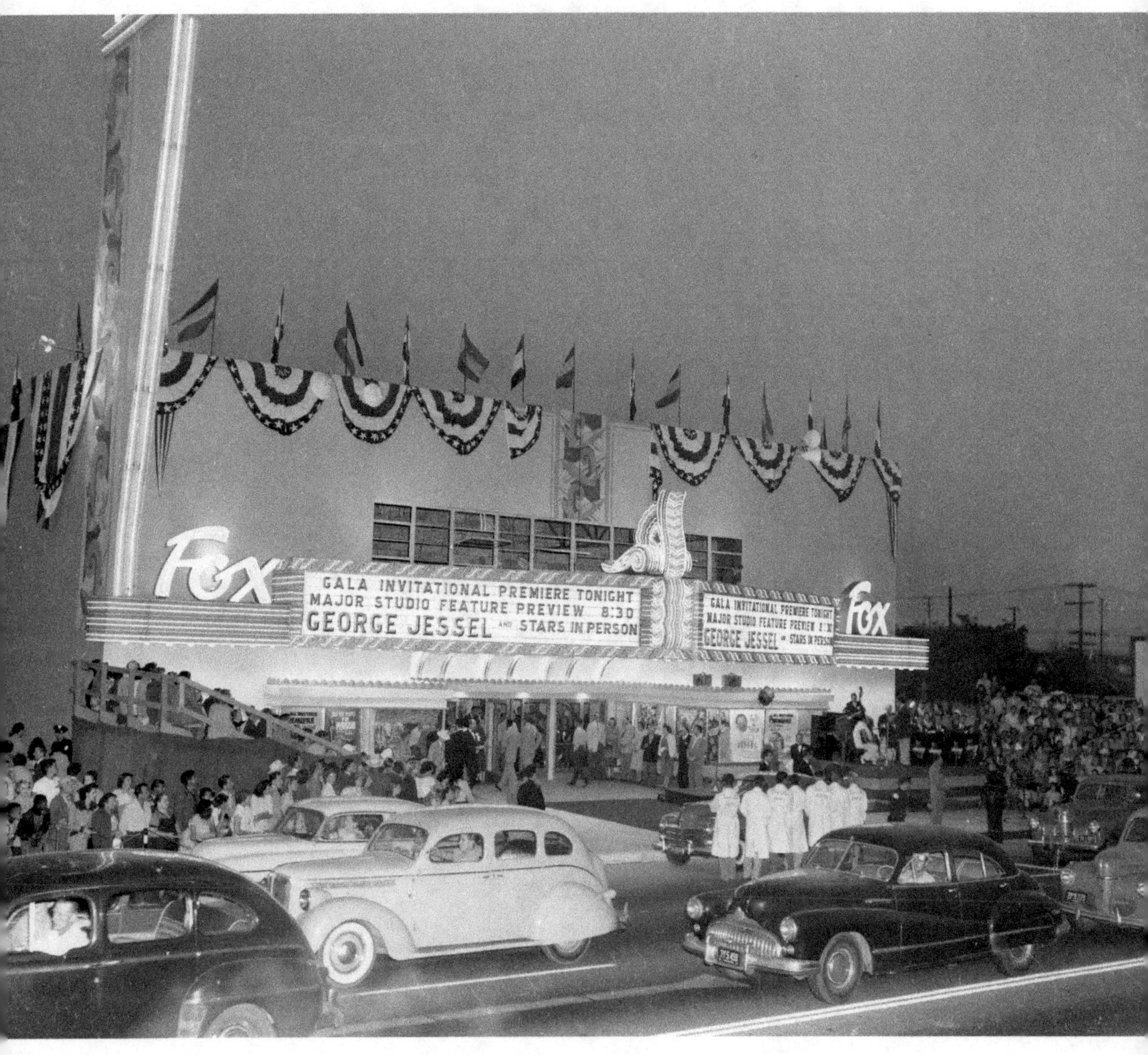

Above and opposite: Crowds gather under the neon of the Fox Venice Theatre for a film preview featuring George Jessel in person. (Circa 1940s, Ralph Morris and Security Pacific National Bank Collection)

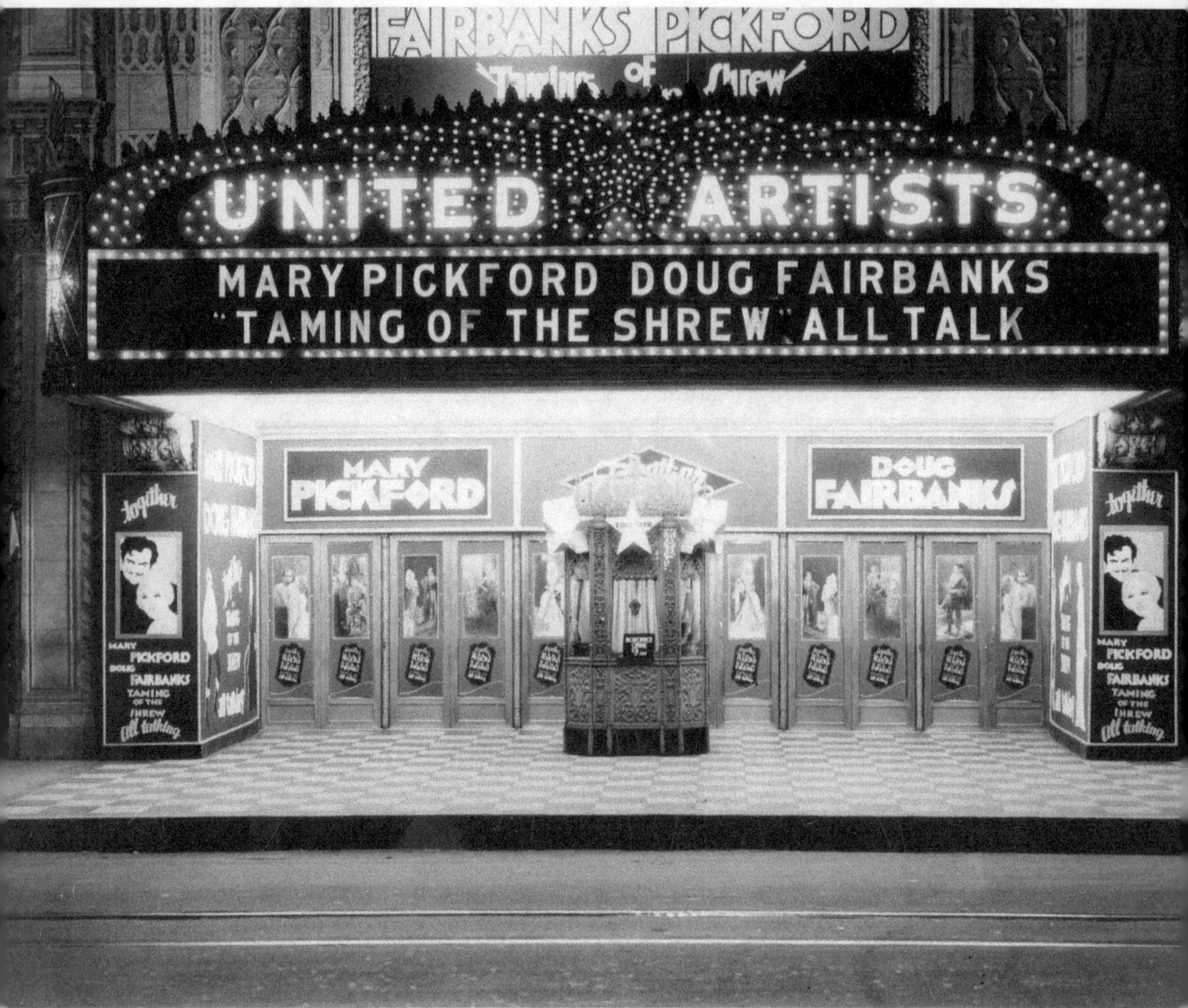

The entrance of the United Artists Theatre in Downtown Los Angeles lights up the many posters of Douglas Fairbanks and Mary Pickford. (1929, Security Pacific National Bank Collection)

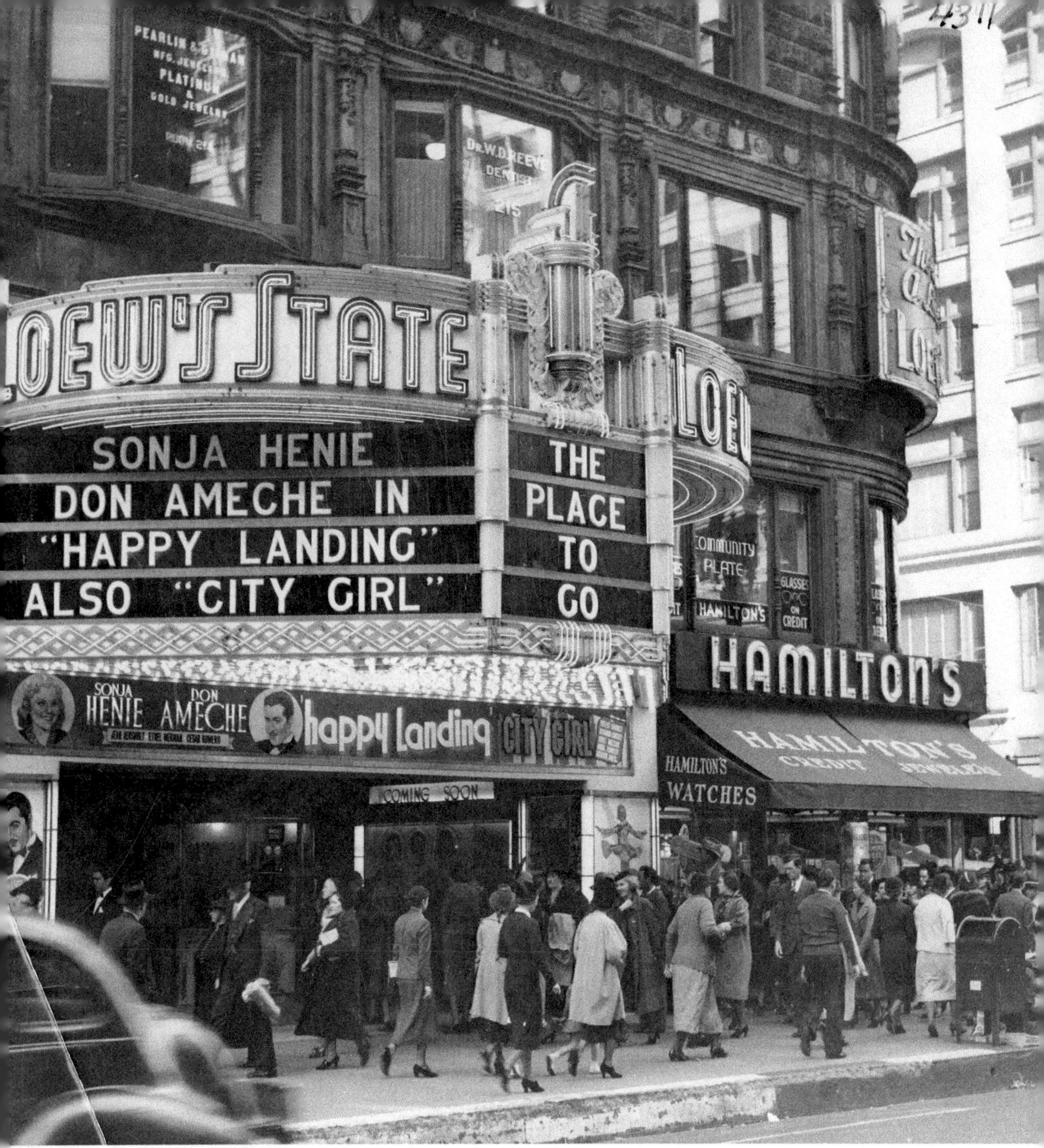

The corner of 7th Street and Broadway is dominated by the neon of Lowe's State Theatre and Hamilton's jewelers. (1938, Security Pacific National Bank Collection)

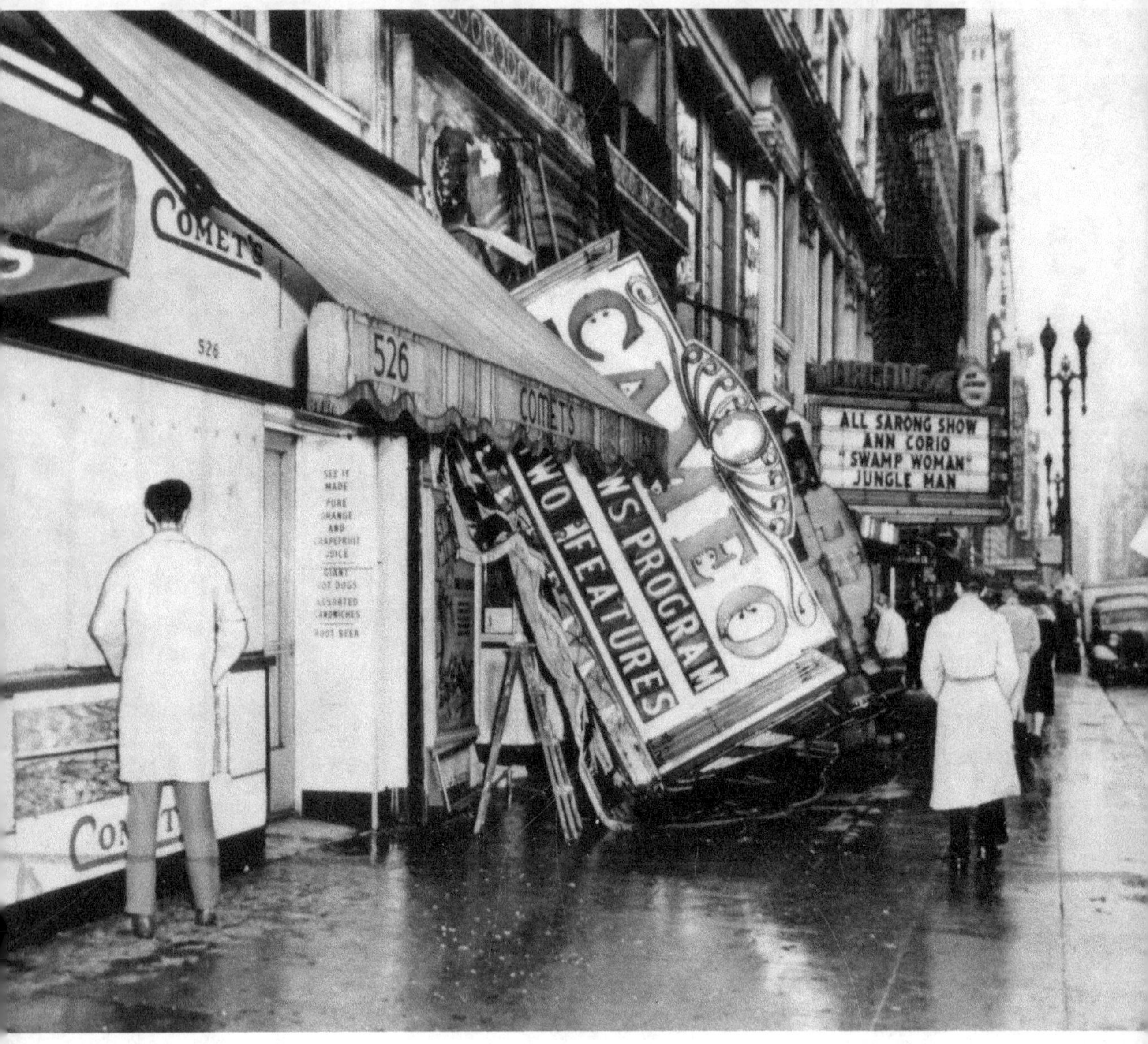

The neon-clad marquee of the Cameo Theatre is down but not out after falling off the building. (1941, Security Pacific National Bank Collection)

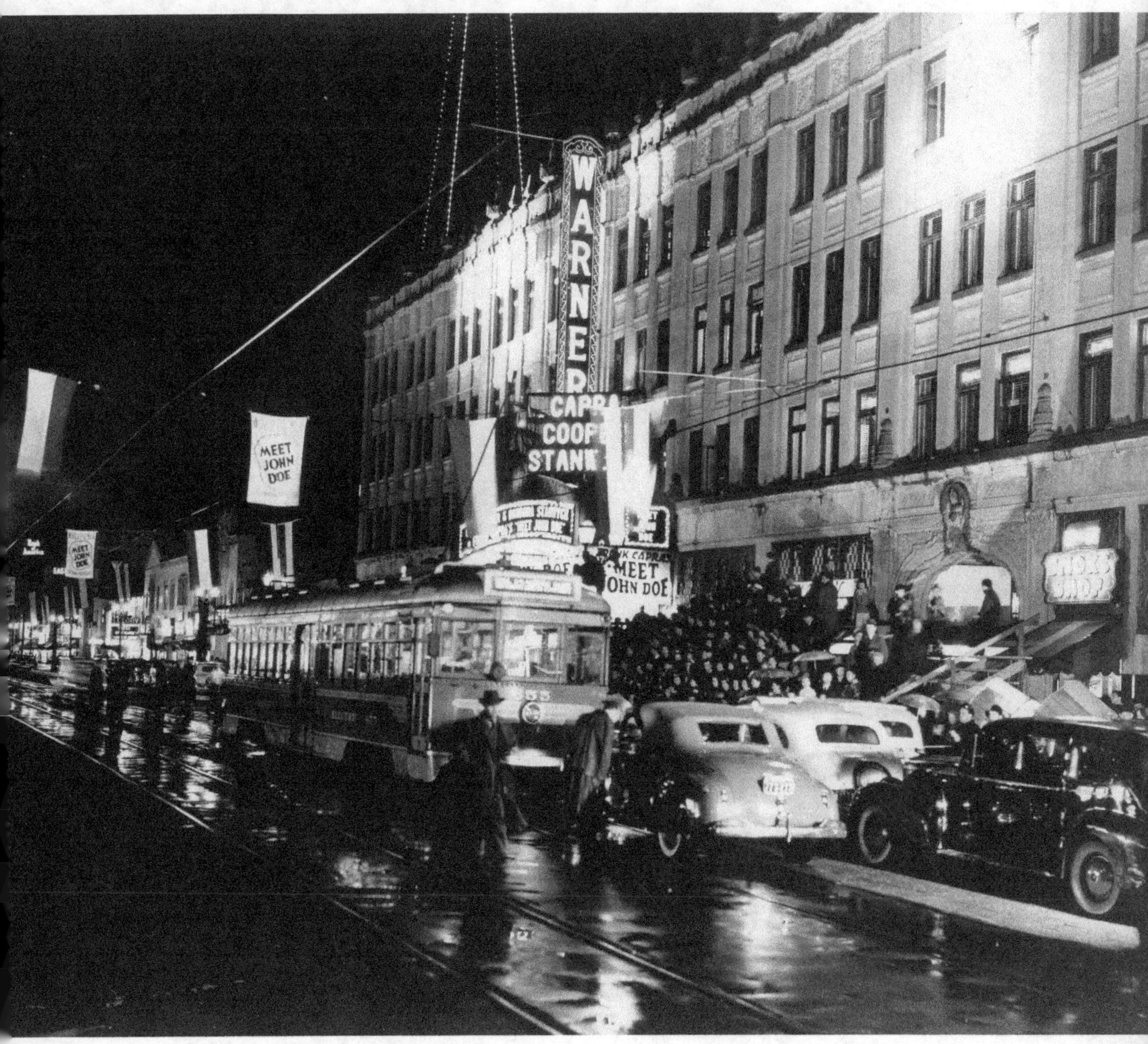

Neon on the Warner Bros. Hollywood Theatre advertises the premiere of *Meet John Doe* starring Gary Cooper and Barbara Stanwyck, directed by Frank Capra. (1941, Security Pacific National Bank Collection)

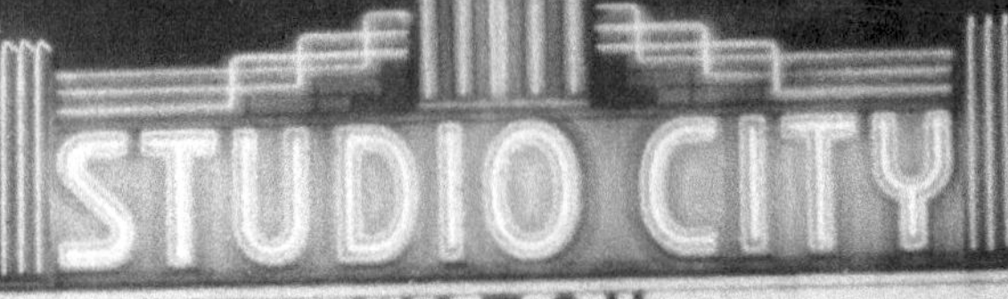
STUDIO
CITY
STUDIO CITY
WATCH
FOR OUR
OPENING DATE
WATCH
FOR OUR
GRAND
OPENING
STUDIO CITY
WATCH
FOR OUR
OPENING DATE
RETURN TO

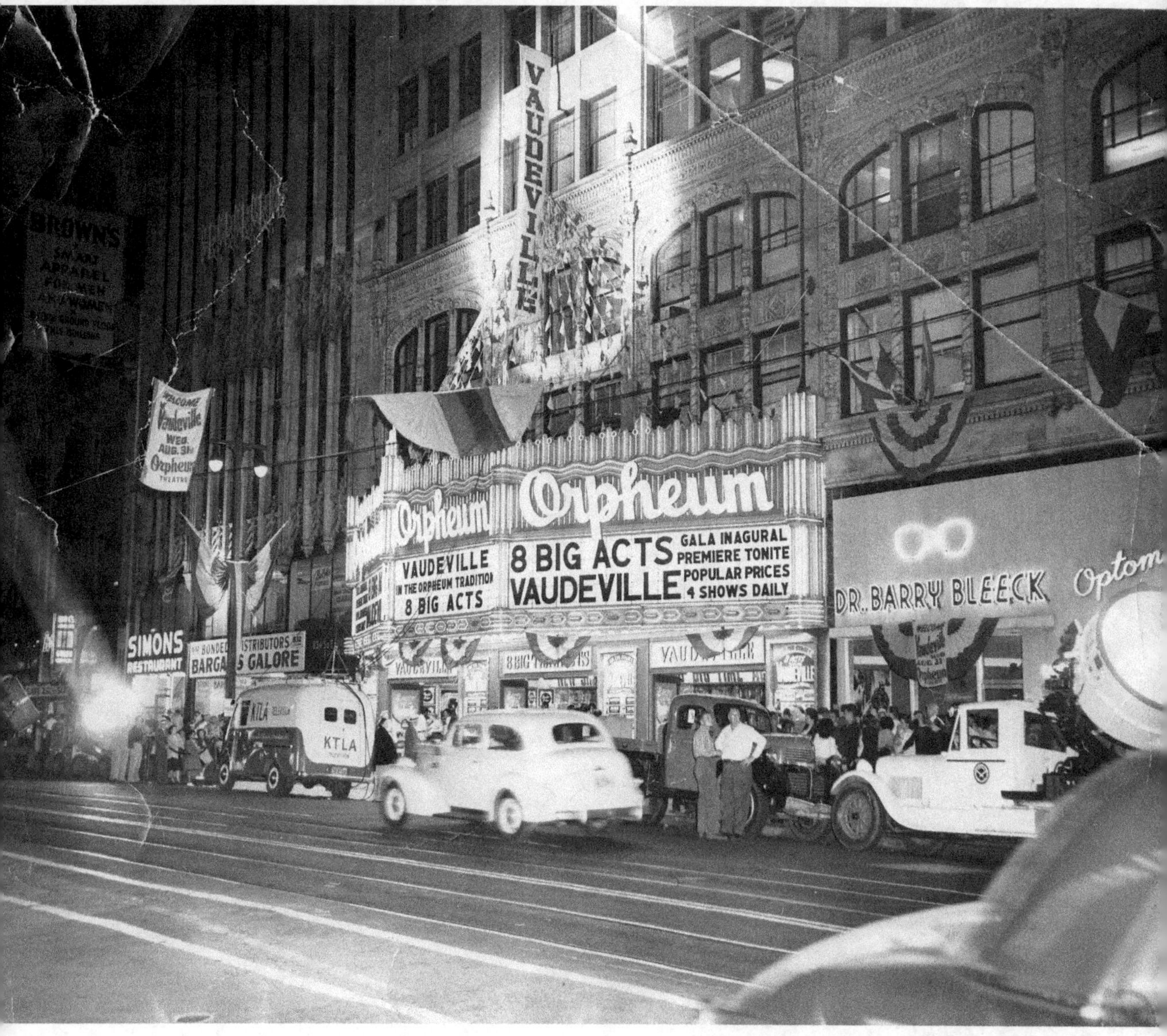

The elaborate neon on the marquee of the Orpheum Theatre in Downtown Los Angeles highlights the announcement that the theater is staying true to its vaudeville roots. (1949, Los Angeles Herald Examiner Collection)

Opposite: A neon marquee and tower are ready and waiting for the opening of the Studio City Theatre. (1938, Security Pacific National Bank Collection)

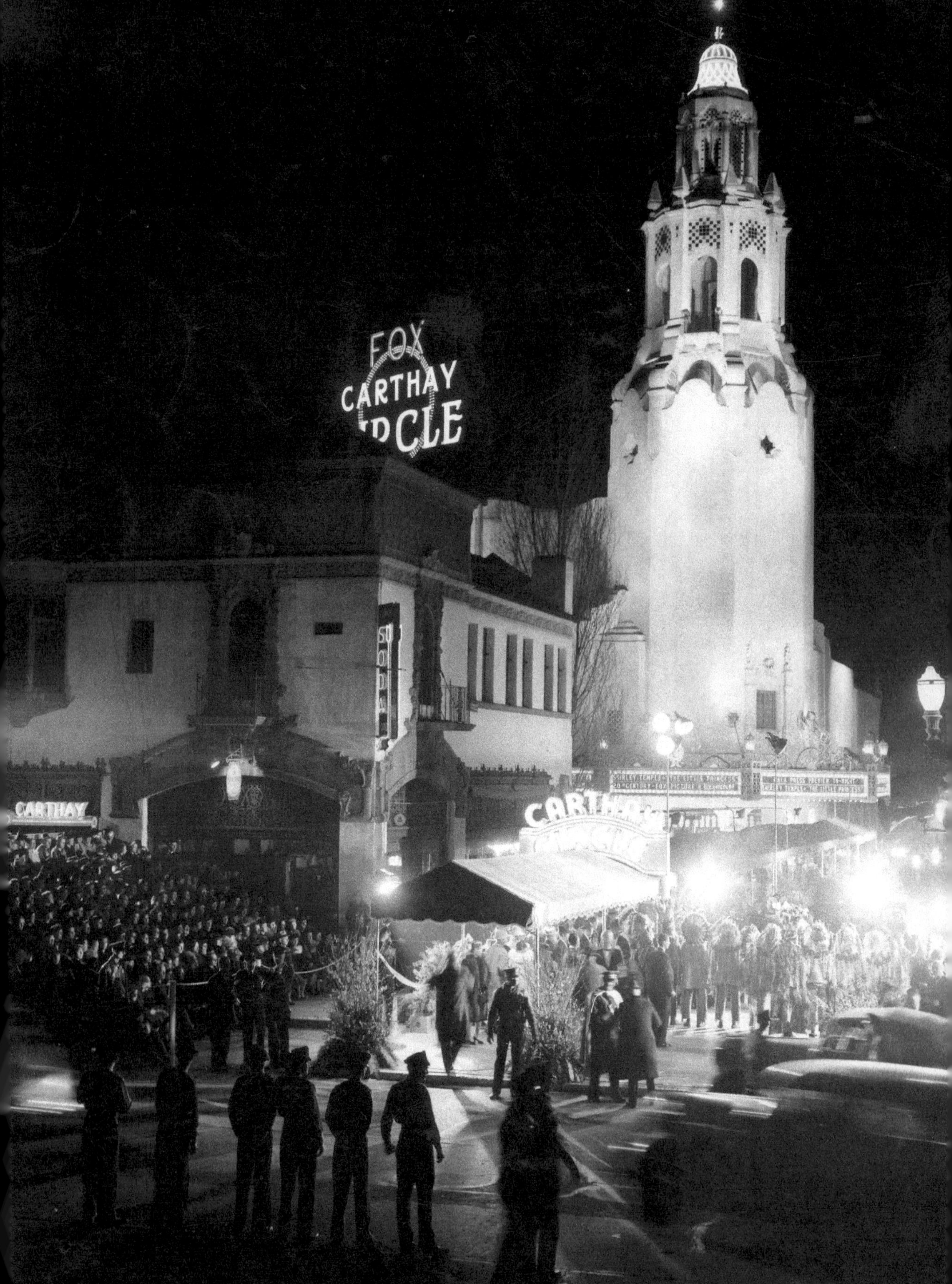
FOX
CARTHAY
SODA
CARTHAY

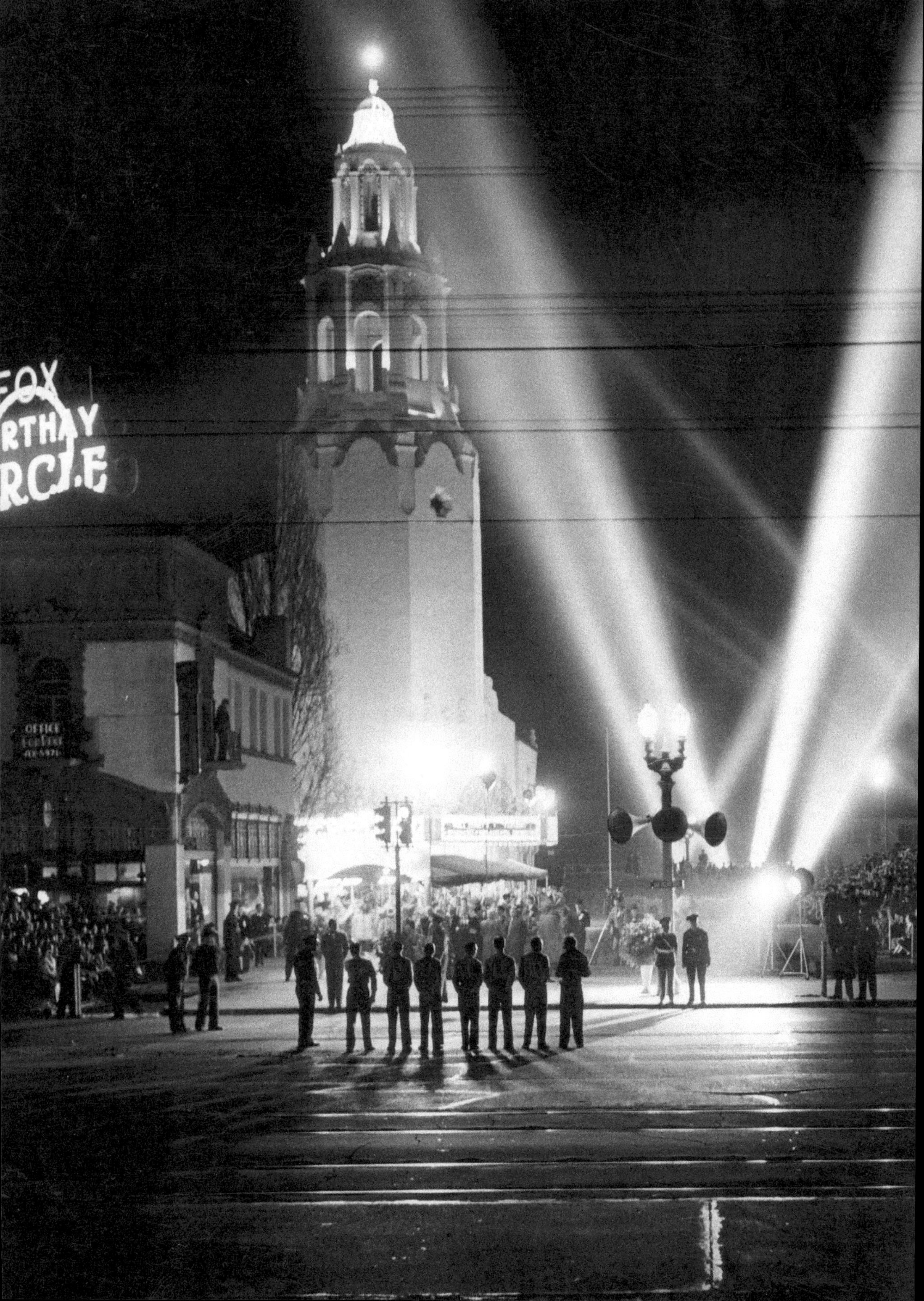
FOX
OFFICE

Page 184: Perhaps the most famous of Los Angeles' lost theaters is the Fox Carthay Circle, once located off of Wilshire Boulevard, west of Fairfax. The movie palace was dedicated to California history and was developed by J. Harvey McCarthy as the centerpiece to his Carthay residential neighborhood. Rivaling Grauman's Chinese Theatre in Hollywood, the Carthay Circle rolled out the red carpet and then some for gala, Klieg-lit movie premieres such as *Romeo and Juliet* (1936), *Snow White and the Seven Dwarfs* (1937), *Marie Antoinette* (1938), *Gone with the Wind* (1939), *Fantasia* (1940), and many more. The iconic theater was demolished in 1969. (1941, Los Angeles Herald Examiner Collection)

Page 185: Crowds gather beneath the numerous neon signs at the Carthay Circle Theatre for the press preview of *The Little Princess* starring Shirley Temple. (1939, Los Angeles Herald Examiner Collection)

Opposite: Tyrone Power and Sonia Henie are interviewed at the Carthay Circle Theatre before stepping underneath a neon arch to view the premiere of *Wee Willie Winkie* starring Shirley Temple. (1937, Los Angeles Herald Examiner Collection)

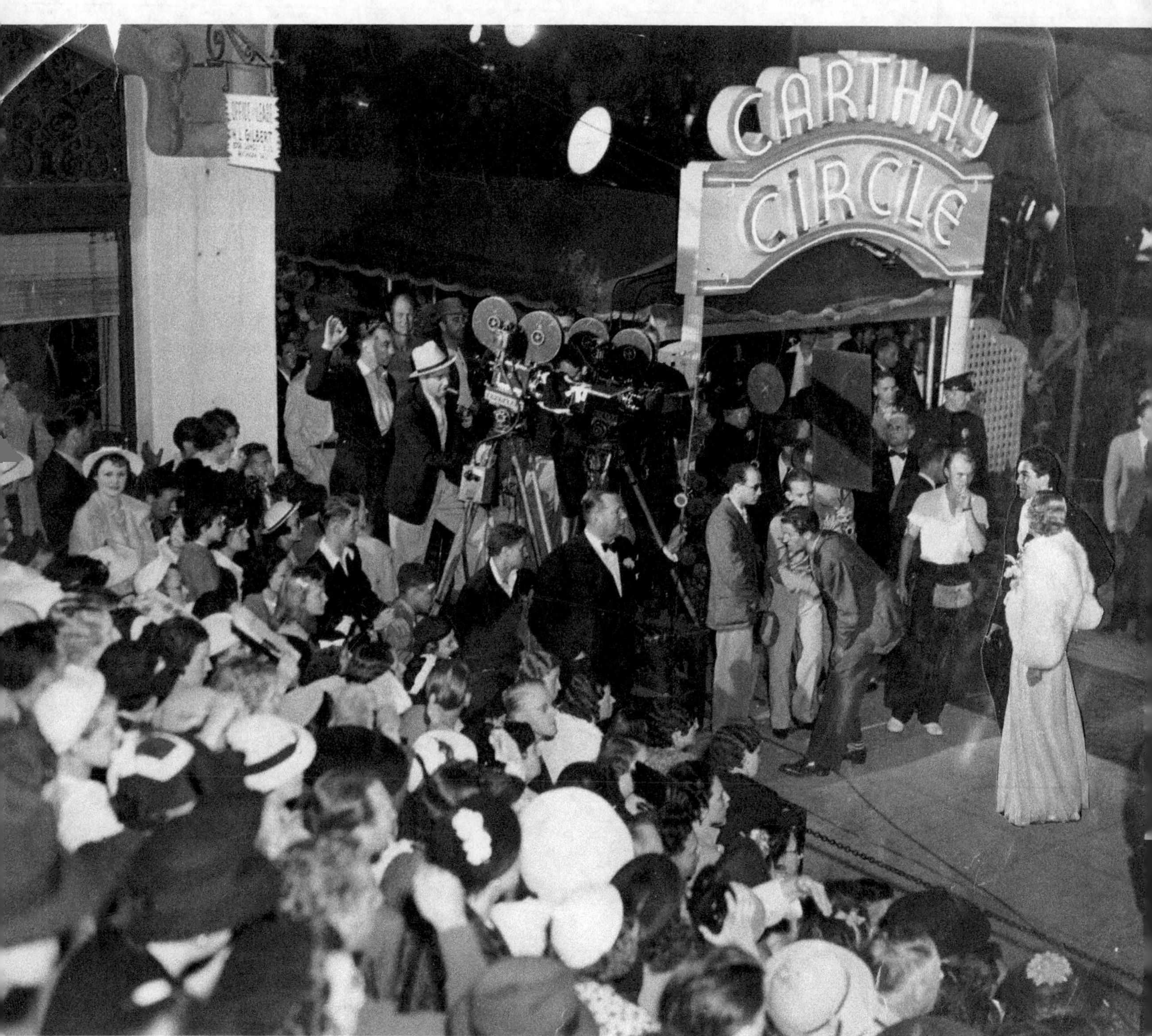
CARTHAY
CIRCLE

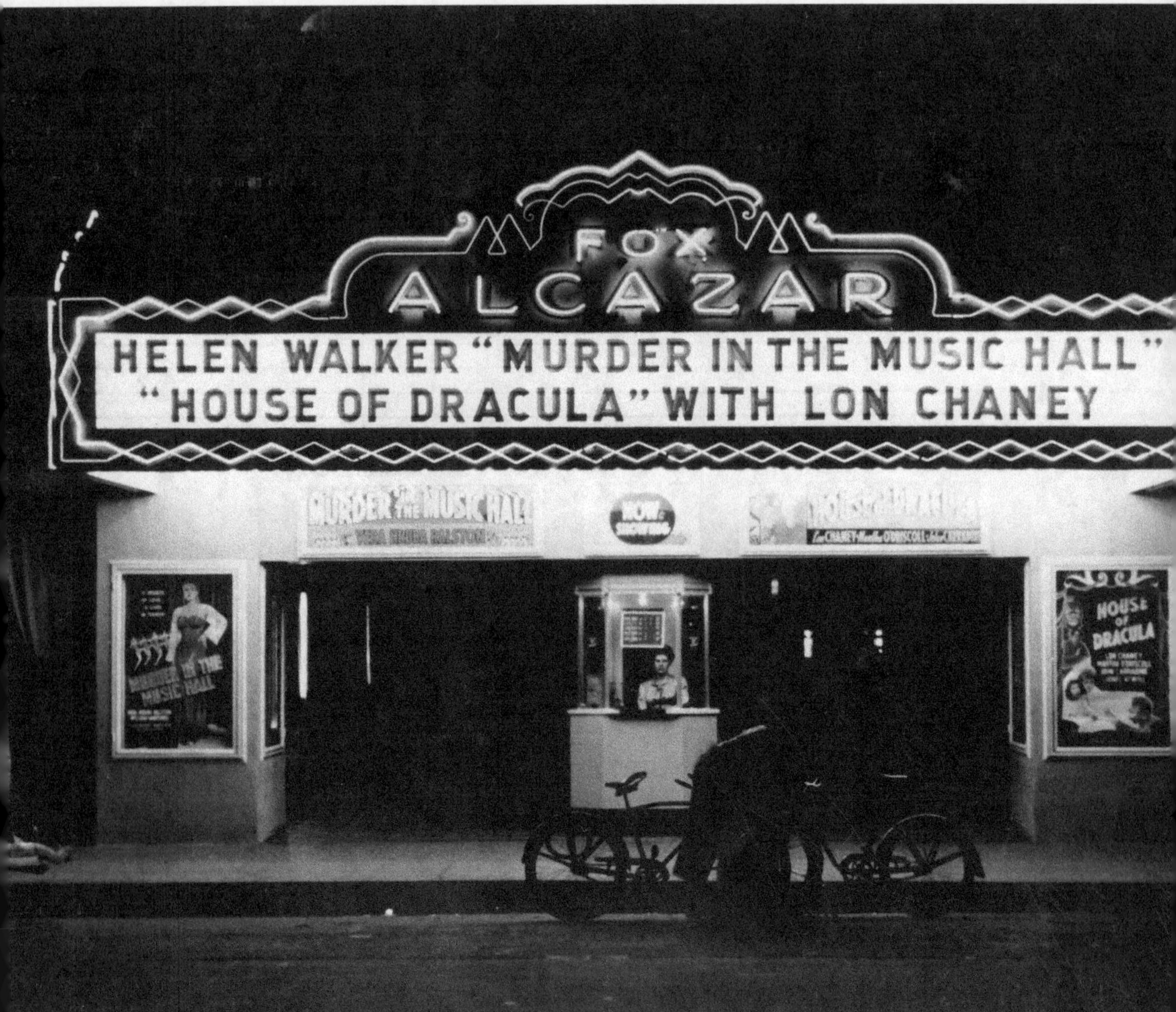
FOX
ALCAZAR
HELEN WALKER "MURDER IN THE MUSIC HALL"
"HOUSE OF DRACULA" WITH LON CHANEY
MURDER IN THE MUSIC HALL
NOW SHOWING
MURDER IN THE MUSIC HALL
HOUSE OF DRACULA

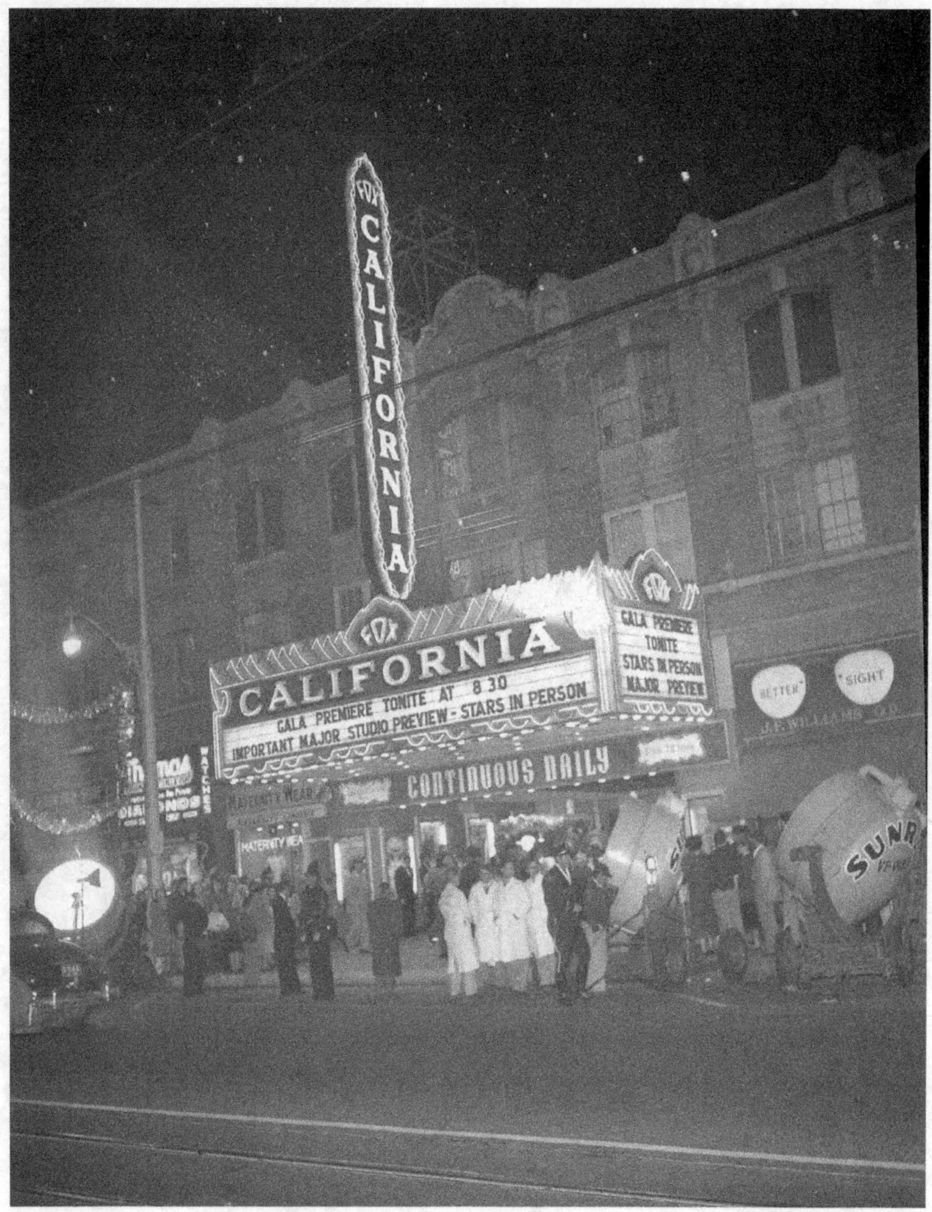

Above, opposite, and pages 190-192: Neon was a staple in urban entertainment districts as well as in smaller communities as exemplified by the Alcazar and Alpha Theatres in the city of Bell, the California Theatre in Huntington Park, the Bijou in Hermosa Beach, and the Tracy in Long Beach. (Security Pacific National Bank Collection & Ralph Morris Collections)

THEATRE
HERMOSA
HERMOSA
GARY COOPER IN
"MARCO POLO" ALSO
DAREDEVIL DRIVERS
GARY COOPER
SIGRID GURIE
BASIL RATHBONE

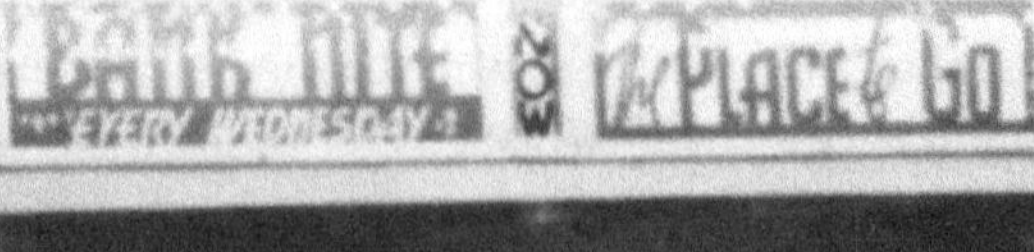
BANK NITE
EVERY WEDNESDAY
NOW
the PLACE to GO

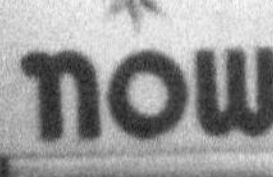
now

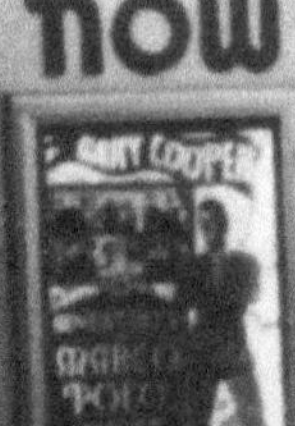
GARY COOPER
MARCO POLO

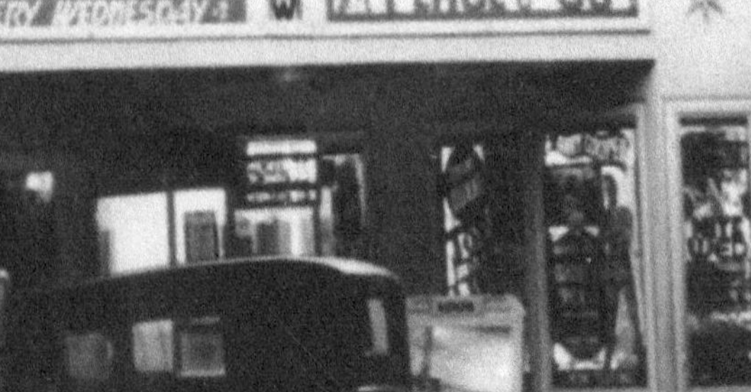

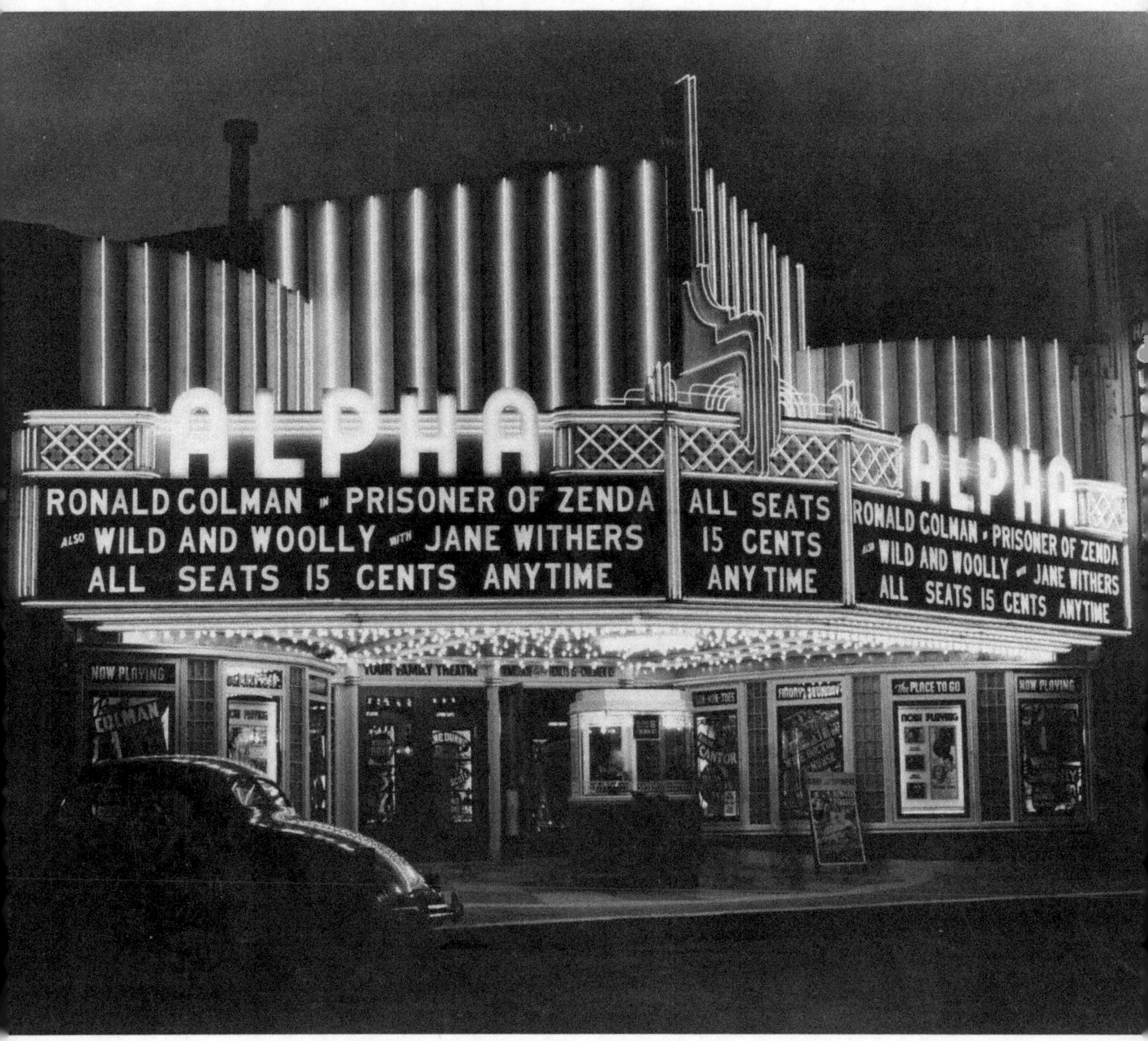
ALPHA
RONALD COLMAN IN PRISONER OF ZENDA
ALSO WILD AND WOOLLY WITH JANE WITHERS
ALL SEATS 15 CENTS ANYTIME
ALL SEATS
15 CENTS
ANY TIME
ALPHA
RONALD COLMAN IN PRISONER OF ZENDA
ALSO WILD AND WOOLLY WITH JANE WITHERS
ALL SEATS 15 CENTS ANYTIME
NOW PLAYING
COLMAN
YOUR FAMILY THEATRE
FRIDAY SATURDAY
The PLACE TO GO
NOW PLAYING
NOW PLAYING
CANTOR

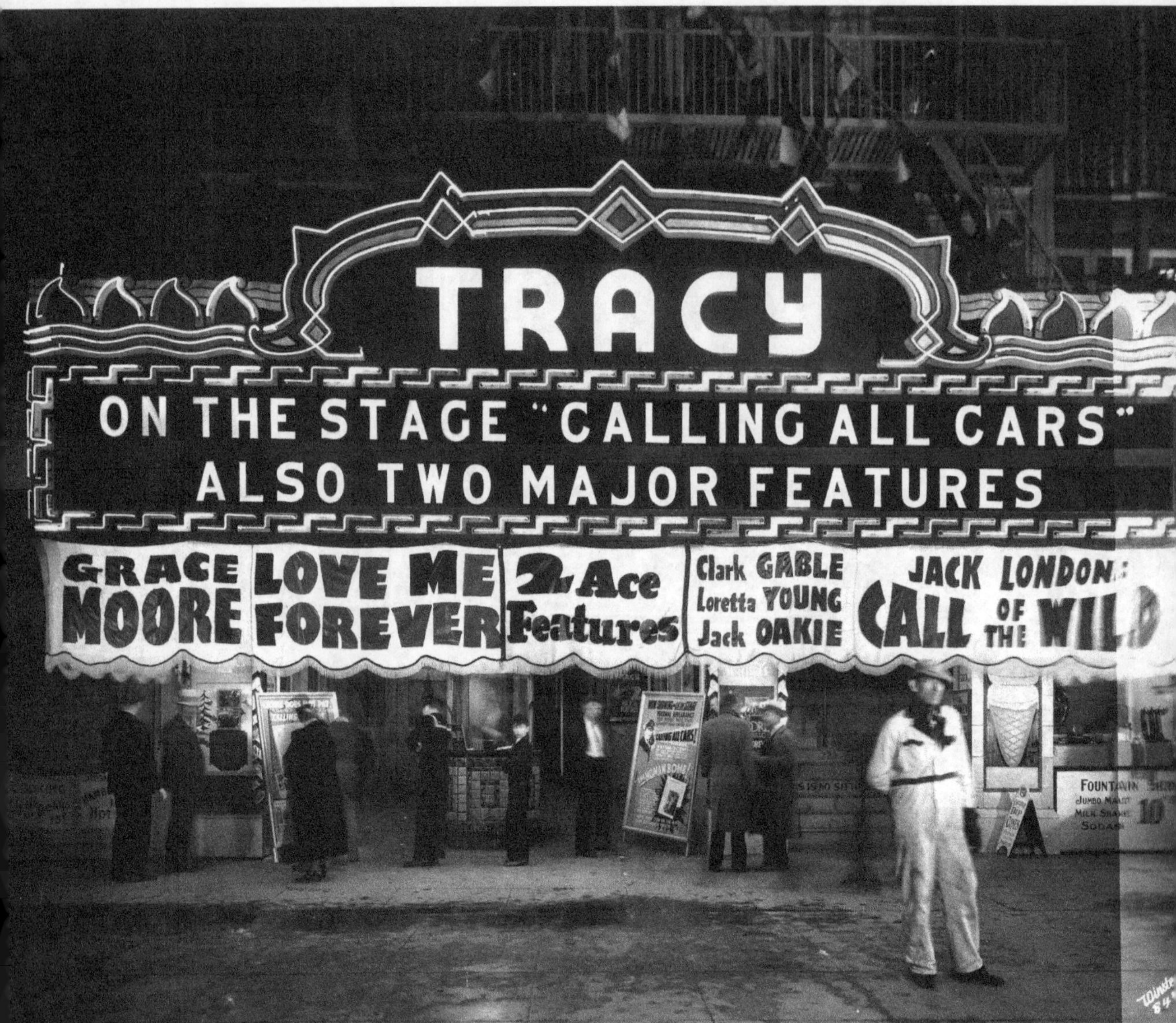

Opposite: Don Nakagiri, the former manager of the Palms Theatre poses below the neon marquee. (1985, Chris Gulker/Los Angeles Herald Examiner Collection)

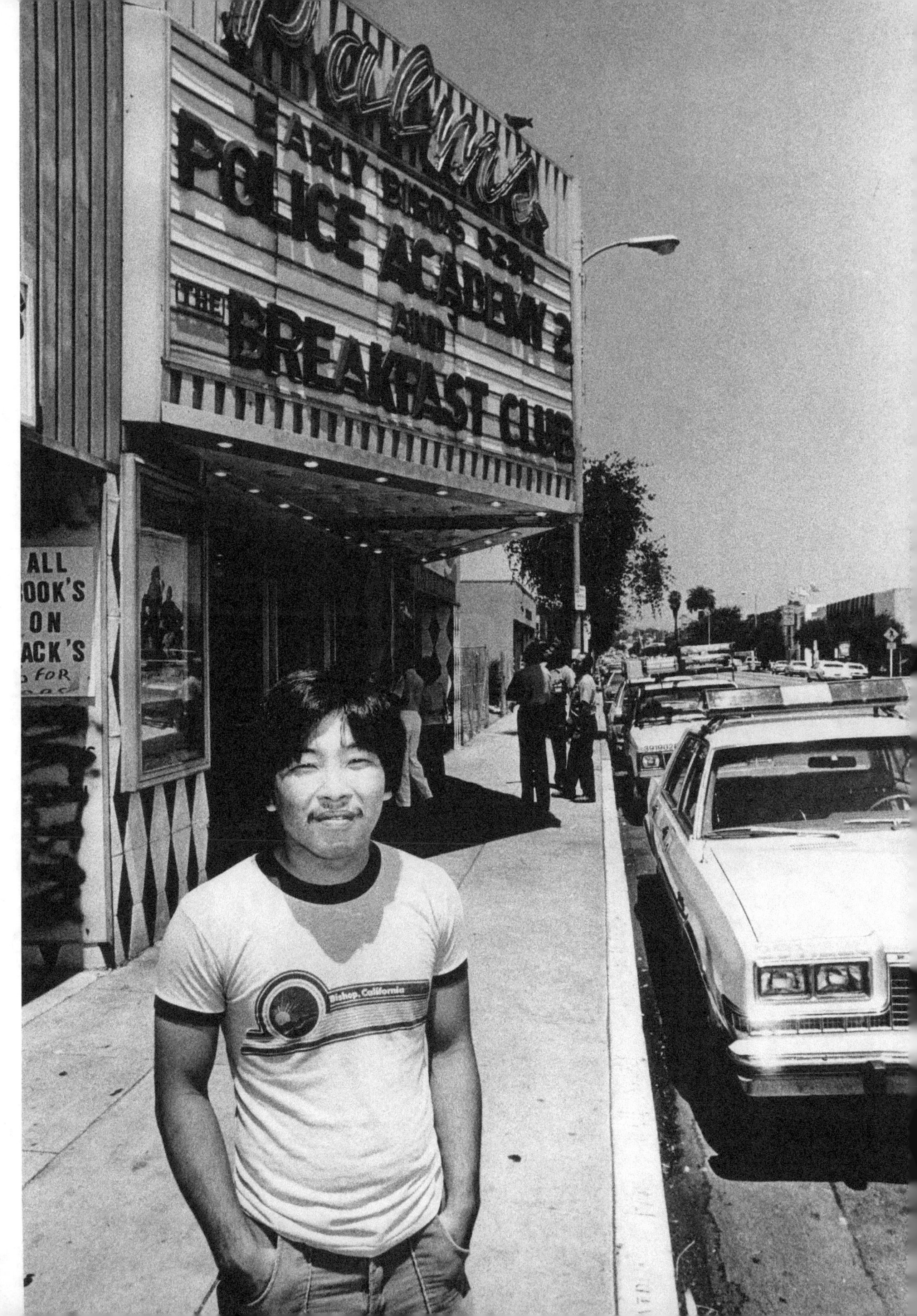
EARLY BIRDS
POLICE ACADEMY 2
AND
THE BREAKFAST CLUB
ALL
ON

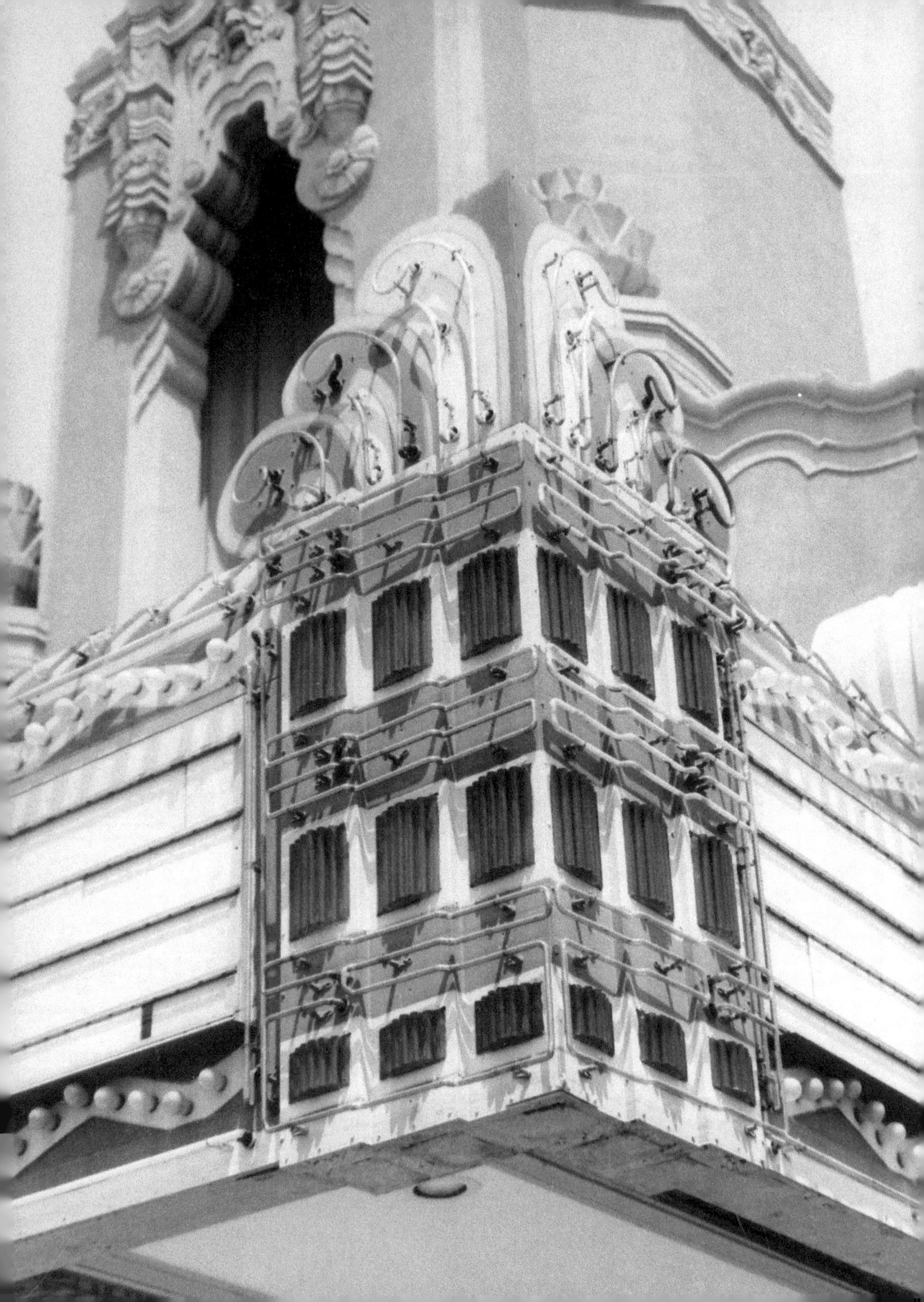

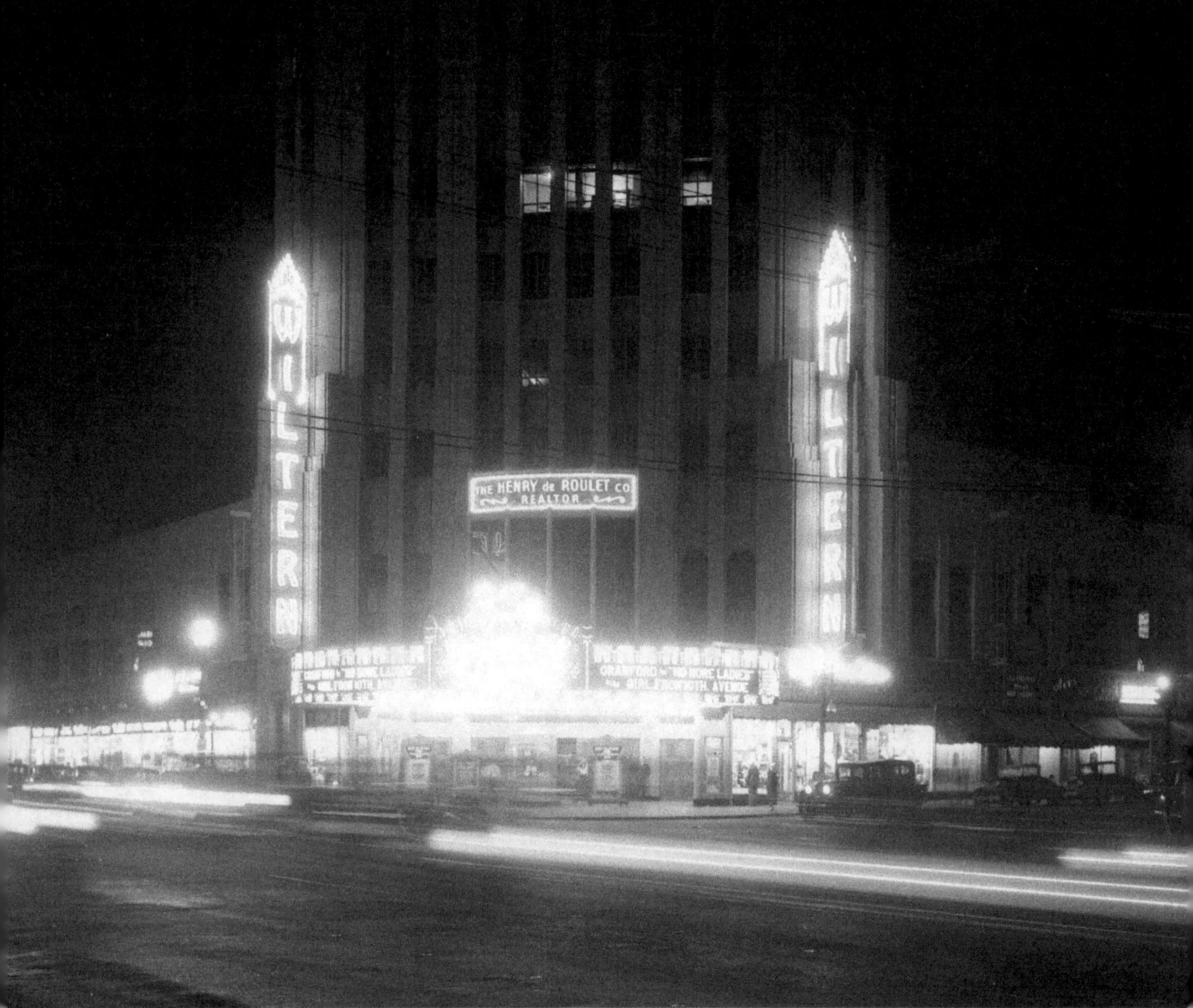

Among the most beautiful Art Deco theaters in the United States, the Wiltern is a survivor that nearly didn't succeed. Upon its debut in 1931 as the Warner Bros. Theatre, the nation was hit by the Great Depression and the neon-lit movie palace shut its doors. By 1935, the Warner Bros. name was dropped and the hyphenated Wil-Tern (Wilshire-Western) name adopted along with a twenty-five cent ticket price to reinvigorate the space. A beacon in the darkness, the twin Wiltern vertical signs remain, but lost are the rearrangeable neon letters for the theater's semi-circular marquee. (1935, Blackstock Negative Collection)

Opposite: Theater marquees could contain elaborate neon designs as indicated in this detailed view of the Leimert Theatre on 43rd Place. (1968, Security Pacific National Bank Collection)

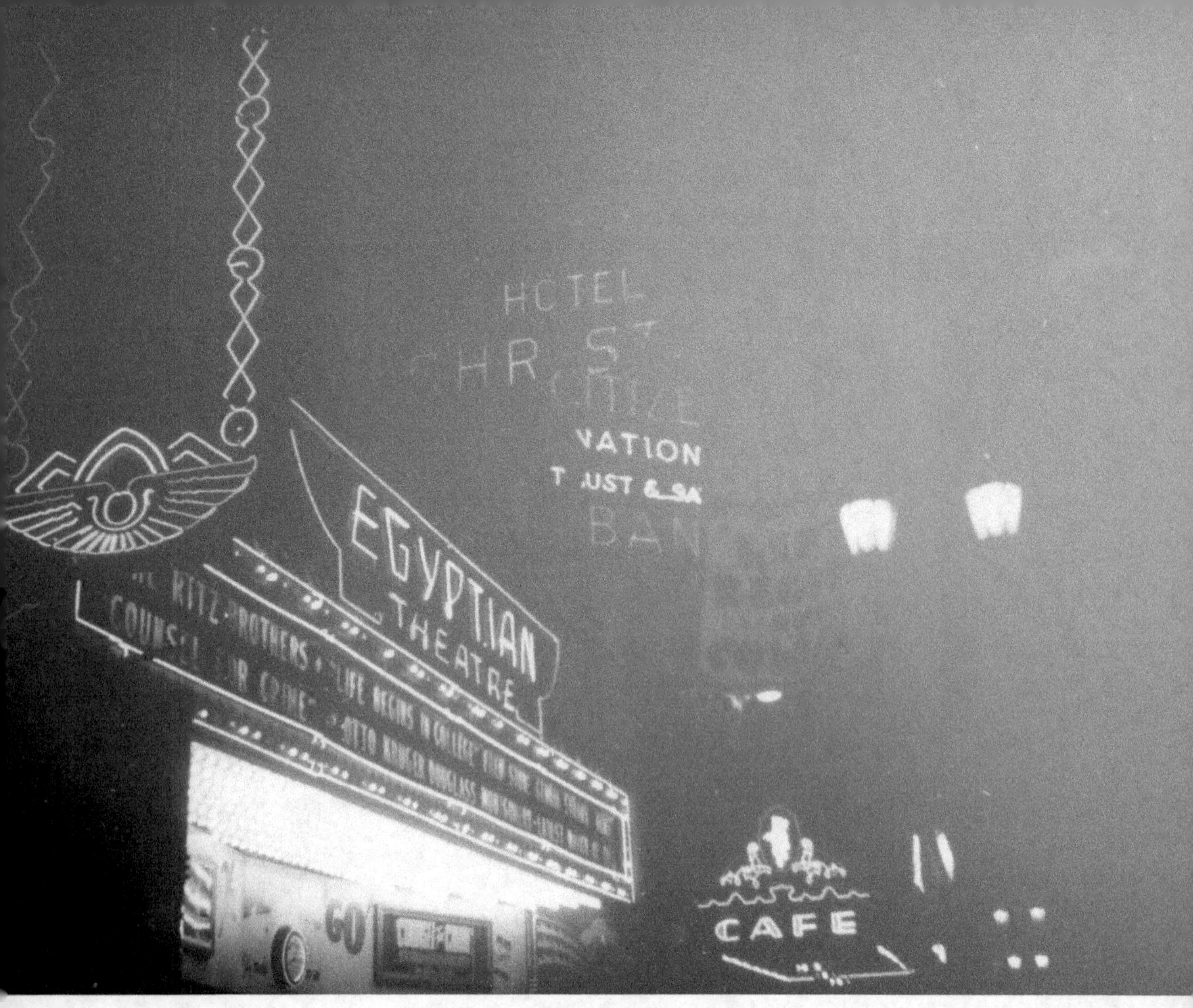

The neon lights blaze in this night shot of Hollywood Boulevard, which includes the Egyptian Theatre, The Pig and Whistle Cafe, the Hotel Christie, and the Citizens Bank. (1937, Herman J. Schultheis Collection)

Opposite: The Mason Opera House on Broadway found later success as a Spanish-language cinema as indicated in the neon signage above the marquee.
(Circa 1950, Julian Mitchell/Shades of L.A. Collection)

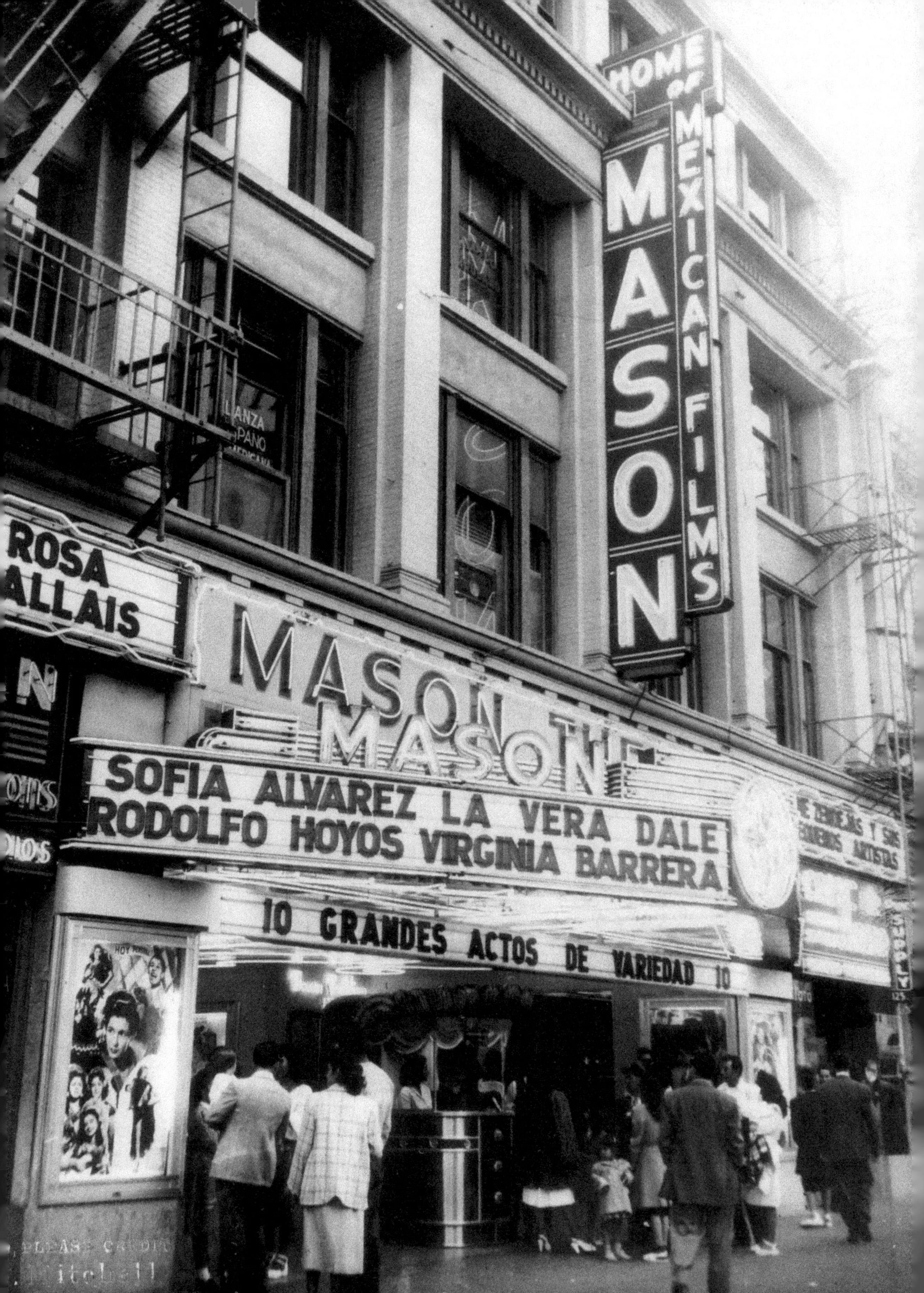
HOME of MEXICAN FILMS
MASON
ROSA
ALLAIS
MASON
MASON
SOFIA ALVAREZ LA VERA DALE
RODOLFO HOYOS VIRGINIA BARRERA
10 GRANDES ACTOS DE VARIEDAD 10
PLEASE CREDIT

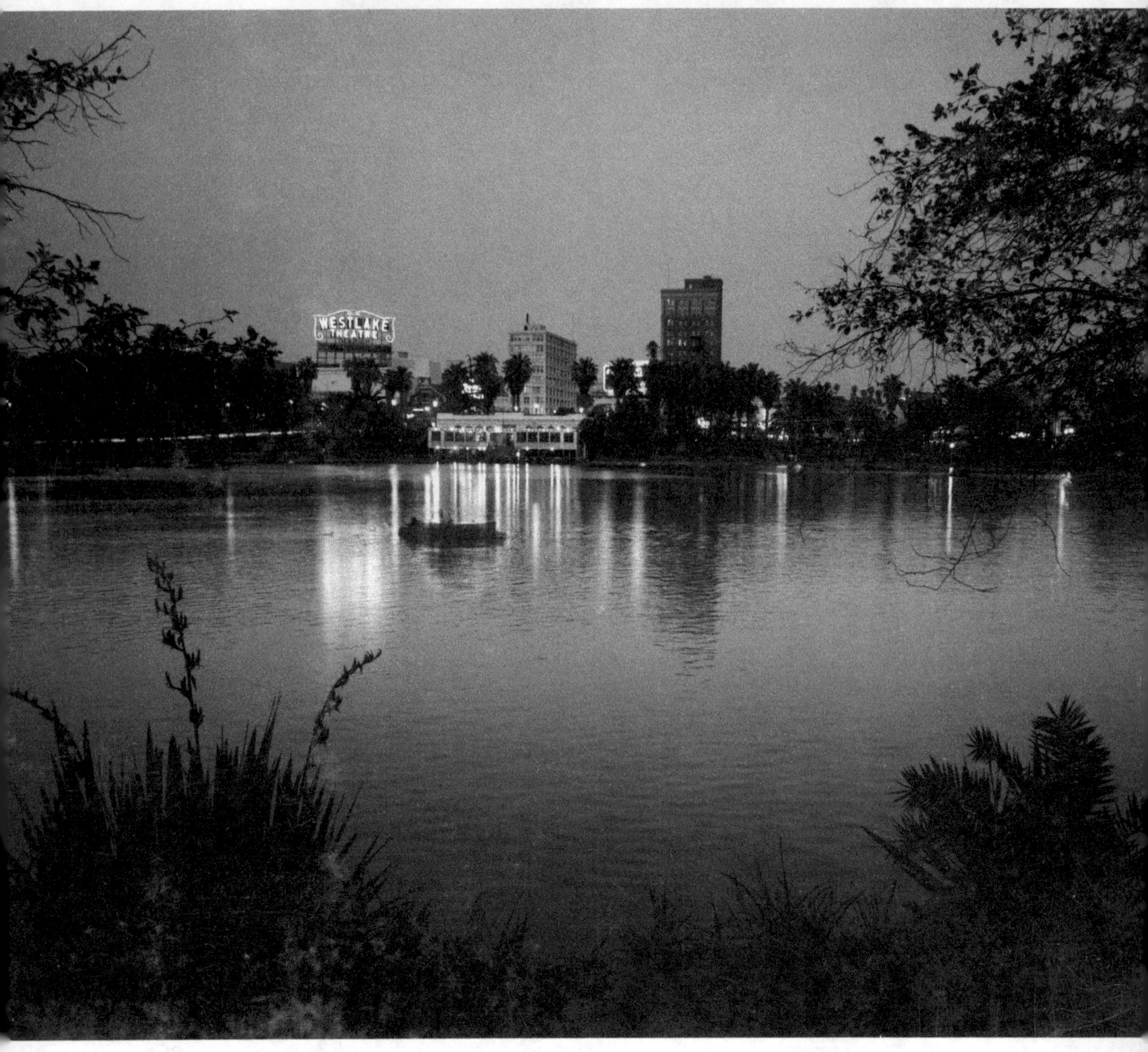
WESTLAKE
THEATRE

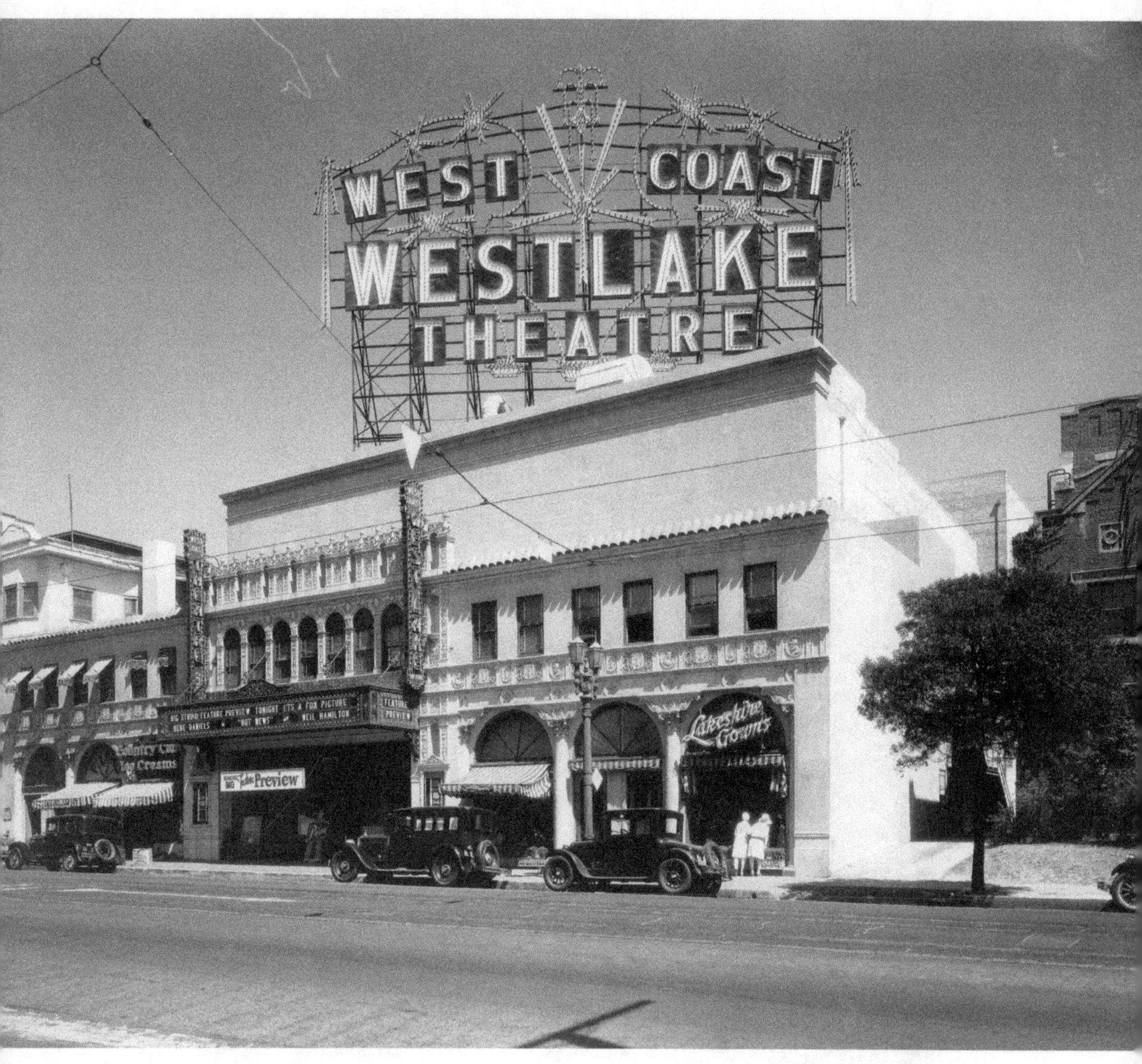

Above and opposite: The rooftop sign of the Westlake Theatre is visible for miles. (Security Pacific National Bank Collection)

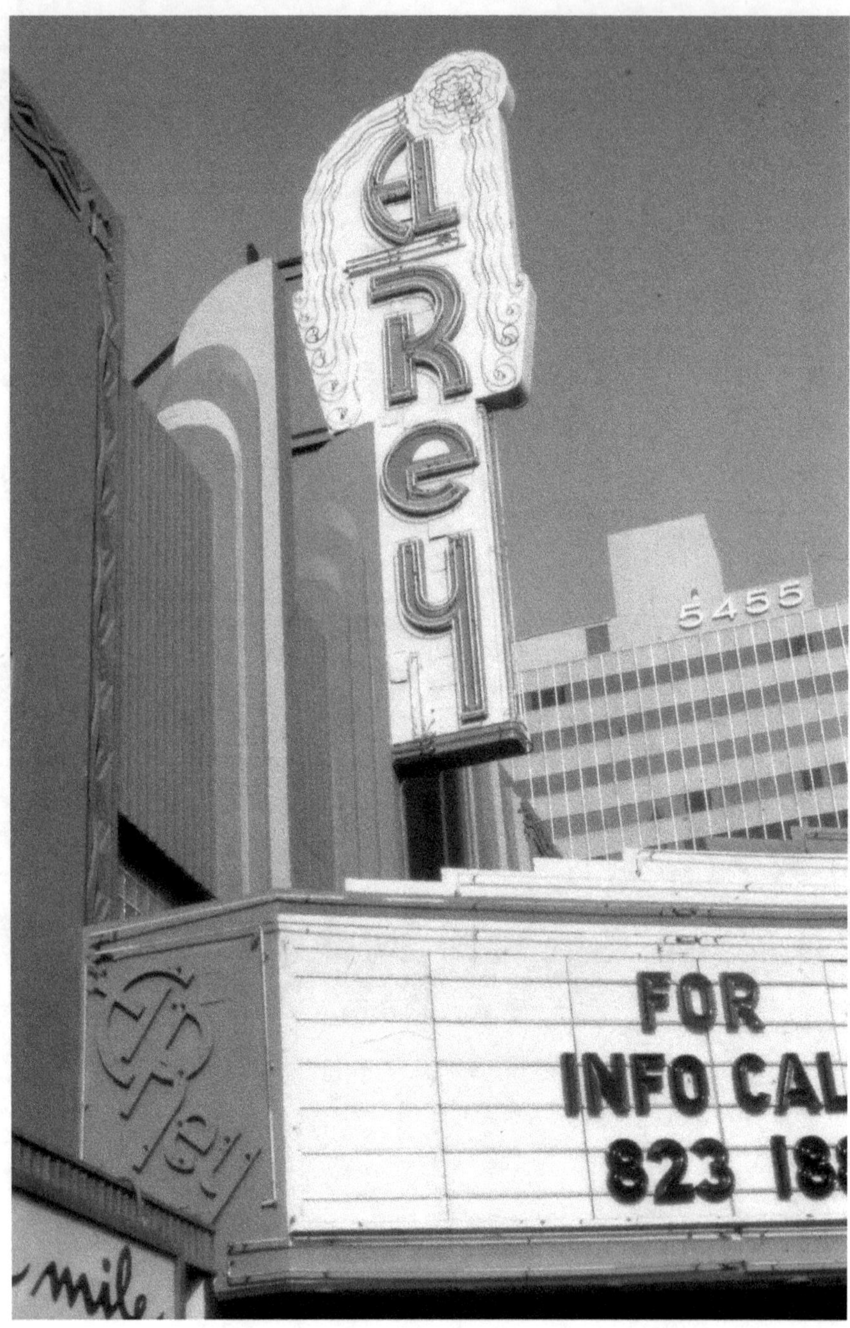

Above and opposite: The neon sign of the marquee shown in the 1970s and the 2000s. (1978, Anne Laskey/Marlene Laskey Collection; circa 2000, Robert Pacheco/Los Angeles Neighborhoods Collection)

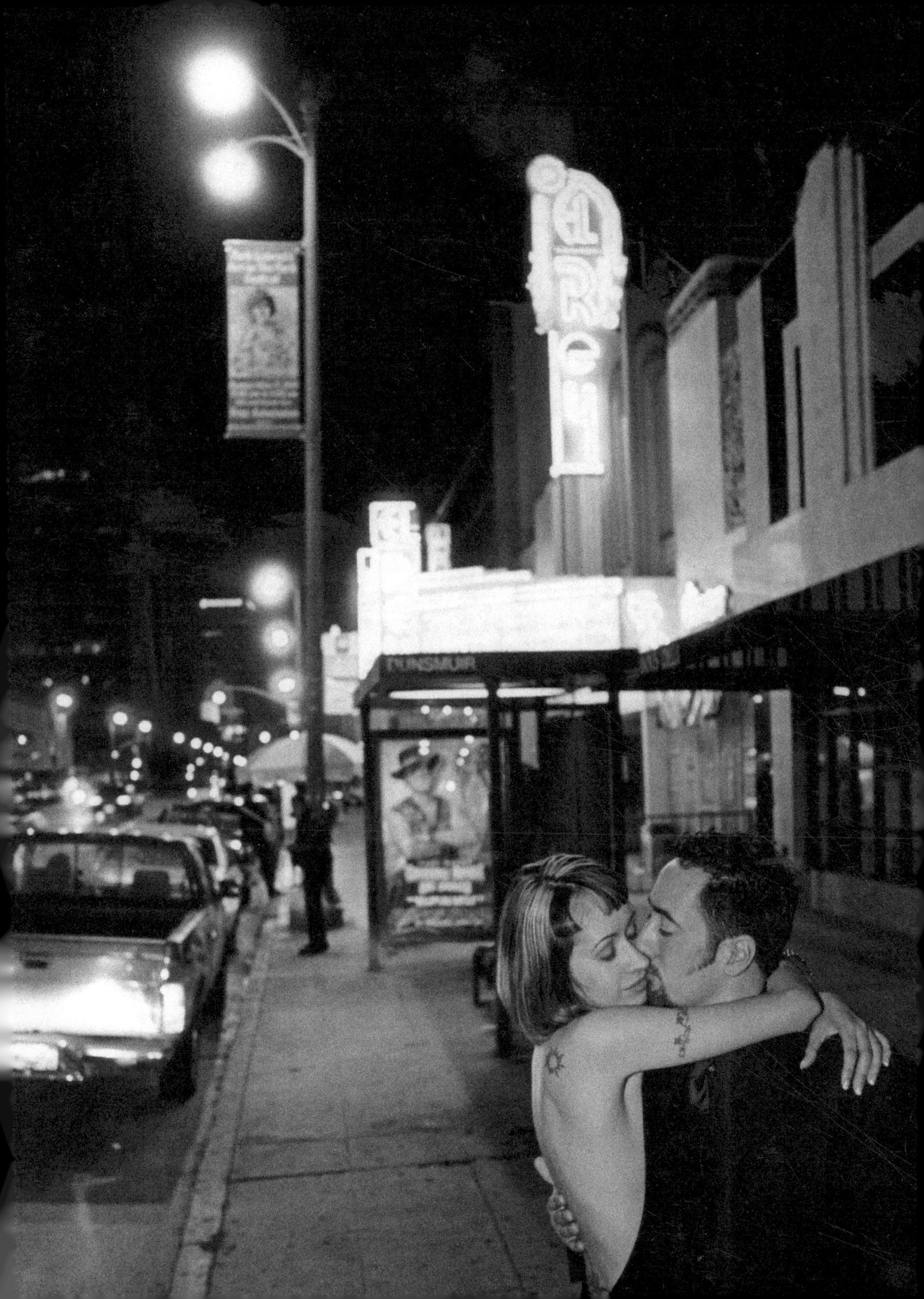

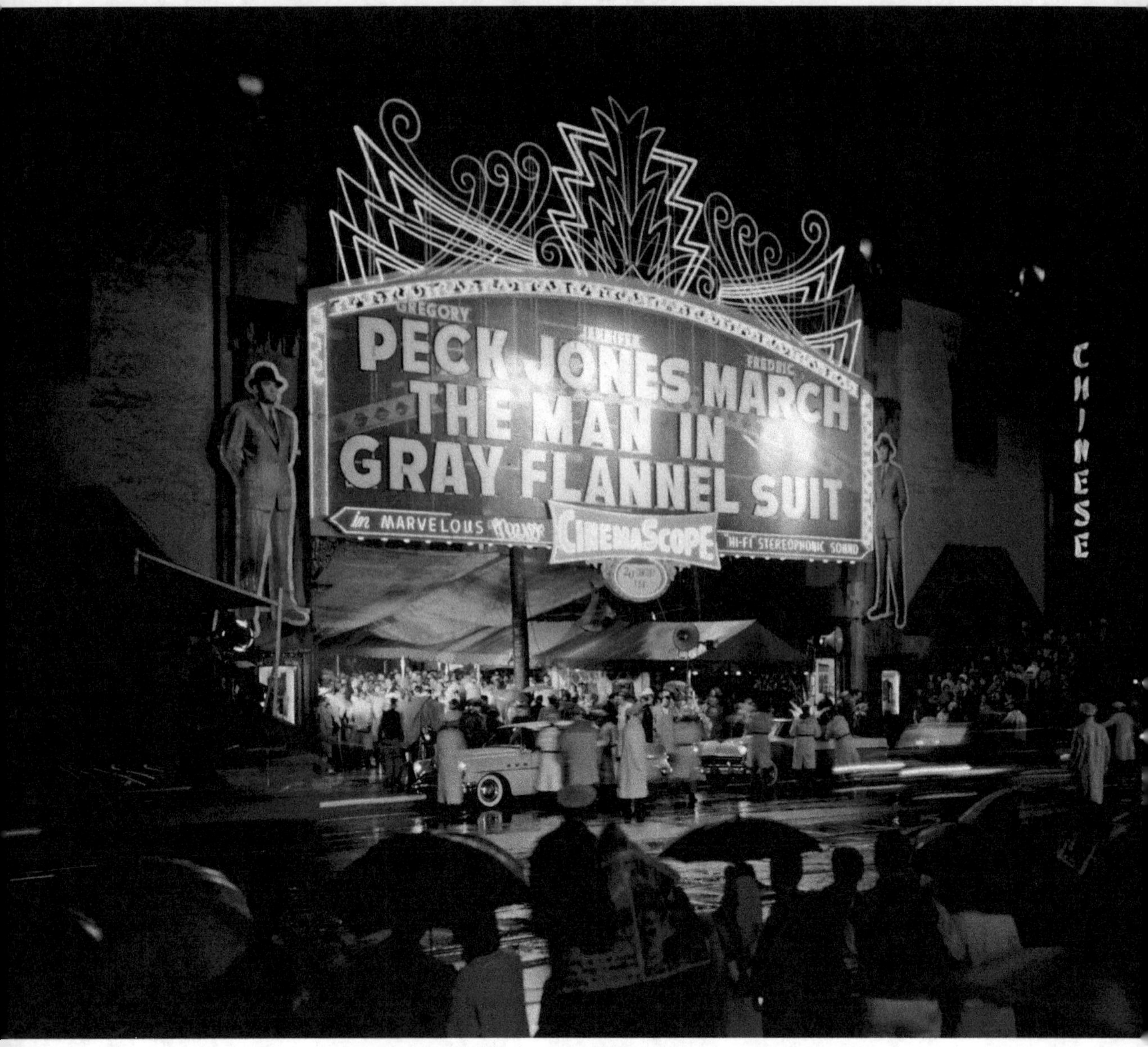
GREGORY
PECK JONES
FREDRIC
MARCH
THE MAN IN
GRAY FLANNEL SUIT
in MARVELOUS
CINEMASCOPE
HI-FI STEREOPHONIC SOUND
CHINESE

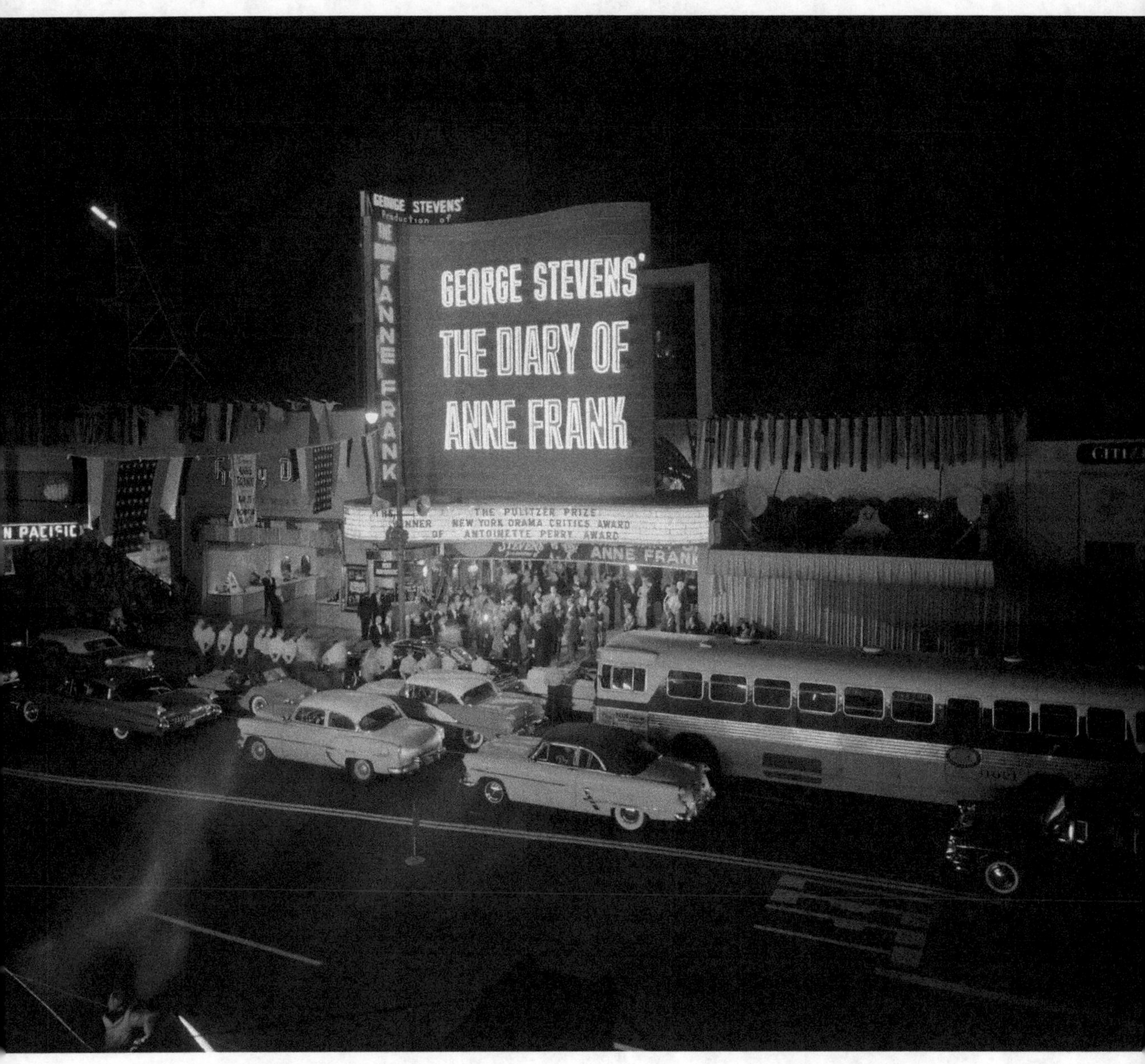

Above, opposite, and page 204: Thirty years after their construction, the Chinese and Egyptian Theatres were obscured by enormous neon billboards designed to promote an ever-growing list of premieres on Hollywood Boulevard. Movies were competing against home television sets and the scale and promotion of the movies got larger and larger – bigger than the movie palaces themselves. (1956 & 1959, Sid Avery Collection)

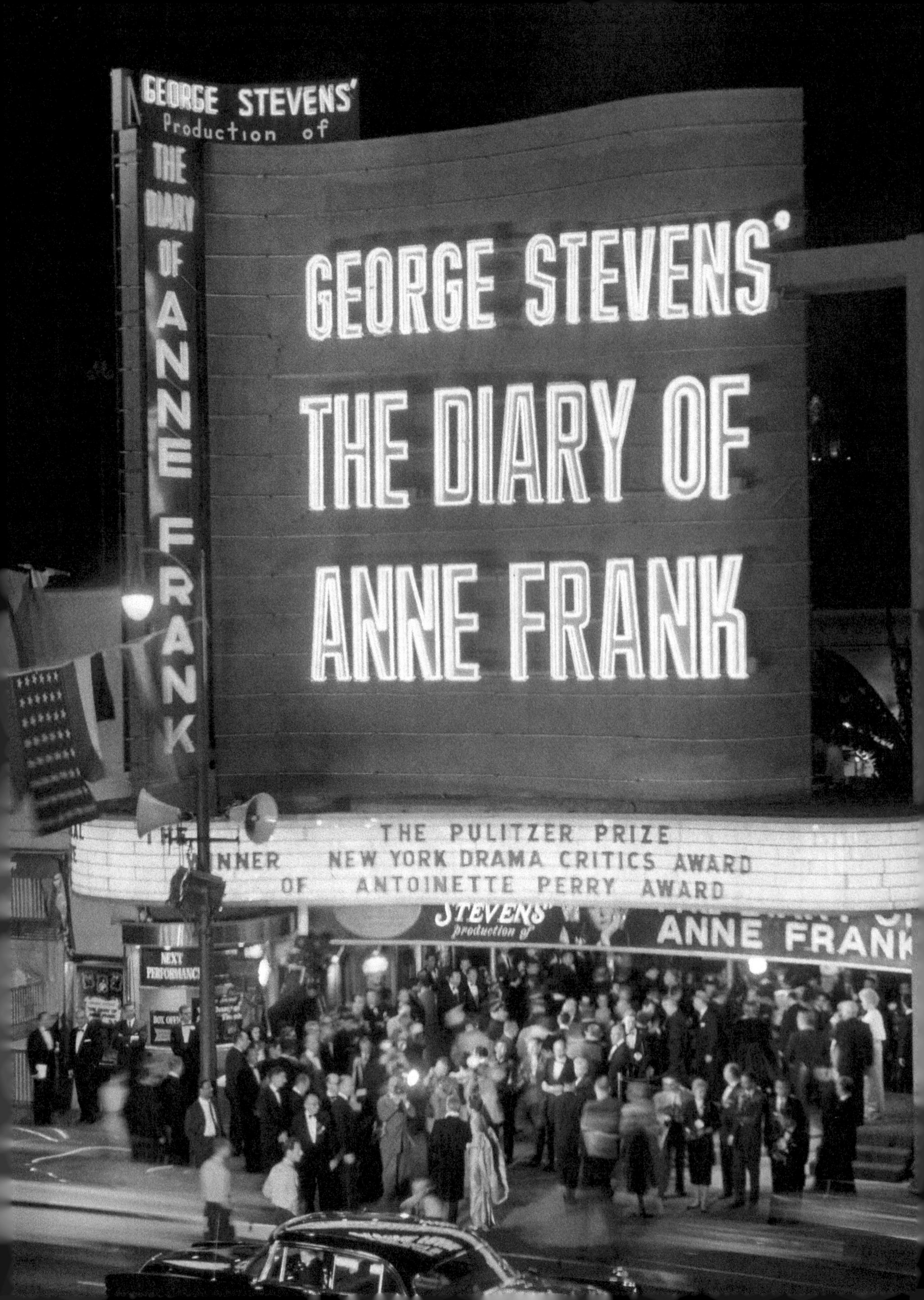

GEORGE STEVENS'
Production of
THE DIARY OF ANNE FRANK
GEORGE STEVENS'
THE DIARY OF
ANNE FRANK
THE PULITZER PRIZE
NEW YORK DRAMA CRITICS AWARD
ANTOINETTE PERRY AWARD
STEVENS'
production of
ANNE FRANK
NEXT PERFORMANCE

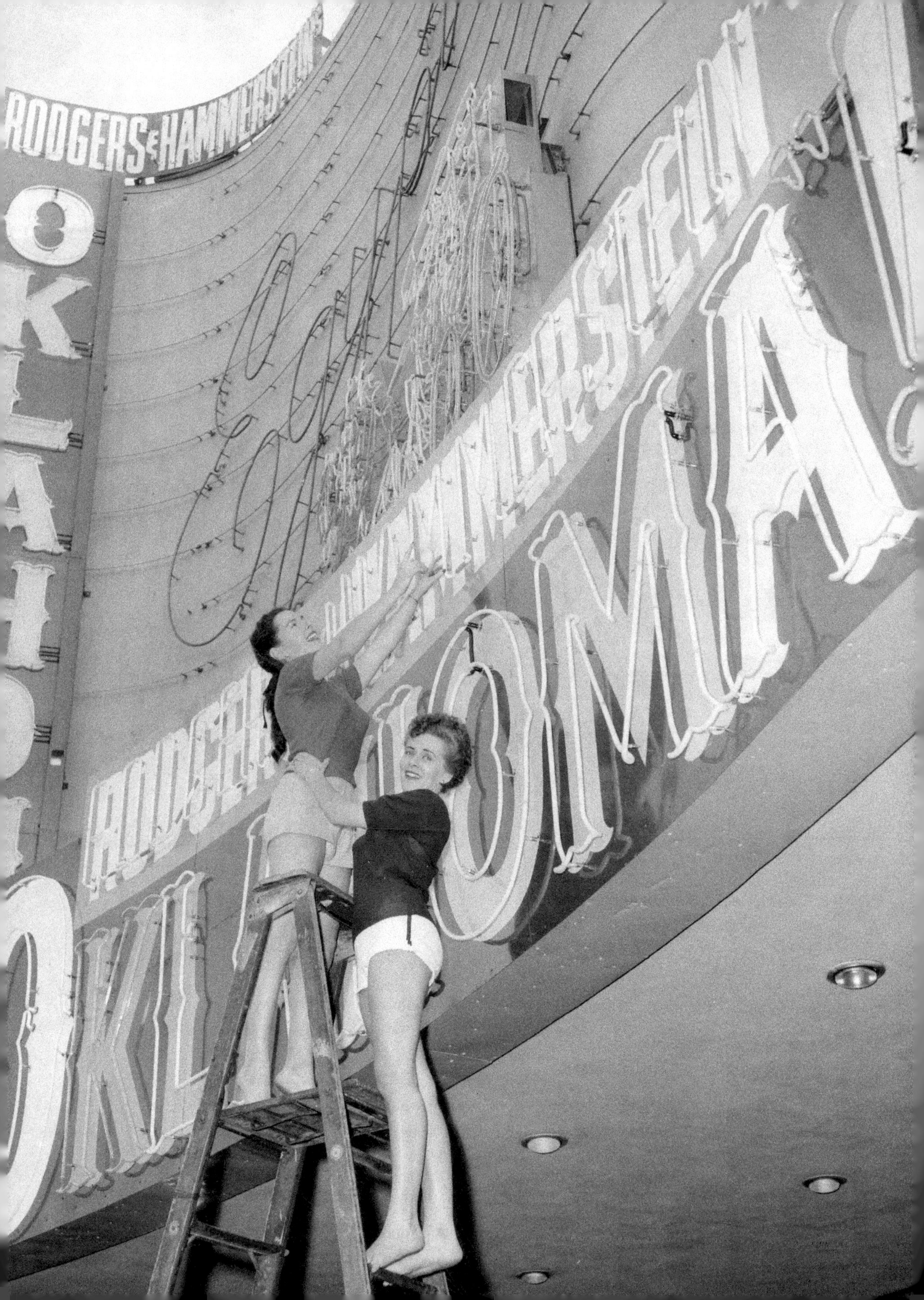
RODGERS & HAMMERSTEIN

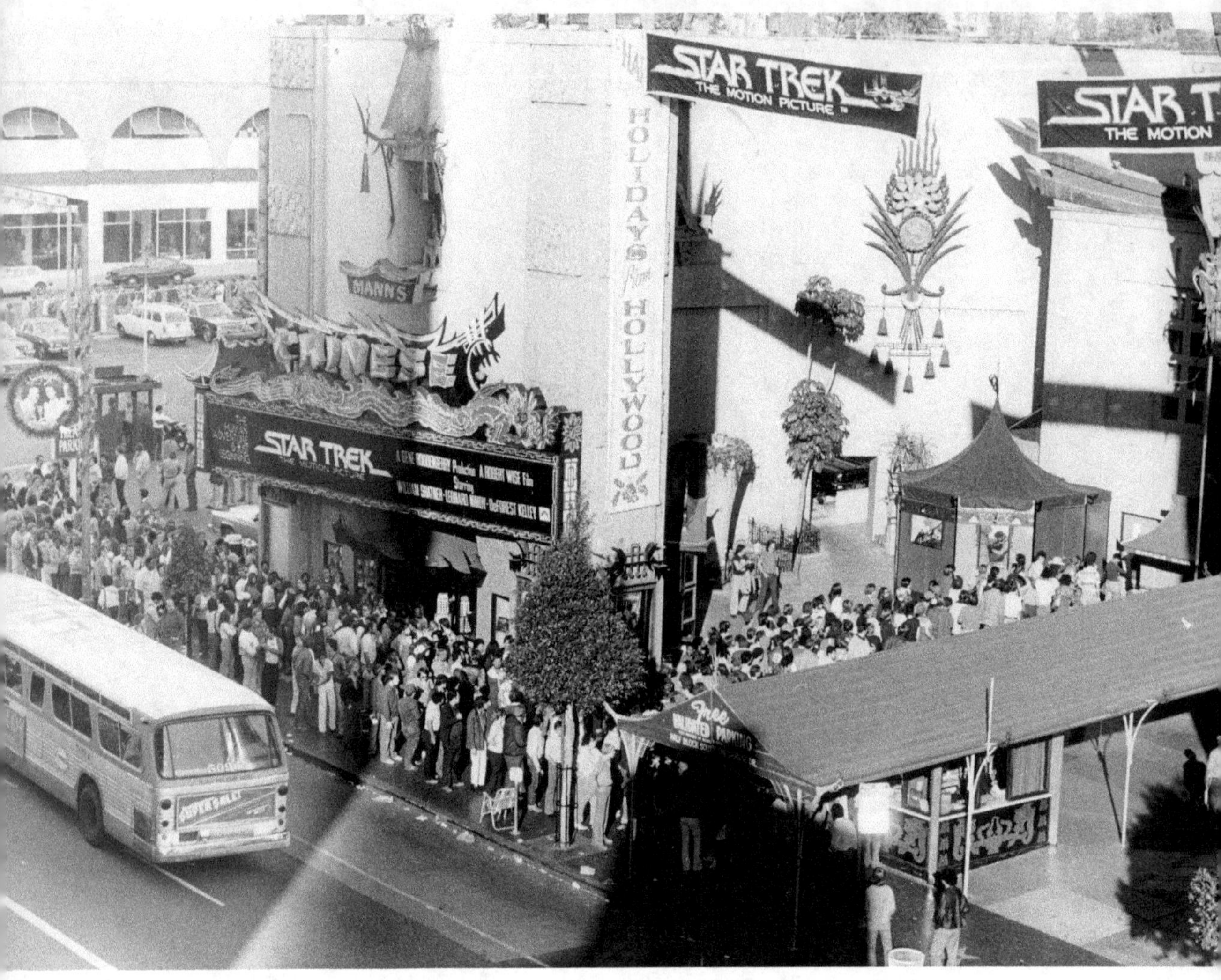

Movie fans line up under the elaborate neon marquee of Grauman's Chinese Theatre while waiting to view *Star Trek: The Motion Picture*. (1979, Los Angeles Herald Examiner Collection)

Opposite: Neon is visible in the courtyard of Grauman's Egyptian Theatre during the premiere of *Don Juan* starring John Barrymore. (1926, Los Angeles Herald Examiner Collection)

Overleaf: Two women help show off neon signs which advertise the film *Oklahoma* at the Egyptian Theatre. (1955, Ralph Morris Collection)

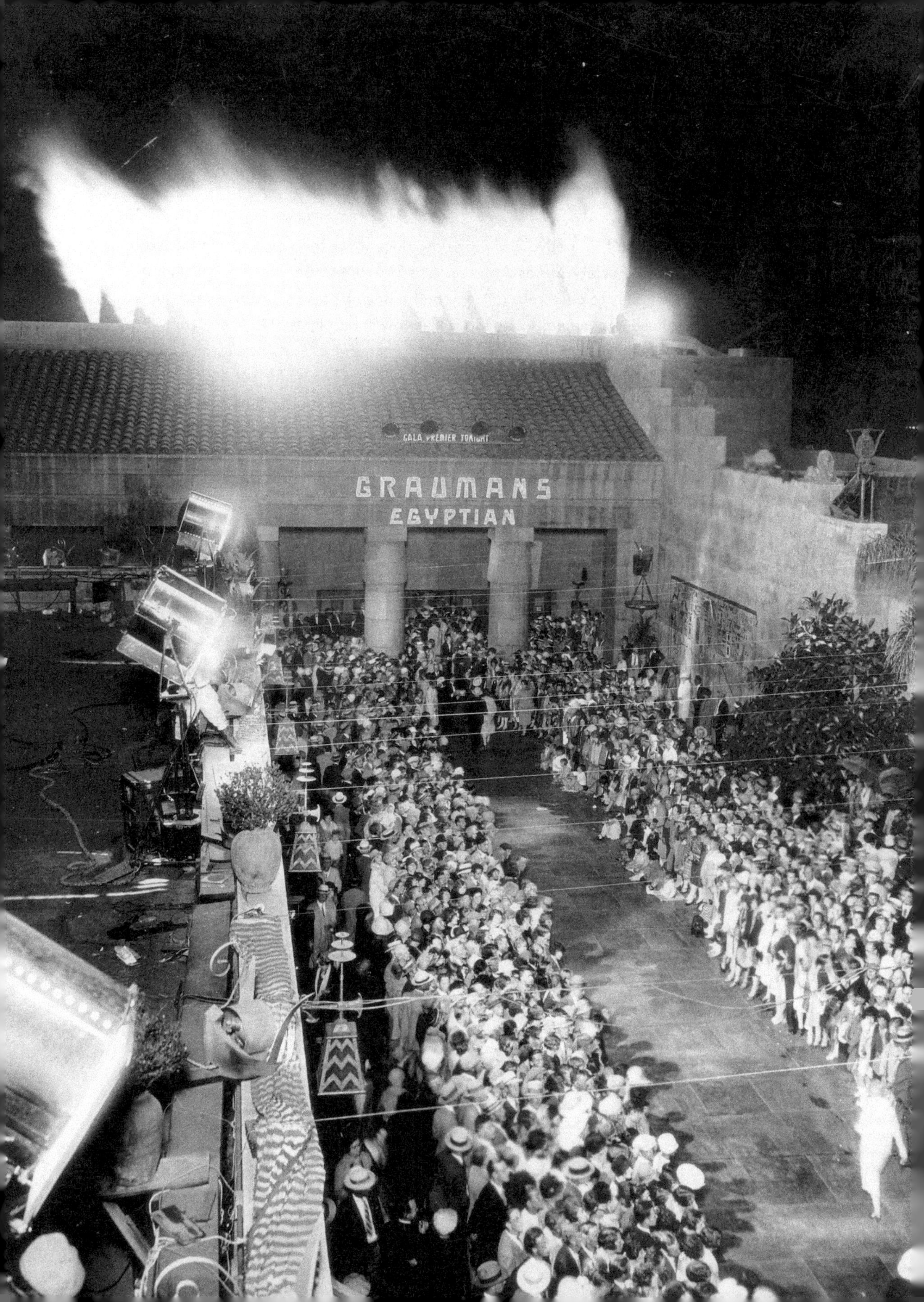

GALA PREMIER TONIGHT
GRAUMANS
EGYPTIAN

ABOUT THE AUTHOR

J. Eric Lynxwiler is an L.A. native and long-time docent for the Los Angeles Conservancy and Art Deco Society of Los Angeles. As a board member for the Museum of Neon Art, he continues to celebrate L.A.'s neon heritage by saving historic neon signs and guides the museum's famed "Neon Cruise" — now in his eighteenth year. Lynxwiler researched the book *Wilshire Boulevard: Grand Concourse of Los Angeles* and coauthored *Knott's Preserved: From Berry Stand to Theme Park, The History of Knott's Berry Farm*. He celebrates the little-known stories of Los Angeles and has just released his third book, *Spectacular Illumination: Neon Los Angeles, 1925–1965* with photographer Tom Zimmerman.

ABOUT THE PHOTO COLLECTION

The Los Angeles Public Library (LAPL) began collecting photographs sometime before World War II and had a collection of about 13,000 images by the late 1950s. In 1981, when Los Angeles celebrated its 200th birthday, Security Pacific National Bank gave its noted collection of historical photographs to the people of Los Angeles to be archived at the Central Library. Since then, LAPL has been fortunate to receive other major collections, making the Library a resource worldwide for visual images.

Notable collections include the "photo morgues" of the *Los Angeles Herald Examiner* and *Valley Times* newspapers, the Kelly-Holiday mid-century collection of aerial photographs, the Works Progress Administration/Federal Writers Project collection, the Luther Ingersoll Portrait Collection, along with the landmark *Shades of L.A.*, which is an archive of images representing the contemporary and historic diversity of families in Los Angeles. Images were chosen from family albums and copied in a project sponsored by Photo Friends.

The Los Angeles Public Library Photo Collection also includes the works of individual photographers, including Ansel Adams, Herman Schultheis, William Reagh, Ralph Morris, Lucille Stewart, Gary Leonard, Stone Ishimaru, Carol Westwood, and Rolland Curtis.

Over 110,000 images from these collections have been digitized and are available to view through the LAPL website at **http://photos.lapl.org.**

ABOUT PHOTO FRIENDS

Formed in 1990, Photo Friends is a nonprofit organization that supports the Los Angeles Public Library's Photograph Collection and History & Genealogy Department. Our goal is to improve access to the collections and promote them through programs, projects, exhibits, and books such as this one.

We are an enthusiastic group of photographers, writers, historians, business people, politicians, academics, and many others, all bonded by our passion for photography, history, and Los Angeles.

Since 1994, Photo Friends has presented a regular series called *The Photographer's Eye*, which spotlights local photographers and their work. In 2011, Photo Friends inaugurated *L.A. in Focus*, a lecture series that features images drawn primarily from the Photo Collection. We have presented programs on L.A. crime, the San Fernando Valley, Kelly-Holiday aerial photographs, and L.A.'s themed environments, among others.

With initial funding from the Ralph M. Parsons Foundation, Photo Friends sponsored *L.A. Neighborhoods Project* by commissioning photographers to create a visual record of the neighborhoods of Los Angeles during the early part of the 21st century (all now part of the collection). To ensure the library's collection will continue to reflect such an important part of Los Angeles's history, a generous grant enabled Photo Friends to hire five contemporary photographers to document present-day industrial L.A. These images have become part of LAPL's permanent collection and are available through the Library's photo database. Photo Friends also curates photography exhibits on display in the History Department.

Photo Friends is a membership organization. Please consider becoming a member and helping us in our work to preserve and promote L.A.'s rich photographic resource. All proceeds from the sale of this book go to support Photo Friends' programs.

photofriends.org

This catalog was published in conjunction with a photo exhibit at
Los Angeles Central Library's History & Genealogy Department,
curated by J. Eric Lynxwiler
Signs of Life: Los Angeles Is the City of Neon
January 18 - July 9, 2017

THANK YOU! Kim Creighton, Christina Rice, Darin Barnes, Amy Inouye, and the Museum of Neon Art in Glendale, California.

Signs of Life: Los Angeles Is the City of Neon
Essay by Eric Lynxwiler • Edited by Christina Rice

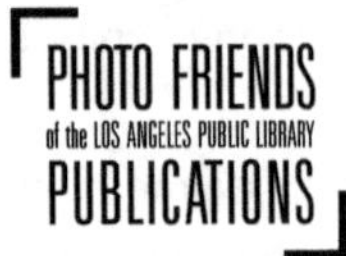

Published by:
Photo Friends of the Los Angeles Public Library
c/o Future Studio
P.O. Box 292000
Los Angeles, CA 90029
www.photofriends.org

Designed by Amy Inouye, Future Studio Los Angeles

Special quantity discounts available when purchased in bulk by corporations, organizations, or groups. Please contact Photo Friends at: **photofriendsla@gmail.com**

ISBN-13: 978-0-9978251-1-4

Printed in the United States

www.ingramcontent.com/pod-product-compliance
Lightning Source LLC
LaVergne TN
LVHW081323110826
845149LV00007B/1579
9780997825114